By the Ore Docks

UNIVERSITY OF MINNESOTA PRESS
Minneapolis • London

By the Ore Docks

A Working People's History of Duluth

Richard Hudelson and Carl Ross

Published by the University of Minnesota Press
111 Third Avenue South, Suite 290
Minneapolis, MN 55401-2520
http://www.upress.umn.edu

Library of Congress Cataloging-in-Publication Data

Hudelson, Richard.

By the ore docks : a working people's history of Duluth / Richard Hudelson and Carl Ross.

p. cm.

Includes bibliographical references and index.

ISBN-13: 978-0-8166-4636-4 (hc : alk. paper)
ISBN-10: 0-8166-4636-8 (hc : alk. paper)
ISBN-13: 978-0-8166-4637-1 (pb : alk. paper)
ISBN-10: 0-8166-4637-6 (pb : alk. paper)

1. Working class--Minnesota--Duluth--History. 2. Ethnic groups--Minnesota--Duluth--History. 3. Labor unions--Minnesota--Duluth--History. 4. Communism--Minnesota--Duluth--History. 5. Farmer-Labor Party (Minn.)--History. I. Ross, Carl, 1913-2005. II. Title. III. Title: Working people's history of Duluth.

HD8085.D88H83 2006
331.8809776'771--DC22

2006026093

Printed in the United States of America on acid-free paper

The University of Minnesota is an equal-opportunity educator and employer.

12 11 10 09 08 07 06   10 9 8 7 6 5 4 3 2 1

contents

preface

AN OUTSIDER, I ARRIVED IN DULUTH IN THE FALL OF 1977 TO take an academic position at a local university. Almost immediately I began to hear comments suggesting that Communists had once played a part in the history of the city. A baby boomer, I had grown up in the 1950s under the shadows of McCarthyism and the bomb, and as a child I had formed a conception of Communists as evil, twisted souls. Coming of age in the 1960s, I became involved in the peace movement against the war in Vietnam. As a peace activist I met and got to know a number of "old leftists," people who had once been members of (or were at least close to) the Communist Party. Though most of them talked too much for my taste, I liked these people. In their fifties, sixties, and seventies when I met them, they were intelligent, informed, idealistic, and active—a far cry from what I had thought Communists were like.

As a peace activist I also had contact with a number of "Marxist-Leninist" groups involved in the "new left" and the peace movement. There was a cultlike atmosphere around these groups. The Leninist principle of democratic centralism gave excessive authority to a few leading individuals. Submitting to the will of the "Party" and the imagined dictates of history, individual cadres abandoned their own good sense and the basic moral requirements of common humanity. I began to see how intelligent, informed, and idealistic activists could have served as Stalin's assassins. Leninist discipline made a powerful weapon—for good or ill.

I fell in love with Duluth from the moment I arrived. The physical setting of the city, overlooking Lake Superior, is beautiful. Though predominantly Yankee and Scandinavian, the city included Finns, eastern and southern Europeans, Native Americans, African Americans, Hispanics, and Asians. Students in my classes carried names from every corner of the world. Many came from families that had been in Duluth for several generations. They had roots in neighborhoods that had once had distinct identities within the ethnic history and class structure of the city. Instead of the familiar Republicans and Democrats of my youth, Duluth had its Democratic Farmer-Laborites and Independent Republicans, living products of some interestingly deviant historical development.

As an academic with some interest in history, I was aware of the often bitter debate among American historians in the 1980s and 1990s about the role of the American Communist Party. On the one hand were those "revisionist" historians who depicted the party as part of a broad populist tradition within American life. On the other hand were the anti-Communists, who affirmed the essential correctness of the 1950s view that Communists were enemies of American democracy. Getting familiar with Duluth and learning a little bit about its history, I began to think of this history in light of these two conflicting views of American Communism. Of course Duluth is only one city, and an understanding of the role of Communists in the history of Duluth cannot be generalized to the nation as a whole. Still, I thought that case studies like the history of Duluth could make a contribution to advancing the level of debate about the nature of the American Communist Party. Just what was the role of the party in the history of Duluth?

As I thought about the history of the city in these terms, it became apparent that the role of the Communist Party in Duluth could not be understood without taking into account the ethnic and labor history of the city. After I came to this realization, I had the good fortune to meet Carl Ross in the spring of 1988. Having grown up in the left-wing Finnish community in Superior, Wisconsin, just across the bay from Duluth, Carl had devoted thirty years to the American Communist Party. With the defeat of the reformist wing of the party in 1957, Carl left the Communists for a career in business. In retirement he had turned to scholarly work, writing historical studies of Finnish America and serving as director of the Twentieth-Century Radicalism Project of the Minnesota Historical Society. Already thinking in terms of a history of Duluth as a local study of radicalism in an urban industrial community, Carl recruited me to join him in attempting to write a history of the city of Duluth. With his personal roots in the local radical Finnish community and his long reflection on the history of radicalism in Minnesota, Carl was able to suggest many ideas that proved fruitful for thinking about the history of the city, and he pointed me to a rich array of sources that had already been collected by the radicalism project.

The study now before you is the result of this collaboration. The impetus was my own question about the role of the Communists in the history of Duluth, but the attempt to answer this question inevitably led us into the ethnic and labor history of the city. The history presented here is only a part of the history of the city, but it is a part that no true history of Duluth can ignore, and we thought it worth telling. Our collaborative work began fifteen years ago. As director of the radicalism project and as someone who had lived through parts of this history, Carl was able to recommend a variety of resource materials and eventually I began to write, sending draft chapters to Carl for his comments. Unfortunately, age and declining health caught up with Carl before the project could be completed; he died on March 1, 2005. He was unable to comment on late revisions to the work, and I hope he would approve of the decisions I made and the words I chose. I would like to conclude this preface with words from Carl that conjure up a view of Duluth familiar to all who love the city as he did:

> A traveler driving toward Duluth from Minneapolis or St. Paul for about 150 miles on Interstate 35 will arrive at a point where the highway appears ready to plunge downward for the next half mile and a distant vista of Lake Superior shoreline opens ahead. On the left side of the freeway is an easily accessible tourist center and scenic overlook, perhaps the very spot from which the French explorer Sieur du Lhut, reputed the first European to arrive at the western terminus of the Great Lakes, gazed over the virgin white pine forest at the expanse of a potential harbor sheltered from the waters of a vast lake that reached beyond the distant horizon.
>
> From this overlook one can gaze over miles of St. Louis Bay, the great harbor serving Superior, Wisconsin, located on a flat alluvial plain created by the St. Louis River on the south shore of Lake Superior, and Duluth, Minnesota, stretched for nearly thirty miles, mostly along a narrow ribbon of land at the foot of the massive rock face rising steeply above the harbor on the north shore of the lake; the city streets running like paved hillside terraces from west to east, the avenues finding their way up the steep incline from lake front to hilltop.
>
> Altogether, this is one of the world's rare natural

settings, inviting the construction of a great city, a setting worthy of universal admiration such as is bestowed on San Francisco or Vancouver. To be sure, the John Blatnik Bridge that spans the harbor connecting the Twin Ports of Duluth and Superior may lack the celebrity of the Golden Gate Bridge. Nonetheless, it matches that bridge in length and height and it stands as a fine tribute to the World War II hero and long-term member of Congress who was the son of a Slovenian immigrant iron miner—and as a tribute to the son of Finnish immigrants [Jack Salo] whose engineering firm [helped design] the bridge.

If my own interest in this project began with the question of Communist influence on the history of Duluth, Carl began with a broader vision. For him there was no question about Communist influence. He knew about that from his own life experience. For him the Communists were only a part of a bigger story. That bigger story had to do with America and the immigrants who helped make America what it is today. The chapters that follow will tell the story of Communist influence in Duluth, but they will do so within the context of this bigger story about immigrants who came here, a story that has more than a little relevance for the present.

R. H.

acknowledgments

ONE OF THE JOYS OF WORKING ON THIS BOOK HAS BEEN THE experience of receiving the generous help of many different people. Supported by the Center for Community and Regional Research of the University of Minnesota Duluth (UMD), several UMD students contributed to the research effort: Susan Perala-Dewey, Eva Johansson, Siri Delange, Josephine Barber, Bruce Myers, Karen Larson, and Richard Aylsworth. Students from the University of Wisconsin-Superior, working with the support of the UW-Superior Foundation, also did valuable research: John Zupansic, Jaclyn Rivard, Robert Sibila, Erin Amdall, Anthony Bennett, and Surath DeAlwis.

My own research has received generous support from the University of Wisconsin-Superior, the University of Minnesota Duluth, and the Minnesota Historical Society. Research took me to several different libraries, and library staff was invariably helpful and generous with time. I would like to express personal thanks to Dorothy Lemke from UMD, Laura Jacobs from UW-Superior, and David Ouse and Kris Aho from the Duluth Public Library. Deborah Miller, director of research for the Minnesota Historical Society (MHS), called my attention to many resources in the MHS collection that I never would have thought to use, and she has provided much valuable assistance along the way. Rudy Vecoli, Timo Riipa, Joel Wurl, and everyone at the Immigration History Research Center (IHRC) provided direction and help in working with that valuable collection. Thanks also to the St. Louis County Historical Society, which has preserved an invaluable collection on local history that is now housed in the Northeast Minnesota Historical Center in the library at UMD.

Colleagues near and far generously shared their knowledge and their time. Ron Mershart, Joel Sipress, and Karl Bahm at UW-Superior have shared their knowledge of regional, U.S., and world history. Jimmy Engren and Lars Olson from Vaxjö University and Per-Olof Grönberg from Umeå University provided special help regarding Swedish Americans and general ideas about immigration and labor history. I learned a lot about the Swedish roots of Duluth's Scandinavian Socialists from Aage Johansson and his colleagues at the local historical society in Ljusne. Similar help with both general ideas and Finnish American history was provided by Michael Karni, Arnie Alanen, and Mayme Sevander. Michael Brooks was generous with his research on Swedish American Socialists. William Millikan shared detailed research information on Duluth from his work then in progress on the Citizens' Alliance. Virginia Hyvärinen did amazing research from her outpost in Cambridge, Massachusetts.

Lionel Davis read and commented on an earlier draft and provided many helpful suggestions. I benefited greatly from detailed comments on earlier drafts by University of Minnesota Press readers Peter Rachleff and Laurie Hertzel and by University of Minnesota Press editor Todd Orjala. The book is definitely better organized, better written, and shorter because of their efforts. I also thank Pieter Martin and Laura Westlund of the University of Minnesota Press for their help in getting the manuscript ready for publication. Thanks, too, to Linda Lincoln for her many helpful editorial recommendations.

Finally, I thank friends closer to home. Tom Selinski has generously shared his research on the labor movement of the region. Larry Sillanpa, editor of *Labor World*, has been a great help over a long period of time. Herb Widell has always been willing to share his memories of Duluth and has been supportive of my efforts to write something about that history. Erik Peterson has been extraordinarily generous with his ideas, his research, and his time; without his detailed criticisms of a grandfather version and his further help along the way, this book would never have been written. Finally, I thank Pat Maus from the Northeast Minnesota Historical Center (NEMHC), whose knowledge of that collection and whose generous support have been a great help from start to finish.

R. H.

abbreviations

ACW	American Clothing Workers
AFL	American Federation of Labor
AFSCME	American Federation of State, County, and Municipal Employees
ASL	Anti-Saloon League
AYC	American Youth Congress
BMU	Butte Miners' Union
CIO	Congress of Industrial Organization
CLP	Communist Labor Party
CLPC	Central Labor Political Committee
CWA	Congress of Women's Auxiliaries
DFL	Democratic-Farmer-Labor Party
DFTA	Duluth Federated Trades Assembly
D&IR Railway	Duluth and Iron Range Railway
DM&N Railway	Duluth, Missabe, and Northern Railway
FLA	Farmer-Labor Association
FLP	Farmer-Labor Party
IHRC	Immigration History Research Center
ILA	International Longshoremen's Association
IOGT	International Order of Good Templars
IWW	Industrial Workers of the World
MCPS	Minnesota Commission of Public Safety
MHS	Minnesota Historical Society
MMSW	Mine, Mill, and Smelters Workers Union
NEMHC	Northeast Minnesota Historical Center
NMU	National Maritime Union
NPL	Non-Partisan League
NRA	National Recovery Administration
SLP	Socialist Labor Party
SNPJ	Slovene National Benefit Society
SSF	Scandinavian Socialist Federation

SWOC	Steel Workers Organizing Committee
TUEL	Trade Union Education League
UGCW	United Gas and Chemical Workers
UMD	University of Minnesota Duluth
UPW	United Public Workers
UW-Superior	University of Wisconsin-Superior
WASP	White, Anglo-Saxon, Protestant
WCTU	Women's Christian Temperance Union
WPA	Works Progress Administration
WPNPL	Working People's Nonpartisan League
YCL	Young Communist League
YPSL	Young People's Socialist League

introduction

THE TWIN PORTS OF DULUTH AND SUPERIOR LIE AT THE WEST-
ern tip of the Great Lakes. Duluth, located on the north shore, is
the larger of the two cities. Until 1854 the north shore was Indian
country, closed to non-Indians by treaties between the Ojibwe
Nation and the United States. While the Treaty of LaPointe, signed
in 1854, opened the north shore for non-Indian settlement, the Civil
War and the depression of 1873 delayed real development of the
region. It was not until the mid- to late 1880s that Duluth really
took off as a city. The location of the city and the time of its development framed its history, which was part of the great expansion
of industry in the United States that characterized the period following the Civil War. The spread of non-Indian people into Indian
country in the years after the war was integrally connected with the
expansion of American industry. The frontier was industrial, providing the lumber, iron, lead, and copper needed by growing industries and the grain needed to feed the growing mass of people who
worked in those industries. Cities sprung up across the West, providing the railroad terminals connecting extracted resources with
eastern industry. Duluth was part of that industrial frontier, providing lumber, grain, and iron ore to a growing America.

The post–Civil War period of industrial transformation was
also a period of turmoil and conflict. Before this transformation,
most industrial facilities were small and produced for a local market. They employed a relatively small number of laborers. Employers often knew the men and women who worked for them. Workers
often possessed skills that gave them a degree of control over the
process and pace of production. Employers and employees were
apt to share religious, ethnic, and cultural traditions. In the process of transformation, industrial facilities became much larger.
Many began to produce for national and even international markets. They employed a larger workforce, often made up of immi-

grant men and women from diverse ethnic backgrounds. Changes in the scale of production were accompanied by changes in the technologies of production, with technologies involving relatively autonomous groups of skilled laborers giving way to mass production by unskilled labor. These new processes eroded the ability of laborers to control the pace and process of production. They also undermined the communities of shared cultural values that once united employers and employees. Many laborers, laboring families, and laboring communities resisted these changes. Many American workers saw the industrial transformation of the United States as a threat to the republican values on which the country had been founded. On their own or in combination with immigrant workers acting out of their own sometimes quite different traditions, these workers fought against the emerging industrial order. Often this resistance took the form of strikes or resistance to lockouts. Sometimes, as in the upheavals on the railroads in 1877 or at the Homestead Steel Mills in 1892, these confrontations turned violent and deadly.[1]

Historical research into this period of transformation and resistance has provided rich insights into the thoughts, feelings, cultural traditions, and actions of diverse groups of American workers. It has also thrown considerable light on the cities and towns these workers inhabited. In many cases, acting on their own or in alliance with small businessmen or farmers, workers were able to assert significant influence over local politics and affairs. Nevertheless, American industry did change. Gradually, in different industries at different times, the new modes of production prevailed. By World War I, this transformation was largely complete and with it the "fall of the house of labor"—the decline of once-powerful unions formed by skilled laborers in American industries in the nineteenth century.[2]

Duluth had its origins in the midst of this industrial transformation and ensuing turmoil. The larger patterns sketched above are reflected in the early history of the city. Overseen by captains of industry and finance, the city was developed as an important outpost on the industrial frontier. Almost from the start, Duluth's multiethnic working class challenged big business for control of the city. For a while, during the 1890s, the working men of Duluth largely set the course of city government through their elected representatives. (At that time women lacked the right to vote.) But all of this changed with the arrival of the steel trust in Duluth, again reflecting the national patterns of development. From roughly 1900 on, the large industrial interests centered around U.S. Steel gained the upper hand. The labor coalition of the 1890s gave way, beaten back by organized business interests and divided by ethnic and religious differences. These business interests would dominate Duluth into the 1930s.

But this is not the end of the story. Opposition to business interests continued throughout the period of business dominance. While this opposition drew on the labor traditions of the past, it was in some respects qualitatively different. In the decade before World War I, a new oppositional current took shape within the city. Based in strong locals of Finnish and Scandinavian Socialists, this oppositional current reached out to unskilled workers in Duluth's multiethnic industrial working class. Informed by an international Socialist movement, this opposition accepted the new industrial technology but sought to capture it for the working class. Modernist in outlook, it looked not to an idyllic past but to a utopian future. Beaten back for twenty years, this oppositional force merged in the 1930s with other currents rooted in the experiences of Duluth's multiethnic working class to form a Popular Front that successfully challenged the long-dominant business interests.

Central to the success of this Popular Front was a new vision of America. Running alongside the transformation of American industry and the labor unrest that accompanied that transformation were concerns about the nature of the American republic and its continued viability. The rapid growth of American industry would have been impossible without massive immigration. In important sectors of American society, there was deep concern about the effect of these immigrants on the fabric of the American republic. Were these immigrants really Americans? Could they be assimilated to American ways? Did they bring ideas and ways of life that would damage or destroy America? These concerns were present within governing circles but also within some sectors of the American labor movement, and they worked to divide the movement. They also led immigrants, particularly immigrants from certain parts of the world, to be relegated to an inferior status within the economic, political, and cultural life of the nation.

The business interests that led America from 1900 to 1930 developed a particular view of America that worked to legitimate their own leadership. On the one hand, they attacked immigrant Socialists as un-American. In a more positive vein, they developed a paternalistic vision of American industry. In this view, business leaders rightfully played a leading role because they had the know-how, the entrepreneurial spirit, and the American values that had made American industry great and brought prosperity to the American people. To varying degrees and in not-altogether-compatible ways, American opinion-makers often linked this know-how, entrepreneurial spirit, and ethical outlook to membership in the Anglo-Saxon "race," or to rootedness in Anglo-Saxon culture. Immigrants from other parts of the world, therefore, were not qualified to lead and rightfully belonged in lower positions, at least until they had become fully assimilated. For decades immigrants from southern and eastern Europe, and especially African Americans and Asian immigrants, labored under the weight of such prejudices.[3] Employers tended to slot particular ethnic groups into particular kinds of work, with "Americans" and their northern European "Nordic" cousins thought fit for supervisory, managerial, and skilled roles, while eastern and southern Europeans were thought fit only for manual labor and sometimes only for specific manual labor.[4] In Duluth such prejudicial assumptions were clearly at work in the steel plant, where skilled and supervisory jobs went to Americans and northern Europeans, while southern Slavs, Italians, and African Americans got the least desirable manual jobs.

The view that some ethnic groups were not really or fully American persisted into the 1930s and beyond, but by the mid-1930s a different, more inclusive conception of America was being advanced in certain quarters. According to this "working-class Americanism," all men and women were created equal and had an equal right to work and share in the bounty of America.[5] This conception of America challenged the legitimacy of business leadership. It also asserted a claim on behalf of every American for work, food, shelter, opportunity, and participation in the economic, political, and cultural life of the nation. In Duluth, Communists and their allies in the progressive Popular Front, which led the Farmer-Labor Party and the CIO, advocated for this inclusive working-class Americanism. Their ideas found deep and wide support among the city's multiethnic industrial working class, where similar thoughts had been percolating in the 1920s within a number of ethnic working-class organizations. This vision of America was instrumental in forging a popular coalition that for more than a decade, from 1935 to 1948, seriously challenged the business interests that had led the city since 1900.

The chapters that follow tell the story of this popular coalition. Chapter 1 begins with an account of the origins of the labor movement in Duluth. Chapter 2 describes the defeat of that labor movement by a coalition of business leaders who would largely govern the city throughout the next three decades. Chapter 2 also explores some of the divisions within the labor movement that made this defeat possible and continued to hamper attempts to challenge the business leadership for years to come. Subsequent chapters reconstruct the formation, temporary ascendancy, and subsequent decline of the popular coalition that challenged business leadership in the 1930s and 1940s. The book concludes with a consideration of what, if any, are the lasting effects on the city of this aspect of its history.

Throughout these chapters the focus is on Duluth and specifically on the history of the labor movement there. From what has been said above, however, it should be clear that this history is part of larger histories—of the United States and of global capitalism. In particular, this history is part of the now not-so-new "new labor history." This is a body of work that attempts to study not just the institutional history of unions but the thoughts, feelings, experiences, values, and cultural expressions that have made up the lives of working-class individuals and communities at different times and places. While there are very clearly large historical forces at work shaping and constraining the lives of working-class communities, such as the structural development of global capitalism and the political development of the nation, the ways that different working-class communities respond to these forces are shaped by the particularities of time and place and the availability of resources drawn from ethnically and culturally diverse traditions.

The history of the labor movement in Duluth presented here is the history of how one ethnically diverse working-class community acted within the framework of larger historical forces. It is neither wholly unique nor wholly typical. Consider, for example, the interestingly similar yet interestingly different experience of the working class in Butte, Montana. Butte and Duluth were both cities on the industrial frontier. Each played a part in metal-mining industries. Each was the site of intense agitation by radicals belonging to the Industrial Workers of the World (IWW) during the World War I era. In each case, Finnish immigrants played a large part in this radical agitation. There were also direct connections between the two cities, with William Dunn, the editor of the radical *Butte Bulletin*, speaking in Duluth and Jack Carney leaving his position as editor of *Truth*, a radical Duluth newspaper, to take over as editor of the *Butte Bulletin* in 1920.[6] But there were important differences in the two cities that caused similar actions by similar agents to produce very different outcomes. For one thing, the "fall of the house of labor" came earlier to Duluth than it did to Butte. In Butte, copper mining dated back to the early 1880s. The work involved skilled laborers, who organized themselves into the Butte Miners' Union (BMU), which was present in Butte almost from its beginnings. The kind of industrial transformation, which undermined unions of skilled laborers across the United States, came somewhat late to the Butte copper mines. In contrast, the iron-mining industry arrived in Duluth in the mid-1890s, well after copper mining had come to Butte. But by the time the iron industry came to Duluth, it had already won the decisive battle against unions of skilled workers in that industry. In Duluth IWW radicals worked among unorganized laborers. In Butte they faced a well-organized union, most of whose members, bound by strong ties of Irish ethnicity, preferred their own conservative leaders to the IWW radicals they viewed as outside agitators.[7] It is not surprising that radical agitation produced different results in these different environments.

Chicago is another city that is interesting to compare and contrast with Duluth. There are several parallels between the two cities. Each emerged from the World War I era with an ethnically fragmented working class. Most of this working class was not part of the organized labor movement. Religious and secular ethnic organizations provided the primary locus for social life. Ethnic organizations provided the social welfare safety net that supported working-class families in times of illness, injury, and death. In both cities during the decade of the 1920s, the development of a shared American popular culture and the emergence of an immigrant second generation at home in that culture worked to overcome ethnic divisions. When the crisis caused by the Great Depression overwhelmed the ethnic safety net, the multiethnic working class in each city rallied to support the revitalized labor movement and the New Deal politics of Franklin Delano Roosevelt.[8]

But while this general framework seems to apply to Duluth as well as Chicago, there are interesting differences. Consider, for example, the role of Swedes. Chicago was home to the single largest Swedish community in the United States; Duluth also had a large Swedish population. In each city, a significant minority of the local Swedish community was made up of radicals who supported unions and some form of Socialism. In each city, many of these radicals had left Sweden after the defeat of a general strike in 1909. Locals of the Scandinavian Socialist Federation (SSF) were formed in each city. *Svenska Socialisten*, the newspaper of the SSF published in Chicago, was read and distributed by members of the Scandinavian Socialist local in Duluth.[9] But Swedish radicals in Duluth operated in an environment very different from that of their comrades in Chicago. Faced with competition for jobs from other ethnic communities and hostility to immigrants in general, Swedes in Chicago appear to have turned inward, toward allies within the Swedish radical community and within the larger Swedish community.[10] In Duluth, where the Swedish community was the single largest foreign-born community in the city and where a large group of radical Swedes found strong allies among the radical Finns, Swedes felt confident enough to reach out to other ethnic groups early on. For example, in 1917, when the Swedes in Duluth launched their own newspaper, they chose to publish in English.

The point of these comparisons between Duluth, Butte, and Chicago is to illustrate that while similar historical forces influenced the history of each city, the particular way those forces were channeled by historical agents differed significantly. The industrial unions of the post–Civil War era, like the Amalgamated Association of Iron, Steel and Tin Workers, never had a strong presence in Duluth. Industrial Duluth was largely developed under the sway of the steel trust after the defeat of the Amalgamated at Homestead in 1892.[11] Duluth was also blessed with large Swedish and Finnish communities, each salted with radicals from the 1906–1909 labor struggles in Sweden and the attempted revolution in Finland in 1905. Socialist and IWW radicals from these two communities led an industrial labor movement in Duluth that was heavily influenced by Marxism. This labor movement adopted an internationalist, rather than an ethnic nationalist, perspective. It looked to a utopian future rather than to a utopian past. In the aftermath of the split in the international Socialist movement into Socialist and Communist wings, Duluth's radical Finns and Swedes threw their lot in with the Communists for the most part. Held in check in the decades before the Depression, in the 1930s this radical current within the local labor movement came to play an important role in the CIO and the Farmer-Labor Party.

It was not only in Duluth that Communists played an important role in the labor movement of the 1930s. Communists also controlled the central labor bodies of the CIO unions in many of the
larger towns in the United States.[12] But what is perhaps different
about Duluth is the extent to which this Communist influence was
homegrown and deeply rooted in the long struggle for industrial
unions waged by Duluth's multiethnic, industrial working class.
When, after World War II, the Communists were largely driven out
of their positions of influence in politics and the labor movement,
we see that despite Communist ineptitude and overwhelming
external pressure to purge the reds, it proved surprisingly difficult
to get rid of them. Communists had deep roots in Duluth and these
roots enabled them to withstand the storm against them for somewhat longer than elsewhere. In the final chapters of this book, we
will examine the eventual purge of the reds, the fall of the Popular
Front coalition of which they were a part, and the consequences of
that fall for the subsequent history of the city.

labor roots

FORMED BY GLACIAL ACTION, LAKE SUPERIOR TODAY IS A SOME-what shrunken version of the ancient lake that once occupied the site. The city of Duluth is long and narrow, built along the steep hillside formed by that ancient lake and overlooking the north shore of the lake that exists today. It is blessed with a fine natural harbor protected by Minnesota Point, a long spit of land protecting the inner bay from Lake Superior. Even before the 1854 Treaty of La Pointe between the United States and the Ojibwe Nation, which opened the north shore for "white" settlement, there was a buzz about the place. Developers were convinced that the western tip of the Great Lakes was destined to become the site of a great city. Promoters envisaged Duluth as a city connected by rail to the great Northwest and by water, following the opening of the locks at Sault St. Marie, to the industrial and commercial centers of the Midwest and the East. Duluth was touted as the future "Chicago of Lake Superior."[1]

Despite the financial panic of 1857, which caused the population to fall from 1,500 to 400, the conviction persisted that Duluth was destined for greatness.[2] Speaking in Boston in February 1858, the real-estate promoter General George B. Sargent maintained that Duluth "must center the trade of Twenty American States yet unborn, and the British trade of the Red River settlements, and of Hudson's Bay." He foresaw a city linking by rail and ship the riches of the Orient brought to the ports of the Pacific and the riches of Europe brought to the ports of the Atlantic. At the head of Lake Superior, Sargent held, "Europe and Asia will meet and shake hands in the genial months of summer."[3]

The city was developed hot-house fashion with lots of outside investment. Especially important was the Philadelphia banker Jay Cooke. Knowing that there were iron ore deposits north of Duluth and convinced of the commercial potential of the area, Cooke began buying up land in 1866.[4] In 1867 he traveled to Duluth, which was then described as "merely a half dozen frame houses and a land office," to discuss with local businessmen the building of a railroad to connect the city with Minneapolis and St. Paul.[5] A number of other eastern investors took an interest in Duluth at this time, so many of whom were from Philadelphia that both the *Philadelphia Evening Bulletin* and the *Duluth Minnesotian* referred to Duluth as an appendage of that city.[6]

With the influx of this outside capital and the building in 1869 of Jay Cooke's Lake Superior and Mississippi Railroad, confidence in Duluth's future was restored. Having come to Duluth to publish a newspaper, Dr. Thomas Foster proclaimed Duluth "the Zenith City of the Unsalted Seas."[7] A brochure produced by the city in 1870 said nature itself intended Duluth for commercial greatness and reiterated the idea of General Sargent, now head of the bank of Duluth, that in Duluth the trade of Europe and Asia would come together.[8] Local newspapers sounded the same theme. The *Duluth Tribune* compared Duluth to Chicago as a gateway for emigration to the West, while the *Duluth Minnesotian* predicted that Duluth would even surpass Chicago, having a hinterland that was more diverse and rich in natural resources.[9] Joshua B. Culver, the first mayor of Duluth, expressed the prevailing local sentiment:

> Duluth commences her existence under most auspicious circumstances. Nature has placed her at the head of navigation upon our great chain of water communication with the Atlantic, and railroads are about to unite her with the Northwest and Pacific Ocean—she stands, admitted by all as destined to be one of the great cities of the west.[10]

Even the *New York Times* agreed, proclaiming that "nature undoubtedly intended Duluth for a great city ... one of the chief cities of the continent."[11]

It is a measure of the strength of this conviction that it persisted despite enormous difficulties. When Representative Proctor Knott of Kentucky ridiculed the Duluth bubble in a famous speech in front of the U.S. House of Representatives, local citizens sent him a wire congratulating him on his speech and offering him the best lot in the city.[12] Later, they would name the industrial suburb of Proctor after him. A far more serious difficulty came with the 1873 financial collapse of Jay Cooke, Duluth's principal financial backer. Following Cooke's failure, work on the Northern Pacific railroad, intended to link Duluth with the Pacific Northwest, came to a halt. The Bank of Duluth, also financed by Cooke, went out of business in 1875. Unable to meet obligations undertaken for local development, the city of Duluth defaulted on $51,000 worth of bonds and in 1877 gave up its charter as a city, not to reincorporate as a city again until 1887. The population of Duluth fell from 5,000 in 1873 to 2,500 in 1875. A Duluth businessman was able to collect only fifteen dollars out of some $2,400 owed to him and Orrin Rice, one of the early settlers at the head of the lakes, could not trade one of his lots on Superior Street for a pair of boots.[13]

Nevertheless, the north shore settlement survived. While shipments and receipts at the port of Duluth declined in the mid-1870s, by the end of the decade both were well above the best years prior to the Jay Cooke failure.[14] By 1886 Duluth's population soared to twenty thousand. Taxable valuation for the industrial infrastructure of the city increased from $669,000 in 1880 to over $4.7 million in 1886.[15] Key to this revival were the grain and lumber industries. With the completion of the Lake Superior and Mississippi Railroad and a part of the Northern Pacific extending out to the wheat fields of the Great Plains, it became possible to bring grain into Duluth for shipment on the Great Lakes. The first grain elevator had been built in 1869 and the 1871 completion of a canal for boat traffic on the Duluth side of Minnesota Point made it possible to load the grain within the safety of the protected harbor. Larger grain facilities followed in the 1870s and 1880s.[16] Grain capacity increased from less than 1.5 million tons in 1880 to nearly 18 million tons by 1886.[17] And by the mid-1880s Duluth's bay front from Rice's Point to West Duluth was lined with large sawmills, cutting some 10 million feet of lumber each year. Five years later, annual production had risen to 150 million board feet of lumber.[18]

By the late 1880s, Duluth seemed well on its way to fulfilling its promise. Its population was growing rapidly and its economy was booming. With all of its debts paid, the city's charter was restored in 1887. Writing in the *Duluth Morning Sun* in April 1887, a local booster proclaimed that a glance at the map, a little history, and a knowledge of production statistics "must convince any person of ordinary sagacity that if nature ever designated any place as a great commercial metropolis, that place is Duluth, Minnesota."[19] Similar estimations of Duluth and its future appeared in *Harper's*

The Alger-Smith Sawmill at Garfield Avenue on Rice's Point was one of the largest sawmills operating in Duluth. Courtesy Northeast Minnesota Historical Center.

Weekly, Cosmopolitan, and newspapers in New York and London.[20] Investors in New York, Boston, and Philadelphia bought real estate in Duluth and in November 1889, a London syndicate invested one million dollars in the city, including property along what is now London Road.[21] Writing in 1910, the authors of the *History of Duluth and St. Louis County* surveyed the origins of Duluth, concluding that it was "inevitable" that a great commercial city would arise at the head of Lake Superior and that its future growth and development as the commercial link between the western plains and the markets of Europe and the eastern United States was equally "certain."[22]

Duluth was made up of several different settlements in the years following the Treaty of La Pointe. From the beginning, there were differences between these settlements that would color the parts of Duluth they would later become. Oneota, located around Forty-Fifth Avenue West, began as an industrial site. In an 1856 diary entry, Reverend Peet describes the place as follows: "The town or city of Oneota contains about 20 inhabitants, three dwellings, three huts for workshops and a store, a dock and steam sawmill building."[23] By 1870, Oneota was well on its way to becoming an industrial and working-class community. At that time it had a population of five hundred, with two sawmills, a furniture factory, a tugboat used for towing stone-laden scows for harbor improvements, and a shipyard.[24] In contrast, Endion, a settlement located on the east hillside overlooking the lake claimed in 1856 by Captain Markland, was platted into suburban lots "for capitalists doing business at Superior."[25]

The natural setting also influenced the future role played by each of these settlements. Efforts to set up boat docks along the lake outside of Minnesota Point failed because they offered inadequate protection from the powerful forces of Lake Superior. After the cutting of the canal in 1871, it became clear that docks for incoming coal and outgoing grain and lumber should be built inside the protection of Minnesota Point. Hence, it was the area surrounding the bay on Rice's Point (including what is now West End) and around the bay to Oneota that became the industrial center of the area. Hence, it was also this area, close to places of work, where the homes of most of the laborers in these industries were located. Along with the lumberyards, sawmills, docks, grain elevators, railroad yards, warehouses, blast furnaces, metal-working shops, tanneries, and other industries were the homes, hotels, boardinghouses, and shanties that housed Duluth's growing labor force.[26]

While the early settlers in the area were largely "American," by 1870 almost 60 percent of Duluth's population was foreign born.[27] Swedes made up by far the largest group among these foreign born. The influx of foreigners into Duluth was largely due to the construction of the Lake Superior and Mississippi Railroad. In the year following the agreement to build the railroad, the population of Duluth had grown from fewer than a hundred to over three

Rice's Point in the late 1880s. Courtesy Northeast Minnesota Historical Center.

thousand.[28] The railroad company advertised widely in both the English-language and foreign-language press in America. The company called for three thousand laborers, promising wages from two to four dollars per day and proclaiming that the lumber companies in the area would furnish "abundant and profitable" winter work. It also called for ten thousand immigrants to settle on land owned by the company along the railroad right of way, offering liberal credit and free transportation from Duluth over the completed portion of the railroad to any who settled on the land.[29]

The first boatload of Swedish immigrants arrived in Duluth on June 16, 1869, greeted by the cheers of local residents.[30] By the end of June, the railroad had finished constructing the Immigrant House, a large wooden structure designed to be temporary housing for incoming immigrants.[31] More immigrant laborers arrived on July 5, July 9, and July 31, 1869.[32] They were put to work clearing land, constructing the railroad road bed, building bridges, laying track, building machine shops, warehouses, loading docks, and a breakwater at the lakefront, all necessary for construction of the railroad.

Housing and other buildings were almost entirely wooden frame structures, built out of lumber milled locally from the white pines surrounding the settlement. Streets were unpaved and ungraded. Superior Street, Lake Avenue, and perhaps a few other streets had sidewalks made up of wooden planks nailed to wooden posts sunk into the mud. Fred Smith, who arrived in Duluth at Christmas time in 1869, described the city as a "haphazard, scraggly and repellent settlement, a mixed combination of Indian trading post, seaport, railroad construction camp, and gambling resort, altogether wild, rough, uncouth and frontier like."[33] A Finnish woman who immigrated sometime later recalled that she cried when she reached Duluth. Expecting a large city, she found instead a primitive town with shacks, brush, stumps, and a few wooden sidewalks.[34]

The Lake Superior and Mississippi Railroad turned to foreign workers to build the railroad because of the lack of laborers and because it was cheaper to hire immigrants than pay the wages necessary to entice American laborers to move to the area. A brochure published by the city of Duluth in 1870 advertised that "labor of all kinds is high and in constant demand," and reported that "common laborers get from $2 to $2.50; carpenters from $3 to $4.50; plasterers, stone masons, brick-layers, $4 per day."[35] However, it appears that actual wages paid were on the lower end of this range, with common laborers getting two dollars and carpenters three dollars per day.[36] In any case, while there were some skilled workers, merchants, and professionals among them, most of the immigrant laborers who were brought to Duluth at this time worked at

Lake Superior and Mississippi Railroad Immigrant House at the southeast corner of Michigan Street and Fifth Avenue West. Photograph by Paul D. Gaylord; courtesy of the Northeast Minnesota Historical Center.

unskilled jobs. The contractors, physicians, real estate brokers, lawyers, civil engineers, and merchants were nearly all Americans or immigrants from Canada and the British Isles.[37]

With the rapid expansion of Duluth in the 1880s, more and more immigrants came to the city. Some sense of the growth of the immigrant communities in Duluth in the 1880s can be gained by considering the churches founded in that decade. Among them were Salem Evangelical Covenant, a Swedish mission church; St. Mary Star of the Sea Catholic; the Swedish Church of Christ; the Norwegian Methodist; the Danish Methodist; St. John the Baptist Catholic; St. Matthew's German Lutheran; Third Swedish Baptist; St. Clements Catholic; the Finnish Evangelical Lutheran; the Swedish Evangelical Lutheran; Zion Lutheran (Norwegian); First German Methodist Episcopal; and the Swedish Methodist Episcopal Church. Impressive as this list is, it is important to keep in mind that many of the immigrants coming to Duluth lived outside the orbits of the various churches. According to one estimate, three-quarters of Swedes emigrating to America maintained no affiliation with any church.[38] Similarly, only one-quarter of Finnish Americans chose to belong to any church.[39] When C. B. Newcombe, superintendent in charge of construction of the first grain elevator in Duluth, attempted to lead his crew of two hundred largely immigrant men in prayer at the start of the workday, "he would get a bootjack, loaf of bread or fish hurled at his head."[40]

The transformation of Duluth from an outpost on the industrial frontier to a thriving city was part of a larger transformation going on in the United States. In the years following the Civil War, the American economy grew prodigiously. From 1860 to 1894, the United States jumped from fourth to first place in the world in the production of industrial goods. The number of laborers in manufacturing industries doubled in the decade of the 1880s, while during the same period the railway mileage in the country nearly doubled, so that in 1890, the United States had more miles of railroad than all European countries combined.[41] With this growth came a qualitative change in the nature of the American economy. Prior to this period, most production was done in small manufacturing establishments. As late as 1870 the average American manufacturing firm employed fewer than ten workers.[42] Products were sold to local and regional markets. The growth in America's manufacturing industries in the 1880s was capital intensive, tripling while the number of workers doubled.[43] By the 1890s large trusts dominated production in several industries, marketing their products on a national scale.

The vast growth of the railroads played a central role in the transformation of the American economy. The railroads required enormous amounts of capital. Cities and states competed to win the favor of major investors with offers of substantial public funding. State and federal land grants to the railroads further sweetened the deals. The railroads, in turn, sold the land to settlers, many of whom were immigrants brought to build the roads. The railroads created whole new towns almost overnight to supply the building of the roads and service the shipments back along the created lines. Further, the railroads created links to national markets, enabling producers to ship their goods to all parts of the country.[44]

This great transformation of the economic system created considerable uneasiness within sectors of the American public. Small businesses were threatened by competition with industrial giants. Laborers came under the control of impersonal corporate bureaucracies, intent on restructuring the productive processes to reduce the costs of production and actively recruiting low-wage immigrant workers. Farmers found their independence reduced. Increasingly dependent on the industrial sector for farm equipment, on the banks for financing, and on the railroads for transportation, farmers were threatened by economic forces beyond their control. Large numbers of small businessmen, laborers, and farmers felt unjustly treated by the emerging giants of commerce. In a message to Congress in December 1888, President Grover Cleveland reflected these public concerns about the changes that had occurred: "As we view the achievements of aggregated capital, we discover the existence of trusts, combinations and monopolies, while the citizen is struggling far in the rear or is trampled to death beneath an iron heel. Corporations, which should be carefully restrained creatures of the law and servants of the people, are fast becoming the people's masters."[45]

Popular indignation at the "robber barons," who owned and controlled the railroads, the trusts, and the banks, led to a series of popular movements to restore power to the people. The Granger movement of the late 1860s and early 1870s organized farmers into cooperatives for purchasing machinery, providing credit, and marketing grain. The Greenback Labor Party, calling for an increase in the money supply to ease the straits of debt-ridden farmers and small businessmen, polled over a million votes in 1878 and elected fourteen representatives to Congress. As part of this broad popular opposition to the dominance of big business, the 1870s and 1880s saw the emergence of a national labor movement in the United States. While labor unions had existed since early in the nineteenth century, particularly among skilled craftsmen, the changes in the American economy led to a labor movement that was different in size and structure from anything that had gone before.

Duluth's earliest labor unions were affiliated with a national organization known as the Knights of Labor. Formed in 1869, the Noble and Holy Order of the Knights of Labor was part of the post–Civil War reaction against the growth in power of big business. Noting the growth of a factory system in which increasing numbers of men and women were trapped in the role of wage laborers, the manifesto of the Knights proclaimed "an inevitable and irresistible conflict between the wage-system of labor and republican system of government."[46] Regardless of race, sex, or nationality, the Knights was open to all working people, excluding only the idle (bankers, speculators), the corrupt (lawyers, liquor dealers, gamblers), and social parasites (all of the above).[47] In its early years, the Knights eschewed both strikes and electoral politics, instead favoring efforts to raise the intellectual and moral qualities of working men and women and educate them on the need to replace the system of wage labor with a cooperative commonwealth that would recognize and reward honorable labor.

The Knights of Labor was present in Duluth from at least 1881, when a contingent marched with the firemen and a cornet band in a Fourth of July parade.[48] During the 1880s, six local assemblies of the Knights were established in Duluth, along with two assemblies across the bay in Superior, Wisconsin.[49] In addition, the Knights in Duluth established a hall at Seventeenth Avenue West and Michigan Street, which served as a meeting place.[50] They also established the Cooperative Mercantile Company at 121 West First Street.[51] By the end of the decade, two Knights of Labor newspapers were published weekly in the Twin Ports, the *Voice of Labor*, published by Fred W. Fry in Superior, and the *Industrial Age*, described as "the accredited representation of all labor organization in and about Duluth."[52]

The extensive presence of the Knights of Labor in Duluth is an indication that the "labor question" that exercised much of the United States in the last quarter of the nineteenth century was raised in Duluth. In the country on average in the 1880s, highly skilled workers in the construction trades could earn four dollars per day. Unskilled workers averaged slightly more than a dollar per day.[53] Because of its geographical remoteness and booming economy, wages in Duluth were considerably higher than this. The Duluth *Tribune* remarked on the scarcity of laboring men in Duluth and the higher wages that resulted.[54] Laborers in Duluth were also aware of the bargaining advantage this situation gave them and they pressed for still higher wages. In May 1882, early in Duluth's limited shipping season, longshoremen rejected an offer of twenty cents per hour, which would have put them well above the national average.[55] Taking advantage of the same seasonal pressures, laborers at the coal docks threatened to strike in May 1883.[56] In October 1883 the longshoremen were getting forty cents per hour and unsuccessfully went on strike to force this rate to fifty cents.[57] In August 1884, men working for the then-privately owned gas and water company went on strike to raise wages from $1.75 to $2.00 per day.[58]

There is thus considerable evidence to support the *Tribune*'s claim that wages in Duluth were substantially higher than the national average. On the other hand, Duluth's remoteness and boomtown economy made for higher-than-average living costs. The *Tribune* itself commented on the prevailing opinion that rents in Duluth were too high.[59] For the nation as a whole, rent for a working-class family averaged about $200 per year. In Duluth, house rental rates were $300 per year and up. It is also likely that costs for food, clothing, fuel, and other necessities were higher in Duluth than in more accessible parts of the country. Given what appears to have been the normal rate for unskilled labor in Duluth of $1.75 per day and a U.S. average working year of 282 days, annual wages for an unskilled laborer in Duluth in the 1880s would have been just under $500 per year.[60] This compares with an annual salary of $900 to $1,200 that the *Tribune* reported for a young businessman in 1884.[61] At the same time, the average annual cost of living for a working-class family in the United States stood at $720 per year.[62] Thus, it is clear that despite the favorable labor market, unskilled laborers in Duluth were hard-pressed to support a family on the prevailing wages. As a result, many single male laborers chose to lodge in boardinghouses, where the costs of living were lower, while others, including whole working-class families, lived in the substandard "shanties" scattered about Rice's Point and the area now known as the West End.

While the *Tribune* held that laborers were doing pretty well in general, it also recognized that some workers, even in Duluth, needed help just to get by.[63] In March 1884 it reported on the formation of a local Ladies' Relief Society to help the deserving poor of Duluth.[64] That same month, wages for lumber pilers and other yard men were reduced to $1.50 per day.[65] By the end of that year, a temporary downturn in business activity had caused a fall in demand for labor and consequently a fall in wages to $1.20 per day for common laborers.[66] The *Tribune* urged its Christian readers to turn from foreign missionary work to the plight of Duluth's own poor:

> Come back to Duluth and look around on some of the back streets, away up on the bleak hillside, or down on the marshy flats of Rice's and Minnesota Points. We may not find "heathen," perhaps, but we shall find many poor families that are absolutely in worse condition. We shall find our own people, honest, industrious and temperate people, too, who work with us and for us for the general prosperity of the city of which we boast—and many of them (more than the average citizen realizes) will be found quite destitute of the comforts of life.[67]

A large portion of Duluth's poor was made up of immigrant laborers. These were the single men and families who occupied many of the homes and shanties on Duluth's hillside and on the flats of Rice's Point and Minnesota Point, below. Among them were men who cleared the way and laid the railroad tracks, and the switchmen who worked in the railroad yards, ducking under moving cars to disassemble and reassemble moving stock. These immigrants also worked at the coal docks, lumber camps, lumber mills, and railroad repair shops. They were the men who made up the construction crews putting up buildings, grading streets, and digging the trenches for water, gas, and sewer lines. They were the women who cooked, cleaned, and did the laundry in the boardinghouses or worked as domestic servants in the homes of the well-to-do. An advertisement in a local newspaper read, "Please tell your Scandinavian hired girls that there will be a Swedish gospel meeting held in the English Congregational church, corner of First avenue and Second street east, every Sunday at 3:30 P.M." A prominent and indignant Scandinavian complained: why didn't the ad say "Scandinavian ladies" instead of "Scandinavian hired girls"? And, he asked, didn't the "professedly pious bucks who are so very anxious to meet the hired girls" bear a good deal of watching?[68] The alignment of class and ethnic divisions created a potentially explosive situation in Duluth.

The Noble and Holy Order of the Knights of Labor attracted many of the immigrant working poor. While the leadership of the Knights was predominantly made up of "American" males, the Knights was open to all working people, male or female, of whatever ethnic background. Its motto, "An Injury to One Is the Concern of All," promised a sympathetic hearing to immigrant laborers confronting English-speaking bosses and English-language laws. The first local assembly of the Knights of Labor in Duluth appears to have had a largely English-speaking membership. W. S. Woodbridge, a local newspaperman, marched with this assembly in the July 4 parade in 1881.[69] Its members included Charles Brennan, a painter employed by the St. Paul and Duluth Railroad, who died in a fall from a moving train, and Francis Holt, injured in a dynamite blast while working on the Duluth and Winnipeg Railroad.[70] In late fall 1882, a second local assembly of the Knights was formed at Rice's Point.[71] This assembly was a "mixed" one, including laborers from several industries.[72] It was the largest and longest lasting of the Knights of Labor groups in Duluth.

As it did across the country, the successful 1885 strike by the Knights against Jay Gould's Southwestern Railroad system stimulated the Knights in Duluth. The local at Rice's Point increased its membership from thirty-four to sixty-six.[73] It was also probably at this time that the local first established its hall.[74] Reflecting on the national impact of the strike in the spring of 1886, the Duluth *Tribune* called the Knights the most powerful secret organization in the country and looked forward to a rumored reorganization of the Knights in Duluth that would resurrect the defunct English-language local, restoring it, rather than the foreign Rice's Point local, to preeminence in Duluth and giving the city a lodge "second to none in strength and importance."[75] When a second struggle broke out between the Knights and Gould's Southwestern Railroad in March 1886, the *Tribune* supported the Knights, calling for the "recognition of rights too long withheld" and predicting that the "widespread and powerful organization of the Knights will compel more just and respectful treatment."[76] The *Tribune*'s support, however, was directed at the national leadership of the Knights, which opposed strikes, favoring arbitration and cooperation between labor and capital.[77] Hence, as the strike wore on and violence broke out in St. Louis, the *Tribune* openly broke with the Knights, charging that Socialists had unduly influenced the order.[78]

The *Tribune* was just as opposed to strikes in Duluth as it was to strikes in St. Louis. In an article entitled "The Trouble at Rice's Point," it disdainfully dismissed the efforts of workmen in the lumber mills to call a strike, and then went on to criticize a similar attempted strike by men working on the coal docks: "About noon a number of men quit work on the Ohio Company's dock and made a raid upon the Northwestern Fuel Company's premises, and, in various foreign tongues, commanded every man to quit." The company bookkeeper called the mayor, who ordered the police to disperse the strikers. A meeting of the strikers was held later that evening, "but all the men were foreigners and the proceedings were conducted in an irregular manner and in a foreign tongue." The men wanted an increase of pay from $1.50 to $1.75 per day; the company refused. Anticipating trouble, Mayor Sutphin telegraphed Governor Hubbard, who wired Captain Henri DeWitt, commander of the Duluth unit of the Minnesota Guard, to be ready to serve the mayor. The strike appears to have broken up without further incident, however. The *Tribune* dismissed the labor trouble as probably the work of one big talker.[79]

Nonetheless, labor agitation in Duluth continued. In the fall of 1886, a Minneapolis-based strike by railroad switchmen connected to the Knights of Labor involved Duluth.[80] Apparently enthused by the militancy of the Knights, two more local assemblies of the Knights were formed in 1887.[81] Trading on the popularity of the Knights, a local entrepreneur began to sell whiskey bearing the Knights of Labor label. The secretary of the district board of the Knights was instructed to inform Brother Schweiger that the label was a fraud and to advise members of the Knights in Duluth that the whiskey was bad and should be left alone.[82]

In 1888 the Knights continued to play an active role. The Knights supported the recently formed Typographers' Union in its dispute with the Duluth *Herald*, passing a resolution supporting the typographers and appearing at a meeting of the city council on their behalf.[83] The Typographers' local had been formed in March 1886.[84] Its president, C. B. King, served as editor of the Knights' newspaper in Duluth, the *Industrial Age*.[85] A few days after the city council meeting, on Memorial Day, the Knights marched east from their hall at Seventeenth Avenue West and First Street, accompanied by a unit from the Knights of Pythias and the West End Band, joining up with the main Memorial Day procession in downtown Duluth.[86] One week later the Knights in the Twin Ports hosted public meetings in both Superior and Duluth. Featured speakers were P. J. McGaughey, chairman of the general co-operative board of the Knights of Labor, and Eva MacDonald, a young working woman and labor activist from Minneapolis.[87] McGaughey called for the unity of all workers regardless of "faction or birth," while MacDonald discussed the plight of working women, who often put in twelve to fourteen hours per day and were paid only one-half to two-thirds of what men were paid. MacDonald called for equal pay for equal work and for a working day of length and pay that would enable all women and men to enjoy the better things life has to offer.[88]

August 1888 found the Knights hosting a dance in Superior, but in Duluth events had taken a more ominous turn.[89] Throughout the summer of 1888, the construction of Duluth's sewer system had been under way, involving many different contractors and large numbers of immigrant workers. On the night of Thursday, August 2, a gang of men working for the firm of Wolf and Truax quit work at a site on the West End.[90] The next day the strike spread, with a gang of strikers going east along Superior Street urging other men to quit work. By the time the strikers reached Fitger's brewery, there were "a good five hundred" men in the crowd. The strikers moved further east, heading up Tenth Avenue and then turning west, picking up other men who had been working on street and sewer construction on Third and Fourth Streets. Eventually they arrived at a vacant lot opposite the Fargusson buildings on the 400 block of West Superior Street, where speeches were made calling for two dollars per day. At this meeting a decision was made to call out the men working on the coal docks and in the sawmills on Rice's Point. The crowd moved down toward the point, picking up city streetcar crews along the way. Despite some minor violence when a sawmill engineer tried to prevent the strikers from shutting down his engine, the strikers succeeded in shutting down the coal docks and sawmills on the point. Headlines in the *Lake Superior News* proclaimed, "A Strike Which Spreads Over the City From End to End" and "Work Is Stopped."[91]

During the evening of August 3, the strikers met in Culbertson Hall at Twenty-Second Avenue West and Superior Street. The meeting was orderly. Speakers urged the men to be disciplined and persistent, predicting that the contractors would have to give in since the demand for laborers in the Dakota wheat fields at that time of year made it impossible for them to bring in replacement workers. Among the speakers were the Reverend Fred Ring, Police Chief Doran, and Knights of Labor activist Joe Schweiger. Also among the speakers was the prominent Oneota Swedish business-man E. G. Swanstrom, who was elected to a committee to represent the strikers, along with Schweiger and four other men.

Following negotiations involving this elected committee, the various contractors, and Mayor Sutphin, another meeting was held at Culbertson's Hall on August 10 with Swanstrom serving as chair.[92] Representatives of the negotiating committee, speaking in English and Swedish, urged the men to accept a deal giving most workers $1.75 per day. This represented a compromise between the $1.50 previously paid by the contractors and the $2.00 demanded by the strikers. This compromise was supported by Mayor Sutphin and Swanstrom. Eventually a vote was taken in which "there was quite a sentiment against taking less than $2.00." Following this vote, the mayor again spoke, bluntly warning the men that as

The E. G. Swanstrom family. E. G. Swanstrom stands in the middle, wearing a black hat. Courtesy Northeast Minnesota Historical Center.

mayor, he would deal severely with any who attempted to interfere with men working for $1.75 per day, using the police force if necessary. Following some angry words directed at certain of the contractors who were unwilling to pay even the $1.75, the strikers agreed to accept the negotiated settlement. While not a total victory, the settlement reflected the emergence of a powerful labor movement in Duluth. It also set the stage for a violent confrontation the following year between Duluth's police and its immigrant labor force.

One year later, in 1889, the bloodiest strike in Duluth's history erupted. Like the previous year, the strike began among laborers working for various contractors building streets and sewers for the city. Again the precipitating issue was wages. The settlement of the preceding year had given way, with the prevailing wage being cut back to $1.50 per day. Many in Duluth were sympathetic to the plight of the laborers. An editorial in the *Duluth Daily Tribune* directly addressed the issue of wages:

> Strikes among laboring men in Duluth are becoming far too frequent and it is high time a more careful investigation of the causes leading to them was had. Unless the strikers are an unreasonable class of men, it is a self-evident fact that the wage system in Duluth is in need of an overhauling. The almost weekly announcement of a strike in Duluth does not rebound to the credit of the city and when the cold facts are given out it certainly does look as though the strikers are justified in their actions. A single man finds it difficult to save a cent from the pay of $1.50 a day after meeting the necessary expenses of living in Duluth. There are few, if any, cities in the country where board is as high, and all incidentals are in proportion. This statement being borne out by the facts, how must a man of family fare on the same wages? Not very well, we imagine. Contractors should take this into consideration when making bids upon work, and if they have not done so, it seems hard that they would intentionally ask the laborer to bear the brunt of their mistake. If we are correctly advised in the premises, we would say that $1.75 is none too much for a day laborer in Duluth.[93]

Construction crews installing water and gas lines in Duluth in 1890, the year after the strike. Courtesy Duluth Public Library.

In light of this and the return to the $1.50 wage, it is not surprising that a strike again broke out among these day laborers.

The strike began on the morning of July 2, when four hundred men employed by the gas and water company on Michigan Street quit work. As had happened the year before, the strikers roamed around the city calling out other workers, including men working at McDougall's shipyards and at the various sawmills. Support for the strike was widespread. By the time the strikers had made the rounds of the various construction sites, the crowd had grown to "fully 2,000 men."[94] As had happened the year before, the men met in an empty lot to consider what to do next. However, while the strikers were following a course similar to the previous summer, the situation confronting them had changed. In 1888 the strike broke out at a time when no other laborers were readily available. In 1889 there were "thousands of laborers in the city" who were "out of employment" and were "glad to work at $1.50 a day or even less."[95] Realizing that this labor market would make it difficult for the strikers to maintain discipline, "the contractors in the Chamber of Commerce and Palladio buildings" demanded that the mayor provide police protection for any crews willing to work at $1.50.

Wednesday, July 3, brought a confrontation between the strikers and the police. Having gathered in a vacant lot, the strikers marched to where a small crew of men was working on First Street, between Fifth and Sixth Avenues East. The strikers compelled the men to stop working and the police interfered, making a show of arms when the strikers approached them and protecting the men who returned to work. The strikers eventually dispersed, meeting again in the afternoon at the Knights of Labor Hall, where a squad of police kept an eye on them. Most of the talk at this meeting was in "Scandinavian."[96] The *Tribune* news story describing these events said the men were "more or less under the influence of Fry the notorious Duluth labor agitator and one somewhat inclined to use violence against men who will not quit work."[97] In an editorial on July 4, the *Tribune* reversed its earlier support for the strikers, holding that while "the men probably were worth $1.75 a day or more," "most of the contractors could not afford to pay more than $1.50 per day," so the strike was "not deserving of sympathy." The editorial also denounced the "blatant and loud mouthed" Fry, the strike leader.[98] This Fry was almost certainly Fred Fry, publisher of the *Voice of Labor*, the official organ of the Knights of Labor across the bay in Superior. The *Daily News*, which like the *Tribune*, had earlier argued that $1.75 was a minimum family wage, now also denounced the strikers, holding that attempts to prevent willing men from working for $1.50 and less were violations of individual rights.[99]

Thursday, July 4, was peaceful. Eighteen hundred people rode special excursion trains to Lakeside and Lester parks, hundreds of them stopping to view the Breutigan's summer garden, where gymnasts from the German Turnverein performed. At Lester Park, "Clan Stewart and friends were out in full force" and the Lakeside Women's Christian Temperance Union ran a refreshment booth. Along Park Point thousands gathered under clear and sunny skies to watch the yacht races out in Lake Superior.[100] On the West End the ladies of Grace Methodist Episcopal Church raised twenty-five dollars selling cake and ice cream.[101] And in West Duluth, the Duluth Maroons came from behind to win a baseball game against the West Duluth team.[102] The only hint of the labor problems simmering beneath the surface came when a drunken man shouting, "Stop the Knights of Labor! I'm a union man!" was arrested for interrupting a bicycle race on Superior Street.[103]

The next morning, Friday, July 5, the strikers again gathered early in the vacant lot opposite the downtown post office. From this lot the crowd moved to the Metropolitan Block, where construction workers were building an addition. When the strikers attempted to get the men working to quit, the police, led by Captain McLaughlin, intervened, making clear their intention to prevent the strikers from interfering with the men. The crowd dispersed but gathered later at the Knights of Labor Hall. Speeches were made in English, "Scandinavian," Finnish, and Italian, and a Laborers Union was formed. Elected officers were P. Morris, president, Ander Soby, vice president, and Clarence Freiburg, secretary-treasurer. In addition, a committee made up of English-speaking men was named to talk to the contractors.[104]

Later in the afternoon the crowd moved outside, this time trying to get men working on sewer construction at Garfield Avenue and West Michigan Street to quit work. When the police again intervened, men in the crowd began throwing rocks at them. In response the police charged the crowd, swinging nightsticks and firing some fifty shots, though without deadly intent. Under this assault, the crowd, estimated at between five hundred and two thousand men, broke and ran away.[105] The *Tribune* took considerable delight in the retreat of the crowd, describing how "one big Scandinavian when the first shot was fired sung out 'val ay tank ay skam' running [*sic*] across the sidewalk and jumped into a vacant lot which was filled with mud and water."[106] Similarly, the *Daily News* reported that onlookers "simply roared with laughter when they beheld the exertions put forth by each runaway to save himself."[107] When it was all over, several policemen had been injured by rocks and sticks and several strikers "were bleeding profusely from wounds about the head made by policemen's clubs."[108] Observing that there were plenty of men in the city out of work, the *Tribune* advised the striking men to accept the $1.50 daily wage and "kick about half a dozen labor agitators out of town."[109]

The strikers had other ideas. Enraged by the police, they began to arm themselves. The *Herald* reported that three hundred to four hundred strikers were out on the streets, including some two hundred men said to be Finns and Italians armed with pistols. The *Herald* warned, "It appears that the strike is now out of the control of the Scandinavians and other cool headed men who were in it at first, and to be now a mob led by Bohemians and Italians, races that are about as undesirable as could be had in a strike or in a town."[110]

About 4:00 that afternoon, July 6, the strikers broke into two groups, each making its way to Michigan Street, where work continued on a sewer between Garfield Avenue and Twentieth Avenue West. Following some maneuvering by both strikers and police, one group of strikers attacked the men working, while another group began to throw stones at a police line formed on West Michigan Street at Twentieth Avenue West. At some point, shots were fired and a gunfight erupted between the strikers and the surrounded policemen. The shooting lasted for over an hour, ending only when the strikers ran out of ammunition and the local guard unit, commanded by Captain DeWitt, arrived on the scene. Nearly half the policemen engaged in the battle were hit by bullets. The strikers were armed only with pistols, however, while the police had some high-powered weapons. This kept the strikers at a distance, and none of the policemen was seriously wounded. Among the policemen, officers Donovan, Walkoviak, Hayden, Clemens, Kilgore, O'Donnell, Harrigan, Smollet, Cummings, and Captain McLaughlin were all wounded. Among the strikers, several people were seriously injured, including two men, Ed Johnson and Matt Mack, both Finns, who later died of gunshot wounds.[111] Frank Zan, identified by the *Herald* as "a very large Italian," was shot in the head but survived. Other seriously wounded strikers included George Peletier, a streetcar driver, Haken Benson, Yorke Castigan, Alfred Anderson, George Peterson, and T. Clemson.[112] The *Herald* estimated that thirty men were wounded and reported that wounded strikers were hiding in the squatters' shacks at Fourteenth Avenue and First Street.[113] Also among the wounded were Pastor Dahl of the Norwegian Lutheran Church, who had three balls pass through his clothing but was only slightly wounded, and Thomas Fitzsimmons, an eighteen-year-old bystander struck by a stray bullet who later died of his wound.[114] The day ended when Mayor Sutphin, supported by the police and local guard unit, ordered the streets cleared and the saloons closed. "Bloody War" was the headline in the *Tribune* the next morning.[115]

This outburst of violence was a tragic climax to the labor troubles that had been simmering in Duluth throughout the 1880s. While the conflict was clearly a labor dispute, it was also an ethnic conflict, pitting foreign immigrants against a largely Irish police force and a predominantly "American" elite in charge of the construction companies, the city government, the press, and the militia.

The ethnic dimensions of the conflict are evident in the newspaper accounts. We have already seen how the *Herald* noted that

MEMBERS OF THE DULUTH POLICE DEPARTMENT WHO PARTICIPATED IN THE SUPPRESSION OF THE RIOT OF JULY 6, 1889.

Alex Gillis

Wm. Walkoviak   Geo. Burke   Patrick McGuire   E. B. Force   Patrick O'Donnell   N. P. Nelson   Martin Keating   Daniel Donovan   John Shea
John Wade   Thomas Hayden   N. L. Moen   Wm. Hocking   G. Kilgore   Edw. Dwyer   Martin Smith   J. F. Horgan   Jacob Rosek
Patrick McManus   Samuel Thompson   Det. Robt. Benson   Sergt. F. Clements   Mayor John T. Sutphin   Chief P. Doran   Capt. Thos. McLaughlin   Thos. Madden
Louis Ratty   Robert Smolett

Members of the Duluth Police Department who participated in the suppression of the riot on July 6, 1889. Courtesy Northeast Minnesota Historical Center.

the strike had slipped out of the control of "cool headed" Scandinavians and into the hands of "a mob led by Bohemians and Italians, races that are about as undesirable as could be had in a strike or in a town."[116] Dr. McNulty, a witness to the events who was hostile to the strikers, told the *Herald* that "[t]he first bullet was fired from the strikers. An Italian did the firing as he stood near Nineteenth Avenue. The police before this had been firing blank cartridges at the strikers."[117] The *Herald* also mentions two Italians who stood in the intersection at Seventeenth Avenue West and Superior Street and emptied their pistols at the police while "exposed to a hail of lead."[118] Finns also figure prominently in the newspaper accounts. The two strikers killed by the police were both Finns, and the *Herald* claimed that the initial rush on the police was led by Finns.[119] Further, on the Monday following the strike, the *Herald* reported the discovery of a plot by Finns to burn down buildings in Duluth.[120] The *Daily News*, having identified several of the injured strikers as Scandinavian or Finnish, reported that "not an American, Englishman, German or Irishman participated in the strike, so far as can be learned."[121]

The idea that some of the strikers may have intended to provoke a wider insurrection was reinforced when Sergeant Clements of the police force found a box of dynamite stored near Second Street and Fifteenth Avenue West. While the dynamite probably was there for use in the ongoing construction work, the police and newspapers believed it had been placed there by a striker with anarchist tendencies.[122] The *News* mentioned the rumors of dynamite and arson and also published a report that strikers had crossed in boats from Twentieth Avenue West to Superior, Wisconsin, where they tried to purchase arms.[123] On the Monday following the strike, the *Tribune* ran an editorial on its front page mentioning rumors that "strikers and anarchists" were arming themselves and supplying themselves with dynamite. The *Tribune* went on to denounce the Knights of Labor and called for further arming the police. The *Tribune* also printed a request from the local chamber of commerce for a mass meeting to discuss ways and means of preserving law and order.[124] Fearing further trouble, local authorities added seventy-five or eighty special police to the Duluth police force and armed them all with rifles and .44-caliber Colt revolvers. In addition, Sheriff Sharvey swore in thirty deputies and Company K of the Minnesota Guard remained on duty.[125]

On Tuesday, July 9, the chamber of commerce went further, running a notice in the *Tribune* calling on all men who believed in law and order to meet at 10:00 A.M.[126] On the same day, a story reported that some four hundred businessmen had already volunteered to serve in a special force to preserve law and order. Many prominent businessmen were mentioned as being among this force.[127] To prevent further violence, Mayor Sutphin also issued a proclamation closing all saloons, stating, "Notice is hereby given to all persons that no gatherings of any kind will be allowed upon the streets, or elsewhere in the city of Duluth, until after the termination of the present difficulty."[128]

Local businessmen rallied behind the police. In the *Tribune* for Tuesday, July 9, a letter from J. D. Ray to Mayor Sutphin was published, praising the valiant police force and pledging one hundred dollars as a reward to be given to the men. In the days that followed, other businessmen followed Ray's lead until by Friday, the reward fund for the police amounted to $3,174.

The business community, however, was not entirely united. On the Monday following the violence on Saturday, the *Herald*, clearly revealing the ethnic dimension of the confrontation, sadly observed that "[i]t is a lamentable fact that several business men—foreigners—of the West End were heard to express sympathy for the strikers."[129] And four days after the violence, the *Tribune* reported that "certain Rice Pointers blamed the mayor for the trouble."[130] These criticisms were aimed at businessmen from the immigrant Scandinavian community, who were sympathetic to the cause of the immigrant laborers. The authorities went so far as to bring charges against Charles Carlson, a real-estate agent from the Scandinavian West End who, according to the *Daily News*, "seemed to have had the greatest influence with the men, if the reports can be believed."[131]

Another "foreign" businessman with some sympathy for the strikers was the prominent West End Swedish businessman and politician, E. G. Swanstrom. The year before, Swanstrom had been elected to serve on the committee representing the strikers in negotiations with the contractors. Swanstrom's support for the immigrant workers continued. At a meeting of the city council on July 1, before the strike, Mayor Sutphin spoke in support of cutting wages for laborers directly employed by the city, from $1.75 per day to the prevailing lower wage rate. Alderman Swanstrom opposed the mayor on this issue, supporting the existing $1.75 per day wage rate.[132] Swanstrom and opponents of the mayor, including the *Daily News*, prevailed.[133]

Developments following the strike cast further light on a political fault line existing in Duluth in the late 1880s. On the one side were Swanstrom and other "foreign" businessmen sympathetic to the laborers and supported by the *Daily News*. On the other side was Mayor Sutphin, supported by the "American" chamber of commerce and the *Tribune*. In the days after the strike, both sides tried to use the strike to their own political advantage. For example, supporters of Mayor Sutphin mounted an attack against Swanstrom and the *Daily News*. While there is no evidence that Swanstrom or the *News* ever encouraged violence, the *Tribune* denounced Swanstrom as largely responsible for the trouble, charging him with a "morbid hatred of Mayor Sutphin."[134] The attack on Swanstrom and the *Daily News* continued with editorials in the *Tribune* blaming Swanstrom and W. H. Burke, president and general manager of the *News*, for the riot.[135] The *Tribune* also laid the blame for the death of the Fitzsimmons boy, hit by a stray bullet, on Burke and S. A. Thompson, treasurer of the *News*.[136]

The *News* responded to these attacks. On July 9 it defended Swanstrom, dismissing the charges against him as the work of "political claqqers for John B. Sutphin who view Mr. Swanstrom as Sutphin's rival."[137] On that same day, the *News* attempted to shift blame for the riot onto its rival, the *Tribune*, by quoting the pre-strike article by the *Tribune* justifying the strike as evidence that the *Tribune* itself was responsible for the violence.[138]

The aftermath of the strike also casts light on the role of organized labor in Duluth politics. Both the *Tribune* and the *Herald* laid part of the blame for the violence on the local Knights of Labor. Resolutions from two local assemblies of the Knights denied any involvement in the strike and accused the *Tribune* and *Herald* of publishing false accounts of the strike.[139] These resolutions by the two assemblies of Knights and post-strike letters in the *Daily News* from master workman A. M. McLean show some emerging divisions within Duluth's working class. On the one hand, the resolutions and letters try to place blame for the violence on one particular ethnic group, the Italians. On the other hand, the resolutions and letters distinguish the respectable, organized labor movement of the Knights from the unorganized movement of the several thousand men involved in the strike.[140] In the end, neither of these attempts was wholly successful. While both the Knights and the *Herald* singled out Italians as responsible for the violence, only one of the strikers arrested or injured was Italian. All the others were Finnish or Scandinavian. Nor are the claims that the Knights had nothing to do with the strike credible. The *News* itself reported that the strikers had met at the Knights of Labor Hall the day before the violence began. This was the meeting at which the *Herald* reported the strikers forming a new Knights of Labor Laborers Union.

While it is impossible to say with any certainty what really happened, it appears that a significant number of recent immigrants, employed in making improvements throughout the city as they had done the year before, turned to the Knights of Labor for help restoring the $1.75 per day wage, this time forming a new union under the umbrella of the Knights. With the support of some local, mainly "foreign," businessmen, the Knights tried to negotiate a solution to the problem similar to the settlement of the year before. When that failed, the established local assemblies of the Knights lost control of the strikers. With the police pledged to prevent work stoppages, fighting broke out and blood was spilled. The Knights then tried to distance themselves from the violence and everyone looked for someone else to blame.

If the initial sympathetic coverage of the 1889 strike by both the *Tribune* and the *Daily News* was right, however, the reduced prevailing wage of $1.50 per day was simply not a living wage. If this was so, it was neither "riotous dagos" nor a handful of labor agitators that prompted Duluth's largely immigrant day laborers to take up arms against the police, but rather hard circumstances.

In Duluth, six men were arrested as leaders of the July 6 confrontation charged with rioting. They were Charles Carlson, Adolphe Embleme, George Peterson, Frank Zahn, Eric Lofgren, and Joseph Frank. The men were formally arraigned on September 9, 1889. The first to be tried was Frank Zahn, the man identified as one of the Italians who instigated the violence. The jury returned a judgment of "not guilty."[141] On January 6, 1890, all remaining charges were dismissed "for want of prosecution."[142] In February, 1890, city elections were held. The labor question entered into the campaign and the labor candidate, M. J. Davis, was elected mayor.[143] Samuel McQuade, whom Davis appointed as the new chief of police, was immediately given responsibility for drawing up a new set of rules to govern the use of force by the police.[144]

from labor town to steel trust

THE BLOODY EVENTS OF 1889 GALVANIZED OPPOSITION TO THE business leaders who had until then provided political leadership for Duluth. In response to those events, a coalition was formed that challenged the business leaders throughout the 1890s. While this coalition included some business and professional men from the different ethnic communities, its largest constituency was working class, and its basic agenda was to elect men to public office who would serve the interests of Duluth's workers and their families. This coalition, however, was laced with internal contradictions. The arrival of the steel trust in Duluth at the turn of the century changed the balance of power. Faced with a strengthened business community and an aggressive anti-union campaign, the fragile pro-labor coalition gave way, leaving Duluth in the hands of leaders drawn from the business community for decades to come.

The immediate outcome of the events of the summer of 1889 was a heated mayoral campaign, with independent labor candidate M. J. Davis overcoming both the Republican, M. O. Hall, and the Democrat, J. K. Shaw, in the February 1890 election. Support for Davis came largely from Scandinavian laborers, who had been alienated by the events of the strike from Mayor Sutphin and his Republican Party, which was traditionally supported by Scandinavian voters.[1] Many, if not all, of these laborers were immigrants. The Davis forces made a concerted effort to get these men to take out "first papers" by formally swearing their intention to become citizens and paying a one-dollar fee; these first papers made the immigrant eligible to vote in local elections. The *Tribune* reported "heavy registration" with a "great crush" of would-be voters trying to register at different precincts in the city. Altogether, some four thousand voters were added to the lists during the three days of voter registration.[2] An article in the *Tribune* described the scene at Captain Pressnell's office, where the immigrants came to take out their first papers. A force of clerks was kept busy asking, "Where were you born? When did you come to this country and where did you land?" Following these questions, the applicant would be "sworn that it [was] his bona fide intention to become a good American citizen." Finally, "after he had left his dollar or the order of some candidate for political honors," the immigrant would be eligible to register to vote. This same article tells us that on this particular day, most of the one-dollar fees were "charged" to candidates for office. It also tells us that among the 115 sets of first papers issued that day, "61 were to Swedes; 20 to Norwegians; 15 to Finlanders; 5 to Polanders; 6 to Englishmen; 4 to Canadians; 2 to Scotchmen; 1 to an Irishman and 1 to a German."[3] The following day, 305 persons took out first papers, with arrangements having been made to transport these future voters for free from the State Bank to the courthouse.[4]

With E. G. Swanstrom of Duluth widely viewed as the dominant force in the Davis camp, the local Republican Party sought to hold at least a part of its traditional Scandinavian base by nominating a promising young Norwegian businessman, M. O. Hall, as its candidate for mayor. This proved to be a singularly misguided choice, for it was Hall who had introduced a resolution condemning the Duluth *Tribune* for instigating the July strike at a July 3 meeting of the chamber of commerce. Angry with Hall, the *Tribune*, traditionally a solid supporter of the Republican Party, now chose to support the Democratic candidate, Shaw.[5] Hall had also been one of the instigators of the campaign to raise money to reward the police force for its role in suppressing the July strike. Davis's supporters were quick to turn this to his advantage:

> "Do you, workingmen, ever get gold medals when you shoot somebody?"—The poor workingmen who were torn to pieces by the well-armed and bloodthirsty policemen.—the blood of the workingmen who were murdered the 6th of July is crying to heaven for revenge upon Mr. Hall, who collected money for the police-murderers.[6]

Not to be outdone in this rhetorical war, the *Tribune* denounced Davis as a "simple minded nonentity" and a "tool for a cunning, tricky politician" and "cunning dictator," Swanstrom.[7] In the same preelection issue, the *Tribune* printed a letter from

"A Workingman," who called Swanstrom "one of the chief instigators of the riot" and described M. F. Wesenberg, editor of *Skandinav*, as a "hairy faced anarchist."[8] For its own part, the *Tribune*
described Wesenberg as "the much-bearded exponent of dynamite
and destruction at the West End."[9]

The election of Davis indicated the depth and breadth of
anger at the police and city administration among laboring men and
their sympathizers in the immigrant communities. Outrage at the
broken agreement governing wages and the willingness of city politicians to use the police force to serve the interests of the contractors produced a reaction within Duluth's multiethnic working class.
Under the leadership of Swanstrom, the large Scandinavian community abandoned its traditional home in the Republican Party and
joined with some Germans, Poles, Irish, and Italians, traditionally
aligned with the Democrats in Duluth, to support the Independent
Labor candidacy of Davis. This coalition, however, was threatened
by internal differences. Besides the obvious problems caused by
differences of language, there were issues concerning religion and
temperance that were rooted in different cultural and ethnic traditions. These issues would persist for thirty years or more. There
were also short-term differences connected to a national contest
between the Knights of Labor and the emerging American Federation of Labor (AFL) over the future direction of the American labor
movement.

In the 1890s, numerous bridges existed between the labor
movement and the temperance movement. A pledge of temperance, the "Powderly Pledge" (named after the head of the Knights
of Labor, Terrance Powderly), was a standard part of the membership oath of the Knights. Temperance was also especially popular
among the Finns and Scandinavians, key groups that had played
prominent roles in the strike of 1889. Connections between the
temperance movement and the Davis candidacy were clear even
before the election. In its effort to derail Davis, the *Tribune* had ridiculed the Davis campaign as a marriage between temperance blue
laws supported by "the basement luminary," Wesenberg, and the
half-baked political economy of "labor philosophers."[10]

Connections between the temperance movement and the
labor movement extended beyond the Davis campaign. Though it
supported Hall, the Republican, over Davis, the Norwegian newspaper *Scandia* consistently expressed both pro-temperance and pro-
labor positions. *Scandia* also mentioned frequent meetings of the

Scandinavian Good Templars in Duluth. The International Order of Good Templars (IOGT) was one of the older fraternal organizations that came to play a significant role in American life around the turn of the century. Primarily focused on the cause of temperance, members pledged to personally abstain from the use of intoxicating liquors, to work toward educating the public about the value of temperance, and to work toward legislative prohibition of the liquor traffic. But the platform of the IOGT clearly placed the cause of temperance within a wider framework, calling for the "cultivation of the ideal of the world-wide brotherhood of man, regardless of race, color or creed, with expanding effort to uplift and educate the members to social needs and obligations."[11] For the Good Templars, the brotherhood of man included women as well. As early as 1864, the IOGT was charged with being a "free love society" because it accepted women as members with equal rights, and from the beginning women were elected to offices in the Minnesota Grand Lodge.[12] By 1890, two Scandinavian lodges of the Good Templars were active in the area: Nordstjärnan Lodge in Duluth and Morgonstjärnan Lodge in West Duluth. While the Good Templar Lodges included many people from business and professional backgrounds, they also included working-class men and women, and as an organization, the Good Templars sympathized with the cause of labor.[13] For example, on May 15, 1891, *Scandia* reported on an IOGT lecture by Dr. Rissen in Duluth supporting both Prohibition and Socialism. It was this Scandinavian reform movement, encompassing both temperance and labor issues and including business and professional men as well as laborers, that provided the foundation for Davis's successful campaign for mayor in 1890. It is thus not surprising that Davis should have supported an early saloon-closing initiative.[14]

Unfortunately for Davis and his Independent Labor Party, temperance was not popular among all working-class communities and the temperance issue quickly became one of those fissures that would divide the labor movement in Duluth for decades to come. Already in the campaign of 1890, significant opposition to Davis surfaced within labor organizations and immigrant groups heavily composed of working-class families. In a meeting of five hundred of Duluth's Germans at Turner Hall, the Democratic candidate Shaw was endorsed for mayor. On the same evening, a meeting of three hundred Poles at Sateski's Hall unanimously endorsed Shaw. Likewise, at Oleson's Hall a meeting of about sixty Italians voted overwhelmingly to endorse Shaw. Unlike the Scandinavians and Finns, each of these ethnic groups was opposed to the Prohibition measures supported by the temperance movement.

Another fissure within the labor movement in Duluth grew out of the national conflict between the Knights of Labor and the AFL, which was rapidly replacing the Knights as the leading labor organization in the United States. Conflict between the Knights and the AFL surfaced within the organized labor movement and had a clear bearing on the mayoral campaign. Late in the 1890 campaign, Frank Bresland, vice president of Painters and Decorators Local 106, came out openly for Shaw, complaining that he had only just found out that the "labor" candidacy of Davis was in fact the creation of a small clique and lacked the official support of organized labor in Duluth.[15] Bresland's discovery was probably due to the opposition to Davis coming from the AFL in Duluth. In the week before the election, August Stirnel, traveling auditor for the Cigar Makers' International, the union from which Samuel Gompers, the national head of the AFL, had come, was in Duluth. In an article in the *Tribune*, Stirnel was quoted as expressing dismay that the *Industrial Age* could claim the authority of the Trades Council in Duluth for its endorsement of Davis.[16]

While Stirnel professed to have no interest in local affairs, in fact his statement reflected the interest of the emerging AFL in separating itself and the American labor movement from the influence of the Knights of Labor. Emil Applehagen, the organizer for the AFL based in Duluth, followed up on the direction provided by Stirnel. Applehagen, who was president of the Duluth Trades and Labor Assembly, called a meeting of union and laboring men. He opened the meeting with an attack on the Davis campaign, claiming that the selection of Davis as the candidate of labor was done at a meeting of "not more than twelve men" at the office of the *Industrial Age*. Applehagen went on to call for an official labor endorsement in the mayoral campaign from the meeting at hand, apparently ignoring the AFL policy against such endorsements. In due course, the meeting adopted a resolution condemning the *Industrial Age* endorsement of Davis as a "star chamber meeting of a few men" and endorsing Shaw for mayor.[17] Thereafter the *Industrial Age* dropped from the head of its editorial columns the endorsement of the Duluth Trades and Labor Assembly.

A third factor dividing Duluth's pro-labor coalition was the fissure between Protestants and Catholics. This religious divide was connected with ethnic divisions and with differences over temperance. In general, Duluth's working class divided into two camps, with Protestant, pro-temperance Scandinavians and Finns on one side, and Catholic Irish, Poles, southern Slavs, and Italians, who were fearful of the temperance movement, on the other. Germans, who were divided on grounds of religion, generally sided with those ethnic groups who were fearful of the temperance movement.

With Duluth's labor movement divided in these multiple ways, Davis ran for reelection in 1892 as the candidate of the People's Party. In February 1892, reform-minded organizations, including the Knights of Labor, the Single-Taxers, the Nationalists (followers of the popular Socialist Edward Bellamy), the Greenbackers, and the Prohibitionists met in St. Louis under the leadership of the Farmers' Alliance. There the People's Party, or Populist Party, was formed. Later, at a convention in Omaha in July 1892, the Populists adopted a platform written by the Minnesota Populist orator and writer Ignatius Donnelly, charging the capitalistic trusts with bringing the country to "moral, political, and material ruin."[18] Running as a Populist, Davis faced stronger opposition than he had two years before. In a speech delivered to a "crowd of Polanders" on the Sunday before the election, Charles D'Autremont, a prominent lawyer in Duluth and Davis's Democratic opponent, said, "The question before you to consider is whether you will turn the government of the city over to the churches and the Scandinavians."[19] Here D'Autremont challenged the role of the Scandinavian temperance movement and the role of (Protestant) Pastor Monten, who had replaced Swanstrom as the political leader of the Swedes in Duluth.[20] The challenge worked. It forced open the split within the labor coalition between the Protestant, pro-temperance, Scandinavians, who rallied around the Knights of Labor, and the Catholic, antitemperance, non-Scandinavians, who rallied around the AFL, giving the victory in the mayoral campaign to D'Autremont.

The divide between Protestants and Catholics also extended beyond the labor movement. With the governing "American" elite being overwhelmingly Protestant, this divide often found expression in negative attitudes directed against those immigrants who adhered to the Roman Catholic faith. Anti-Catholicism was deeply rooted in Protestant America and had flourished in overtly political form in the Know-Nothing movement of the 1850s. In the late nineteenth century, anti-Catholicism again appeared in political form in the American Protective Association (APA). Founded in March

1877, the goal of the APA was to protect Protestant America against the influence of the pope, priests, and the Catholic religion. Members of the APA took an oath pledging not to employ any Catholic if a Protestant could be found, to exclude Roman Catholics from all collaborative efforts, and to oppose all Catholics for public offices. Members of the APA believed that a secret order had gone out from the pope calling for the massacre of Protestants on the day of the feast of St. Ignatius in 1893. When the massacre did not happen, the APA blamed it on the trickery of the Jesuits, who hoped to lull the Protestants into a false sense of security.

APA publications also printed forged documents, purportedly written by the pope, absolving all Catholics of the need to obey oaths of citizenship to the United States. In the climate of economic distress and political instability caused by a national economic depression in the early 1890s, the APA became a force to be reckoned with in the national Republican Party. In a handful of American cities, including Duluth, the APA briefly dominated local politics.[21] In elections for city council held in February 1893, APA Republicans won all elected offices except city treasurer, for which F. J. Voss ran unopposed. This gave members of the APA overwhelming control of the council. Acting on APA principles, the council then refused to appoint Catholic bishop James McGolrick for a second term to the Library Board and apparently blocked a promised sale of land for the construction of a new cathedral in Duluth.[22]

The APA in Minnesota was especially popular among Scandinavian immigrants.[23] While it is impossible to say with any certainty how many of the Scandinavian immigrants in Duluth voted for the APA Republicans, it is certain that the APA Republicans could not have gained control of the city council without substantial support from them. The sweep of the APA Republicans indicates that a significant number of working-class, Protestant, pro-temperance, Scandinavians broke with the significantly Catholic, antitemperance, Democratic, German, Irish, and Polish AFL. The coalition born of the strike of 1889 broke apart on overlapping grounds of religion, ethnicity, and support for temperance. Still, despite these various divisions, the forces of class interest expressed in the aftermath of the strike of 1889 remained at work beneath the political surface.

The decade of the 1890s was a time of considerable economic and political stress. In Duluth as in the rest of the nation, American industry continued the restructuring process in which small-scale production for local markets was being replaced by large-scale production for national and international markets. Producers struggled to survive by cutting the costs of production. Wage cuts and layoffs were common. In 1894 in the United States, between two and one half and three million workers, perhaps as many as one out of five, were unemployed.[24] In the presidential election of 1892, the Republicans, blamed for hard times and favoring the rich, experienced a massive defeat. The Democratic administration of Grover Cleveland, however, was largely viewed as equally unresponsive to the needs of the people, and in the election of 1896, the Populist crusade against corruption and big corporations appeared on the verge of capturing the White House. In these hard times, people were eager for radical change. In Duluth the ongoing depression helped revive the labor coalition.

The coalition was also helped by the arrival in Duluth of Sabrie Akin, the founder of the *Labor World* newspaper, launched in April 1896. Promising that "the labor question will be handled without gloves by the *Labor World*, and if need be with knife in

The dining room at the Children's Home in Duluth, circa 1895. With no welfare safety net, the unfortunate events of death, illness, or injury of a parent often forced the surviving parent to place small children in an orphanage. Photograph by the Eclipse View Company; courtesy of the Minnesota Historical Society.

hand," Akin went on to predict that in the afterlife, "the monop-olist, the gold-bug and the slimy capitalist robber will sink into an oblivion deeper and darker than hell itself, there to remain till the crack of doom."[25] Born in either 1867 or 1869, Mrs. Akin, an experi-enced journalist, arrived in Duluth in March 1895 along with a child by a previous marriage. She also brought an interest in the cause of labor and a commitment to social justice in the broadest sense.[26] Aware of the divisions present in the labor movement, Akin prom-ised in the inaugural issue of the *Labor World* to fight for the cause of all working men and women and in support of all labor unions. Under her ownership and editorial control, the *Labor World* cham-pioned the cause of laundry girls, immigrant ore trimmers, and immigrant workers in the lumber mills, all largely ignored by the existing trade unions. Given standing as a delegate to the Duluth Trades Assembly (the first woman present at assembly meetings), she played an active part. At a meeting of the assembly soon after the launching of *Labor World*, Akin gave a report on behalf of the committee supporting organizing among immigrant miners on the Iron Range, urging support for a home for "friendless women," and

This photograph of Sabrie Akin was reconstructed from scraps found in a bound 1900 volume of Labor World. *Courtesy* Labor World.

Many of the men loading lumber on the docks were Scandinavians. Sabrie Akin was involved in efforts to organize a union among these lumber pilers; although there were several such attempts, no union survived. Courtesy Minnesota Historical Society.

Laundry workers, 1911. Sabrie Akin began her work to organize "laundry girls" in the late 1890s. Courtesy Minnesota Historical Society.

introducing to the assembly Sylvester Kelliher, general secretary for the American Railway Union (ARU), who had gone to jail with the ARU's Eugene V. Debs in the aftermath of the Pullman strike in Chicago.[27] (Debs was soon to become the popular leader of the American Socialist Party. The *Labor World* says that at the mention of Debs's name, "the assembly fairly went wild with applause.") Akin was also a labor organizer, speaking to a crowd of four hundred unorganized freight handlers in Duluth and another crowd of four hundred unorganized sawmill workers in Cloquet in one week in July.[28]

Akin provided a valuable bridge between the labor movement and reform elements outside the labor movement. As the nineteenth century drew to a close, large numbers of men and women across America joined an array of fraternal and social organizations. In Duluth, in addition to the strictly ethnic organizations of the various immigrant groups, the Masons, Good Templars, Knights of Pythias, Elks, Moose, and Eagles provided social contact that to some extent cut across ethnic and class divisions. While many of the groups had a largely social purpose, almost all of them had at least some commitment to working for the improvement of the social order, and some, like the temperance-oriented Good Templars, had a commitment to social reform as their primary purpose. The Twentieth Century Club, formed in September 1898, was another such group. Bringing together women from various literary clubs, the Twentieth Century Club aimed to focus the intellectual and spiritual resources of women on the cause of making a better world. Like the Women's Christian Temperance Union, the Twentieth Century Club called on women to step out of the home and play a role on the wider public stage. The club included women from the highest social circles in Duluth, but its members were liberal-minded and made a deliberate effort to reach out to people in other walks of life and other parts of the world. In the women of the Twentieth Century Club, Sabrie Akin found kindred spirits. She enthusiastically embraced the club, becoming its corresponding secretary and bringing to its members some of her experiences in the labor movement.[29] Following Akin's untimely death in January 1900, several members of the club wrote moving tributes to Akin that were published in the *Labor World*.[30] Ida Thompson, a club member who was especially close to Akin, continued to work with the Trades and Labor Assembly after Akin's death, forming an organization of women supportive of unions and speaking at a meeting of the Trades Assembly.[31] In organizations like the Twentieth Century Club, the Good Templars, and many of the ethnic lodges, the labor movement found allies for its efforts to reform the social order.

In response to the ongoing depression and with the help of such allies and an able core of local leaders, Duluth's labor coalition revived and the organized labor movement grew rapidly. In 1896 alone, three thousand new members were added to the unions affiliated with the Trades Assembly.[32] Labor Day celebrations in Duluth that year included a parade two and a half miles long, composed of between two and five thousand marchers. There were thirty-seven unions, four bands, platoons of police and firemen, laundry girls and waiter girls riding in carriages, and about a hundred floats. Later that day, the street railway company carried between twenty-five hundred and three thousand people to the picnic grounds at Fond du Lac.[33] At Fond du Lac, the popular congressman Charles Towne, who had deserted the Republicans to run on the Populist-Democrat ticket in the upcoming election, was the orator of the day. In the campaign that followed, *Labor World* gave strong support to Towne and Populist-Democratic presidential candidate William Jennings Bryan. Later that fall Bryan came to Duluth and spoke at the streetcar barn in the West End, where he drew a crowd of twenty-five thousand men. (Because of the expected crush of the crowd, a separate appearance had been scheduled for the ladies at the Lyceum Theater, where workers had recently won a complete victory after a year-long strike.[34]) Later that same month Eugene Debs also drew a crowd of thousands when he spoke in Duluth and Superior.[35]

On the national scene, the Populists went down to defeat in the election of 1896, but in Duluth a revitalized labor movement regained control of city hall, electing Henry Truelson, a Populist-leaning Democrat, as mayor. The son of an immigrant German brewery worker and married to a Swedish wife, Truelson ran for mayor as the candidate of Duluth working men, who were locked in battle with the "millionaire interests" of "the wealthy families who populated Duluth's east side."[36] Victorious in the election, Truelson invited the common people of Duluth to accompany him the following evening in a procession to city hall, which they did to the accompaniment of "roman rockets, kazoos, drums, and large quantities of beer and whiskey (provided by the retail liquor dealers)." From the balcony of city hall, Truelson proclaimed his election "a

Henry Truelson. Photograph by Rudolph Zweifel; courtesy Northeast Minnesota Historical Center.

victory of plain people over organized capital."[37] He was elected again two years later. Truelson's success showed that despite deep fissures, the labor insurgency galvanized by the strike of 1889 remained a potent force in Duluth politics. During the decade of the nineties, the Republican Party, which had largely controlled Duluth prior to the strike, was able to place its man, Ray Lewis, in office for only two of the ten years, from 1894 to 1896. At the end of the century, Duluth was a labor town.

But things would soon change. During the dramatic strike by construction laborers in July 1889, the Duluth *Evening News* had given front-page coverage to the coming launch of the second vessel built by the American Steel Barge Company in Duluth.[38] Number 102 was built to carry iron ore from the Lake Superior mining sites to Cleveland for shipment to the iron mills of western Pennsylvania and eastern Ohio. As dramatic as the events of July had been, news of the growing ore trade was big news in the Duluth of 1889, seeming to provide yet more evidence of the city's future commercial grandeur. Even a special edition of the *Evening News* devoted to the strike found space to cover a report on the iron market that had been just released by the *Cleveland Iron Trade Review*, and the front page of a number of issues of the Duluth *Daily News* covering the aftermath of the strike included stories on continued heavy ore shipments from the Great Lakes ports of Escanaba, Marquette, St. Ignace, Ashland, and Two Harbors.[39]

As early as the winter of 1847–48 the Jackson Mining Company had set up a forge and bellows and had begun making iron from ore mined near Negaunee, Michigan, close to the shores of Lake Superior.[40] In the years that followed, the iron-mining industry of the Lake Superior region developed rapidly, with the establishment of mines on the Marquette, Menominee, and Gogebic ranges of Northern Michigan. These rich iron deposits fired the vision of speculators and developers. Speaking in Boston in February 1858, George B. Sargent, the Duluth-connected land developer associated with Jay Cooke, maintained that the ores of the Lake Superior region could be developed "on a scale of magnitude, and in a state of purity, almost unprecedented." Sargent told his audience that "the undeveloped wealth of the Lake region offers reward beyond calculation, to those who have the energy and enterprise to secure it."[41] There were also rumors of vast deposits of ore in Minnesota, north of Lake Superior. Exploring that region in 1866, surveyor George Stuntz found significant iron ore deposits on the Vermilion Range, returning with ore samples and a detailed map showing the location of the deposits, as well as valuable timber stands in the region. With the support of Charlemagne Tower, a Philadelphia-based financier, the Minnesota Iron Company was formed to exploit the ore deposits on the Minnesota side of the lake, and on July 31, 1884, the first shipment of Minnesota ore left the Vermilion Range for the docks in Two Harbors. Eight years later, in October 1892, financed by borrowed money raised by the Duluth-based Merritt Family, the Duluth, Missabe, and Northern (DM&N) Railway was formed to ship ore from the Mesabi Range to Duluth.

In the depression of 1893–97, however, many small iron-mining companies followed the Merritt interests into financial ruin. Only the very large concerns could weather such hard times. By the time the economic storm was over, only four large concerns dominated the iron ore industry in northeastern Minnesota: the Oliver Iron Mining Company, created by investment in Mesabi ore lands in 1892 by the farm implement manufacturer Henry Oliver and backed by the Carnegie Steel interests; the Minnesota Iron Company, owned by Charlemagne Tower and his associates, which had extended its holdings into the Mesabi Range; John D. Rockefeller's Lake Superior Consolidated, which had swallowed up the Merritt interests and was the largest of them all; and the Lake Superior Company, backed by James J. Hill of the Great Northern Railway, which had begun buying large holdings on the Mesabi Range in 1897.[42]

The opening of the Minnesota iron ranges occurred in the midst of rapid growth and change in America's iron and steel industries. Large capital outlays were required to manufacture iron and steel, which were used mainly in the construction of railroads and structures, which could be delayed when times were bad; demand for steel thus fluctuated greatly with the ups and downs of the economy. Idle mills meant idle capital. To keep his mills operating over the years, iron and steel magnate Andrew Carnegie had cut his costs of production as much as possible, underpricing his competitors and taking their share of the diminished markets during hard times.[43] This ruthlessly competitive strategy had driven many small producers out of the iron and steel production industry, causing them to view Carnegie's entry into the mining industry with concern. Under the direction of financier J. P. Morgan and his hand-picked advisor, Judge Elbert Gary, a Chicago attorney who had negotiated previous consolidations in the steel industry, the Carnegie, Rockefeller, and Tower interests were combined to form the United States Steel Company. Established in spring 1901, the company was valued at over a billion dollars.[44] In a country already apprehensive about the appearance of million-dollar trusts, the appearance of the gigantic steel trust was viewed with alarm.[45]

The newly organized U.S. Steel Company controlled more than half of all the known iron ore–producing resources in the United States.[46] Some independent iron ore–mining companies remained. Cleveland Cliffs, Pickands, Mather and Co., and M. A. Hanna and Co., all, like Rockefeller, with roots in Cleveland and each with holdings on the iron ranges of Northern Michigan, acquired mines on the Minnesota ranges. But the Mesabi Range, connected by the DM&N Railway to the ore docks in Duluth, was largely controlled by U.S. Steel, competing only with James J. Hill's Lake Superior Company, which retained leases on a number of Mesabi mines.[47] The Oliver Iron Mining Company, now a wholly owned subsidiary of U.S. Steel, owned 65 of the 104 mines on the Mesabi Range that were shipping ore in 1901. It also owned five railroads and 112 ore boats, capable of supplying two-thirds of all the ore needed by U.S. mills.[48] This control over access to Mesabi ore gave U.S. Steel dominance in the iron and steel industry that was even greater than its size. It controlled both the DM&N and the Duluth and Iron Range (D&IR) Railways, the two railroads bringing ore to the ore docks at Duluth and Two Harbors. It also owned the docks and the boats that carried the ore to the mills below. Sensitive to possible antitrust action by the government, U.S. Steel did supply ore to its competitors in iron and steel manufacture, but while it hauled its own

Ore boats loading at the docks in Duluth, circa 1900. Courtesy Minnesota Historical Society.

Coal docks at Duluth, circa 1915. Courtesy Minnesota Historical Society.

ore at cost, it made a profit of $1.20 per ton for raw materials supplied to its competitors.[49]

With the rich Mesabi ore flowing through Duluth, more and more men were needed to work on the railroads, ore docks, and ore carriers. In addition, men were needed to work on the coal docks, where the fuel for the railroads and mining operations came into Duluth, and in the numerous shops that supplied and repaired the machinery used in the mines, railroads, and boats. High wages for skilled laborers, foremen, and executives attracted able and ambitious men to Duluth to work for U.S. Steel, while labor agents serving the iron-mining industry recruited immigrant laborers, especially in Finland and Scandinavia, to do the manual labor.[50]

Duluth was the base of operations for the Minnesota iron-mining industry. Here corporate attorneys and executives directed the operations of the companies active on the Iron Range. Meanwhile, on Michigan Street, bars and labor recruitment agencies competed for the attention of the newly arrived immigrants. Boardinghouses served the needs of the single men who worked in the mines on

Workers at coal docks, circa 1900. Courtesy Minnesota Historical Society.

the range in the summers and in the lumber camps in the winters. Despite the depression of 1893–97, Duluth grew rapidly, from a population of 33,000 in 1890 to 53,000 in 1900. Its future looked even brighter when the trade journal *Iron* predicted that Duluth would soon become the greatest steel center in the United States.[51] As early as 1895 rumors circulated that agents for John D. Rockefeller were scouting the country looking for a site to construct a new center for steel manufacturing to compete with Pittsburgh. Chicago, Cleveland, and Duluth were thought to be the main possibilities. Pittsburgh had been king in the three decades after the Civil War, but by 1890, the center of industrial activity had moved westward. Why ship ore all the way to Pittsburgh and then ship the finished iron and steel back west? Why not locate mills in Duluth and ship from there? In 1907 the steel trust announced that it would indeed build a major new production facility in Duluth.

The development of the iron-mining industry in northeastern Minnesota changed the balance of power between labor and capital in Duluth. The labor policy of the old Carnegie Steel Company was simple enough: "If a workman sticks up his head, hit it."[52] Charles Schwab, the president of Carnegie Steel, who went on to become the first president of U.S. Steel, was intransigently opposed to labor unions, and Carnegie executives William E. Corey and Alva C. Dinkey, both of whom went on to hold high positions at U.S. Steel, were even opposed to company-controlled unions.[53] J. P. Morgan, the financier most responsible for creating the steel trust, was similarly committed to maintaining an open shop.[54] Charlemagne Tower's Minnesota Iron Company, which opened iron ore mining in Minnesota, had an explicit company rule prohibiting the employment of anyone belonging to a union and calling for the immediate dismissal, with forfeiture of all wages owed, of any employee discovered to have joined a union or supported a strike.[55] With such a militantly anti-union steel industry venturing into a labor town like Duluth in the 1890s, it is not surprising that difficulties arose.

Labor conflicts appeared almost as soon as the mines were opened. In the Mesabi Range town of Eveleth, the average wage for a miner was $1.00 per day, well below the $1.50 per day rejected by construction workers in Duluth in 1889.[56] In Norway, Minnesota, miners went out on strike, demanding more than the 92 cents per day they were earning.[57] When these already low wages were cut even further, as they often were, miners frequently responded by downing tools and refusing to work. There were around fifty such strikes in the first decade of mining operations on the iron ranges of Minnesota.[58] Often the mining companies would break these strikes with immigrants hired in Duluth. Sometimes the St. Louis County sheriff, based in Duluth, would hire deputies, arm them, travel up to the location of the strike, and use the armed deputies to protect scab crews hired by the companies. Sometimes violence broke out and sometimes striking miners lost their lives.[59]

These early strikes were unorganized. In April 1896, mine managers on the range put up posters forbidding employees to join unions and began firing employees who were thought to belong to a union trying to organize in the Lake Superior region. The Duluth Federated Trades Assembly took up the cause of the miners and the very first issue of the *Labor World* denounced the firing of union miners as a violation of the rights of labor.[60] The struggle between management and labor continued on the Minnesota Iron Range, with the *Labor World* reporting that the companies continued to discharge men who either joined unions or voted for reform candidates.[61]

Similar anti-union policies began to take hold in what would become U.S. Steel operations in Duluth. William Morrison, president of the Ore Trimmers' Union, spoke to the Duluth Federated

Trades Assembly, complaining that union men were no longer allowed to perform the work of ore trimming at the Duluth docks, which were then owned by Rockefeller. The ore trimmers worked in the holds of the ore boats, moving the ore that had been dumped into the boats from the ore docks into an even and stable load.[62] The Duluth Trades Assembly joined with Mayor Truelson, who had proclaimed his election "a victory of plain people over organized capital," in urging that union men be employed on the Duluth ore docks.[63]

The merger of the Morgan, Carnegie, and Rockefeller interests to produce the giant steel trust, U.S. Steel, was announced in April 1901. From its formation, "trouble on the corporation's boats on the Great Lakes threatened to halt the movement of ore."[64] That trouble had to do with a strike by the Marine Engineers based in Duluth against all of the fleets operating in the city, a strike that ended with contracts for the smaller independent fleets, but without a contract for "the steel trust's big fleet."[65] A national strike led by the Amalgamated Association of Iron and Steel Workers later that same year was no more successful in overcoming the giant trust. In fact it was a rout, with the Amalgamated further reduced in influence and U.S. Steel more steadfastly committed to a policy opposing any attempts to further unionize its plants.[66] The experience of these failed strikes led the *Labor World* to reflect on the immense power wielded by the steel trust and the possible futility of the strike as a means for opposing it.[67]

Events the next year seemed to confirm this assessment. In May, Licensed Lake Tugmen based in Duluth went out on strike, completely shutting down all lake traffic.[68] Eventually a settlement was reached with all the smaller independent operators, but again the union was unable to win recognition or contracts governing boats belonging to the steel trust. When a trust tug was beaten to an incoming boat by a union tug, boys on Lake Avenue greeted the trust tug with hoots and laughter. Frustrated, the trust tug captain fired a revolver "recklessly up Lake Avenue" at the boys. No one was hurt in that incident or in the gunfire aimed at the union tug *Record* from the trust tug *Dowling* out on Lake Superior.[69] A more serious incident, however, occurred when another captain of a trust tug shot and seriously wounded a union man he claimed was throwing rocks at his boat.[70] The tugboat captain charged with the shooting was released on $3,000 bail. Meanwhile, the bail for J. F. Mullaly, a union man arrested for passing out "unfair" lists of

Tugboat crew for Stevens Tug Line, an independent line, circa 1905. Courtesy Northeast Minnesota Historical Center.

companies to be boycotted by supporters of the unions, was set at $17,500.[71]

In his study of steelworkers in America, David Brody comments on the extensive role of steel company executives in the local affairs of the communities where plants were located.[72] This was certainly true in Duluth. Company officials played important roles in government, commercial clubs, civic affairs, and volunteer organizations. Arriving in Duluth in the 1890s, the lawyers, executives, and engineers of the mining companies, mining railroads, and ore-shipping companies joined the Commercial Club, the Kitchi Gammi social club, the Northland and Minnesota Country Clubs, the local bar association, and the local churches and fraternal orders. Many of them served on local civic boards and many were active in local Republican politics.[73] The increased presence of this business elite helped turn the tide against the powerful labor movement that had dominated Duluth politics in the 1890s. In the election of 1900, J. W. Allen, a former secretary of the Duluth Trades Assembly, was removed from the list of Republican Party nominees. He was replaced by Andrew Miller, the only elected representative from Duluth to vote in favor of a bill in the Minnesota legislature restricting the rights of labor organizations to boycott establishments doing business with products made by nonunion labor. The *Labor World* complained that the switch had been made at the insistence of D. H. Bacon, a member of the board of directors of Minnesota Iron Company.[74] Some twenty years later an official for the generally pro-business *News Tribune* conceded that Republicans in northeastern Minnesota were "necessarily forced" to select candidates acceptable to the steel company.[75]

At the turn of the century, powerful trade-union organizations could be found in many American cities. In strong labor towns like Duluth, local unions and trades assemblies often engaged in boycotts against firms doing business with nonunion companies or against firms involved in labor disputes with other unions. In many cities, as in Duluth, local labor organizations, still imbued with the non–trade union orientation of the Knights of Labor, were not fully under the control of the national and international unions that made up the AFL. The absence of labor discipline made the ordinary conduct of business difficult.[76] Boycotts and wildcat strikes were common. Across the United States, businessmen began to organize to fight against labor organizations. Through the American Anti-Boycott Association and the National Association of Manufacturers, businessmen sought injunctions in the courts and legal reform in the state legislatures to curb the power of the unions. These organizations also lent their support to employers facing strikes, urging and sometimes demanding that the employers hold the line against the unions.[77] This "open-shop drive" gathered momentum in the early years of the twentieth century. In the fall of 1907, following a bitter strike on the Iron Range and strikes at the ore docks at the head of the lakes, U.S. Steel "dramatically joined" the open-shop drive, expelling "all remaining unions from its own plants" and influencing "whatever mines, docks, ships, haulers, and construction operations it could to do the same."[78]

In December 1907, Zar D. Scott, the owner of a local firm supplying the construction industry and the chairman of the Commercial Club in Duluth, began lobbying local businessmen to join the national open-shop drive.[79] With the support of U.S. Steel, businessmen in Minnesota launched a special open-shop drive specifically targeting the strong labor movement in Duluth. Under pressure from U.S. Steel, which refused to sell to unionized contractors, members of Duluth's Builders' Exchange, an alliance of local contractors, refused to do business with any local firm recognizing and negotiating with a union. Soon union workers faced lockouts throughout Duluth. The city became the focus for the confrontation between organized labor and the now-organized employers in the state of Minnesota.[80]

While many of the trade unions in Duluth survived this offensive, the open-shop drive significantly weakened the power of the labor movement in Duluth. A 1910 booklet designed to promote Duluth as the "new steel city," published by the Public Affairs Committee of the Commercial Club in Duluth, summarized the success of the open-shop drive:

> Manufacturers and others two years ago united to assert their independence of labor organizations. The movement was a complete success and while no man is barred from employment for membership in a labor union, the walking delegate carries no dread to the manufacturer and the bugbear of the sympathetic strike or the boycott have no terrors. All concerned in the movement believe that conditions have materially and permanently improved and that the personnel of their working forces has been raised by that decisive stand.[81]

class struggle and ethnic conflict

THE LABOR MOVEMENT THAT EXERCISED SIGNIFICANT POLITI-
cal power in Duluth in the 1890s was based on unions, largely in
the building trades, and on unorganized immigrant laborers. With
the development of the iron-mining industry in the region, there
was considerable growth in the number of unorganized immigrant
laborers. The unions that survived the open-shop campaign of the
early 1900s were craft unions largely made up of "American" workers, or workers of German, Irish, Scandinavian, or Polish descent
who had been in Duluth for some time. These workers and their
unions were affiliated with the American Federation of Labor and
belonged to the Duluth Federated Trades Assembly. They were surrounded by a much larger group of unorganized workers, many of
them immigrants who had recently arrived in Duluth. These newer
immigrants made up the largest part of Duluth's emerging industrial working class. Working in unorganized industries hostile to
unions, many of these workers turned a sympathetic ear to what
was said by radicals from the Socialist Party and the Industrial
Workers of the World. In the years leading up to World War I, these
immigrant radicals waged several important battles with U.S. Steel
and other industries in the region. These conflicts concerned both
class and ethnicity, and they laid the foundation for the popular
movement that led to the establishment of the Farmer-Labor Party
and the powerful labor movement of the 1930s.

In the early decades of the twentieth century, Duluth bore
some resemblance to a city in a third-world country, its economic
life dominated by external interests and its managerial and laboring classes divided by nationality. The city existed primarily as a
port for extractive industries. Lumber, though now harvested in
declining amounts, continued to be milled in Duluth and loaded
onto boats headed to ports on the lower Great Lakes. In increasing amounts, grain from the plains of the upper Midwest made

its way into the elevators that ringed the bay for shipment down the lakes. Above all, iron ore from Minnesota mines poured into Duluth, where it was dropped into boats for transport to Chicago, Cleveland, and Pittsburgh.

U.S. Steel dominated the lucrative iron ore industry in the area. In addition to its mines on the Vermilion and the Mesabi ranges, it owned the ore docks in West Duluth, the railroads that transported the ore from the mines to the docks, and the largest share of the ore boats that moved the ore down the lakes. From offices in New York and Cleveland, the aides of Elbert Gary, J. P. Morgan, and John D. Rockefeller managed the affairs of the company's far-flung interests, deciding, for example, to build a massive steel manufacturing works in Gary, Indiana, and entering into an agreement with the state of Minnesota to build a smaller manufacturing works in Duluth in exchange for favorable tax laws governing its iron-mining operations in the state.[1] The Lake Superior interests of the company were centered in Duluth with offices for U.S. Steel subsidiaries all located there: the Oliver Iron Mining Company, the Minnesota Iron Mining Company, Minnesota Steel, American Wire, Universal Portland Cement, the Duluth and Iron Range and the Duluth, Missabe and Northern Railways, the ore docks and coal docks, and the American Steel Barge and Pittsburgh Steamship companies. A cadre of able executives, engineers, and attorneys, men like Chester A. Congdon, William J. Olcott, Thomas F. Cole, John C. Greenway, William A. McGonagle, John Howard McLean, Herbert W. Brown, Jed L. Washburn, Joseph Bell Cotton, and William D. Bailey managed these local subsidiaries. They sent their children to eastern schools, built fine homes in Duluth's fashionable East End, belonged to the Commercial Club, the Gitchee Gammi Club, the Northland Country Club, and the Duluth Boat Club, and they were active in Republican politics. In contrast, immigrants did most of the manual labor at the mines, the steel plant, the wire plant, the cement plant, the ore docks, the ore boats, and the railroads. Agents for the mining companies recruited workers from Europe. In 1907, 84.5 percent of Oliver Iron Mining Company's twelve thousand employees were foreign born.[2]

This same year, 1907, witnessed a major confrontation between the steel trust and its immigrant workforce. The trouble began with a strike by immigrant sawmill workers in Cloquet, a city located some twenty miles south of Duluth. In part in reaction to force used against the sawmill workers, laborers on the ore docks in Duluth also went out on strike. By July 18, 1,500 men were out on strike in Duluth.[3] From there the strike spread to the Mesabi Range, where the Western Federation of Miners, which had been organizing for about a year, hurriedly called a strike in response to the ore dock strike in Duluth. Fueled by anger over inferior pay and the poor treatment of immigrant laborers, the strike spread rapidly, shutting down all the mines on the Mesabi Range and involving 20,000 miners.[4] Oliver Iron Mining Company responded by firing 300 strike leaders and by importing immigrant workers as strikebreakers. In August alone, the company brought in 1,124 scabs.[5] In addition, the company hired and armed hundreds of "man killing thugs brought here by the United States Steel Corporation."[6] A climate of violence and intimidation surrounded the towns and mine sites on the Mesabi Range. *Labor World* complained that the sheriffs of Itasca and St. Louis counties were tools of the mine owners and berated the local press for depicting strikers as violent anarchists.[7] In the end, however, having paid out over $250,000 for scabs and "detectives," the steel trust had its way. The strike was broken and militant strikers, most of them Finns, were blacklisted.[8]

While most of the drama unfolded on the Iron Range north of Duluth, Duluth was involved in the events of the strike as the headquarters for Oliver Iron Mining Company and as the government center for St. Louis County. Ironically, the strike by the ore-dock laborers in Duluth, which hurried the strike on the range, was settled peacefully, though without union recognition. Duluth's ore docks, protected by armed guards, became the staging area for the shipment of strikebreakers to the range.[9] Duluth was also the site of a mass meeting organized to support the striking miners. Chaired by William McEwen, editor of the *Labor World*, and held at the armory during a heavy rain, the meeting featured Mother Jones, the famous labor agitator, Charles Mahoney, Vice President of the Western Federation of Miners, Joseph Shartel, from the Duluth Federated Trades Assembly, and Morris Kaplan, a grocer and Jewish Socialist who had helped to organize relief efforts for the striking miners. The meeting also featured the Finnish Band playing the Marseilles.[10]

Finns played a leading role in the strike of 1907. Many of the Finnish miners involved in this strike had made their way through Duluth to the Minnesota Range from the copper-mining region around Hancock, Michigan, where Finns had worked in the mines

William McEwen, an active member of the Plumbers and Steamfitters Union, took over as owner, publisher, and editor of Labor World *following the death of Sabrie Akin in January 1900. Courtesy Minnesota Historical Society.*

as early as 1865.[11] Joined by new immigrants from Finland, some of these Finns stayed in Duluth and Superior, Wisconsin, establishing the Twin Ports as a base for Finnish life in the western Lake Superior region. In Duluth, there was an early settlement of Finns in the West End and a settlement in West Duluth, but the bulk of Duluth's Finnish population had settled along St. Croix Avenue (renamed South First Avenue East in 1912), which ran next to Lake Superior, from the base of Duluth's hillside to the ship canal. A Finnish historian called the area "the worst part of town."[12] St. Croix Avenue itself was lined with houses and boardinghouses. There was a Finnish church, a few saunas, one or two saloons, and some other retail businesses. Across the street from the boardinghouses there were a number of houses of prostitution, frequented by men of various nationalities. Near the ship canal, on Lake Avenue parallel to St. Croix Avenue, was another area of Finnish saloons.[13] Many of the men who frequented the boardinghouses and saloons in the neighborhood were lumberjacks. Other Finns worked on the boats, the ore docks, the coal docks, in construction, or in the factories ringing the bay from the base of the point to West Duluth.[14] About one-third of the Finns emigrating to the United States were women, many of whom came to the Midwest as a result of courtships that began with want ads placed in the Finnish-language newspapers.[15] Finnish women also worked in the boardinghouses and in the restaurants and other businesses that served the needs of the Finnish settlement, and some ran successful businesses of their own.[16] Besides these Finns, who were relatively stable residents of Duluth, there was a large population of Finnish men who passed in and out of Duluth. The employment offices located near the Union Depot on Michigan Street routed men to jobs in the iron mines on the Minnesota Range, to lumber camps near and far, to the harvest fields of the West, to railroad construction camps, and to a host of other jobs in the Midwest and the West. An ad placed in a Duluth Finnish newspaper in the fall of 1905 sought five hundred Finns for railroad work, offering them $2.25 per day in wages, less $4.00 per week for food and shelter.[17]

If Duluth's "Finn Town" on St. Croix Avenue was indeed "the worst part of town," Duluth's Finnish community was not without significant cultural resources. Finnish settlements in Northern Michigan and the northeastern part of the United States had already begun to form a network of cultural institutions to serve the needs of Finnish Americans. Among these institutions was the Finnish Socialist Federation. The Finnish Socialist movement was born out of a broad cultural awakening among Finnish people, both in Finland and North America, in the late nineteenth and early twentieth centuries. Finnish nationalism, feminism, temperance, and Socialism were all manifestations of this general cultural awakening, rooted in a shared conviction about the possibility of constructing a new and better world and an idealistic commitment to bringing this possibility into real earthly existence.[18]

In the 1890s and early 1900s, Finnish American socialists focused on the idea of creating Finnish utopian communities organized on cooperative principles, but by 1903 Marxist ideas had begun spreading among the Finnish socialists in both Finland and America. The Duluth group championed the new Marxist orientation and, with the support of Finnish locals in other cities, persuaded the Finnish Socialist Federation to adopt the cause of international Socialism and affiliate with the American Socialist Party at a convention of the Finnish Socialist Federation in Hibbing in 1906.[19] One year later, thousands of striking Finnish miners had marched behind the red flag of Socialism during the Mesabi strike of 1907. The *News Tribune* gave the red flag front-page coverage:

"Blood Red Flag Is Flaunted by Federation Strikers"; "Finns march through streets of Sparta, led by Amazon wearing the emblem of anarchy—other females also sport the gory color."[20]

Galvanized by the events on the Mesabi Range and an equally bitter strike by Finnish copper miners in the Upper Peninsula of Michigan in 1913, enthusiasm for Socialism swept through the Finnish communities of northern Michigan, northern Wisconsin, and northeastern Minnesota. While as Socialists these Finns embraced an internationalism calling for the unity of all working people, as Finns they also embraced the progressive Finnish culture of the late nineteenth and early twentieth centuries. Finnish Socialist halls, often former temperance halls, became centers for a rich assortment of cultural organizations, attracting Finns to plays, concerts, lectures, and athletic events. While it is true, as some critics have maintained, that for many Finns the cultural aspects of this "Hall Socialism" were more important than the ideology of Socialism, it is also true that the ideology of Socialism was important to enough for them to support two Socialist daily newspapers with a combined circulation of twenty-five thousand and to generate a substantial number of votes for Socialist candidates for public office.[21]

The large Finnish Socialist Federation would become the leading force within the local Socialist Party, but the Finns were not the only Socialists in Duluth. Other early Socialists in the city were members of the largely German-speaking Socialist Labor Party (SLP).[22] The SLP appears not to have survived in Duluth beyond 1902. In that year an English-speaking local of the American Socialist Party (SP) of Eugene V. Debs was founded in Duluth, probably incorporating the local German Socialists. Sabrie Akin, the founder of *Labor World* who died in 1900, had been an early supporter of Debsian Socialism.[23] This Socialist Party also found support within the local carpenters, painters, and longshoremen's unions.[24] Important Socialist Party locals were also formed among Jews and Scandinavians in Duluth.

Jews had been present in Duluth since the earliest years of white settlement and had established a number of successful businesses and a temple. But a Jewish immigration into Duluth after the turn of the century significantly changed the nature of the Jewish presence in the city.[25] The earlier Jewish immigration to Duluth had been made up of "German" Jews from Germany and the German-speaking regions of Hungary and Bohemia. Many of them came from families that had been living in the United States for some time.[26] In contrast, the new immigrants were "Russian" Jews from the Ukraine, Lithuania, and other parts of the Russian empire. The German Jews in Duluth had been heavily influenced by secular thinking and American ways. Many of them belonged to Temple Emanuel, a Reform congregation that had incorporated some of these new ways of thinking into Jewish religious life. The new Russian Jews were Orthodox Jews who preserved the strict religious practices and rituals of daily life found in the Judaism of eastern European cities and villages. These new immigrants established their own Orthodox synagogues in the neighborhood around Third Street and Third Avenue East, where many of them settled.[27] Irene Paull, who grew up in the Orthodox community of "Russian" Jews, summed up the difference this way: "We were 'Jews without money.' The aristocratic German Jews had their temple in the stylish section of town and looked down their noses at the newcomers on the high hill (awf en barg), called 'Little Jerusalem,' a motley ghetto."[28] Many of these Jews found employment in the flourishing local garment industry. Among the local factories were the F. A. Patrick Knitting Mill and the Garon Knitting Mill. Located at 101 Thirtieth Avenue West, the Garon Knitting Mill was originally organized in 1902 as the Great Northern Spinning and Knitting Company by Israel Garon, himself an immigrant from Lithuania.[29]

In 1911, local Jews formed a branch of the Arbeiter Ring, the Workmen's Circle, a Jewish fraternal order with a secular and Socialist orientation. Founding members of Duluth Branch 353 included Issac Jaffe, Jacob Lussan, and Nathan Schneider.[30] Jews also formed a Jewish local of the Socialist Party. The founding meeting was held at Odd Fellows Hall in September 1914. Two hundred and fifty people showed up to hear speeches by Richard Jones, a prominent figure in the English language local, and H. Levy. The program for the evening included readings by S. Dietsch and H. Singer and singing by Jacob Meyers. Others who were active in the Jewish local included Mrs. H. Singer, George Goldfarb, Max Sander, and Ida Sukof.[31] It is noteworthy that women were among those playing an active role in the affairs of the local.

The Duluth Scandinavian Socialist local was established sometime between 1904 and 1907 and was one of the most active Socialist Party locals in Minnesota.[32] Estimates of the size of the local vary from four hundred to six hundred members, with an active core of around forty.[33] The Scandinavian comrades met weekly to discuss business and political affairs, and at least one lecture and one "entertainment" were held each week. Meetings, entertainments, dances, and lectures were usually held at Woodman Hall, located at Twenty-First Avenue West and First Street in the heart of the Scandinavian West End. The lectures sponsored by the local brought many of the nationally and internationally prominent figures in the Socialist movement to Duluth.[34] The Scandinavian Sewing Circle, an organization of Socialist women, regularly put on dances, fundraisers, parties, and entertainments. Scandinavian women also acted as subscription promoters and financial contributors. One of the women, Sabina Rodberg, served as a member of the local's collective that was responsible for publishing *Truth*, an English-language Socialist weekly.[35] In addition to their duties as wives and mothers, many of the women active in the local worked as domestics in the homes of the affluent residents of Duluth's East End. The son of one of these women recalled his mother speaking of the "East Enders" with neither affection, nor respect. The active core of the local consisted of a close-knit group of people of similar age, situation, background, and outlook. They shared one another's lives, often visiting and eating meals together. Summer Sundays were usually occasions for group picnics. Families in

Members of the Scandinavian Socialist local at a summer outing. The newspapers the men are holding are copies of Svenska Socialisten, *the national publication of the Scandinavian Socialist Federation published in Chicago. Courtesy Northeast Minnesota Historical Center.*

the group did not attend church, though during World War I a secular Socialist Sunday school was organized for the children.[36]

The Scandinavian local was deeply involved in a strike by streetcar workers in 1912. A newspaper story printed in June, a few weeks before the strike, noted, "There are dozens of Socialists in the employ of the Duluth Street Railway company. Perhaps a great majority of the conductors and motormen are believers in the faith."[37] Another newspaper story published during the strike noted that "nearly all of the present strikers are Socialists."[38] According to an account of the strike written by William E. Towne, a leader in the Scandinavian local, Socialists were busy speaking to streetcar workers in the summer just before the strike broke out, and during the strike, "the Socialists held the largest street meeting ever assembled on a Duluth Street corner."[39]

Streetcar work was among the least desirable work in Duluth, and since the 1890s there had been attempts to organize the streetcar workers. By 1912 many of the streetcar men were recent Scandinavian immigrants. Little had changed since the 1890s. Streetcar men continued to work long hours, often fifteen or sixteen hours per day for low pay, and they continued to be subject to a system of surveillance and fines for petty infractions.[40] Turnover remained high. The Duluth Street Railway Company continued to be opposed to any unionization and it used a system of spies to weed out union activists.

The strike itself was precipitated in early September when, informed by managerial personnel who broke in on the meeting, the company fired nine men who had met at the home of Alex Peterson to discuss the affairs of a newly formed union.[41] The streetcar workers stopped work, demanding reinstatement of the nine men, recognition of the newly formed union, and a ten-hour day. These demands were refused and scab crews, some hired before the strike actually broke out, were brought in to run the cars.[42] What happened next was described by Towne:

> Duluth is divided into two parts by an enormous point of rocks. The car barns [for streetcars] are west about twenty blocks, in a business district, which is also populated by thousands of workers. The majority of these are Scandinavians, hardworking, sober and slow to wrath. However, on Monday evening, September 9th, three thousand working people in this district woke up from

their seeming lethargy and proceeded to smash the transportation system. The attack came with such suddenness that it paralyzed the street car officials. Cars were derailed, scabs were shown the error of their ways and the fear of God was put in their hearts.[43]

Towne's estimate of three thousand people is corroborated by a story in the *News Tribune*. By the third and fourth day of the strike, the size of the mob and the level of violence had increased. One report from the *News Tribune* estimated that fifteen thousand people were involved in a mob at the car barns. Streetcars manned by scab crews were stoned, blockades were set to stall and stop running streetcars, and cars were pulled from their tracks and overturned.[44] Headlines in the *Herald* proclaimed, "Police Unable to Quiet Mobs of Strikers' Friends" and "Enough Men to Man the Cars But They Dare Not Take Them from Barns."[45] On Friday, September 13, shots were reportedly fired at a scab motorman.[46] Although the streetcar company had hired Thiel Detectives to ride in the cars along with the scab crews, attacks on streetcars making their rounds continued until as late as October 6.[47]

Opposite the strikers stood Herbert Warren, the general manager of the Street Railway Company. Warren maintained that the company had a right to treat its employees any way it wished, that the company would not allow anyone to interfere with its right to determine its own labor policies, that it would not negotiate with any of the men, and that it had a right to fire any man for any reason.[48] This position did not have widespread public support, but in the end, having the law on its side, it prevailed. Despite this failure by the strikers, the strike appears to have had an energizing influence on local Socialists.

A strike by ore-dock workers in 1913 also had a deep influence on the labor movement in Duluth. The ore-dock strike began on the night of July 31, 1913, after an accident at the Allouez dock on the Superior side of the bay killed two men and seriously injured two others.[49] The accident involved a system of signaling used by ore-dock workers opening pockets under the ore cars so that the ore could slide from the cars through the ore pockets and into the boats waiting below. Miscommunication had nearly led to tragedy in the past and the men had asked that the system of communication be changed, but they failed to get a positive response from the Great Northern Railway. Angered by this failure to act and the con-

sequent deaths and injuries to fellow workmen, five hundred workers on the Allouez dock immediately went on strike.[50]

The next day the men met at a West Superior ballpark, where
they drew up a list of three demands: that one man from each shift
be selected to supervise the switching of railroad cars on the ore
dock, that ore pockets be closed when not in use, and that workers should have the right to enforce the discharge of foremen they
had reason to believe were objectionable.[51] The men also resur-
rected a Union of Ore-Dock Workers, which had formed in 1907
but subsequently disbanded, applying $300 remaining from the
old union to the treasury of the new and collecting $1.50 initiation
fees from the men present, which was to be used to take care of the
workers injured the day before.[52] At this point, organizers for the
Industrial Workers of the World (IWW), a national radical labor
organization, became involved in the strike. Exactly how the IWW
became involved is not clear, though organizers for the IWW had
been involved in a strike by the ore-dock workers the year before.[53]
For some reason, Frank H. Little, a nationally known IWW organizer, appears to have been in the Duluth-Superior area for several
weeks before the 1913 strike began.[54] Whatever the circumstances
of his involvement, Little quickly came to play a prominent role in
the strike. A number of other IWW organizers joined Little, including James P. Cannon, who would go on to become one of the leaders of the American Trotskyites.[55] Leo Laukki, one of the teachers
at the Finnish Work People's College in Duluth, played a prominent
role among local leaders of the strike.[56]

Frank Little spoke at the meeting in the ballpark on the morning after the accident. Following his speech, the men voted unanimously to stay out until their three demands were met. Later the
men added a demand for a pay increase. In fact, the company did
offer some concessions on the safety issues and did eventually
offer a moderate increase in pay. This offer was turned down by the
strikers by a vote of 244 to 95.[57] At this point, the Great Northern
Railway began to bring in strikebreakers to do the work on the ore
docks, as well as armed guards to protect the workers. By August
5, work on the ore docks had resumed.[58] The next day, some six
hundred workers on the Duluth, Missabe, and Northern ore docks
in West Duluth went out on strike in sympathy with the strike in
Superior, refusing to load boats diverted from the Allouez docks.[59]
W. A. McGonagle, president of the DM&N Railway, which was a
subsidiary of U.S. Steel, blamed the strike on outside agitators con-

nected with the IWW.[60] A cartoon in the *News Tribune* depicted the heel of public opinion crushing an IWW snake.[61]

Backed by public opinion, the Great Northern and the DM&N Railways withdrew all offers to negotiate and issued an ultimatum requiring the men to return to work or lose their jobs.[62] The companies also turned to an aggressive use of force. Private guards hired by the Oliver Iron Mining Company attacked Leo Laukki when he tried to speak to strikers near the DM&N ore docks. Sergeant Roberg of the Duluth Police Department witnessed this attack and was quoted in the newspaper as saying, "In my opinion the special police had no business to interfere because Chief Troyer [Chief of Police in Duluth] had sufficient men to handle the situation; furthermore the strikers were on city property and not infringing on the company's rights."[63] A similar disregard for the niceties of the law was also evident on the Superior side. Frank Little, the most prominent of the IWW organizers involved in the strike, was kidnapped and taken to a farm near Holyoke, where he was held under armed guard.

As it happened, Little's place of captivity was discovered and he was rescued by a group of IWW supporters.[64] His recovery led to a triumphant mass meeting at the armory in Duluth, which was sponsored, significantly, not by the AFL, but by the Socialists of Duluth and Superior. Little delivered a short speech that brought rousing cheers and flying hats from the crowd of assembled strikers and supporters that filled the armory to capacity.[65] Despite the enthusiasm of the crowd, however, the strike had been essentially lost by this point. The next day, McGonagle, the president of the DM&N, announced that those men who had failed to return to work were no longer employees of the company.[66] On the Superior side of the bay, the Great Northern Railway gave the men one last chance to return to work, promising them a raise of ten cents a day on October 1 and an additional ten cents a day on October 15. The company promised to hire back all of the striking dockworkers except the Finns: no Finnish people were to be rehired under any conditions.[67] The strikers refused the offer.[68] Later, by a vote of the striking men at the Finnish Socialist Hall at 417 West Superior Street in Duluth, the strike was officially called off.[69]

While the strike itself was defeated, the ore-dock strike of 1913 left the IWW with a permanent foothold in Duluth and Superior. As early as 1909, immigrants had constituted a majority of the industrial working class in the United States.[70] Most of them worked as unskilled laborers and the vast majority labored outside the organized labor movement. Frustrated with the AFL's neglect of the mass of industrial workers, radicals of various stripes had gathered in Chicago in 1905 to organize the IWW. The fundamental aims of the IWW were to organize the industrial working class, including the mass of unskilled immigrant workers, and to replace the system of capitalism with an economic system based on workers' control of the means of production. The IWW aimed at organizing all workers into "one big union" that would eventually take control of all processes of production. A group of talented and charismatic organizers crisscrossed the country organizing textile workers, lumberjacks, woodworkers, dockworkers, seamen, iron miners, and agricultural workers. The IWW found organizers who could speak the languages of the immigrant workers. They led multiethnic strikes and included women and African Americans. They pioneered tactics of mass civil disobedience in strikes and free speech fights from East to West and from North to South. Their spirit was captured by IWW songwriter Joe Hill, who, just before his death by a firing squad in Utah, said, "Don't mourn, organize!"

The IWW had first appeared in Duluth during a free speech fight initiated by Duluth's Socialists in the summer of 1911. When police arrested the Socialist speakers, Vincent St. John, national General Secretary of the IWW, sent a telegram to the national IWW newspaper, Solidarity, asking for "reinforcements ... on [the] ground as soon as possible" for a free speech fight in Duluth.[71] Apparently a good number of IWW activists, known as "Wobblies," responded to St. John's call. A News Tribune headline proclaimed, "Free Speakers Invade Duluth," and Solidarity proclaimed, "Free Speech in Duluth" and "Superior on IWW Map."[72] It was not until 1913, however, following the ore-dock strike in Duluth, Superior, and Two Harbors, that the IWW firmly established itself at the head of the lakes.

Leaders of the American Socialist Party, like Eugene V. Debs, were among the founders of the IWW. Nevertheless, by 1913 there were deep divisions between the Socialist Party and the IWW. For one thing, many Socialists wanted to retain a working relationship with the AFL, but the IWW was anathema to the AFL, which saw the IWW as an attempt to split the American labor movement. Second, the Socialist Party itself was infected by racist attitudes toward non-Nordic immigrants from eastern and southern Europe.[73] Third, the IWW was increasingly drawn to a philosophy of "direct action," which favored strikes, and was moving away from the electoral strategy favored by the Socialist Party.[74] Finally,

Men outside IWW headquarters in Duluth. Courtesy Tom Selinski.

like Socialist parties in Europe, the American Socialist Party began to divide into "reformist" and "revolutionary" wings. These multiple divisions tended to overlap, forming within the Socialist Party a "right wing" and a "left wing." The right wing was reformist, supported electoral politics, tended to share racist attitudes toward the new immigrants, and favored cooperation with the AFL. The left wing was revolutionary and favored direct action over electoral politics; it found a base of support among the new immigrants, and favored cooperation with the IWW.

In 1910 the American Socialist Party changed its constitution to permit immigrant Socialists who belonged to foreign-language Socialist federations, like the Finnish Socialist Federation, to join the Socialist Party as a group. This decision profoundly affected the Socialist Party, opening it up to a flood of immigrant workers attracted to the cause of Socialism. By 1915, immigrants constituted 45 percent of the membership of the Socialist Party and by 1919, it was 53 percent. The increasing weight of the foreign language groups would have a decisive effect on the development of the Socialist Party in Duluth, with its large Finnish and Scandinavian Socialist Federations.

The question of the IWW was a particularly important issue among the Finns. As early as 1906, at the founding convention of the Finnish Socialist Federation in Hibbing, the primary issue was whether to support the newly formed IWW.[75] With its commitment to organizing industrial unions among immigrant workers, the IWW was attractive to the Finnish Socialists. Many of them, however, shared the electoral politics of the European Social Democrats and the American Socialist Party. Events in Finland pushed many Finnish American Socialists toward the direct-action standpoint of the IWW. Finland was under the political control of the Russian Empire in the years before World War I. Many of the Finns who came to the United States did so to escape conscription and the greater degree of control imposed on Finland by the czar during the period of Russia's war with Japan and the turmoil of 1905. The collapse of reformist hopes and the imposition of a new period of repression in Finland in 1909 had a radicalizing effect on Finnish Social Democrats in both Finland and America.[76]

Many of the newly radicalized Finns immigrated to the United States. Among them was Leo Laukki, who had participated in the 1905 revolutionary uprising in Finland and looked favorably on direct action.[77] Laukki, an experienced newspaperman, a forceful orator, and a former cavalry officer, became an instructor and director at the Finnish Work People's College in Smithville, a western industrial suburb of Duluth. The Work People's College served the needs of Finnish radicals, giving practical training and ideological instruction to Finnish men and women. Laukki, a charismatic and influential figure, strongly supported the direct action wing of the IWW. It was Laukki who worked with the IWW leaders Frank Little and James P. Cannon during the strike by ore-dock workers in Duluth, Superior, and Two Harbors. Under his leadership, a pro-IWW faction grew within the Finnish Socialist Federation. Radicalized by bitter defeats on the Mesabi Range in 1907 and in the copper country strike of 1913, increasing numbers of Finnish Socialists followed Laukki's lead in moving in the direction of the IWW and direct action.

The issue came to a head in the aftermath of the copper and ore-dock strikes of 1913. Some Finnish Socialists favored the IWW and direct action, while others held firmly to the strategy of electoral politics. Unable to resolve the issue, the Finnish Federation split into two wings. The Finnish Socialist newspaper, *Työmies*, remained in the hands of the political wing, while a new newspaper, *Socialisti*, published in Duluth, became the paper of a coalition of "political radicals" and pro-IWW direct actionists. By 1916, the IWW faction had gained the upper hand and completely controlled the newspaper, renaming it *Industrialisti*. With a daily newspaper, with control of the Socialist Publishing Company based in Duluth, and with a strong presence at the Finnish Work People's College in Smithville, the pro-IWW Finnish Socialists had powerful resources at their disposal.

With the support of the large and active Scandinavian Socialist Local, which also supported the IWW, pro-IWW Finns gained control of the Socialist Party in Duluth. The power shift at the center of the local Socialist movement was evident as early as 1913, when the Socialists ran their own mayoral candidate, Morris Kaplan, against the AFL-backed William McEwen, a sharp critic of the IWW in his role as editor of *Labor World*. McEwen lost by a handful of votes, throwing the election to W. I. Prince, the candidate of the big business wing of the Republican Party. Left-wing control of the local Socialists was further evident at the May Day celebration in the Duluth armory following the election. The meeting was chaired by John A. Johnson, a member of the left-wing Scandinavian Local.[78] Speeches were given in Finnish, Scandinavian, and Polish, with the featured English-language speech given not, as in the past, by pro-AFL local Socialists P. G. Phillips or Richard Jones, but by Allen Strong Broms, a prominent left-wing pro-IWW Socialist from Minneapolis.[79] Indeed, by October 1914 the central committee of the St. Louis County Socialist Party, now firmly under the control of

Work People's College in Smithville. The curriculum included accounting, mathematics, and Marxism. Under Leo Laukki's influence the college became firmly connected to the IWW. Courtesy Immigration History Research Center.

District meeting of the Scandinavian Socialist Federation in Duluth. The SSF was an organization of Scandinavian-American Socialists and, like the Finnish Socialist Federation, included many supporters of the IWW and the left wing of the Socialist Party in the United States. Courtesy Northeast Minnesota Historical Center.

the left-wing Finns and Scandinavians, recommended that Richard Jones, elected to the Minnesota Legislature from Duluth as a Socialist, be expelled from the party for pandering to non-Socialist votes. This recommendation was supported by a referendum vote of the members of the Socialist Party of St. Louis County, showing that support for the left-wing position was widespread.[80]

At the national level, the growing rift between the right and left wings of the Socialist Party led to a 1912 amendment to the party constitution calling for the expulsion of any member who opposed electoral politics or who supported direct action in the form of sabotage or violence. This amendment was clearly directed at IWW leaders like William D. Haywood and Vincent St. John and their supporters within the Socialist Party. Within a year, between June 1912 and June 1913, more than fifty thousand members left the Socialist Party, many of them expelled as supporters of the IWW.[81]

These expulsions had less of an effect on the Socialists in Duluth than one might expect. Undoubtedly under pressure to act from the national executive committee of the American Socialist Party, in January 1915 the national leadership of the Finnish-American Socialist Federation did act to expel the left-wing Finns. A story in *New Times*, the official organ of the Socialist Party of Minnesota, reported the expulsion of "the group of Finns supporting the *Socialisti* including most of Minnesota's Finnish locals."[82]

It is one thing to "expel" by removing someone's name from a national membership list, however, and it is something else to remove the person from an active role on the ground at the local level. In Duluth and Superior, many Finns and Scandinavians remained active in the local Socialist Party and continued to be supporters of the IWW.[83] In fact, by the time these expulsions were ordered, the left-wing Finnish and Scandinavian Socialists were already firmly in control of the Socialist Party in Duluth. In June 1915, five months after the expulsion order, Eugene V. Debs, the popular figurehead of the American Socialist Party, spoke to a crowd of three thousand at the auditorium in Duluth. W. E. Towne of the pro-IWW Scandinavian local served as the chair of the meeting. And in the back of the auditorium, local Socialists sold left-wing literature, including a pamphlet written by IWW leader William Haywood, who had been expelled from the Socialist Party.[84] A month later Haywood himself was the featured speaker at the annual picnic of the Duluth Socialists at Fairmount Park. A headline in *Labor World*, the pro-AFL and anti-IWW newspaper published in Duluth, proclaimed, "Duluth Socialists Disgrace to Party." The accompanying story charged the Socialist Party in Duluth with succumbing to the control of a disgraceful IWW gang.[85] But like it or not, left-wing radicals were firmly in control of the Socialist Party in Duluth and the surrounding region. In November 1915, John J. Kolu, the Finnish organizer involved in both the Mesabi Range strike of 1907 and the copper country strike of 1913 and a supporter of the pro-IWW *Socialisti*, served as chairman of the Socialist Party in Duluth.[86] And at the state convention of the Socialist Party of Minnesota, held in Duluth in early 1916, an amendment to the state constitution was passed permitting the left-wing Finnish locals expelled from the national Finnish Federation to receive charters directly from the Minnesota Socialist Party, now also under left-wing control.[87]

With the support of the Finnish and Scandinavian Socialists in Duluth, the IWW opened an office at 907 West Michigan Street, in the midst of the bars and employment agencies frequented by lumberjacks and transient workers. There they began a campaign to organize the multiethnic industrial working class in northern Minnesota, Wisconsin, and Michigan, distributing literature in five different languages.[88] By the summer of 1916, this local office was deeply involved in support for another strike on the Mesabi Range, one that brought in nationally prominent IWW leaders such as Sam Scarlet, Carlo Tresca, Joe Schmidt, Frank Little, Joe Ettor, and Elizabeth Gurley Flynn. A telegram from William D. Haywood, the general secretary of the IWW, set the tone for the strike: "War has been declared against the steel trust and the independent mining companies of Minnesota, by the Industrial Workers of the World."[89]

In many ways the 1916 strike was a continuation of the 1907 strike, only now the remaining radical Finns were joined by thousands of South Slavs, many of whom had come to the range as strikebreakers in the earlier strike. The central issues remained wages and the contract system, which made it possible for mining captains to demand bribes from miners in exchange for favorable assignments. As in 1907, the miners paraded and formed pickets around mine sites. Oliver Mining Company, with the cooperation of John Meining, the sheriff of St. Louis County, responded by hiring a thousand private guards, arming them with carbines, high-powered police revolvers, and nightsticks, and sending them out to break up the parades and picket lines of the strikers.

Violence and the threat of violence became a daily part of the strike. On June 22, John Alar, a miner, was killed in Virginia. Quoting Oliver officials, the *Duluth Herald* reported that Alar had been armed with a Winchester rifle and was killed in a gun fight with Oliver guards.[90] An account less sympathetic to the mining company maintained that Alar was unarmed and was shot by a mine guard because he and some other miners did not disperse when ordered to do so.[91] Subsequent reports on the strike by state and federal officials seem to confirm the second view, placing responsibility for the violence on the mine guards. No charges were ever brought in this case, despite the fact that, in the words of the *Duluth News Tribune*, "Alar was the whitest man in the location."[92] Alar's funeral was held at the Finnish Socialist Hall in Virginia because, contrary to the requests of Alar's widow, no Catholic priest would consent to perform the service. A large red banner proclaimed: "Murdered By Oliver Gunmen."[93]

While no charges were brought in the Alar case, charges were filed in another case involving the death of Deputy James Myron, a fifty-nine-year-old salesman and former city assessor from Duluth.[94] In this case, officials brought murder charges against four Montenegrin miners: John Orlandich, Joe Cinnogomenich, Joe Michech, and Philip Masonovich, all of whom were present in the house where Myron was killed. Myron, along with other deputies, was investigating a report of illegal sale of alcohol. Mrs. Mikela Masonovich, the wife of Philip Masonovich, was also charged with murder. St. Louis County officials used Myron's death as grounds for an attack on the local IWW. A number of IWW leaders who were nowhere close to the scene were arrested and charged with fomenting the murder through their strike agitation. As with the Alar case, the circumstances surrounding the death of Deputy Myron were murky. The *Labor World* blamed the incident on the overly aggressive behavior of Nick Dillon, a mine guard who, according to *Labor World*, had received his training as a bouncer in a brothel in Virginia.[95] Despite the fact that the coroner's jury refused to name anyone as responsible for the death, St. Louis County prosecutor Greene pursued the case.[96] Eventually a deal was reached. Charges against the IWW leaders, Mrs. Masonovich, and two of the miners were dropped and it was agreed to sentence the remaining three miners to terms of one to three years for manslaughter. The miners agreed to this plea bargain only to have Judge Cant unexpectedly hand down sentences of five to twenty years.[97]

In the end, the 1916 strike was broken. Newspapers and officials in Duluth were widely perceived as subservient to the interests of the steel trust. Even the *Labor World*, though highly critical of the IWW, ran stories critical of the coverage of the strike by the local press, charging it with gross distortion and bias on behalf of the mining companies.[98] Contrary to the Duluth newspapers, a report by the Minnesota Labor Commission blamed the mine guards for most, if not all, of the violence.[99]

Likewise, a report done by George P. West for the United States Commission on Industrial Relations was decidedly on the side of the striking miners. According to the West report, "The city of Duluth, the county of St. Louis and the state of Minnesota, as represented by Gov. J. A. A. Burnquist and other public officials, have joined hands in a relentless effort to crush out the strike of 15,000 miners." The report went on to say, "With the support and good will of the United States Steel Corporation and affiliated interests in the state, Governor Burnquist, Sheriff John R. Meining of Duluth, County Prosecutor Greene, and the Duluth chief of police are playing at ducks and drakes with the most sacred rights of the foreign workmen who mine the ore that goes down to the ships at Duluth for shipment to the Pittsburgh mills."[100] West and others sympathetic to the strikers were critical of Governor Burnquist for backing up Sheriff Meining in his deputizing of large numbers of men paid by Oliver Iron Mining Company. The West report also stressed the subservience of local officials to the steel trust, claiming that "Duluth, ambitious and hungry for Eastern Capital, is notoriously with the companies and against any interest opposing them."[101]

Duluth businesses were also charged with serving the interests of the steel trust by cutting off credit to range businessmen, many of whom openly sided with the miners. The *Mesaba Ore*, a Hibbing newspaper, reported that "Range business men have received a circular letter notifying them of the no more credit resolution and it was signed by Bridgeman-Russell Company, Gowan-Lemaing-Brown Company, Haugsrud-Markanaen Company, Rust-Parker Company, Stone-Ordean-Wells Company and Tuohy-Eimon Mercantile Company."[102] All of these companies were leading Duluth businesses.

Like the strike of 1907 and the copper country strike of 1913, the 1916 strike had a great impact on immigrant radicals in Duluth. Some, like John Kolu, the head of the Socialist Party in Duluth, were directly involved. In 1916 he took over leadership of the strike when the national IWW organizers were jailed.[103] Finnish Socialists in Duluth clearly supported the strike. Over two thousand of them attended a rally for the striking miners on July 9.[104] In addition, IWW activity in Duluth may have had an effect on shipments of ore from the Duluth docks. In June and again in July, IWW organizers were trying to foment a strike among the ore-dock workers in Duluth.[105] IWW organizers were also active at the gates of the steel plant in Duluth and at the ore docks in Superior.[106] Frank Little, one of the IWW organizers unjustly charged in the killing of deputy Myron, spoke at IWW headquarters in Duluth.[107] The local press consistently denied any IWW success at the docks. Still, in August 1916, the *News Tribune* reported that ore shipments from Duluth in July were down by 400,000 tons. The *News Tribune* explained this decline as being due to the excessive heat.[108] Whether this is true, or whether the decline was due to reduced ore from the strikebound mines or slowdowns on the docks or some combination thereof, cannot be determined. In any case, it is clear that on the eve of World War I, radicals sympathetic to the IWW were the dominant force in the Socialist Party in Duluth, with widespread support on the Iron Range of Minnesota.

war and revolution

THE FIRST WORLD WAR BEGAN IN EUROPE IN AUGUST 1914. THE
war pitted Britain, France, and Russia on the one side against Germany, Austria-Hungary, and Turkey on the other. On the western
front, the war settled into a deadly stalemate of trench warfare and
poison gas. On the eastern front, German armies pushed onto the
soil of the Russian empire, inflicting enormous casualties. Americans were divided in their sympathies. Some, like former President
Theodore Roosevelt, clearly sided with the British. Many German
Americans supported Germany's side in the war. Irish Americans,
opposed to British rule over Ireland, were often anti-British, many
virulently so following the British suppression of the Easter Rising
in Dublin in 1916. Scandinavians and particularly Swedish Americans also tended to side with Germany, reflecting cultural ties with
Germany and long-standing Swedish hostility to Russia. *Posten*, the
mainstream newspaper of Swedish Americans in Duluth, strongly
opposed United States involvement right up to the declaration of
war in April 1917.[1]

Once the United States did enter the war against Germany,
the vast majority of Minnesotans, like the vast majority of Americans, united behind the war effort. Many of the eighty-one Duluth
men killed in action during the war were sons of immigrants, like
David Wisted, killed at Belleau Wood, and Adam Kucharski, killed
in the battle of the Argonne.[2] *Posten*, like the rest of the Scandinavian press, dropped its opposition to the war, urging readers to
support their new country.[3] Most of the noncitizen immigrants,
the "aliens" working in American mines, fields, and factories, did
their part to support the American war effort. Immigrants bought
more than their share of the liberty bonds sold to raise money for
the war.[4] Leaders among the various ethnic groups formed organizations, like the John Ericsson League of Patriotic Service, that
worked among Swedish Americans to educate them about Amer-

ica's aims in the war and to win their support for the war effort.[5] Duluth's Serbs were among the first in Duluth to show their support for the war. Just weeks after the declaration of war, before the organized state and city efforts were under way, two Serbian societies arranged a patriotic program in Gary-New Duluth. Directed by John Widih, the program featured a speech by Mayor C. R. Magney and much waving of the stars and stripes.[6] Relatively few immigrants gave up citizenship "first papers" to avoid the draft, though they could have.[7]

While in reality most immigrant aliens loyally supported the war effort, public perceptions did not accurately reflect this support. Before the war, immigrants were largely ignored by the American public, except when they pressed for a radical agenda. In the labor press, and to a lesser extent in the mainstream press, immigrants were sometimes perceived as a threat to the American standard of living because of their supposed willingness to accept lower wages. A racist view of immigrants from southern

War bonds rally in Duluth during World War I. Courtesy Northeast Minnesota Historical Center.

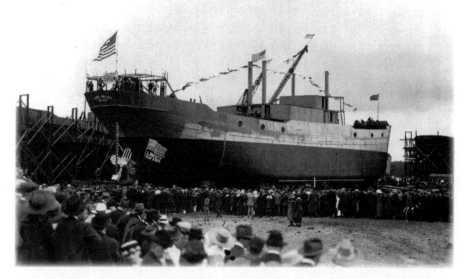

The shipyard at Riverside also supported the war effort. Photograph by Hugh McKenzie; courtesy Northeast Minnesota Historical Center.

Serving in a racially segregated army, African American soldiers leave Duluth's Union Depot. Courtesy Northeast Minnesota Historical Center.

and eastern Europe as being inferior to Anglo-Saxons was also widely accepted. With the coming of the war, public perceptions of immigrants changed. Many Americans began to see the aliens living among them as potential enemies. "Americanization" became the watchword of the time, referring to both a training in American ways and a deliberate program to stamp out all remaining loyalties to foreign lands. Former president Theodore Roosevelt recommended that unpatriotic German Americans be shot or hanged and demanded the deportation of anyone who could claim that 10 percent of his affections still belonged to his native land.[8] Roosevelt also called for a ban on all foreign-language newspapers.[9] In a similar vein, President Woodrow Wilson said that "[a] man who thinks of himself as belonging to a particular national group in America has not yet become an American," and he expressly warned against the dual loyalty of "hyphenated Americans."[10]

Fear about the potential disloyalty of German Americans, Swedish Americans, and other "hyphenated" Americans was definitely present in Minnesota. Prior to the declaration of war by Congress, German Americans and Scandinavian Americans had openly expressed their opposition to American entry into the war. Even elected public officials, many of whom had opposed American involvement, were suspect. At least one source denounced eleven of the twelve Minnesota congressmen as "Kaiserites."[11] Determined that Minnesota would do its part to support the American war effort and worried about the loyalty of many of its residents, the Minnesota legislature created a special agency, the Minnesota Commission of Public Safety (MCPS), which was granted sweeping powers to ensure that Minnesotans loyally supported the American war effort. John McGee, the chairman of the commission, described the bill that created it as having "teeth in it eighteen inches long."[12]

Through a network of subordinate county organizations, the commission arranged for the sale of war bonds and published propaganda supporting the war in English and in the languages of the various immigrant groups. In Duluth, John Jenswold and Hans B. Haroldson were recruited to serve as pro-war speakers for Swedish audiences; O. J. Larson and J. H. Jasberg spoke to Finns; and Rev. S. A. Iciek spoke to Poles.[13] County Public Safety Commissioner William Prince also requested twenty thousand copies of a speech in Swedish by Rev. Gustav F. Johnson of Willmar, a speech that encouraged Swedish support for the war effort.[14] In addition,

WATER-FRONT PASS.

Port of........Duluth........

Pass ......Frank Runca........

Residence....1110 ... 3rd St........

Nationality....Italian....No. Papers........

Occupation....Laborer........

Employed by ...The Clarkson Coal & Dk.Co

Date....April 17th 18.Location........First Ave.........

No. 31548........JR. A. Kessel........

United States Marshal

Waterfront pass for Frank Runca, a laborer on the Clarkson Coal Dock. Fearful that disloyal aliens would sabotage the docks, the local public safety commission placed armed guards around the docks and issued passes for men who worked there. Courtesy Iron Range Historical Society.

the public safety commission passed emergency decrees restricting the sale of alcoholic beverages and the operation of dance halls. It also passed decrees requiring the registration of all aliens and all property owned by aliens. Fear spread among immigrant communities that people were to be imprisoned or deported and their property confiscated. In Duluth approximately fifteen thousand aliens and their property were registered.[15] The commission also restricted instruction in foreign languages in public schools to one hour per day.[16] And in a state where hunting was widespread, the public safety commission passed an order forbidding aliens to have firearms or explosives.[17] Although ostensibly motivated by concerns about the wartime loyalty of aliens and others, these various measures were also aimed at suppressing the labor movement in Minnesota. In general, the commission served the interests of elements within Minnesota's corporate world that favored an active anti-union agenda.

Already in February 1917, before American entry into the war, William McEwen, the editor of *Labor World*, had complained that the real power in Duluth lay in the hands of big business, not in the hands of elected city officials.[18] The history of the MCPS seems to bear him out. Bypassing elected public officials, the Public Safety Commissioner wrote to Colonel H. V. Eva at the Commercial Club in Duluth asking him to recommend someone to serve as St. Louis County commissioner for the MCPS. William Prince, former president of the Commercial Club and former mayor of Duluth, was appointed on the basis of this recommendation.[19] The Commercial Club also drew up a list of names to be included in the local Council of National Defense, actually displacing a list already prepared by the elected mayor of Duluth.[20] The MCPS called on the Commercial Club to finance its specially formed military force.[21] It was at the Commercial Club in Duluth that "representatives of all the mining companies operating throughout the district" met to discuss a plan for "centralizing and promoting" fund-raising and support for the war effort.[22] And it was at the Commercial Club that the St. Louis County director received all communications from the MCPS.

The commission used a network of detective agencies in its employ to root out pockets of disloyalty and to spy on labor leaders throughout the state. It encouraged the passage of vaguely drawn vagrancy ordinances that could be used to arrest labor organizers. It encouraged local authorities to use their police powers to prevent public meetings by radical groups. And it led to the formation of a Minnesota Home Guard, which could be used as an independent police force against labor unrest. On the whole, the antilabor agenda of the commission appears to have outweighed its official purpose of mobilizing Minnesota for the war effort. When this antilabor agenda ran afoul of federal labor policies, the commission showed a willingness to risk undermining federal war mobilization efforts to promote its own antilabor agenda.[23]

In the state of Minnesota, concerns about the loyalty of aliens and "hyphenated" Americans were intertwined with the antilabor and antiradical agenda of the public safety commissioners. While in southern Minnesota the commission focused on German Americans, in northern Minnesota the focus was on the left-wing Finns and Scandinavians active in the IWW, the Socialist Party, and the Non-Partisan League (NPL), a Populist reform movement that had recently moved into Minnesota following considerable success in North Dakota.

Like the American Socialist Party with which they were affiliated, the Finnish Socialist Federation and the Scandinavian Socialist Federation maintained a position of opposition to the war even after the U.S. entry.[24] In Duluth, *Industrialisti*, the newspaper of the Finnish IWW, was uncompromising in its opposition to the war.[25] So too, *The Labor Leader* (later renamed *Truth*), the English-language weekly published by the Scandinavian Socialists in Duluth, took a firm stand against the war.[26] With such open opposition to the war in the background, St. Louis County Attorney Warren E. Greene said in an October 1917 letter to the members of the MCPS that a section of the law creating the commission could arguably be construed as outlawing "all kinds of anti-war talk."[27]

The imposition of a military draft also drew the Finnish and Scandinavian Socialists into dangerous territory. Opposition to conscription was strong among the Finns. In the early 1900s, many of them had fled to the United States to avoid conscription into the army of the Russian Empire. There was also some confusion about the requirement to register among non-English-speaking Finns. Whether because of a general opposition to conscription or simple misunderstanding, a significant number of Finns failed to register for the draft as required by law.[28] There was also some resistance to the draft among the Scandinavians.[29] A newspaper article from March 1919 lists some sixty young men from Duluth, all Scandinavians and most from West Duluth, who gave up citizenship "first papers" to stay out of the draft.[30] Nationally, few Scandinavians gave up citizenship papers to avoid the draft. One study of those who did revealed that most of them were young Socialists who had recently immigrated from Sweden.[31] Thus individuals among both the Finnish radicals and the Scandinavian radicals in Duluth were probably among the "slackers" who avoided registering for the draft. One of the tasks of the public safety commission in Duluth was to round up these slackers and force them to either register or go to prison. To some degree they were successful. A newspaper story in June 1917 reported the arrest of many Finns and Austrians (South Slavs) for being draft resisters and IWW cardholders.[32]

The passage of the Espionage Act by Congress in June 1917 further increased the dangers confronting the Socialists and the IWW. That act made all utterances considered damaging to American foreign policy punishable by heavy penalties. This could conceivably have made wartime labor agitation an act of espionage. Further repressive possibilities were introduced by a 1917 amendment that allowed for the deportation of aliens guilty of supporting or belonging to groups advocating the violent overthrow of the government.[33] The primary target of these measures was the IWW. At a meeting in St. Paul that included the governor, members of the MCPS, officials from Duluth, and officials from the Iron Range, it was decided that "northern Minnesota communities must preserve order and keep out the disturbing influences of the IWW propaganda in these war times." Local authorities were instructed to "keep down" the IWW.[34] This directive put the MCPS on a collision course with the Finnish and Scandinavian radicals in the city, who were strong supporters of the IWW.

With the blessing of the MCPS in St. Paul, the St. Louis County Public Safety Commission tried to implement the proposed suppression of the IWW, but the task was not easy. In addition to the sheer size of the county and the extensive IWW presence there, the county commission had problems finding local officials who were willing to cooperate. Many of the elected officials were more tolerant of the IWW than was the MCPS. A detective in the service of the MCPS complained that Mayor Boylan of Virginia "would allow IWW every liberty if it were not for Commissioners."[35] In a similar vein, John Pardee, secretary for the MCPS in St. Paul, wrote to William Prince, chairman of the St. Louis County Commission. Expressing sympathy for Prince in his difficult situation, Pardee went on to say, "I understand that you have appointed a Vice-Chairman for the Range but I do not know whether he has ever done one blessed thing or not."[36] The diversity of languages also presented a problem. George Brozich, a cashier at the First State Bank of Ely, wrote to Prince complaining that the "Why We Are at War" circulars, which were distributed on behalf of the commission by the Oliver Iron Mining Company in five different languages, did not include a Slovenian version.[37] Language may also have provided a pretext for immigrant officials to avoid serving on the commission. In late August, John Suihkonen, clerk of the town of Embarrass, wrote to Prince, respectfully declining to serve as the local official for the St. Louis County Commission on the grounds that he did not speak English.[38]

Despite these difficulties, the St. Louis County Commission began a campaign to suppress the IWW. Detectives were hired to keep tabs on local radicals and report on the activities of radical organizations. File cards assembled by Thomas G. Winter, the Director of Intelligence for the MCPS in St. Paul, kept track of these agents' reports. Among the cards covering the summer of 1917 are reports on the activities of Leo Laukki, editor of *Industrialisti*, and William Reynolds, editor of *Labor Leader*. Detectives reported the move of Charles Jacobson, a Finnish IWW organizer, from Virginia to Duluth; they kept track of the activities of Joel Lichten, an activist in the Jewish local of the Duluth Socialist Party; they filed

William I. Prince, a banker, Republican Party activist, and former mayor of Duluth, was chairman of the Public Safety Commission in St. Louis County. Courtesy Northeast Minnesota Historical Center.

reports on Sigmund Slonim, an attorney who defended Duluth radicals; they kept a constant watch on Arthur Thorne, secretary of the Duluth IWW; and they consistently monitored local IWW and Socialist activities.[39]

Duluth officials took other steps to suppress the IWW. The city council passed a vagrancy ordinance in June based on model legislation proposed by the MCPS.[40] The ordinance made it a crime to oppose or be about to oppose full support of the war. It was used against the IWW almost immediately. The nationally prominent IWW leader Elizabeth Gurley Flynn was in Duluth, having been invited to speak at the annual Finnish Socialist picnic on the range in early July. She met with local IWW officials at their office in Duluth. The local IWW leaders were concerned for her safety and decided to take her by car to a private home in Virginia. Before she could check out of the Holland Hotel where she was staying, local police arrested her and local IWW leaders under the recently passed vagrancy ordinance.[41] Among the fifteen local leaders arrested were Leo Laukki, Charles Jacobson, and Marie Baxter, organizer for the Domestic Workers Union, a branch of the IWW.[42] County officials also took action against the IWW, banning IWW members, many of whom worked for the county highway department, from being employed by the county. State Senator Charles Adams urged private contractors to follow this example as well.[43]

The campaign against the IWW continued to heat up. On August 1, Frank Little, the IWW organizer who had led the 1913 ore dock strike in Duluth, was kidnapped in Butte, Montana, where he was organizing copper miners. Six masked men broke down the door of his hotel room and he was murdered, lynched from a railroad trestle outside of Butte. Little was part Indian. He

Red Torch *was an IWW annual published in Duluth by the Workers Socialist Publishing Company from 1916 to 1941. As this cover indicates, the IWW opposed the war. Courtesy Immigration History Research Center.*

Members of Duluth Domestic Workers Union, 1909. This may or may not be the same union as IWW Domestic Workers Local 115, which was present in Duluth in 1919. Marie Baxter was probably a member of Local 115. Courtesy Immigration History Research Center.

spoke of himself as "a real American" and "a real Red." "The rest of you are immigrants," he said. Pinned to Little's body was a note threatening several men among the striking local miners and electrical workers.[44] On August 4, just after Little's murder, the *Duluth Herald* editorialized that "[t]o solve the problem of the IWW, we shall probably have to forget rights and liberties and constitutional guarantees for which our fathers fought and suffered and died. A nation at war cannot let itself be hampered and perhaps defeated by internal revolution and in self defense it will suppress the internal enemy."[45] The *Herald* was owned by Anton C. Weiss, one of the seven members of the Minnesota Commission of Public Safety.

Despite the pressure, the IWW remained active in Duluth. The annual Finnish Socialist Picnic at Fairmount Park was held on July 7, with Leo Laukki, recently released from jail on the vagrancy charge, as the principal speaker. The *Labor World* reported a "fair crowd," with over five hundred coming from the range.[46] An ore dock strike, supposedly influenced by the IWW, resulted in the arrest of 139 men at the Allouez docks in Superior.[47] Still, the repression continued. The Duluth police force raided the local IWW office at 530 West First Street in early August, but a detective reporting to the Public Safety Commission noted that the office was reopened.[48] On August 18, the same day this report was filed, about one hundred members of the Third Regiment of the Minnesota National Guard launched another attack on the IWW office in Duluth. At about five o'clock in the afternoon the guardsmen marched in formation to IWW headquarters, where they assaulted four IWW members, destroyed furniture and office equipment, and burned all office records. Afterward the guardsmen formed into ranks and marched away. Duluth police took no action to protect the IWW members or the office and none of the participating guardsmen was arrested.[49] St. Louis County Public Safety Commission director William Prince commented on this incident in a letter to MCPS secretary Pardee:

> The wiping out of the I.W.W. head-quarters last Saturday evening, while theoretically a lawless act, is generally approved of, and is much more in line with public sentiment than the course pursued with reference to such head-quarters by municipal officials. The existence of the place should not have been tolerated for some time past and wiping it out meets with general public approval.[50]

Following this attack, Duluth Chief of Police McKercher announced that no future IWW meetings would be tolerated in the city.[51] A few weeks later, on September 5, 1917, Federal Bureau of Investigation officers raided IWW offices throughout the nation and the federal government indicted 166 important leaders of the IWW.[52] Among those indicted were several local IWW activists, including Leo Laukki, editor of the Duluth newspaper, *Industrialisti*, and a teacher at Work People's College; Fred Jaakkola; Arthur Boose; William Tanner; Frank Westerlund; and Charles Jacobson.[53]

The MCPS also targeted the Non-Partisan League (NPL), a Populist political coalition appealing to farmers in North Dakota and Minnesota and to some labor activists both inside and outside the AFL. Although the NPL officially endorsed President Wilson's war policy, its support was less than enthusiastic. Like the IWW and the Socialists, the NPL saw the war as serving the interests of big business. The NPL called for the conscription of wealth as well as the conscription of men. In July 1917, Charles A. Lindbergh, who had served as a United States congressman from Minnesota and who would go on to be the NPL candidate for governor

Prisoners support group. The photograph is from Ahjo (The Forge), *September 1917, an IWW quarterly published by Work People's College. The newspaper visible in the photograph is* Industrialisti. *Courtesy Immigration History Research Center.*

in 1918, published a book on the war that forcefully presented this point of view.[54] In May 1918, as a gubernatorial candidate, Lindbergh was scheduled to speak at the Shrine Auditorium in Duluth. The executive committee of the Shrine canceled the lease agreement, citing protesters who were coming to their officers and saying that "the auditorium was leased under a misapprehension of the character and purpose of the meeting." Denied the use of the auditorium, local Lindbergh supporters, many of whom were Scandinavians, arranged for him to speak at Woodman Hall in the West End. Despite the fact that the rental fee had already been paid and despite the presence of a crowd of eight hundred persons assembled on short notice, the trustees of the hall refused to open it for the meeting. Police Chief McKercher had advised them not to allow it.[55]

Because of their prewar opposition to American entry into the war and because of their support for the NPL, Swedish Americans were considered suspect in the eyes of Judge McGee, the dominant personality on the Minnesota Public Safety Commission.[56] Speaking before a U.S. Senate Committee on Military Affairs, McGee said,

"A Non-Partisan League lecturer is a traitor every time. In other words, no matter what he says or does, a League worker is a traitor." McGee went on to criticize the U.S. attorney in Minnesota for lacking a fighting stomach, adding that "[w]here we made a mistake was in not establishing a firing squad in the first days of the war. We should now get busy and have that firing squad working overtime." He went on to summarize the loyalty problems in his state, saying, "The disloyal element in Minnesota is largely among the German-Swedish people. The nation blundered at the start of the war in not dealing severely with these vipers."[57]

To be sure, later McGee would retreat from these words.[58] Most Swedes in Minnesota were, if possibly reluctant, at least conscientious supporters of the war. Few Swedes evaded the draft. Few spoke out against the war, even if they did support the NPL. And, as a group, Swedes purchased their share of war bonds.[59] But the Scandinavian local of the Socialist Party in Duluth did justify the wildest fears of McGee and those who thought like him. Its members did publicly oppose the war. At least some of them publicly refused to purchase war bonds. They opposed conscription and they publicly supported the IWW.

On May Day 1917, following the U.S. entry into the war in April, the Scandinavian local in Duluth began publishing *The Labor Leader*, an English-language weekly newspaper. In part, the decision to publish the newspaper grew out of frustrations with the *Labor World*, the privately owned newspaper supportive of the AFL. In April, about three weeks after the United States entered the war, Duluth Local 165 of the Boilermakers, Shipbuilders and Helpers Union went out on strike. The strike affected an industry with potential military significance. At first the employers refused to negotiate and called in strikebreakers. The union held firm, rejecting a later settlement offer made by the employers at a meeting at the Commercial Club. Scandinavian Socialists played a significant role in the strike. Meetings of the union were held at Sloan Hall, in the middle of a neighborhood that was heavily Swedish and known to harbor large numbers of Socialists.[60] About one month into the strike, the Scandinavian Socialists held a benefit for the striking Boilermakers in the same neighborhood.[61] Over two months later, the strike was settled on terms advantageous to the union.[62]

Believing that the *Labor World* had not been sufficiently supportive of this strike and believing in the need for a Socialist press in Duluth, the Scandinavian local launched the *Labor Leader*. From the beginning, the newspaper opposed the war and fought against the loss of civil liberties threatened by conscription, the espionage law, and proposed censorship. The very first issue of the paper also complained that no laboring men had been included among the special deputies recently sworn in to guard the ore docks and other port facilities. In June, the paper was publicly voicing "left wing" Socialist criticism of P. G. Phillips, a "right wing" Socialist city commissioner who had helped pass the vagrancy ordinance urged by the Minnesota Public Safety Commission. It also protested the use of this ordinance against the IWW in Duluth.[63] Also in June, Ole Hjelt, an organizer for the Scandinavian Socialist Federation, spoke in Duluth to a combined crowd of Swedes and Finns.[64] Around the same time, a private detective employed by the MCPS began tailing the new editor of the newspaper.[65]

During the summer of 1917, the Scandinavian local sharpened its defense of the beleaguered IWW and called attention to the work of the People's Council for Peace and Democracy, a national organization supporting a negotiated peace and defending civil liberties against wartime hysteria. Other local newspapers took a somewhat different view of the council, denouncing it as "striking daggers into the back of liberty," comparing it to rats gnawing at the vital organs of America, and calling upon readers to "crush the traitors."[66] Undeterred, the *Labor Leader* denounced the Minnesota Public Safety commissioners as dictators, ridiculed the witch hunt against the IWW, and defended revolutionary direct action in the spirit of the Boston Tea Party.

Some sense of how radical this position was at that time can be gained by noticing that during the same period the *Labor World*, which had for twenty years been the voice of the labor movement in Duluth, denounced the IWW as reckless, treasonous, and made up only of un-American aliens.[67] In August 1917 *Labor World* struggled further to distinguish itself and the moderate labor movement of the AFL from the radicalism espoused by the IWW: "There are at least precious few Americans who claim membership in this bandit organization. The aliens who predominate in the I.W.W. are so divided over national differences that there is no chance for them to get together on a strike that would tend to weaken their respective countries during the war. The Finns are the only alien workmen who could put up a solid front in a strike of iron miners at this time and it is said that even they are divided among themselves." Further, having observed that the Finns had no love of country and wouldn't abide by the rules governing the legitimate labor movement, *Labor World* concluded by saying that "[t]hey [Finns] are both political and industrial outlaws and should be treated as such until they learn that labor's first duty is to support this country at all costs and at all times, and that any movement for labor's freedom in the United States ... [should be by] ... evolution and not revolution."[68] AFL-affiliated unions in Superior, Wisconsin, actively volunteered to help prevent IWW strikes at the coal and ore docks.[69] In Duluth, J. G. O'Neill, a long-time activist in the local AFL Longshoremen's Union, took a similarly proactive stance, writing to the Minnesota Commission of Public Safety to inform against activists in the Non-Partisan League.[70]

In September 1917, in keeping with repression of the Socialist press throughout the United States, the U.S. Postmaster ruled that the *Labor Leader* was not entitled to the second-class mailing permit normally extended to all newspapers. The last issue of the *Labor Leader* was published on October 5, but on October 12, the newspaper was reborn as *Truth* with the same editor, the same editorial policy, and the same backing from the Scandinavian local. The local also continued its fight for peace and civil liberties through the local People's Council. On November 16 this local brought Scott Nearing to Duluth, one of the national leaders of the People's Council. A crowd of over eight hundred showed up to hear Nearing speak, only to have fifty local police close the meeting and arrest Nearing, along with several of the local leaders.[71] Despite the uncertainty of civil liberties, the life of the Scandinavian local continued. Ties with the national and international Swedish Socialist movement are indicated by the continued availability in Duluth of *Social Democraten* and *Svenska Socialisten*, in spite of the harassment of such newspapers by the Post Office.[72] Some three hundred Scandinavians turned out to hear O. E. Thompson, one of the leaders of the Duluth local, speak in Superior, Wisconsin.[73] At a meeting of all of Duluth's Socialists, a meeting that closed with the singing of "The International" simultaneously in English, Finnish, Swedish, and "Jewish," party leaders claimed a membership of one thousand.[74]

In fall of 1918, mainstream newspapers in Duluth became even more shrill in their attacks on local radicals. The *Herald* directly attacked *Truth* as pro-German, while the *Tribune* chose this time to give tacit support to extra-legal repression of the IWW. Contrasting the lynching of Frank Little with the drawn-out trials of

Bill Haywood and other IWW leaders in Chicago, an editorial in the *News Tribune* concluded: "Maybe Montana's way with the I.W.W. agitators is better than Chicago's. Little's trial was shorter and it had no such aftermath as Haywood's."[75] A few weeks later, on the night of September 18, Olli Kiukkonen, a young Finn thought to have renounced his claim to citizenship to avoid military service, was dragged from his room by "Knights of Liberty" and forced into a waiting car. He was not seen again until September 30, when his tarred and feathered body was found hanging from a tree in Lester Park. The death was ruled a suicide.[76] A little more than a month later the war came to an end. However, threats of prosecution, deportation, and extra-legal harassment, born of the wartime hysteria, continued to hang over the Finnish and Scandinavian radicals in Duluth. During the war, America had come to see a part of the foreign population within its borders as an internal enemy, but it was never very clear in the public mind just how substantial this enemy was. Sometimes it was said to be a handful of agitators who were rejected by the great mass of foreigners within the nation's borders; other times everyone who spoke a foreign language was thought to be suspect. World War One was waged on two fronts—in Europe and at home.

The Communist revolution in Russia added fuel to the turmoil in Duluth. From the beginning, radicals in the United States were enthusiastically supportive of the Bolshevik revolution, though there was considerable confusion about what was going on and what kind of Socialism the Bolsheviks were creating in Russia. *Truth*, the newspaper published by the Scandinavian local, first used the term "Bolshevik" in a December 1917 story concerning the abolition of titles and corporate profit.[77] In the months that followed, *Truth* published journalists' reports about what was happening in Russia as well as pronouncements by Lenin and Trotsky, including the text of Lenin's "Letter to the American Working Class."[78] By November 1918, one year after the Bolsheviks seized power, *Truth* had come to see the Russian Revolution as the first step in a worldwide Socialist revolution.[79] One year later, when the American Socialist Party split into Socialist and Communist camps, the Duluth Scandinavian Socialists voted to join the Communists, and the Communist hammer and sickle appeared on the masthead of *Truth*.[80]

Alarmed at the enthusiasm for Communism spreading among immigrant radicals in the United States, the Department of Justice

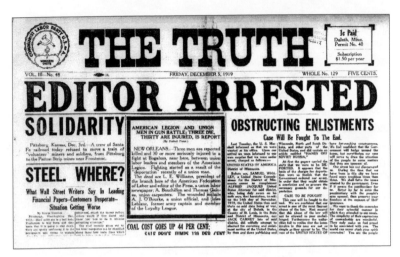

By luck, editor Carney eventually made his way back to Ireland without serving any lengthy time in prison. The Scandinavian Local in Duluth became one of the founding locals of the Communist Party USA.

struck back. On the night of January 2, 1920, federal agents arrested thousands of suspected alien radicals. "Agents Bag 3,896 Reds in 35 Cities" was the headline in the *Duluth News Tribune* the next morning. No raids were conducted in Duluth, but local newspapers announced that deportation proceedings had been initiated against Jack Carney and Carl Haglund, two leaders of the Communists in Duluth. Headlines in the *News Tribune* proclaimed: "List of Alleged Duluth Reds Is Sent to St. Paul" and "Definite Steps to Stamp Out the Communist Labor Party Being Taken."[81] More raids were conducted elsewhere on January 6 and later that month charges were brought against Communist leaders, including Carney, for violating an Illinois sedition law by attending a Communist meeting in Chicago.[82] In response to this legal repression, the Communists went underground. With mere membership in the Communist movement being construed by the authorities as sufficient grounds for deportation, the many members of the Scandinavian local who were not yet citizens were in serious danger. In the midst of the raids and arrests, the Communist insignia disappeared from the masthead of *Truth* and a notice appeared: "In view of the reactionary laws about to be passed and the possible misuse of the powers of the Constitution, it has been deemed advisable to disband the Communist Labor Party of Minnesota."[83]

In fact, as was clear to any reader, the paper remained connected to the Communist movement and the local Communists continued to function. In Duluth the Communists purchased the Bricklayers' Hall in West Duluth, renaming it Workers' Hall.[84] This hall became the site for a steady stream of nationally renowned speakers, such as Kate Richards O'Hare and Ella Reeves Bloor, both nationally prominent Communists who appeared in the fall of 1920, though authorities would not allow Robert Minor, another Communist of national importance, to speak.[85] Dances and entertainments were frequent. So, too, were talks by local leaders like Albert Thalin, Bertha Van Hove, O. E. Thompson, Matt Daly, and J. O. Bentall, who replaced Carney as editor of *Truth* when Carney moved to Butte, Montana.[86] Other prominent outside speakers included Elizabeth Gurely Flynn and Helen Keller.[87] Flynn's appearance in Duluth was part of a vigorous local campaign against the execution of Sacco and Vanzetti, two immigrants sentenced to death on dubious grounds.[88] Area Communists also formed an active chapter of the Friends of Soviet Russia, an organization devoted to raising aid for Russia, which had been torn by civil war and famine. The organization was active in Duluth between September 1921 and June 1922, raising more money in Duluth than was raised in Cleveland and almost as much as was raised in Detroit and Boston.[89] Duluth also hosted a district convention of the Scandinavian Socialist Federation, now almost completely gone over to the Communists, in September 1921.[90]

The local Communist movement was greatly strengthened by the adherence of the Finnish Socialist Federation to the Communist cause. When the Socialist Party shattered in August 1919, the Finnish Socialist Federation did not immediately affiliate with the Communists. Clearly sympathetic to the Communist International but unwilling to affiliate with either of the warring Communist factions in the United States, the Finnish Federation voted to leave the American Socialist Party at a national convention in December 1920, remaining independent until it joined the newly formed Workers' Party, a legal offshoot of the Communist Party USA, at the end of 1921.[91] The affiliation of the Finnish Federation brought valuable resources to the Communists. With between 7,000 and 8,500 dues-paying households, members of the federation made up about 40 percent of the membership of the Communist Party in the early 1920s. The Finns also brought a well-established left-wing press, adding a circulation of 40,000 to the Communist press in the United States.[92]

IWW activists also joined the local Communists. Though there was a split within the national IWW over the issue, a large part of the IWW in the Duluth area rallied to the Communist cause. Bill Haywood, the prominent national leader of the IWW, gave his support to the Communists.[93] Out on bail in the summer of 1920, Haywood spoke to an IWW rally in Billings Park in Superior, raising a thousand dollars to be split between *Truth* and the IWW.[94] Leo Laukki, the editor of the Finnish IWW newspaper *Industrialisti*, also embraced the Communist movement and wrote an extensive history of the Russian revolutionary tradition that was published by the Workers' Socialist Publishing Company in Duluth in 1919.[95] On May Day, 1921, IWW members in Hibbing circulated handbills and stickers calling on their fellow workers to join the Bolsheviks.[96] Another significant step in moving local Wobblies to the Communists took place in the summer of 1921, when George Hardy, one-time national secretary-treasurer of the IWW, spoke in Duluth. Hardy had been critical of the Bolsheviks but changed his mind after a visit to Russia in early 1921. Now an enthusiastic supporter of the Communists, Hardy spoke at the Finnish Workers' Opera House in Duluth and at the IWW hall at 328 Tower Avenue in Superior.[97] Arthur Boose, the former secretary for the IWW in Duluth who had been recently released from prison for his IWW activities and had converted to Communism, also spoke in Duluth at the Workers' Opera.[98] Boose was invited back to speak (in English) at the Duluth Finnish Workers Federation Summer Festival at Fairmount Park two weeks later.[99] Boose also spoke twice more that summer at the Communist Workers' Hall in Duluth's West End, once appearing the same week as William Z. Foster, the prominent leader of the 1919 national steel strike, who had secretly joined the Communists.[100]

By the spring and summer of 1922, the Communists of Duluth and Superior had established the Workers' Party as a going concern. They had established a Workers' Hall at Nineteenth Avenue West and First Street in Duluth and another Workers' Hall in Superior at the corner of Fifth and Tower.[101] In Superior, where a Young Workers' League was being organized, a city central committee had been formed with representatives from the English and Finnish branches and from the Superior Scandinavian local, which was expected to officially join the Workers' Party shortly and in fact did so.[102] Organizers for District Nine of the Communist Party, first Frank Miner and then H. E. Keas, drew the local Communists into contact with the national program of the Workers' Party.[103] A Sunday outing at Fairmount Park in August 1922 featured Ella Reeves Bloor as the speaker, with music by the Workers' Band, exhibitions by the Workers' Athletic Club, a recitation by Miss Francis Hoffman, a speech by Miss Sophie Niskin of the Young Women's Hebrew Association, and singing by the Workers' Male Choir.[104] The year ended with the District Nine Convention of the Workers' Party at Finnish Hall in Superior.[105] With the trials and tribulations of the red scare and the factional fighting behind them, local Communists could begin to think about the battles ahead.

americanization

IN THE DECADES BEFORE WORLD WAR I THERE WAS CONCERN
in some circles about the effects of continued immigration on the
nation. In particular, concern focused on the "new immigrants"
coming from southern and eastern Europe. People like Jews, Italians, and South Slavs were thought to be significantly different
from the northern Europeans who had made up the bulk of earlier immigration to the United States. For one thing, the eastern
and southern Europeans were different from the largely Protestant
northern Europeans in their Jewish and Catholic faith traditions.
In addition, they were different according to the "scientific" theories of race promulgated in the leading universities of the time.
Roughly put, these theories claimed a hierarchy of the races, with
the Nordic peoples of northern European at the top, followed in
descending order by central Europeans, southern Europeans,
Asians, American Indians, and Africans. With the publication in
1910–11 of its forty-volume *Dillingham Commission Report*, which
supported restrictions on immigration, the United States Senate
gave its endorsement to these theories.

The sense of racial status became an inescapable fact of life
in early twentieth-century America. In Duluth, to a greater or lesser
extent and in subtle and not-so-subtle ways, this sense affected
people's lives. Though many of them worked at the steel plant,
Duluth's South Slavs were not welcome in Morgan Park, the model
development that U.S. Steel built for its employees in Duluth. In
the early years, Morgan Park and its United Protestant Church
were reserved for American-born workers and immigrants from
northern European backgrounds, many of whom held technical
or supervisory positions. South Slavs, Italians, and African Americans who worked for U.S. Steel lived outside Morgan Park, mostly
in Gary and New Duluth.[1] South Slavs were aware that the northern Europeans in Morgan Park "always thought they were better

than those in New Duluth and Gary."[2] An article in the *Duluth Rip-saw* blamed the high rate of repatriation among Duluth's Croatians on the insults and harsh treatment they received in Duluth's factories.[3] South Slav children, often unable to speak English, found themselves in English-speaking classrooms in Stowe Elementary School and Morgan Park High School, where teachers shared the prevailing prejudices against them and where fellow students called them "Hunkies."[4]

Scandinavian mothers living in "the Glen" allowed their children to play with the Italian children, but forbade them to go into the Italian grocery stores, where the smells of garlic and oil seemed menacing.[5] Outsiders simply assumed that Little Italy and the mixed South Slav and Italian neighborhood on Raleigh Street in West Duluth were dangerous, though in fact neither was anywhere near as dangerous as its reputation.[6] We have already seen how the *Duluth Herald* commented in its coverage of the violent confrontation between strikers and police in 1889 that control of the strike had slipped out of the hands of the "cool headed" Scandinavians and into the hands of "a mob led by Bohemians and Italians, races that are about as undesirable as could be had in a strike or in a town."[7] Reflecting similar racial prejudices, a *Duluth Tribune* article in 1884 referred to a tenement filled with Italian laborers as "a nuisance to everybody in the neighborhood."[8] In St. Paul, where the Catholic church was controlled by Irish and German clergy, Italian Catholics were forced to meet in the basement of the Cathedral.[9] Similarly in Duluth, the 1901 Cathedral parish directory lists the Italian congregation separately from the other congregants and a 1914 history of the Catholic diocese lists Irish and Polish organizations, but none of the Italian organizations.[10]

Even children were aware of their racial status. In "To Die among Strangers," Irene Paull writes about the humiliation experienced by a little Jewish girl on her first day of school, and in "The War against the Gentiles," she writes about matching insults with Polish kids in her neighborhood.[11] A woman who grew up on Raleigh Street recalled as a child never admitting to strangers where she lived.[12] Another Duluth woman of mixed Italian background recalls how other children in a predominantly German-Catholic elementary school looked down on Italian kids. Still another Italian girl was so indoctrinated into her own sense of inferiority that she believed that only Italian girls menstruated.[13]

As "new immigrants" from eastern and southern Europe,

Duluth's Jews, South Slavs, and Italians bore the economic, social, and psychological burdens imposed by their status as members of undesirable races. Because of their supposed inferior status and because of their religious differences compared to the predominantly Protestant "American" and northern European people in Duluth, they were largely excluded from social contact with Duluth's economic and social elite. The Kitchi Gammi Club and the Northland Country Club—both important for their business, political, and social contacts—specifically refused to accept Jews, South Slavs, and Italians, as did fraternities and sororities in Duluth's high schools.[14]

The First World War heightened concern among many Americans about the aliens in their midst. Immigrant support for radical social change fueled anxieties about these aliens. But while there were some who thought that immigrants from southern and eastern Europe could not be assimilated into the American way of life, there were others who were at least willing to make the effort. The state of Minnesota had created the Minnesota Commission of Public Safety to lead the state through the ordeal of World War I. The Commission of Public Safety in turn created the Minnesota Americanization Committee, which was charged with inculcating American values and the knowledge of American ways into the foreign-born population of the state. In Duluth, yet again bypassing elected officials, the Commission of Public Safety turned to the Commercial Club to organize the Duluth branch of the Americanization Committee in August 1918.[15] Headed by Judge William A. Cant, who had legal experience in the naturalization process, the Duluth Americanization Committee included forty-four members, most of them drawn from the commercial and social elite of the city. The committee also included prominent representatives of some of the most important ethnic communities, like Father S. A. Iciek of the Polish Catholic church, O. J. Larson, the Finnish lawyer and politician, A. Castigliano, the Italian consul, and John Movern of the Slovenian community, who worked on the staff of the county auditor.[16]

The Duluth Americanization Committee's first efforts centered on organizing night-school classes in the English language, American history, and American government. Classes were developed in cooperation with the Duluth Board of Education and the local YMCA and YWCA. In addition, over the next four years the Americanization Committee sponsored a series of talks in factories,

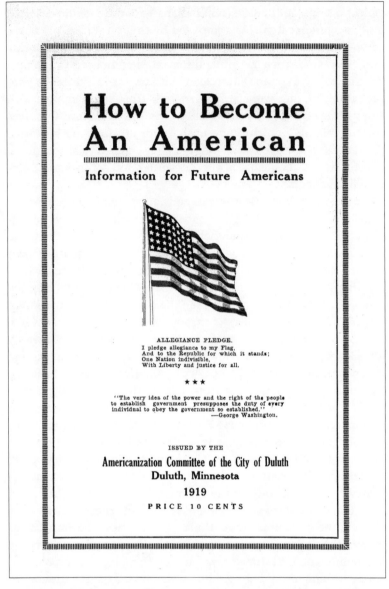

How to Become An American

Information for Future Americans

ALLEGIANCE PLEDGE.

I pledge allegiance to my Flag,
And to the Republic for which it stands;
One Nation indivisible,
With Liberty and justice for all.

★ ★ ★

"The very idea of the power and the right of the people
to establish government presupposes the duty of every
individual to obey the government so established."
—George Washington.

ISSUED BY THE

Americanization Committee of the City of Duluth
Duluth, Minnesota
1919
PRICE 10 CENTS

An early publication of the Americanization Committee of the City of Duluth. The phrase "under God" was not part of the Pledge of Allegiance in 1919. Courtesy Northeast Minnesota Historical Center.

lodges, and churches where the foreign-born were found. Albert Clarfield, the executive secretary for the committee, gave a series of talks at the Missabe Ore Docks, at noon for the day shift and at midnight for the night shift. His talks covered the advantages of American citizenship, what it means to be an American, and who makes the laws in America. Another series of talks was given at the Marshall-Wells Company, covering the workings of American government at the federal, state, county, and city levels.[17] The Americanization Committee relied heavily on Duluth's employers. Employers financed the work of the committee, provided opportunities for representatives of the committee to speak to alien workers, and encouraged their employees to participate in the programs the committee offered. A list of "Suggestions to Employers" distributed by the committee includes the establishment of company representatives, the placement of bulletin boards to inform workers about classes, sponsoring talks by representatives of the committee, monitoring employees' attendance at Americanization classes, and publicly recognizing those employees who attend.[18]

Born of wartime hysteria, the Americanization movement included many, like national leader Theodore Roosevelt, who wanted to eliminate the use of foreign languages, the foreign press, and all traces of loyalty to the homeland from the hearts of the foreign born.[19] These sentiments found expression in the annual report of the Duluth Americanization Committee for August 1919, which said that Americanization aimed to create "undivided loyalty" to America among the aliens, and that "[t]he foreigner [was] to be taught that the greatest of virtues is gratitude and the most magnificent of passions is loyalty to the flag that protects them."[20] But alongside this conception within the Duluth Americanization Committee was a kinder, gentler understanding of Americanization, one that valued diversity and aimed to preserve the cultural identity of the immigrant within the naturalized citizen.

The International Institute movement incorporated this understanding of Americanization. Edith Terry Bremer, the national leader of the movement, stressed the importance of preserving the immigrant's connections to the ethnic community and the ethnic family. Organized by the YWCA in many major cities before the war, International Institutes provided social services to the immigrant communities. With the coming of the war and the campaign to make immigrants into American citizens, it was natural for the International Institutes to add classes and provide guidance to assist immigrants to become American citizens.

In Duluth, both the YMCA and the YWCA were involved in Americanization work from the beginning, offering night classes in

English, American history, civics, and preparation for the natural-ization examination at their downtown locations.[21] Attendance at these classes, however, was not good. To make the Americaniza-tion process more accessible to the foreign born, the Little Gray House, an International Institute center, was opened in September 1919 in Gary-New Duluth, an industrial neighborhood on the west-ern edge of the city with a heavy concentration of South Slav and Italian immigrants. Although the Little Gray House was organized as a branch of the local YWCA, funding was initially provided by the Duluth Americanization Committee from contributions made by employers of the foreign born.[22] The executive secretary of the International Institute in Duluth was described by a national offi-cial of the YWCA as "an ex-office secretary who had a kind attitude toward foreign people; no training whatever; [and] no contact at any time with [the] International Institute or social work."[23] Never-theless, a kind attitude and a convenient location in the community seemed to help. Attendance at Americanization meetings was much

An "Old World market" sponsored by the International Institute in 1927. Photograph by Hugh McKenzie; courtesy Northeast Minnesota Historical Center.

higher at the Little Gray House than at other locations.²⁴ Reflecting on her personal experience, an Americanization teacher in Eveleth noted that "[t]he biggest breakthrough in the program to educate and Americanize the adults came when it was realized that it was wrong to try to tell them that all their customs and traditions had to be discarded. The teachers started to tell them to bring the best of their country with them, but leave their old hatreds and prejudices behind. This attitude changed the picture entirely."²⁵ Americanization workers in Duluth came to this realization from their own experience with immigrants and by establishing regular ties with the International Institute movement. By 1920, ethnic festivals celebrating traditional dress, food, and music had become regular parts of Institute life.²⁶

Americanization work continued well into the 1930s at the International Institute's center in Gary, at a downtown branch that opened later, and at its Neighborhood House on Raleigh Street in West Duluth.²⁷ However, the institute in Duluth moved beyond Americanization work to become, like the original International Institutes in other cities, a broad social service agency devoted to serving the needs of the foreign-born community. The institute provided a wide range of services: there were Americanization classes and English-language classes as well as facilities for a variety of clubs and organizations. One of the earliest was a Girls' Club, formed on September 24, 1919, with twenty-two girls representing fourteen different nationalities.²⁸ An Italian Mothers' Club, a Slovenian Mothers' Club, and a Finnish Mothers' Club were also among the early organizations formed. There were cooking classes and sewing classes, with the institute providing sewing machines for the women's use. There was a variety of recreational activities for children. The Neighborhood House on Raleigh Street organized basketball, football, and baseball teams for neighborhood boys.²⁹ Girls played basketball at Gary. Girls from Raleigh Street wrote and performed plays.³⁰ Later, at both the Gary and Raleigh Street centers, physicians gave talks and provided baby clinics for the children in the neighborhood. Financial support for these clinics was provided by the Masonic Shrine.³¹ In January 1922 the institute was planning to open a "women's exchange," where needlework and crafts made by foreign-born women could be sold. Women also played cards at the Raleigh Street center.³² Men came to both locations in the evenings for night classes and for meetings. Beginning in September 1921, a Catholic Croatian lodge rented the Gary center for its meetings. By the late 1920s and early 1930s, men were holding political meetings at both the Gary center and the Raleigh Street Neighborhood House, and there were frequent parties and ethnic festivals. Beginning in October 1921, the institute put on an "International Revue," featuring costumed performers from the various ethnic groups. The revue was staged downtown for an "American" audience. It was intended as a fundraiser for the work of the institute. It appears to have been successful, despite the Croatian Orchestra's refusal to perform, saying the audience appeared too "intellectual" for their music, and despite the fact that the performance of the accordion soloist had to be canceled because he was too intoxicated.

The monthly reports of the institute staff provide a view of life in the immigrant communities they served, though this view is to some extent filtered by the values and presuppositions of the women who did the institute's work. An early entry comments on the low moral standards of the Finns and the "colored" people of Lake Avenue. Another describes the Montenegrins as the "lowest" of all the ethnic groups served by the institute. When Nationality Secretaries, who were local staff members assigned to work with specific ethnic groups, observed what they took to be cases of child neglect or abuse, they informed the Child Welfare Agency. In at least some cases, children were removed from their homes. The monthly reports contain frequent references to the "squalor," "filth," and "appalling conditions" they encountered in the homes they visited. In one case a nationality secretary threatened to remove an infant child from a mother's home unless the house was cleaned up. A subsequent monthly report mentions the mother running after the secretary on the street, insisting that she come and see how the house had been cleaned. It is not surprising that in some cases people refused to let staff from the institute enter their homes. The institute also faced a high level of distrust and noncooperation from some of the Catholic priests active in the communities of the foreign born. Despite a donation of Slovenian books that somehow ended up in a library established by the institute, Father Pirnat of St. Elizabeth's Slovenian Church urged his flock to have nothing to do with the institute, as did Father Schultz, a Polish priest from West Duluth. In both cases, the decidedly Protestant character of the YWCA, of which the institute was officially a branch, appears to have been the stumbling block.

The Americanization Committee grew out of the need felt

by dominant elites to "Americanize" resident aliens. But "Americanization" was not just a top-down process; it worked the other way, too. Immigrants to America were both agents and objects of Americanization. Consider, for example, the benevolent societies formed by the Italians in Duluth. The Christopher Columbus Society, founded in 1893, was composed primarily of relatively prosperous northern Italians. Duluth's first lodge of the Sons of Italy was formed in 1910–1913 by merchants in Gary-New Duluth. Another Sons of Italy lodge, this one composed mainly of working-class members, was formed some years later in the central part of Duluth. Yet another Italian fraternal organization, the Societa' M. S. Besaglieri, or Sharpshooters, was organized in West Duluth in 1919.[33] In the early twentieth century these groups were divided by the relative prosperity of their members and the location of their neighborhood base in Duluth. In the wake of the First World War, concerns about the need to Americanize the immigrants and the codification in American immigration law of racist views concerning the inferiority of southern Europeans led Italians in Duluth to work together to promote a more positive image of themselves. The celebration of Columbus Day became particularly important in this regard, with Columbus serving as a symbol of the role Ital-

The Glen was an Italian neighborhood around Twelfth and Thirteenth Avenues West. Courtesy Northeast Minnesota Historical Center.

ians played in opening the New World to European science and culture. As early as 1923 the Christopher Columbus Society and the lodges of the Sons of Italy cooperated to put on a parade and banquet in Duluth to celebrate Columbus Day. Led by the Sons of Italy brass band, the parade began at Eleventh Avenue West and Superior Street in Duluth's "Little Italy" and made its way east on Superior Street and back on First Street. Banquet speeches were delivered by the Italian consul, Attilio Castigliano, Italian police captain A. G. Fiskett, and Reverend Father Egidius Allais, rector of St. Peter's Catholic Church. Musical entertainment was provided by the Boudini brothers, local accordionists. More than four hundred local Italians participated in these festivities.[34]

It is clear that this campaign to celebrate Columbus Day was very important to the Italians in Duluth, who also played a significant role in the campaign to build a memorial to Columbus on the grounds of the State Capitol. A report presented to a meeting in Hibbing in June 1933 indicates that the relatively small Italian community in Duluth contributed over four thousand dollars to this campaign, more than the three thousand dollars contributed by the much larger Italian community in Minneapolis and second only to the six thousand dollars contributed by the Italians of St. Paul.[35] An effort of this magnitude required the cooperation of a large part

Sons of Italy from Gary in early 1920s. Courtesy Alex Batinich and Immigration History Research Center.

By the late 1920s, a Sons of Italy band had been formed that included men from differ-ent Italian neighborhoods in Duluth. Courtesy Iron Range Historical Society.

of the Italian American community and presupposed a common identity as "Italian Americans" that would not have been present among Duluth's earliest Italian immigrants, whose identities were centered not on Italy, but on the particular regions in Italy from which they had come. By the early 1930s, this new sense of them-selves as Italian Americans led to the formation of the Italian-Amer-ican Club of Duluth, an organization aimed at providing fellowship among all Italians in Duluth and at promoting the image and inter-ests of Americans of Italian heritage.[36]

The Federation of Jugoslav Societies, formed in Decem-ber 1931, served a similar role in Americanizing Duluth citizens of South Slav background. Like the Italians who had made their way to Duluth, the South Slavs in Duluth originally formed a number of different fraternal societies to provide fellowship and insurance benefits to their members. In 1920 there were twelve different fra-ternal lodges in Duluth serving the needs of South Slavs.[37] By 1925, John Movern, who had served on the Duluth Americanization Committee, led an effort to form an organization that would include all Yugoslavs in Duluth and would work to Americanize them, including educating them and encouraging progressive political action on their behalf.[38] But it was not until December 1931, about the time the Italians of Duluth were coming together in the Italian-American Club, that the South Slavs in Duluth joined together to form the Federation of Jugoslav Societies.[39] Like the Italian-American Club, the Duluth Federation of Jugoslav Societies served as an institutional realization of the process of Americanization, in this case of South Slav immigrants, who had come to think of themselves as Yugoslav-Americans. At the same time, by advancing the image of Italians and South Slavs as Americans, the Italian-American Club and the Federation of Jugoslav Societies were also transforming the image of America itself. In this sense, the process of "Americanization" was simultaneously a process of "Italianization" and "Slavification."

Similarly complex processes were at work in the world of popular culture. By the 1920s, movie theaters showing silent films had largely replaced the vaudeville and burlesque shows of earlier years. These movies were especially popular with children, who flocked to Saturday matinees. Small theaters like the Sunbeam, Astor, and Diamond provided only a piano player to accompany the film, while larger theaters like the Garrick replaced the single piano player with an orchestra of ten musicians. Patrons often lined up for blocks to see a film. At one time there were twelve different movie theaters operating in Duluth.[40] In the darkened movie houses the children of diverse immigrant groups saw the same films in the same language, English. They also acquired common heroes and a common culture. Similar "Americanizing" forces were at work in sports, radio, the advertising of large companies, and the emerging chain stores, which began to displace the small neighborhood retail groceries and clothing stores. In all of these influences there was a leveling tendency that replaced the traditional ways and material culture of distinct immigrant groups with a shared "American" mass culture.

The second-generation Finns, Slavs, Jews, and Italians—the sons and daughters of the "new immigrants" of the early twentieth century—were coming of age in the 1920s. They were especially open, by reason of their youth, to the influences of the new technologies and the developing mass culture. To some extent, many of them lost aspects of their ethnic identity. The sons and daugh-

Young people at the Finnish Work People's College pose in a relaxed, "American" style in the 1920s. Courtesy Northeast Minnesota Historical Center.

ters of immigrants who attended high school in the 1920s had been grade-school students during World War I, when "speak English" campaigns had been in full swing. Under pressure from the authorities and out of a desire to be "American," many of these second-generation immigrants became English-only speakers.[41] Children often asked their mothers to prepare "American" foods and the sons of immigrants abandoned the European-style gymnastics of their fathers in favor of the "American" sports of baseball, football, and basketball.

Still, even these signs of the apparent loss of ethnic identity can have a surprising complexity about them. Phonograph recordings spread ethnic music as well as mainstream music. Consider also the enthusiasm for American sports that infused second-generation immigrants in Duluth in the 1920s. Bill Wickstrom, who graduated from Denfeld High School, was admonished by his father, John, a leader of the Scandinavian Socialist local, for being caught up in the trivialities of football and baseball and for ignoring more important things, such as, presumably, Socialist ideology.[42] On the other hand, the young Finns of Duluth and Superior, who abandoned traditional Finnish gymnastics for basketball, combined their interest in the American sport with the political traditions of their parents. In Duluth, the Finnish American Athletic Club Hall provided a meeting place for radicals and a platform for speakers, while in Superior the Young Communists organized the Labor Sports Union with the idea of using friendly competition in sports to build solidarity in the labor movement.[43]

Sports also provided an arena for the assertion of ethnic and neighborhood pride. Second-generation immigrant children in the Raleigh Street area took pride in the accomplishments of their athletic teams. Lazo Chumich, a heavyweight boxer and all-around athlete, was a hero for all of West Duluth.[44] The Finnish American

Performing with John Rosendahl, Viola Turpeinen (standing) was a musical sensation in the Finn Halls of the Lake Superior region. She produced a number of recordings and developed a national reputation in the 1930s. Courtesy Immigration History Research Center.

Athletic Club and its hall were at the center of Finnish cultural life in the late 1920s, a time when the Finnish basketball team was the one to beat in amateur competition in Duluth.[45] Gary-New Duluth teams participated in intra-city competition at least by 1923, when its "People's Meat" basketball team represented the neighborhood. In 1929 the decade-long enthusiasm for sports in Gary-New Duluth led to the formation of the Gary Athletic Club, with Dan Bubalo as its first president. The Gary Athletic Club served not only as the vehicle for community pride through athletic competition, but as a center for community life for the South Slavs, Italians, and others who lived in the neighborhood, featuring musical and theatrical performances as well as athletic competition.[46] To view this embrace of "American" sports as a process of Americanization in which ethnic identity was simply lost would be to miss the complexity of what was actually happening. In the Finnish American Athletic Club and the Gary Athletic Club, Duluth's immigrant communities created institutions in which people did more than absorb American ways—they contributed to the changing of America.

Who is an American? What does an American look like? How does an American dress? What does an American eat and drink? What does an American think? Where does an American worship? Concerns about the changing face of America touched on all of these factors and often linked them together. The "new immigrants" from central and southern Europe were thought to be darker than the northern Europeans who made up the American "native stock." On the Iron Range, the term "white men" came to mean men of northern European ethnicity, while southern Europeans were known as the "black races."[47] Hard menial labor was often thought to be beneath a man of northern European background. A manager for the Great Northern Railroad sent a message saying, "White men coming to Duluth will not work. Dagoes only men who will work.... Send more dagoes and shut off white men."[48] The new, non-Nordic, immigrants were also thought to be more emotional and childlike, and for that reason more susceptible to drink and the ideas of radical agitators. The radicalism of the Socialists, Communists, and members of the IWW was often blamed on undesirable immigrants.[49] Finns aside, the "new immigrants" were also more apt to be Catholics, who were thought to be subservient to papal authority. They also drank more than many people thought was proper for an American.

Some sense of how these various issues became intertwined

can be gained by considering the campaign for Prohibition, which culminated in the Eighteenth Amendment to the U.S. Constitution adopted on January 29, 1919. For decades the Women's Christian Temperance Union (WCTU) had led the fight for Prohibition. The WCTU had been active in Duluth since at least the 1890s.[50] While temperance was its central cause, other issues of concern to the WCTU included suffrage for women, equal pay for equal work, the protection of young girls against rape by raising the "age of consent" from ten to sixteen years, banning obscene pictures from saloons, encouraging exercise and practical dress for women, creating juvenile courts, providing jails for women, and hiring women police matrons.[51] In Duluth, the WCTU regularly sent temperance literature to lumber camps and mining locations, but it also provided food, clothing, and fuel to poor families in Duluth whose "destitution has been caused by the neglect of a drunken husband and father."[52]

During the war years, the national campaign for Prohibition was largely taken over by the Anti-Saloon League (ASL), a male-led organization that has been described as "virtually a branch of the Methodist and Baptist churches," but which in fact had the support of almost all the Protestant churches in the United States.[53] For the ASL, the struggle for Prohibition was an effort to preserve an "American" way of life against a rising tide of Catholic immigrants. Speaking during the election of 1928, which pitted the Catholic "wet" Al Smith, against the Protestant "dry" Herbert Hoover, Southern Methodist Bishop James Cannon, a man who played a national role in the Anti-Saloon League, told people at a rally that Smith courted

> the Italians, the Sicilians, the Poles and the Russian Jews. That kind has given us a stomach-ache. We have been unable to assimilate such people in our national life, so we shut the door on them. But Smith says, "give me that kind of people." He wants the kind of dirty people that you find today on the sidewalks of New York.[54]

In a similar, if less virulent fashion, the view of Prohibition as an instrument of Americanization captured the campaign for Prohibition in Duluth. When the Forty-second Annual Convention of the Minnesota WCTU was held in Duluth in September, 1918, virtually the whole program was given over to patriotic speeches and the work of "Americanization."[55]

Concerns about Americanization also helped fuel the revival of the Ku Klux Klan in the United States. The Klan of the 1920s is often called the "second Klan." In 1915 a new Klan organization was created through the efforts of William J. Simmons, a traveling salesman, organizer of fraternal societies, and Christian minister. Where the first Klan had relied primarily on extralegal terror to intimidate the leaders emerging from among the former slaves, the second Klan functioned more like a secret fraternal society devoted to the cause of white, Protestant America. Klan organizers called on white, Anglo-Saxon, Protestant (WASP) men to be exemplars of real American manhood, to reject the lures of sexual debauchery and liquor, to be responsible husbands and fathers, to be true followers of Jesus, and to protect their wives and children from the supposed evil machinations of foreigners, Bolsheviks, Catholics, and Jews.

The second Klan was part of a broader movement among white Protestants in the United States to preserve their version of America from what was perceived to be the corrupting influences of foreign religions, foreign ideologies, and foreign immigration. Viewing liberal "modernists" as betrayers of Christian orthodoxy, a Southern California oil tycoon financed the publication, beginning in 1910, of a series of twelve pamphlets attacking the liberal clergy and defending the literal truth of the Bible. Known as *The Fundamentals*, these pamphlets were made available to readers in Protestant churches throughout the United States, providing the foundation for a fundamentalist movement that remains part of the fabric of American culture today. Weaving together support for Christian fundamentalism, moral purity, and America, revivalists like Billy Sunday touched the hearts of many American Protestants. Speaking before massive audiences, Sunday poured out a torrent of words. Pretending to imitate "modernist" ministers, he minced about the platform, squeaking in a falsetto voice.[56] What the church really needed, he said, was fighting men of God, not "hog-joweled, weasel-eyed, sponge-columned, mushy-fisted, jelly-spined, pussy-footing, four-flushing, Charlotte-russe, Christians."[57] He attacked the forces of evil corroding the moral fiber of the nation: high society, worldly amusements, filthy habits, pliable politicians, liberal preachers, trashy immigrants, and the booze traffic.[58] "If I had my way with these ornery wild-eyed socialists and IWWs, I would stand them up before a firing squad," he said.[59] According to him, "Christianity and patriotism are synonymous terms, and hell and traitors are synonymous."[60] When Billy Sunday came to Duluth in

May 1918, eighteen thousand people came to hear him preach at the opening service.[61]

In the Americanization movement of the post–World War I era, this identification of Americanism with Christianity and with Protestant Christianity in particular was widespread. The revived KKK did not itself forge this identification in public consciousness, but it did exploit it. In the early 1920s the Klan marketed itself as pure Americanism. Organizers were paid on commission, getting a percentage of the dues of each member they recruited. They often focused their recruitment efforts on local clergymen, knowing that parishioners would follow their pastors into the Klan. Contributions from the Klan, sometimes ostentatiously delivered by robed Klansmen who appeared during Sunday services, made their way into the collection plates of Methodist, Presbyterian, Baptist, Quaker, and other Protestant churches. Though neither actually joined the Klan, prominent preachers like Billy Sunday and Bob Jones were among those who accepted Klan donations and endorsed Klan principles.[62]

Today we tend to think of the Klan as made up of misfits, alienated souls on the fringes of society, but this was not true of the Klan of the 1920s. Klan members were often lay leaders or clergymen from the main Protestant churches. They were often members of the principal fraternal lodges that were common across America. Simmons, the founder of the second Klan, made his living as an organizer for fraternal lodges and as a salesman of fraternal regalia. He claimed to have earned fifteen thousand dollars in a single year as a district manager for the Woodman of the World. In addition he belonged to several varieties of Masons and to the Knights Templar.[63] Similarly, Elizabeth Tyler and Edward Clarke, the professional fund-raisers who joined Simmons in organizing the second Klan and who earned three hundred thousand dollars in the first fifteen months of their involvement with the Klan, had a long background of working with the fraternal orders.[64] The second Klan was itself organized along the lines of the fraternal societies modeled on the Masons, taking its place in towns and cities across the Midwest alongside the Masons, the Odd Fellows, the Knights of Pythias, the Woodman, the Elks, the Moose, and a host of other fraternal organizations. Klan members often belonged to several of these organizations simultaneously. They came from diverse walks of life; some were factory laborers, while others were business or professional men. They were often pillars of their communities. Masonic lodges, which tended to be made up of educated and prosperous men who were leaders in civic affairs, were recruiting grounds for the KKK in the 1920s.[65]

Unlike the original Klan, which was largely confined to the South, the second Klan had support in virtually all parts of the country. It was particularly strong in the Midwest. Though never as strong as in Indiana, where the Klan controlled state politics for a number of years in the 1920s, the Klan did make its presence felt in Minnesota. A headline in the Klan newspaper, *The Minnesota Fiery Cross*, in February 1924 proclaimed "Ku Klux Klan Is Sweeping Gopher State as Thousands Answer Call," and the paper's editorial called for a policy of staunch Protestant Americanism.[66] Appealing to the "scientific" racism of Lathrop Stoddard, a respected scholar and author of *The Rising Tide of Color*, the Minnesota Klan newspaper called for the white supremacy of Anglo-Saxon, Nordic, and Teutonic people over all other people both within and outside the United States.[67] Speaking to a large audience at Albert Lea, the editor of the newspaper described America's founding fathers as representatives of the Nordic race, contrasting those noble forebears with the inferior foreigners entering the United States from southern and eastern Europe. He appealed to the *Voice*, a publication of the Methodist Episcopal Church, to support his view that discrimination against southern Europeans was justified and necessary because while Nordic immigrants could be assimilated in America, others could not.[68]

In an attempt to defeat George Leach, the incumbent mayor of Minneapolis, the Klan ran its own candidate and charged Leach with having an illicit sexual affair. Libel charges were brought against the Klan candidate, who was successfully prosecuted by Floyd B. Olson, who would later become governor of Minnesota. This prosecution broke the power of the Klan as a statewide organization, but the group retained strength in parts of the state, including northeastern Minnesota and the city of Duluth.[69] In northeastern Minnesota, as in the rest of the Midwest, the primary targets of Klan hostility were non-Nordic immigrants and the Catholic church, to which many of these immigrants belonged.[70] Of course the Klan was pervasively hostile to blacks, but in northeastern Minnesota, as in much of the upper Midwest, immigrant Catholics were more numerous, and therefore perhaps more worrisome to Klan members, than black Americans. A Klan poem captured the spirit of Klan Americanism:

I would rather be a Klansman
in a robe of snowy white,
Than to be a Catholic Priest
in a robe as black as night;
For a Klansman is an American
and America is his home,
But the priest owes his allegiance
to a Dago Pope in Rome.[71]

The Duluth chapter of the Ku Klux Klan was organized at Owl's Hall in the spring of 1921 with seven hundred members.[72] A few years later, in spring of 1925, a local chapter of the Women's Ku Klux Klan may have also been organized.[73] The Klan was a secret organization and no official membership lists are known to exist; however, lists of purported members of the Duluth Klan for 1925 and 1926 made their way into the papers of Bishop Thomas Welch of the Catholic Diocese of Duluth, presumably assembled by a spy. While there are some changes in the lists between 1925 and 1926, most of the names remain the same. There are approximately two hundred and fifty names on each list, and they are Anglo, German, and Scandinavian. Addresses range from the East End to West Duluth, with relatively high concentrations in Lakeside and the eastern parts of the city. Many of the men on the lists held some kind of public office or worked as public employees. Among them are a city clerk, a municipal judge, two sitting county commissioners and one former county commissioner, several public school teachers, two city commissioners, a county auditor, an assistant city attorney, officers of the board of education, two elected members of the school board, two local officials of the federal Internal Revenue Service, several postmen, and several members of the police and fire departments. The list also includes physicians, dentists, attorneys, journalists, a local clergyman, businessmen, and laborers from a variety of trades and places of work. Often several members of one family residing at the same address are listed as members, as well as several employees of one business firm.[74]

The *Labor World*, like the national AFL, bitterly opposed the Klan. In the spring of 1925 the newspaper charged the local Klan with distributing fraudulent campaign literature against candidates who were Catholics.[75] Among those targeted was William Murnian, the labor-supported Commissioner of Public Safety whose "no shoot" order bore much of the responsibility for the lynch-

This sheet music celebrating the Ku Klux Klan was composed and published in Duluth and given away to patrons of a local music shop. Courtesy Northeast Minnesota Historical Center.

ing of black circus workers in Duluth in 1920. Murnian was not the only target of the Klan; much of its local work appears to have been focused on purging Catholics from public office and replacing them with KKK members or sympathizers.

The pages of the *Labor World* give us a window on the activity of the Klan in Duluth and northeastern Minnesota in the mid-1920s. In May 1925, the Klan succeeded in ousting the Catholic postmaster.[76] In August 1925, the Klan fought against welcoming a convention of the Knights of Columbus to Duluth and appears to have succeeded in scaring off elected officials who might otherwise have provided a word of welcome to the convention. With W. A. McGonagle, president of U.S. Steel's Duluth, Missabe and Northern Railrway, giving the welcoming address in place of city officials, the local Klan burned a cross on the hillside above the convention hall and disrupted the parade put on by the visiting Knights.[77] In October 1925, the area Klan held a much publicized ceremony at Pike Lake to initiate new members. Claiming to be one hundred percent American, initiates took an oath pledging their loyalty to white people and to Protestant Christianity. With five flaming crosses in the background, one hundred and forty initiates joined up. About seventy-five of the new Klansmen came from Duluth and the rest were from the Iron Range. Most of the initiates were young men between the ages of eighteen and twenty.[78]

William A. McGonagle, president of the Duluth, Missabe and Northern Railway, defied the Ku Klux Klan to give a welcoming speech at a Knights of Columbus convention in Duluth. Courtesy Northeast Minnesota Historical Center.

In Hibbing, where WASP leadership was being challenged by increasingly successful coalitions of immigrants, the Klan was especially popular. Klan-supported candidates made a strong showing in the 1925 Hibbing elections. Following a near sweep by Klan candidates, fifteen Catholic firemen and twenty-four Catholic policemen, some of them World War I veterans, were fired.[79] The following June, a Klan candidate, Pal Brown, ran for sheriff of St. Louis County. Brown, a former professional boxer, ran in the primary of the Farmer-Labor Party, a reform party claiming to represent the interests of farmers and laborers. He outpolled the labor-endorsed candidate, winning the primary election. While the *Labor World* complained that this was in part due to workers' fears of asking for the Farmer-Labor ballot, particularly in mining towns where a miner might be fired if he were a known supporter of the Farmer-Labor Party, Brown could not have won the primary without significant support from within the Farmer-Labor Party.[80]

The school board elections in 1926 provide another example of how the KKK operated in Duluth. In July 1926 the local Klan put out a bulletin attacking school board members David Clough and Robert Coole and others on the board, blaming them for forcing KKK-supported candidate A. G. Anderson out of the school board race. The Klan was also angry at them for voting down a KKK-supported resolution calling for daily Bible readings in the schools, charging them with un-Americanism. The KKK bulletin urged voters to support its official candidate, Walter Gladson, saying, "Walter Gladson, whom we also recommend that you support, is, or should be well-known to all our membership. He is past master of T. W. Hugo lodge, and is very active in Masonic and Protestant circles in Duluth. He, too, believes in every thing in which we believe, and would, in our opinion, make an ideal member of the school board."[81] In this case the Klan-backed candidate lost the election.

In August 1926 the Klan held a picnic and rally in a field at the intersection of the Miller Trunk highway and the Floodwood-Grand Rapids road. The picnic was attended by Klansmen and Klanswomen from the Iron Range and Duluth. The KKK bulletin distributed at the picnic included ads from Matt Johnson, salesman for a local furniture business, and Val Anderson, president of Paramount Service, Inc.[82] As had been the case with the anti-Catholic American Protective Association in the 1890s, much of the support for the Klan in Duluth came from Scandinavians. William McEwen, editor of the *Labor World* and an implacable critic of the Klan, expressed sympathy for the misguided but well-meaning Scandinavians who got mixed up with it and reminded these same Scandinavians that in the South, they were as much despised by the Klan as the Irish Catholics were in Duluth.[83] In December 1926 a lawyer who was the main organizer for the Klan in Duluth left town, taking KKK funds with him.[84] This development took considerable wind out of local Klan sails, but even so, the organization retained enough strength through its members and supporters on the city council to force the appointment of KKK member Sievert Hanson as fire chief over "Silent Jack" Fisher, a Catholic who had the support of former Fire Chief Randall.[85] In this last success, the Klan surprised its critic, McEwen, who thought the scandal of the stolen funds had put an end to the Klan in Duluth.

The experience of the Klan in Duluth was reflected in other cities as well. Because the Klan was largely created by organizers out to make money, scandals were common. But because the Klan tapped into prejudices that were deep and widespread, its program could survive these scandals. The Klan of the 1920s must be understood as just one expression of these underlying prejudices. In the period following the World War I, Protestant Americans were deeply troubled about the effects of new immigrants and their Catholic faith on the future of America, and the Klan was an expression of that concern. In 1924 the federal government passed legislation finally ending the open immigration that had characterized the previous history of the United States. The law was a "Nordic victory," clearly influenced by prejudices against Catholics and new immigrants, and it was strongly supported by the KKK.[86] The law's underlying premise was that persons from parts of the world other than northern Europe were not welcome in the United States. The prevailing presumption that such people could not be assimilated into American life left the new immigrants who were already in the United States in a difficult position. Were they not Americans? What would become of them?

World War I had aroused a spirit of martial idealism. In the postwar period this martial idealism was enlisted in a broad crusade to preserve the moral fiber of American life. Americans had viewed the war as a war to preserve democracy, to preserve the American way of life against the forces of evil. Almost without exception, the American clergy endorsed the war as a noble cause. From his pulpit in Washington, D.C., Randolph H. McKim proclaimed, "It is God who has summoned us to this war.... This conflict is indeed a crusade. The greatest in history—the holiest. It is in the profoundest and truest sense a Holy War."[87] YMCA director Henry B. Wright provided a meditation for young soldiers who had qualms about bayonet drills, saying that "[i]n the hour of soul crisis, the [YMCA] Secretary can turn and say with quiet certainty to your lad and my lad, 'I would not enter this work till I could see Jesus himself sighting down a gun barrel and running a bayonet through an enemy's body.'"[88]

Assured by the clergy, the press, and public officials of the transcendent nobility of their cause, many American soldiers acquired an understanding of their own experience in terms that were simultaneously patriotic and religious. This gave meaning to the very real danger and horror of the battlefield. In the war men found in themselves and in their fellow soldiers the real nobility of American, Christian manhood. In Duluth the Northwest Warriors Association sought to preserve the fraternal idealism of this wartime experience. Organized in November 1920, the Warriors were World War I servicemen who, having served in the war against external enemies, now enlisted in the fight for Americanism.[89] This spirit of martial idealism extended beyond the soldiers themselves, touching the older men who volunteered for service in the home guards, the thousands of men and women who served in the Red Cross, and the millions who bought war bonds or in other ways acted to support the nation in its time of crisis. In one way or another, all participated in a larger, noble, civic life. It was a powerful force, for good and for ill.

Consider, for example, the Cloquet fire in the fall of 1918. On October 12, 1918, grass fires caused by passing trains broke out in southern St. Louis County. The fire spread rapidly, fanned by high winds. Smoke filled the air surrounding Duluth, so much so that it was possible to look directly at the sun. In the morning people from the surrounding rural area came streaming into Duluth, fleeing from the raging forest fires. The wind drove the fire around the city, threatening the Woodland, Hunters Park, Glenn Avon, and Lakeside neighborhoods on the northern and eastern edges of the city. Wind-blown cinders began to fall in these areas. By late morning, the authorities decided to evacuate two thousand homes in the eastern end of the city. By the middle of the afternoon it appeared that the whole city might be engulfed by the flames. It was not until eleven o'clock in the evening, when the wind died down, that it became clear that the city would survive. Morning revealed a des-

Gilbert's Store in Duluth was a victim of the fire of October 1918, which for a while threatened the entire city. Photograph by Hugh McKenzie; courtesy of Northeast Minnesota Historical Center.

olate scene: some homes were destroyed in the northern and eastern neighborhoods, and the surrounding countryside was a "black cinder," with scores of human corpses and many buildings reduced to ashes.[90]

In this crisis, with the city threatened by the fire and with refugees pouring in, the Duluth Home Guard and the local Red Cross sprang into action. With military discipline and organization, the Home Guard, created during the war to protect the shipyards and ore docks in Duluth, took charge of the refugees and the evacuation of parts of the city. Private cars and trucks were confiscated. Public and private buildings were taken over. With the help of the Red Cross, the guard arranged to bring in the needed food and clothing and together these organizations took charge of relief efforts. In the words of William E. Caulkin, president of the St. Louis County Historical Society and a witness to these events, "The war boys and women at home were foremost in everything," and the crisis was "handled by the home war organizations in a manner beyond praise."[91]

In the case of the 1918 fire, the spirit of martial idealism served a noble purpose. In other cases, however, it served ends of a morally questionable nature, as in the flagrantly illegal attack on IWW headquarters in Duluth by units of the Home Guard in August 1917. Another troubling case was the terrible lynching of three black circus workers in Duluth in June 1920.

On the night of June 14, Irene Tusken, age eighteen, met James Sullivan, a recent high school graduate, at the circus grounds in West Duluth, where Wheeler Field is now located. Having made the rounds of the various sideshows in the company of other young people, the couple lingered to watch as crews struck the tents and loaded animals and equipment for the trip north to Virginia, where the circus was next scheduled. Sullivan escorted Tusken home, where she greeted her parents and went to bed by 11:00 P.M. Having seen Tusken home, Sullivan went home, changed clothes, and reported to the DM&N ore docks, where he worked the midnight to 8:00 A.M. shift. Shortly after 1:00 A.M., Sullivan told his father, the night superintendent at the docks, that Tusken had been raped that evening by six Negroes who worked for the circus. This report set in motion a sequence of events that would lead to the brutal deaths of three black youths.

The next morning, as reports of the alleged rape spread throughout West Duluth, an angry mob began to form. A truck belonging to thirty-eight-year-old Louis Dondino, owner of an auto transfer business in West Duluth, began to cruise the West Duluth business district, spreading word of the supposed attack. A growing parade of angry men followed the truck. By late afternoon, when the parade reached the downtown area, rumors of a lynching had reached the police department. By nighttime the mob had grown to include thousands of Duluth's citizens. One report estimated the the crowd at ten thousand, one-tenth of the entire population of the city. The mob attacked the police station where the young black men were being held. Ordered by William Murnian, the elected Commissioner of Public Safety, not to use firearms, the police fought back with billy clubs and fire hoses. Despite the pleas of police, several clergymen, and two local judges, the mob broke into the police station, seized three black prisoners, dragged them to a light pole at Second Avenue East and First Street, and lynched them.[92] In all probability the murdered men were innocent of the alleged rape. At least one of them, Isaac McGhie, was being held as a potential witness and was not even a suspect in the case. Beyond this, there is considerable doubt as to whether there was any rape at all. The examining physician doubted that a rape had occurred, and there are a number of implausible factors about the supposed attack and the subsequent behavior of the young couple.[93] Despite the physician's doubts and the implausibility of the whole story, which were noted in the *Duluth Ripsaw* at the time, a local jury convicted two of the surviving accused black men of rape.

In his valuable account of the lynching and its aftermath, Michael Fedo suggests some factors that may have contributed to this tragedy. One was the supposed racial tensions arising from the hiring of black workers at U.S. Steel in Duluth. Fedo comments: "Ever since U.S. Steel, the city's largest employer, began importing black field hands from southern plantations to work at the mill, and thereby quelling strike threats by white workers, an uneasy tension existed—especially in the western sectors of the city, where the mill was located, and where most of the city's blacks resided."[94] In keeping with this idea, Fedo stresses the working-class composition of the mob and offers speculative hypotheses about the motives of key actors in the lynching. For example, Fedo suggests that Public Safety Commissioner Murnian, who gave the police the order not to use firearms to resist the mob, was motivated at least in part by his empathy with the working-class constituency that had elected him. Further, he suggests that Leonard Hedman, one of the leaders of the mob, might have been motivated by anger at blacks, whom he thought had taken jobs at the steel plant away from his friends.[95]

Fedo's book is the breakthrough treatment of the lynching. Still, no direct evidence is cited to support the idea that resentment against black workers at the steel plant fueled the lynching and Fedo presents this idea only as a possibility. In the course of the book Fedo does mention the experiences of Edward Nichols, a black man living in Duluth at the time of the lynching.[96] In a 1974 interview, Nichols discusses the lynching and the experience of black workers at the steel plant:

> I first come to the steel plant in 1916. There was quite a
> bit of unrest between the workers. And the white work-
> ers wanted more wages. The owner of the steel corpo-
> ration refused to pay them more wages, and they sent
> their employment agents down South and they brought
> hundreds and hundreds even thousands of Negroes up
> to the northern cities such as Gary, Indiana, where the

steel mills, and [*sic*] also to the steel plant in Duluth and all through the east. They brought these Negroes up and they used them as strike breakers. I did the same work as a white man in the steel plant. I got twenty-five cents an hour and the white man got thirty cents an hour. But you see, he still felt that he was superior to me because he was getting a nickel more an hour. The Negroes lived in a shanty town called Gary, where there was just tumbledown shacks. The white people lived in a model city made out of concrete blocks called Morgan Park.[97]

Nichols's recollections do lend support to the idea that resentment against black workers at the steel plant may have been a factor in motivating the mob. It is also true that most of the men indicted for their involvement in the lynch mob came from West Duluth, where some employees of the steel plant lived. However, there are several reasons for doubting the importance of such resentment in accounting for the lynching.

It is true that blacks were working in the steel plant. The *Twin City Star*, a black newspaper, ran an ad seeking black workers on behalf of U.S. Steel in Duluth in June 1916, the year that Nichols remembered beginning work there.[98] There is no evidence, however, that Nichols and other black workers were in Duluth as strikebreakers. The strike on the Iron Range did not erupt until later that summer and there is no record of any strike or any attempted strike at the steel plant in Duluth at that time during the year. While it is possible that strike talk was circulating among white workers and that black workers were brought in to head off the strike, there is no evidence of this in interviews with white workers who worked at the steel plant at the time.[99]

It is not clear how many blacks came to work at the steel plant in 1916 or in the years leading up to the lynching. With World War I under way and the United States engaged in a brisk trade with the warring countries, business was booming at the steel plant. There was no hint of strike talk by white workers in the plant at this time. Black workers were indeed used as strikebreakers during the great steel strike of 1919, but that was in other cities.[100] There was no attempt to strike at the plant in Duluth. Still, it is possible that white workers resented blacks at the steel plant, blamed blacks for breaking the 1919 national steel strike, and lashed out at the innocent black circus workers because of these feelings. Nichols suggests some such scenario when he mentions Gary, Indiana, and other cities in the East.

While all of this is possible, there remain other reasons for doubting the importance of such resentment as a motive for the lynching. Employment at U.S. Steel was hierarchically structured. At the top were managers of "American," English, and Scottish background. Beneath them was a layer of foremen and skilled workmen composed of "Americans": other native English speakers, Scandinavians, and other "old" immigrants. At the bottom, doing the hardest, dirtiest, and most dangerous manual labor, were the "new" immigrant workers. In Duluth these workers were mostly South Slavs, Italians, and African Americans, and this ethnic hierarchy was reflected in the difference between Morgan Park and Gary-New Duluth. Morgan Park was a model company town built by U.S. Steel to house employees at the local plant. The managerial elite lived in spacious houses on the edge of Morgan Park overlooking the St. Louis River. Middle-level employees—foremen, skilled workmen, and "old" immigrant workers—lived in less spacious housing located further away from the river. With few exceptions, these employees were either "Americans" or from Scandinavian or other "old" immigrant groups. They were also almost all Protestants; they worshipped together at the United Protestant Church in Morgan Park, built by U.S. Steel to serve the spiritual needs of its employees. South Slavs and Italians were not welcome in Morgan Park. Like the African American steel workers, they lived in Gary-New Duluth or West Duluth, neighborhoods near the steel plant but not built by U.S. Steel. They worshipped at St. Elizabeth's Catholic Church or at St. George's Serbian Greek Orthodox Church.

During World War I, black workers across the United States began to displace eastern Europeans in the worst jobs in the steel industry, with eastern Europeans beginning to move up to better jobs.[101] When black men came to work at the steel plant in Duluth, they came as part of this national influx. In Duluth, most of these black workers settled in the Gary-New Duluth area and worked in the least desirable jobs, many of them in the dirty and unhealthy coke ovens.[102] Given the expansive conditions prevailing in the steel industry during the war, it is not likely that these black workers took any jobs away from white workers, and if they did compete for jobs with white workers in Duluth, it would have been with the South Slavs and Italians. There is no evidence of any of these South Slavs being displaced by black workers, either during or after the war. If it were true that resentment against black workers at the steel plant inflamed the lynch mob in Duluth, one would expect to find evidence of bad feeling between the blacks and the South Slavs in Gary-New Duluth. In fact, blacks and South Slavs appear to have gotten along reasonably well. A number of blacks attended the reunion, years later, of the mainly South Slav families who had lived in the Gary-New Duluth area and none of the known interviews with people, black or white, who lived in the area at that time point to tensions between black and South Slav families. The tensions mentioned in the interview by Nichols refer to discrimination against blacks in Morgan Park or at the steel plant, not to problems in Gary-New Duluth.[103]

Near the end of his book, Fedo sketches an imagined scene at Christmas time in 1920 in a speakeasy in Oliver, Wisconsin, where many steelworkers went to drink during Prohibition. Fedo imagines a group of possibly "Italian, Serbian, and Slavic" men drinking their whiskeys, with a need to "exorcise the shreds of guilt" they felt on account of their participation in the lynch mob.[104] Such a scene is in keeping with the hypothesis that steelworkers' resentment fueled the lynch mob, as South Slav steelworkers were the men most likely to be in competition with blacks for jobs at the steel plant in Duluth. But Fedo makes clear this scene is only one possible scenario.

In fact, if one examines the identities of the approximately twenty men indicted for their roles as leading participants in the mob, not one of these men was a South Slav or Italian steelworker. Louis Dondino, the owner of the truck that led the parade and one of the two men sentenced to prison for his role in the mob, may have been Italian, but he did not work at the steel plant; he ran his own auto-transfer business. Leonard Hedman, whom Fedo identifies as having one of the most active roles in the mob, worked as a railroad brakeman while he saved money for law school. Fedo speculates that perhaps Hedman felt that blacks were taking jobs at the steel plant from his friends, but he offers no evidence to support this contention. Among the members of the mob who were arrested, only one is identified as working at the steel plant. Nate Natelson was a retail clerk in a family-owned business. Albert Johnson was an accountant for the Duluth Street Railway Company. Gilbert Henry Stephenson, the only member of the mob other than Dondino to go to prison, was a truck driver. William Rozen, possibly a South Slav, was a fry cook. Carl Miller was a boilermaker's helper. Bill Hughes was a teamster and Pat Olson was a meter inspector.[105] Of twenty-three men indicted for their participation in the lynch mob, only one, George Morgan, can be identified as an employee of the steel plant, and he was an engineer, a skilled workman, hardly threatened by competition from black laborers.[106] While it is likely that other men who worked at the steel plant were among the thousands that made up the lynch mob, there does not seem to be evidence to support the claim that resentment on the part of workers in the steel plant was a significant motive for the lynching. It should also be noted that coverage of the lynching by the Duluth press at the time makes no mention of such resentment as being a significant factor.

If we leave behind the hypothesis that the lynching was the work of resentful steelworkers and look at the identities of the men known to have participated in the mob, two facts confront us. First, the men present a fairly broad cross-section of occupational categories in the working class and the lower middle class. Second, the men are mostly white, Anglo-Saxon, and probably Protestant. With one, and possibly two exceptions, all have Anglo and "old" immigrant names. What could have motivated these men to be a part of a murderous mob?

Fedo suggests that many of these men were veterans of the war and that part of what motivated them was a desire to relive the martial idealism of the war:

> What the anxious, bored veterans desired was a return to battle and another crack at heroism and its heady sensations—the hugs and kisses from girls, the tear-stained faces of old men and women gratefully waving small American flags.... For some veterans flushed with battlefield successes, working as teamsters, boilermakers, meter inspectors, railroad brakeman, or short order cooks was rife with ennui.... Among these men were those itching for a cause.[107]

Here Fedo seems to be on firmer ground. Newspaper accounts of the time commented on the role of veterans in the mob. *Labor World* described the mob as "composed largely of disciplined ex-service men."[108] While there is reason to think that *Labor World* may have exaggerated the role and discipline of the veterans in an effort to defend the actions of Public Safety Commissioner Murnian, it does seem likely that veterans were significantly present in the mob and that the spirit of martial idealism animated at least a number of the key participants. Hedman, identified as one of the key leaders of the mob, and Rozen, charged with murder, were both veterans.[109] When arrests for involvement in the mob were first made, the nine men arrested practiced military drills in the local jail.[110] Of course, this is not to say that all of the men in the mob were veterans or that all of Duluth's veterans were in the mob. In fact, reacting to press reports about the involvement of veterans in the mob, the American Legion in Duluth offered two thousand men to assist police in restoring order to the city.[111] But a misplaced sense of martial idealism put to the defense of American womanhood may explain the behavior of some of the men in the mob.

Another factor, mentioned by William McEwen, editor of *Labor World*, concerned the climate of violence that prevailed in Minnesota during the war. McEwen pointed to violent attacks on supporters of gubernatorial candidate Lindberg, the suppression of rights of speech and assembly, tar-and-feather assaults on persons suspected of disloyalty, the attack on IWW headquarters in Duluth, and the lynching of Olli Kiukkonen as examples of wartime violence tolerated by the authorities. McEwen concluded that the lynching was in part an outcome of this general loosening of the rule of law.[112] The lynching in Duluth was not an isolated incident. Across America there was indeed a spate of lynchings in the post–World War I period. While the fundamental cause of this violence was the racism against African Americans deeply rooted in American history, with such fuel present, misplaced martial idealism and a general loosening of respect for law may have provided sufficient causes to ignite the blaze of violence.

No doubt the underlying cause of the lynchings was racism. In the racial hierarchy of the times, blacks were at the bottom. They were seen as alien beings present in America, but not of America. Their status left them vulnerable to injustices both violent and nonviolent. But it is important to understand that the racism of the times was not the simple racism of black and white, colored and noncolored. The racism of the times was a fine-grained racism, according to which each ethnic group had a place in a supposed hierarchy of the races. To a greater or lesser extent, blacks, Jews, South Slavs, Italians, Indians, Poles, Irish, and even Finns all suffered from the prejudices and discriminatory practices of the times, prejudices that were given "scientific" legitimation in the leading universities and were reflected in federal immigration law in 1924. In Duluth, as in much of the rest of the United States, men and women from these "lesser races" made up the bulk of the industrial working class. The struggle for justice waged by these people was a matter of both class and ethnicity. It was also a matter of religion, as the role of the Ku Klux Klan in Duluth made clear. In organizing the Italian-American Club and the Jugoslav Federation, Italians and South Slavs in Duluth organized to defend both their ethnic and their class interests. Similar concerns for both economic and racial justice flowed through the local chapter of the NAACP, which was formed in Duluth some ten years earlier in the wake of the lynchings.[113]

In the climate of the 1920s, the difficulties facing these outcast groups were large. They labored outside the protection of the existing AFL unions, many of which explicitly discriminated against them. And just as in the 1890s, the Scandinavian-dominated movement for reform and social justice—first the Knights of Labor and then the Farmer-Labor Party—remained strongly colored with pro-temperance and anti-Catholic sentiments that served to divide the working class.

the farmer-labor party

THE WARTIME ECONOMY OF 1917–19 RAISED WAGES FOR MOST American workers. With thousands of men in the armed forces, the supply of labor was reduced and with American industries working overtime to meet the needs of the military, the demand for labor was increased. In addition to these normal market forces, government policies contributed to a rise in wages. In an effort to stabilize production and avoid strikes, the Wilson administration intervened in labor-management relations. The National War Labor Board, under the leadership of former President William Howard Taft and labor lawyer Frank P. Walsh, adjudicated over twelve hundred labor disputes during the war. In addition, the War Labor Policies Board, under law professor Felix Frankfurter, began to establish standardized wages and hours in American industries. In general, these government agencies served the interests of American workers, enforcing an eight-hour day, decent working conditions, and living wages. During the war and immediately after, membership in the American Federation of Labor grew by more than fifty percent, reaching 3.2 million by 1920.[1]

Conditions in Duluth reflected these national trends. War production needed vast amounts of steel and much of the ore for this steel passed through the docks of Duluth and Superior. At the same time, vast amounts of coal required to fuel the ore trains and the iron-mining industry came into the Twin Ports. Production of navy ships at the booming shipyards in Duluth further stimulated the local economy, as did government orders for wartime supplies from the knitting mills in Duluth. Wages went up, reaching the rate of $2.50 to $3.00 per day, a rate that William E. Culkin, a contemporary who wrote about these times, considered "very high." Culkin observed that "[m]en grew particular about their jobs."[2]

The same conditions that allowed men in Duluth to be particular about their jobs provided bargaining leverage to Duluth's unions. For example, the United States declared war on Germany on April 6, 1917. Almost immediately, Duluth Local 165 of the Boil-ermakers, Shipbuilders and Helpers Union, an AFL union that included many Scandinavian workers and a strong contingent of Scandinavian Socialists, went out on strike. The strike involved 250 men at seven shops in Duluth and Superior.[3] One week later, in a meeting at the Commercial Club, the union rejected an offer of the employers.[4] The next week, bypassing a list of names pro-posed by the mayor, the Commercial Club itself drew up a list of members for a new Committee of National Defense to be formed in Duluth.[5] This committee would have some authority over labor disputes during the course of the war. The Commercial Club was determined to hold the line on wages, but the Boilermakers, with support from the Duluth Socialists and some elements within the AFL, stood firm.[6] In late June the strike was settled with the Boiler-makers winning ground.[7]

While the union won in this case, such wartime strikes made the labor movement a target for charges of disloyalty. Open oppo-sition to the war from the Socialist Party, some of whose mem-bers were active within the AFL, increased the vulnerability of the AFL itself to such charges. At a July convention of the Minnesota Federation of Labor, conflict erupted between Socialists and their opponents within the AFL. The Socialists introduced resolutions opposing the war and conscription, calling for a repeal of the law establishing the Minnesota Public Safety Commission and protest-ing the use of nonunion labor at Fort Snelling. William McEwen, editor of the *Labor World*, staunchly opposed these resolutions, calling them "un-American." McEwen approvingly reported both the defeat of the resolutions, 220 to 80, and the subsequent walk-out of the Socialists.[8] As the war years unfolded, McEwen worked hard to distinguish in the eyes of the public the "loyal" AFL unions from the supposed disloyal and un-American radicals in the IWW and the Socialist Party. In August, the *Labor World* denounced IWW literature distributed to miners on the Iron Range as "overtly treasonous," and declared that the Finns who provided the back-bone for the radical labor movement were "political and indus-trial outlaws who should be treated as such until they learn that labor's first duty is to support this country at all costs and at all times."[9] Incensed by McEwen and the conservative leadership of the local AFL, the Machinist and Boilermakers locals, both heavily influenced by the Socialists, withdrew from the Federated Trades Assembly in Duluth.[10]

Despite the alignment of the influential McEwen with the conservative leadership of the Minnesota Federation of Labor, disruptive elements continued to assert themselves within the labor movement in Duluth throughout the war years. In September 1917 unorganized laborers on the Great Northern ore dock in Superior successfully struck to win a pay raise. In November 1917 the AFL Freight Handlers Local 64, an affiliate of the International Longshoremen's Association (ILA), which included a number of Finnish IWW members, staged a three-week strike. The ILA International did not support the strike and it was ended only after George Lawson, secretary of the Minnesota Federation of Labor, went behind the back of the local and signed an agreement with members of the Public Safety Commission and the Great Lakes Transit Company, an agreement that acquiesced in the arrest and internment of Local 64 activist Frank Wasserthal for the duration of the war.[11]

Other strikes in the Twin Ports also threatened necessary wartime production. The steel trust paid less than union boats, maintained a blacklist against union seamen, and refused to comply with wartime federal recommendations regarding labor conditions. Seeing an opportunity to strike back at the lake fleet of the steel trust, Great Lakes seamen based in Superior called for a strike in July.[12] This threatened strike appears to have been averted, but a later strike at the Allouez ore docks in Superior was not. In August 1918, Finnish workers on the docks, at least some of them members of the IWW, struck for higher wages, an eight-hour day, and overtime pay for extra work. The strike completely shut down the movement of ore at the Great Northern ore dock, posing a potentially serious threat to military production. The authorities were quick to react, arresting one hundred and forty of the strikers in their homes during the night. The *Labor World* called the strike foolish, claiming that the men could have won their demands from government arbitrators without resorting to the strike.[13] Fearing that the disruptive strike fever might spread to the equally sensitive coal docks, Judge McGee of the Public Safety Commission issued a proclamation forbidding any strike there.[14]

With the end of the war, the government regulation of labor and management relations also ended. The stage was set for a battle between the unions, determined to maintain or build on gains won during the war, and management, determined to check or reduce rising labor costs. In Duluth, as elsewhere in the country, this battle was intense. The first strike of the postwar period occurred among

Punching ore on the ore docks to get the ore to flow into the pockets below was difficult and dangerous work. Photograph by Hugh McKenzie; courtesy Northeast Minnesota Historical Center.

the iron molders at Clyde Iron Works in March 1919. The strikers demanded a minimum wage of eighty cents per hour, an eight-hour day, and the exclusion of women core makers, who had presumably been hired and trained during the war. Clyde Iron refused to give in and hired strikebreakers. The strike dragged on well into the summer. Other strikes followed. In May, five hundred members of the Building Trades in Superior went out. In Duluth, members of the Cabinetmakers and Millmen's Local 1284 went on strike against the Duluth Showcase Company after the company fired a union organizer, a veteran who had lost an eye in the war. In both the Clyde Iron strike and the Duluth Showcase strike, support was provided to the employers by the anti-union leadership of the large and influential Marshall-Wells Company.[15]

August 1919 brought a series of wildcat strikes that threatened to shut down several major Twin Ports industries. Five thousand workers walked off their jobs in the railroad repair shops in Duluth, Superior, Proctor, and Two Harbors. This was followed by strikes by over 2,000 men on the coal docks, 450 men from the

Allouez ore docks, waitresses at the Spalding Hotel, and in September, freight handlers on the Duluth docks.[16] Confronted by this wave of strikes by unorganized and mainly "foreign" workers, the *Labor World* expressed sympathy for the strikers, who had seen their earnings undermined by postwar inflation and empty promises, but also cautioned workers against too-frequent recourse to strike action.[17]

The strikes that led some 7,000 workers to walk out in the Twin Ports in the month of August 1919 were part of a nationwide wave of strikes that swept the country as labor and management fought to position themselves in the postwar era. The year 1919 saw over four million workers, or 22 percent of the nation's workforce, out on strikes.[18] On the national scene, the struggle between labor and management over the terms of their postwar relationship came to a dramatic showdown in the great steel strike of 1919, the largest strike in the nation's history. Under pressure from outside forces to do something to alleviate the terrible conditions prevailing in the steel industry, the American Federation of Labor acquiesced in a proposed drive to organize the industry. The drive was led by William Z. Foster, who had led an imaginative and partially successful campaign to organize the ethnically diverse packinghouse industry in Chicago. Foster was even then perceived as a radical, and he would go on to become a leader of the American Communist Party.[19]

The steel industry in the United States was an open-shop bastion. It employed a large number of immigrant workers from a variety of ethnic backgrounds. With speakers of different languages working side by side in dangerous conditions, it is not surprising that accident rates were high. At the South Works, operated by U.S. Steel in Chicago, one-quarter of the non–English speaking immigrants employed there were injured each year.[20] Twelve-hour shifts and low wages were common. A 1910 study done by Pittsburgh Associated Charities found that a steelworker who worked twelve hours per day, 365 days per year, could still not earn enough to provide the barest necessities for a family of five.[21] By 1909, U.S. Steel had succeeded in getting rid of the unions in shops it had inherited in the process of its formation and the company publicly announced its commitment to an "open shop."[22] The company used an extensive network of spies to identify union sympathizers, and it used its economic clout to gain the support of the local business communities, churches, and governments in the towns where its plants were located. Contributions to churches were common and, not surprisingly, a federal investigation found "some warrant" to the belief among union sympathizers that many churches supported the company. At one point, the YMCA, which in many areas supported progressive causes, refused to support a campaign to do away with twelve-hour shifts in the steel industry on the grounds that to do so would alienate important financial backers.[23]

The confrontation between labor and management in the steel industry in the fall of 1919 took on almost mythic proportions. Immigrant workers were so eager to strike that some of them went out before organizers were ready. Essentially the strike pitted the steel trust, an oligopoly including one of the largest corporations in the world, against a mostly immigrant workforce. The strike was big, long, harsh, and bloody. Even before the strike began, seven organizers were murdered within a few days.[24] Propaganda produced by the steel companies during the strike characterized the immigrant steel workers as undesirable foreigners.[25] It depicted strike activists and organizers as Bolsheviks or reds. Fannie Sellins

Work in U.S. Steel's wire mill in Duluth, 1923. Courtesy Northeast Minnesota Historical Center.

was one of the union organizers murdered during the strike. Four years after her death, a jury hearing the case acquitted her accused killer on the grounds that the death was justifiable due to Sellins's "bolshevik activities."[26] The steel corporations portrayed the strike as an attempt by radicals to control the industry. They succeeded in persuading government agencies to intervene against the strikers and federal troops and state militias were used to break up picket lines. Violent confrontations were common.

In Duluth work continued as usual at the steel plant run by Minnesota Steel and at the Atlas Cement Plant, both subsidiaries of U.S. Steel. Mainstream newspapers in Duluth took this as a sign of workers' satisfaction with local conditions.[27] In fact, labor peace in Duluth and on the Iron Range appears to have been due to a deliberate decision by strike leaders not to strike in the Duluth and Birmingham, Alabama, districts in order to focus their resources.[28] In its coverage of the national strike, *Labor World* provides a glimpse of local conditions, which were no better than elsewhere: "In the Duluth plant they [employees] work 11 hours during the day and 13 hours during the night, with one day off in every seven." The same article commented on the "open shop" policy of Minnesota Steel: "When it is known that a workman is identified with a union, be it far remote from the steel industry, he is summarily discharged. Particularly is this true with relation to the Duluth plant." The article went on to hope that the national strike would at least put an end to the system of company police, labor spying, and hired gunmen that prevailed in the steel industry.[29]

With the great confrontation in steel as a backdrop and the spate of local wildcat strikes in the spring and summer, local businessmen formed a Duluth chapter of the Citizens' Alliance in October 1919. The Citizens' Alliance was committed to the principle of the "open shop." In theory, the idea of the open shop was that a place of work was open to any individual who contracted to work there. Individual employees did not have to belong to a union, if it existed, in contrast to a "closed shop," which required all employees to belong to the union. In practice, "open shop" employers often took steps to rid their shops of any employees who were members of or sympathetic to trade unions. In the fall of 1919 when the Duluth chapter was formed, the Citizens' Alliance was an emerging national movement, with a strong base of support in Minneapolis, where the movement was led by the energetic O. P. Briggs.[30] The Duluth Citizens' Alliance included between four and five hundred "of the foremost business and professional men of the city."[31] They were, according to the *Labor World*, the same men who had conducted the 1907 open-shop campaign in Duluth.[32]

The alliance included representatives from Duluth's leading manufacturers, such as Oliver Iron Mining Company, Marshall-Wells, Clyde Iron, Diamond Calk, and Scott Graff Lumber, as well as representatives from each of the city's four leading banks: First National, American Exchange National, Northern National, and City National. The support of the banks was crucial for two reasons: because their control over commercial credit could be used to discipline businesses that wavered in their support of Alliance aims, and because their financial resources could support the Duluth Guaranty Fund, which aided employers engaged in labor disputes. With the aid of O. P. Briggs, the Duluth Citizens' Alliance also established a Builders' Employer Council to supply skilled nonunion workman for the contractors of Duluth. Edward Whalen became the labor agent for the Citizens' Alliance and was responsible for supplying nonunion workmen, many of whom were shipped in from out of state. The alliance worked closely with the Builders Exchange, an alliance of Duluth contractors. It also hired the Russell Detective Agency to provide information about the membership and activities of the local labor movement.[33]

Like the Citizens' Alliance in Minneapolis, the Duluth Citizens' Alliance published a monthly bulletin expounding the open-shop philosophy and presenting news about the open-shop movement in the city, state, and nation. During strikes and at other critical moments, the alliance issued "Special Bulletins" to its members, coordinating the fight against the unions. When strikes were finally won by the employers, the alliance would establish a blacklist to inform employers about union members and labor activists. Throughout the 1920s the Citizens' Alliance proved its clout, winning confrontations with the Meat Cutters, the Painters, the Bricklayers, and the unorganized coal-dock workers, and imposing wage cuts on the building trades.[34] The alliance was also successful in pressuring the school board and the city council to cancel union contracts and defeat a proposed minimum wage for work contracted by the city.[35]

The most important confrontation between labor and management in this period, and one in which management, backed by the Citizens' Alliance, again prevailed, was the strike by railroad shopmen in 1922. In 1921, in response to requests from American railroad companies, the Railway Labor Board had approved large wage cuts for most railroad workers and given companies permission to contract out work to nonunion employers. Especially hard hit by this decision were workers in the shops where cleaning, painting, maintenance, and repair work was done. Many of these workers belonged to unions; in fact, some sixteen different unions had members working in the railroad shops. In July 1922, 400,000 of these railway workers went out on strike, the first nationwide rail strike since 1894.[36] In Duluth, one thousand railroad shopmen

Interior of the Duluth, Missabe and Northern Railway shop in Proctor, circa 1915. Photograph by W. W. Kemp; courtesy Minnesota Historical Society.

MEN WANTED!

— on —

GREAT NORTHERN RAILWAY

A number of the Great Northern Railway Company's regular employes having left its service, it is necessary to hire men to fill their places.

Employment is offered to:

Machinists   **Boilermakers**
Blacksmiths   **Sheet Metal Workers**
Electrical Workers   **Car Repairmen**
Carpenters

at wages and working conditions prescribed by the United States Railway Labor Board, effective July 1, 1922.

Rates for journeymen and leading men range from 63 to 82 cents per hour, and for helpers 47 cents per hour, with time and one-half after eight hours and for Sundays and holidays. Applicants who are not Mechanics will be given employment and will be trained in all branches of the trades.

Seniority and pension rights of new employes will date from the time of entering service. Former employes may return to work, if their places have not already been filled, and so many of the former employes as return to work promptly will be allowed a record of continuous service for seniority and pension rights.

Concerning the matter of entering the employ of the Railway Company to take the place of men now on strike Chairman Hooper of the United States Railroad Labor Board has publicly announced:

"In the past, a man who took up the work of another who was on strike against wages and working conditions, was termed a 'scab' or 'strikebreaker'— terms to which much opprobrium was attached. In the present situation created by the strike of railroad shopcraft workers, men who assume the work of the strikers cannot be justly reproached with such epithets. This is not a customary strike in which the employer tries to impose upon the employe unjust wages and unreasonable working rules. In this case the conflict is not between the employer and the oppressed employes. The people of this country, through an Act of Congress, signed by President Wilson, established a tribunal to decide such disputes over wages and working conditions which were submitted to it in a proper manner. It is the decision by this tribunal against which the shopcrafts are striking. REGARDLESS OF ANY QUESTION OF THE RIGHT OF THE MEN TO STRIKE, THE MEN WHO TAKE THE STRIKERS' PLACES ARE MERELY ACCEPTING THE WAGES AND WORKING CONDITIONS PRESCRIBED BY A GOVERNMENT TRIBUNAL AND ARE PERFORMING A PUBLIC SERVICE. THEY ARE NOT ACCEPTING THE WAGES AND WORKING CONDITIONS WHICH AN EMPLOYER IS TRYING TO IMPOSE. FOR THIS REASON, PUBLIC SENTIMENT AND FULL GOVERNMENTAL POWER WILL PROTECT THE MEN WHO REMAIN IN THEIR POSITIONS AND NEW MEN WHO MAY COME IN."

APPLY AT NEAREST SHOP, or at DIVISION SUPERINTENDENT'S OFFICES

Advertisement for strikebreakers to work for the Great Northern Railway from the Duluth News-Tribune, *July 9, 1922.*

walked out, including a number of women who worked cleaning railroad cars.[37] With the full support of the Citizens' Alliance, the railroad companies responded to the strike in the Duluth area by hiring strikebreakers and guards to protect them. Further, the company secured injunctions from the courts to prevent picketing by the strikers.

The injunction against picketing greatly weakened the ability of the strikers to enforce the strike. Nevertheless, they held out, filling the Shrine Auditorium to hear speeches by R. A. Henning from Minneapolis, Congressman William Carss, and *Labor World* editor William McEwen.[38] Later that week, five hundred Proctor shopmen and their families gathered to hear speeches by Carss, McEwen, and John P. Jensen, Duluth chairman of the striking shopmen.[39] But in the face of functioning repair shops and Judge Page Morris's injunction against picketing, such speeches could accomplish nothing. The striking shopmen held out, but by September it was clear that the railroads had won a crushing victory. The strikers lost their jobs and were blacklisted.[40] The defeat in Duluth mirrored the defeat of the shopmen nationwide. In one last insult hurled a year after the strike, a federal judge enjoined the blacklisted shopmen from ever even talking to the strikebreakers who had replaced them.[41]

With the loss of support from the federal government, the loss of bargaining strength caused by large-scale unemployment, and a determined and well-organized open-shop campaign waged by employers, the American labor movement suffered a major defeat in the period between 1921 and 1923. In addition to the failed shopmen's strike, the labor movement suffered significant defeats in the packinghouse and coal-mining industries as well. In 1920 membership in the American Federation of Labor had reached its peak. By its national convention in 1923, the AFL had lost 25 percent of its membership. The Machinists Union, to which many of the striking shopmen had belonged, lost 70 percent of its members between 1920 and 1923.[42]

In Duluth, as elsewhere, the open-shop philosophy of the Citizens' Alliance prevailed. Weakened by the battles of 1921 and 1922, the labor movement in Duluth was largely impotent for the remainder of the 1920s. In the construction trades, the open shop prevailed, with wage cuts and the restoration of the ten-hour day. The Citizens' Alliance proudly claimed credit for this turnaround.[43] It also pointed to a booming construction industry in Duluth as evi-

View of Duluth in 1924. Photograph by Hugh McKenzie; courtesy Northeast Minnesota Historical Center.

dence of the wisdom of the open shop, which the organized employers had managed to enforce in Duluth in contrast to Superior, where the union shop still reigned in the construction trades.[44]

That the open shop was the "American Plan" or the "American Way" was a fundamental tenet of the Citizens' Alliance. Supporters of the Citizens' Alliance believed that businessmen had a patriotic and moral duty to support the open shop, in addition to their duty of self-interest. A publication of the Duluth Citizens' Alliance from January 1929 listed companies committed to the open shop and concluded with this admonition: "If you believe in the American Plan insist that your work be done by open shop contractors. Ask your Architect to provide in specifications that 'ALL WORK MUST BE DONE OPEN SHOP.'"[45]

The business leaders who embraced the open-shop philosophy of the American Plan did so because they thought it was good for business and good for the American people. Many of the men who made up this elite, men like Chester Congdon and Guilford Hartley, two of Duluth's most weighty business leaders, were self-made men who by their own initiative and energy had risen from a threadbare existence to great wealth.[46] Their own life experience had convinced them of the greatness of American industry, the validity of the business ethic of individual initiative, and their own fitness to play a leading role in the affairs of the world. The mining men and railroad men of Duluth were truly captains of industry. The industrial technology of the region was cutting edge, developed on a scale that surpassed mining operations in any other part of the globe. From their offices in Duluth, men like Chester Congdon, Guilford Hartley, Thomas Cole, and John C. Greenway directed

Duluth contractors state their support for the Open Shop "American Plan" in 1929. Courtesy Minnesota Historical Society.

vast mining operations in the Lake Superior region, Arizona, Mexico, and Brazil.[47] For men like this and the sons and associates who took over for them in the 1920s, American industry, American business, and the "American plan" of economic organization had proven their merit.

Many business leaders of the 1920s also believed in the "welfare capitalism" pioneered by Elbert Gary, the founding chairman of the board of U.S. Steel. According to this philosophy, the captains of industry had paternalistic responsibilities toward their employees and toward society as a whole. Gary thought that business leaders had an obligation to work together, to avoid the dangers of ruinous competition, and to replace the anarchy of the market with intelligent planning. In Gary's public pronouncements, this vision of paternalistic capitalism had been supported by appeals to the Christian duties incumbent upon men of wealth. In *The Man Nobody Knows*, a 1925 bestseller, advertising executive Bruce Barton reinforced this vision, depicting Jesus as a businessman adept at advertising his message to a mass audience and managing a corporate organization.[48] For their part, many American business leaders proclaimed their willingness to follow Jesus. A spokesman for the United States Chamber of Commerce rejected "the old dog-eat-dog theory of business competition" in favor of the intelligent and cooperative management of industry by the leaders of the great corporations, locating the foundational principles for this new phi-

Women's Bowling League sponsored by the DM&N Railway in 1927–28. Supporting activities for families of employees was part of the paternalistic philosophy of U.S. Steel. Photograph by Hugh McKenzie; courtesy Northeast Minnesota Historical Center.

losophy of American industry in "the fundamentals of decent and right conduct laid down by Jesus of Nazareth."[49]

Duluth businessman Julius Barnes held similar views. Barnes, the owner of the Klearflax Linen Company and the Barnes-Duluth Shipyards in Duluth, had risen to the position of president of the U.S. Chamber of Commerce. In 1924, he explained the American plan in his book, *The Genius of American Business*.[50] Forcefully underlining the accomplishments of American industry, Barnes argued that to a great extent, the success of America was founded on the American philosophy of "fair play," which set the ground rules for American industry and commerce. Barnes understood this philosophy to be that of a free enterprise system founded on individual rights and the open shop. While unions had no place in this scheme of things, Barnes and the business elite who agreed with him were convinced that unions and foolish strikes by deluded laborers could accomplish nothing. In their view, it was the open-shop system and the benevolent management of American business leaders that would help working people and their families to prosper.[51]

The pro-business philosophy of Duluth's elite did not go unchallenged. Business leaders had been directly confronted by the wave of strikes in Duluth that followed the end of World War I. With the help of the Citizens' Alliance, this uprising had been met and decisively defeated by the end of the shopmen's strike in 1922. But another challenge, a political one posed by the Farmer-Labor Party, continued to threaten the leadership claims of Duluth's business elite throughout the 1920s.

The Farmer-Labor movement in Duluth had its origins in the political campaigns waged by the Non-Partisan League (NPL) in Minnesota in 1918. The Non-Partisan League had its roots in North Dakota, where immigrant farmers had organized to elect public officials who would side with small farmers against the railroads and grain companies, which they believed were taking advantage of them. By 1918, the NPL had expanded into Minnesota, still largely supported by farmers. During the political campaign that year, the NPL backed Charles Lindbergh for governor. Lindbergh had written a book blaming "the money trust" for pushing the United States into the First World War. Despite this assertion, Lindbergh held that every American had a duty to support the war effort. Nonetheless, Lindbergh and his supporters were attacked throughout his campaign as traitors to America. Lindbergh was scheduled to speak at the Shrine Auditorium in Duluth in May 1918 when, at the last minute, permission to use the auditorium was withdrawn. Arrangements were quickly made for Lindbergh to speak at Woodman Hall, located in the middle of the heavily Scandinavian and heavily Socialist West End. Under pressure from the chief of police, the trustees of Woodman Hall also backed out of the agreement, making it impossible for Lindbergh, a popular candidate for a major public office, to speak in Duluth.[52] Though Lindbergh was defeated, the activity of the NPL in Minnesota in 1918 led to the unexpected formation of a new political movement in Duluth.

As early as February 1918, some of the Socialists in Duluth were interested in cooperating with the NPL. While the Socialists had their base in Duluth's urban working class, they shared the NPL view that America had become a plutocracy governed by the wealthy capitalists and they sympathized with the NPL's defense of the common people. They also admired the success of the NPL in North Dakota. The question of whether to cooperate with the NPL split the Socialist Party in Duluth. Jack Carney, the Irishman brought in to edit the party newspaper, *Truth*, rejected all cooperation with the NPL, arguing that it was not a working-class party and that it had compromised itself by giving qualified support to the war.[53] Other Duluth Socialists, in particular Juls Anderson, E. P. Towne, and Joel Lichten, were more interested in building electoral alliances.

In March 1918, *Labor World* reported that Anderson had attended an NPL campaign rally in St. Paul. Anderson, who left the Socialist Party, was a member of the Typographers' Union, which was affiliated with the American Federation of Labor and the Duluth Federated Trades Assembly, the local central body of the AFL.[54] One week later, *Labor World* reported that the Federated Trades Assembly had decided, for the first time in its history, to endorse candidates for the state legislature and for the U.S. Congress. Juls Anderson and Joel Lichten, a Duluth Socialist who belonged to Painters and Decorators Local 106, were each named to the committee charged with organizing the endorsement process.[55] On May 18 the AFL in Duluth announced its support for four candidates for the Minnesota legislature on a Union Labor Party ticket: John Bennett, a plumber; Henry Dworschak, Jr., a member of the Typographers' Union and son of a founder of the Socialist Labor Party in Duluth; Juls Anderson, the former Socialist and also a typographer; and Emil Erickson, a locomotive fireman and engineer.[56] At

The Message of
Union Labor

W. L. CARSS

CONTAINING
UNION LABOR PARTY'S PLATFORM AND
13 REASONS WHY YOU SHOULD VOTE FOR

CARSS For CONGRESS

*Poster for William Leighton Carss from 1918 Union Labor Party campaign. Courtesy
Northeast Minnesota Historical Center.*

this point, the newly formed party still lacked a candidate for U.S.
Congress. The Union Laborites met again at Woodman Hall in the
West End in June under the leadership of the Duluth Socialist William E. Towne.[57] It was not until August 3, however, that the Union
Labor Party announced its nomination of William Leighton Carss
for Congress.[58] Carss was a locomotive engineer from Proctor.

The Union Labor Party of Duluth was the creation of activists
from the AFL and the Socialist Party, but neither the AFL nor the
Socialists gave unified support to the fledgling political party. The

local Socialist Party had come under the control of radicals sympathetic to the IWW and was disdainful of electoral politics. The AFL, on the other side, had long been governed by the philosophy of a "pure and simple" trade unionism that rejected the idea of a "labor" political party. Coverage of the Duluth Union Labor Party campaign was relegated to the back pages of the AFL newspaper, *Labor World*, and it was persistently attacked by the Socialist newspaper, *Truth*. Nevertheless, despite its divided base and late start, the Union Labor Party campaign gained strength. In July, the Minnesota Federation of Labor, angered at the anti-union policies of the Minnesota Commission of Public Safety, pushed for the AFL unions of Minnesota to enter state politics and called for a special convention in August to name a slate of labor candidates. Meeting simultaneously with a reconvened convention of the NPL, the two groups agreed on a list of candidates for some state offices. Reflecting the farm constituency of the NLP and the labor constituency of the AFL, the candidates appeared on the ballot under a "Farmer-Labor" party designation.[59]

Despite this clear break with pure and simple unionism by the Minnesota Federation of Labor, the Duluth AFL and *Labor World* were slow to join the move to electoral politics. Duluth delegates left the special August convention before action was taken.[60] As late as October 8, John Thompson of the NPL wrote to Carss mentioning forthcoming help from the NPL and complaining about the lack of support from the AFL in Carss's district.[61] In the race for governor, the *Labor World* endorsed Fred Wheaton, the Democrat, rather than Lindbergh, the NPL candidate, and it did not officially endorse Carss for Congress until October 26, when little more than a week remained in the campaign. Nor was the Duluth Union Labor Party campaign itself completely in line with the politics of the newly formed "Farmer-Labor" alliance between the AFL and the NPL at the state level. The Carss campaign had two central themes: it attacked the incumbent congressman, Clarence B. Miller, as an antilabor tool of U.S. Steel, and, echoing the persistent attacks on the NPL candidate Lindbergh, it attacked Miller as being of doubtful loyalty and being insufficiently supportive of the war.[62] Nonetheless, despite the apparent isolation of the Duluth Union Labor Party from both local and state politics, the campaign picked up strong support in Duluth and Saint Louis County, accomplishing a stunning upset victory when Carss was elected to Congress in November.

William Leighton Carss was a remarkable candidate. Born in Iowa in 1865, he had some training as a civil engineer and had worked as a locomotive fireman at one time. In 1893 he moved to Proctor, where he worked as a locomotive engineer until his election in 1918. He was a member of the Brotherhood of Locomotive Engineers and the Episcopal Church. He was a thirty-second-degree Mason and a noble of the Mystic Shrine. He had a daughter who graduated from Carleton College and went on to teach high school English in Spokane, Washington. Carss himself, of English background, was well grounded in English literature. He could recite selections from Shakespeare, Carlyle, and Burns by memory. In Congress, Carss supported legislation favorable to organized labor. He championed a system of old-age pensions, like the Social Security system, which would not be won until the New Deal years. He supported women's rights. He also supported the Prohibition amendment to the United States Constitution over the objections of some of his trade-union supporters.[63]

Letters from the district to Congressman Carss in Washington reveal something about Carss's political base and the attitudes of the times. A letter to Mrs. Carss from Helen Rawlings, Carss's Washington secretary, shows the pervasiveness of racism: "Say, our little Duluth girl, of the dark brown mahogany shade, never did call back. I still have her letter waiting here, but Miss Byrd 'aint never showed up.'"[64] Men soliciting Carss's help were not above appealing to their ties to Carss as fellow Masons.[65] The divide between Protestants and Catholics also figures prominently in papers dealing with political appointments and problems at the post office, with Carss's supporters complaining about discrimination against Protestants.[66] A letter from J. H. Bacon of Gheen, Minnesota, complains about Catholic discrimination against Masons and Klansmen.[67] While there is no evidence that Carss himself was either pro-Klan or anti-Catholic, these letters from supporters, like the letter from Carss's secretary, say something about the cultural milieu of Carss's base of support.

The surprising success of the Carss campaign and the approval of political action by the Minnesota Federation of Labor generated new interest in the Duluth Union Labor Party. While the radical leadership of the Duluth Socialists continued to oppose cooperation with the AFL in the Union Labor Party, Socialists like Joel Lichten and John A. Johnson at least temporarily left the Socialist Party to join the new coalition.[68] At the same time, more of the leaders of the AFL unions took an interest, among them William F. Murnian of the Electrical Workers and James A. Farrell of the Plumbers. Murnian and Farrell both came from the more conservative wing of the AFL.[69] Both were also Catholics. The involvement of such men in the Duluth Union Labor Party broadened the party's base, but also weakened the unity of that base.

The 1919 political season started with John Johnson, William Murnian, and James Farrell all filing to run in the primary election for seats as city commissioners. Johnson, the former Socialist, was thirty-nine years old, married, and a homeowner. He had worked as a farmer, a harvest hand, a lumberjack, a sawmill man, a fisherman, and a grocery clerk before turning to his present work as a salesman.[70] Murnian, fifty-four, also married and a homeowner, had come to Duluth from Prince Edward Island in 1897. He had worked as a lumberjack before becoming an electrician and a leader of the electrical workers' union. Farrell, also married and a homeowner, had worked as a timber cruiser before becoming a plumber and he eventually went to work for the city engineering department.[71]

Again, the Duluth Union Labor Party had significant success, with Murnian and Farrell both winning office. The *Labor World*, which was particularly interested in the election of Murnian, noted, "The so-called radical members of organized labor stood loyally behind Mr. Murnian, a conservative. Such men as Joel Lichten, Samuel F. Esse, and M. J. O'Rourke, all consistent Socialists, worked for Mr. Murnian as hard as if he were their own party candidate."[72] Farrell would go on to hold city office off and on throughout the 1920s and 1930s. Murnian, who as Commissioner of Public Safety gave the fateful order not to use deadly force against the lynch mob attacking the jail in 1920, was defeated for reelection in 1923 and again in 1925. In a letter to the *Labor World*, Jack Carney, the radical editor of the Socialist newspaper *Truth*, claimed some responsibility for the defeat of the Socialist defector, Johnson, who was the one Union Labor Party candidate to go down to defeat in 1919.[73]

With another successful election behind them, delegates from the AFL unions met at the Owl's Club to discuss the future of the Duluth Union Labor Party. They decided to form a permanent party, which with representatives from the various unions would parallel the Trades and Labor Assembly in structure and which would deal with electoral politics, leaving industrial matters to the assembly.[74] One month later, at the Minnesota Federation of Labor Convention in New Ulm, the state AFL committed itself to join the Non-Partisan League to form the Working People's Non-Partisan League (WPNPL) of Minnesota.[75] This left the situation in Duluth somewhat unclear. Traditionally, the NPL strategy had been to run progressive candidates in the Republican primary elections and then elect them as Republicans in the fall general election. The Duluth Union Labor Party had chosen a different strategy, running independently under its own label in the general election. In 1920, the Minnesota WPNPL had a complex strategy involving running some candidates in the Republican primary and some as independent candidates in the fall election. In September 1919, the WPNPL announced plans to open a Duluth office. Following up on this announcement, Thomas Van Leer and George Lawson, representing, respectively, the "left" and the "right" wings of the Minnesota WPNPL, appeared together at Owl's Hall in October to meet with Duluth labor activists. Van Lear and Lawson presumably urged the Duluth group to join the WPNPL.[76] It was not until February 1920, however, that the Duluth Union Labor Party officially took this step.[77] By this time, the Duluth WPNPL was in the hands of more conservative labor leaders. Of the eight men who represented Duluth at the 1920 WPNPL state convention in St. Paul, only John E. Jensen remained from the early leaders of the Duluth Union Labor Party.[78] All of the Socialists and former Socialists who had played leadership roles in the Union Labor Party in 1918 were gone from the 1920 Duluth WPNPL leadership group.

At its state convention, the WPNPL chose Henrik Shipstead as its candidate for governor, and following the common NPL practice, it ran him as a WPNPL candidate in the Republican primary election. This strategy created some difficulties for the WPNPL in Duluth. As a progressive, pro-temperance, Protestant, Scandinavian Republican, Shipstead was appealing to the large Scandinavian working-class vote in Duluth. He could even count on the support of moderates among the Scandinavian Socialists. But he was much less attractive to progressives who were non-Scandinavian, anti-temperance Catholics, who had traditionally supported the Democratic Party. The Duluth Union Labor Party had brought together progressive labor activists from both of these two camps. Having evolved into the Duluth WPNPL, the organized electoral wing of the labor movement in Duluth found itself in a difficult position by 1920. Under the leadership of AFL activists like Murnian, Farrell, and Henry Pereault, each of whom was Catholic and wet with roots in the progressive wing of the Democratic Party, the local WPNPL was officially committed to support a pro-temperance, Protestant Republican.

Not surprisingly, the election was a bitter disappointment. Despite overflow crowds to hear Shipstead and the other WPNPL candidates at Woodman Hall in the Scandinavian West End, the entire WPNPL slate went down to defeat. In the primary elections in Duluth, the Republican candidate for governor, Jacob A. O. Preus, defeated Shipstead by a margin of more than two to one.[79] William Carss, running as an independent in the fall general election, lost to O. J. Larson, the Republican, by a narrow margin of two hundred votes.[80] Shipstead, also running as an independent in the general election, was defeated as well. While it is difficult to say with certainty why Shipstead fared so poorly in Duluth, his earlier identification as a Republican and the association of the WPNPL with the Republican Party may have caused the WPNPL candidates to lose some Democratic votes.[81]

Despite the setback of 1920, enthusiasm for a third-party movement spread. In 1922 the WPNPL decided to run two candidates for state office under the Farmer-Labor Party designation: Magnus Johnson for governor and Henrik Shipstead for U.S. Senate. With the two progressive camps in Duluth reunited behind the Farmer-Labor Party banner, both candidates ran well, with Shipstead defeating a strong Republican incumbent, Frank B. Kellogg. For the next two decades, the Farmer-Labor Party was established as a strong third-party alternative to the Republicans and the Democrats.[82]

The third-party movement in Minnesota was part of a national effort by progressive forces within and outside the AFL to change the face of American politics. At a Progressive Political Action conference in Cleveland in December 1922, representatives of the major unions from all over the United States met to consider the possibilities for labor politics. There was a debate between a minority, who favored forming a separate Farmer-Labor Party to contest the Republicans and the Democrats, and a majority, who favored working within the two existing parties. The Minnesota WPNPL, led by William Mahoney, favored the minority strategy of forming a third party. In 1924, with enthusiasm rising in progressive labor circles for a presidential bid by Robert LaFollette of Wisconsin, Mahoney called for a national convention in St. Paul in June to launch a national Farmer-Labor Party with LaFollette as its presidential standard bearer.

There were a number of serious obstacles to this effort, how-ever. One was the role of Communists within the Farmer-Labor movement in Minnesota. While Communists had been banned from participating in the Cleveland conference, radicals within the AFL, like John Fitzpatrick of Chicago and William Mahoney of Minnesota, who wanted to move quickly to form a third party, had shown a willingness to work with the Communists. The Commu-nists, however, had shown themselves to be difficult allies, packing a Farmer-Labor convention in Chicago in 1923 and seizing control of an organization rendered insignificant by their doing so.[83] For Mahoney and the Minnesota Farmer-Laborites, the presence of Communists within their movement would have consequences that damaged their hopes for establishing a national third-party presi-dential campaign in 1924.

Having initially attacked the coalition between the AFL, the NPL, and moderate Socialists emerging in Minnesota in 1924, the Communists tried to gain control of the movement. In the spring primary campaign, they ran candidates publicly identified as Com-munists in the Farmer-Labor primary. Communists also held lead-ership positions within the FLP in Minnesota. Clarence Hathaway, the leader of the Communist Party in Minnesota, was a member of the state Executive Committee of the Farmer-Labor Federation.[84] Seeing the involvement of Communists in the Farmer-Labor move-ment in Minnesota, LaFollette announced, before the June con-vention in St. Paul even convened, that he would not accept the nomination of such a convention and would not have anything to do with it because of the involvement of Communists. With the hopes of launching a LaFollette campaign punctured, interest in the St. Paul convention declined, leaving the committed Commu-nist minority in a position to control the convention, which it did, denouncing LaFollette and even rejecting William Mahoney for the office of chair of the convention.[85]

Despite the convention fiasco, the Minnesota Farmer-Laborites persevered. Floyd B. Olson, the Farmer-Labor candidate for governor, lost but only by a small margin, while a number of other Farmer-Labor candidates were elected to office. In Duluth, William Carss, now running on the Farmer-Labor ticket, regained his congressional seat, which he held until 1929. While Communists had openly participated in the Farmer-Labor campaign in Duluth and St. Louis County, their involvement seems not to have been as damaging as it was at the St. Paul convention. *Labor World* warned its readers of the Communist attempt to take over the emerging

Farmer-Labor Party, but dismissed preconvention charges that the FLP was infiltrated by reds as the old "bug-a-boo" of the red menace.[86] Even after the disastrous St. Paul convention, the *Labor World* continued to urge its readers to stay in the Farmer-Labor Party and keep control of it in non-Communist hands. An article run in the same issue, just after the convention, proclaimed harmony in the Farmer-Labor primary campaign in St. Louis County, briefly highlighting the actvities of the various FLP candidates and including the comment that J. O. Bentall, the Communist candidate for Congress running against Carss, had "had several meetings during the week advocating closer relations between the workers and the Communist movement."[87]

This attitude toward the local Communists is particularly notable because it presumably came from William McEwen, the owner, publisher, and editor of the *Labor World*. Until the 1924 campaign, McEwen and the *Labor World* had held back from the third-party effort in Duluth, covering local developments but often relegating local third-party activity to the back pages and only endorsing selected third-party candidates for office. With the 1924 campaign, McEwen wholeheartedly embraced the idea of labor politics, providing more enthusiastic coverage of the Farmer-Labor Party and at the same time serving as the local manager of the LaFollette-Wheeler Progressive Party presidential campaign, which was run independently from the Minnesota FLP because of LaFollette's refusal to associate with Communists.[88] McEwen's attitude toward Duluth's Communists was also significant. Previously an implacable critic of the Communists, McEwen appears to have changed his mind and become willing to cooperate with them. Equally significant is the apparent willingness of the Communists in Duluth and St. Louis County to cooperate with McEwen. Despite the recommendations of Communist leaders in the United States and in Minnesota in particular, Moscow had given orders for American Communists to repudiate the whole LaFollette campaign from the time of the convention.[89] Yet in August, well after the convention, the Communists in Duluth invited McEwen and William Carss to speak at a party picnic in Fairmount Park, where Max Bedacht, a nationally important Communist leader, was also a scheduled speaker.[90] Carss had defeated the Communist candidate Bentall, who had finished a strong second, in the Farmer-Labor primary. By inviting Carss and McEwen to speak, local Communists were exercising a degree of independence from the national leadership

Though outside the Farmer-Labor Party in the late 1920s and early 1930s, Communists retained local support, especially among Finnish Americans. Here staff and supporters pose outside the offices for Työmies *in Superior. Courtesy Immigration History Research Center.*

of the party and from Moscow. Wanting the Farmer-Labor Party to succeed, the local Communists were willing to ignore Moscow's ban on cooperation with the LaFollette Progressives, while at the same time and for the same reason, the local LaFollette Progressives were willing to ignore the LaFollette campaign's ban on cooperation with the Communists.

Two years later, by the time of the 1926 gubernatorial campaign, the issue of the Communist presence within the Farmer-Labor Party had been dramatically resolved, with the Minnesota Farmer-Labor Party explicitly banning Communists.[91] William McEwen remained, serving as the state campaign manager for Magnus Johnson, the strong but unsuccessful gubernatorial candidate for the Farmer-Labor Party.[92] McEwen also served as chair of the 1927 state Farmer-Labor convention.[93] The FLP had some success in Duluth. Farmer-Labor candidates were elected to the state legislature, like Henry Morin, the former Democrat who had tried to lure Carss onto the Democratic ticket and who had apparently abandoned the sinking Democrats to join the rising Farmer-Labor Party.[94] Farmer-Laborites were also elected as city commissioners, like Christ Evens and James Fourbister, defeating Bert Wheeler, a popular Prohibitionist city commissioner who had opposed a minimum wage ordinance supported by the Farmer-Laborites.[95] The Republicans still won most elections in Duluth, but the Farmer-Laborites won a few and they made credible showings in most others. By the mid-1920s, the Farmer-Labor Party had supplanted the Democrats as the major opposition party in Duluth and St. Louis County.

The Farmer-Labor Party in Duluth was a coalition of forces. Members of the Brotherhood of Railway Engineers were an important part of this coalition. William Carss, whose 1918 election to

Like Communists around the world, Työmies *considered the Bolshevik revolution the harbinger of a better world. From* Työmies, *January 2, 1926. Courtesy Työmies Society.*

*Finnish consumer cooperatives flourished in the western Lake Superior region,
with their center of operations in Superior. Labels from co-op products testify to
the breadth of support for the Russian Revolution. Courtesy Immigration History
Research Center.*

Congress had galvanized the third-party movement in Duluth, was
a locomotive engineer. Many of Carss's closest political allies, who
played leading roles in the early Farmer-Labor Party, were also engineers. Among them were B. H. Farley of Virginia and J. L. Peterson
of Proctor, who each served terms as chair of the St. Louis County
Farmer-Labor Association; H. W. Dart of Proctor; P. F. Demore of
Duluth; and Michael O'Rourke of Duluth. A number of men from
the Brotherhood of Railroad Trainmen also played active roles in
the Duluth area FLP in the 1920s; among them were C. F. Hannigan
of Proctor, George Lockhart of Duluth, W. G. Moffatt of Duluth, and
A. A. Buirge of Proctor.[96]

Another important group in the Farmer-Labor coalition were activists from certain of the AFL unions that had, for one reason or another, been somewhat radicalized. The Duluth Painters Local 106 had suffered under the open-shop campaign against the building trades in 1907 and the similar open-shop campaign launched by the Citizens' Alliance in 1920. John E. Jensen, Joel Lichten, and Elling Munkeby all came from the Painters' Union. Carpenters Local 361 was another union that had suffered under the open-shop drives. It, too, included a number of activists who played leadership roles in the FLP in the 1920s. Otto Tarun was especially important, having served as president of the Carpenters Union and president of the Federated Trades Assembly. Christ Evens, who was elected as a city commissioner in Duluth, came from the Carpenters. Another carpenter, Charles McKinnon, had been active in labor politics in Duluth before the FLP and had remained active in the FLP throughout the 1920s. Perhaps the most celebrated of the Duluth Carpenters was J. H. Baker. Baker was a Civil War veteran, a member of the Carpenters Union since 1857, a leader of the Knights of Labor in Duluth, and a founding member of Carpenters Local 361. At age ninety-two, he was the guest of honor for the Labor Day celebration in Fairmount Park, where Farmer-Labor Congressmen Carss and Paul John Kvale from the Seventh District of Minnesota spoke to a crowd of fifteen thousand people.[97] It was perhaps fitting that Baker, who in 1890 had championed political action against the pure and simple unionism of Emil Applehagen, Gompers's ally in the Duluth Trades Assembly, should live to see the renewal of labor politics in Duluth.

Other unions that contributed radicalized activists to the FLP included the Boilermakers, the Machinists, and the Railroad Shopmen. The Boilermakers, many of whose members worked at the Marine Iron and Shipbuilding Company, had been radicalized before the First World War. There were a number of Socialists in this union and a strike by the Boilermakers had led to the launching of *Truth*, the newspaper of the Scandinavian Socialists, in the spring of 1917.[98] Robert Sermon, a member of the Boilermakers and a Socialist who would go on to operate his own engineering firm, played a leadership role in the Duluth FLP. The Machinists and the Railroad Shopmen, both unions that were decimated by the failure of the Shopmen's strike in 1922, also contributed leaders to the Duluth FLP. Of particular importance were Ingworth Erickson of the Machinists and Arthur Siegler of the Shopmen. Siegler, an electrician working in the Northern Pacific yard repairing railroad cars in 1922, had been president of the striking Carmen and one of the leaders of the Federated Shop Crafts in the shopmen's strike.[99]

Leaders of the conservative AFL craft unions joined the third-party movement after the victory of Carss in the 1918 campaign. William Murnian of the electrical workers and Henry Pereault of the Cigarmakers were two of the most important leaders. Both entered the third-party movement in Duluth as early as 1920, when each appeared as a member of the Duluth delegation to the WPNPL convention in St. Paul.[100] Both had long played roles in the Duluth and Minnesota labor movement. Other important conservative AFL figures in the FLP were Charles Esse of the barbers' union, Robert Olson of the motion picture operators union, and Charles Olson, who ran for secretary of state on the Farmer-Labor ticket in 1926.

Women also had a significant place in Duluth's Farmer-Labor Party. In 1922, just two years after the passage of the nineteenth amendment to the Constitution gave women the right to vote, Anna Dickie Olesen from Cloquet ran an unsuccessful but impressive campaign for the U.S. Senate on the Democratic ticket. Her strong showing opened the door to the involvement of women in local politics. A Farmer-Labor Women's League was officially formed in January 1925.[101] Although this league appears to have functioned as a women's auxiliary to the regular Farmer-Labor Party, a number of women played important roles in the predominantly male party, serving on committees and being elected as delegates to represent the organization at higher levels of the party.[102] Mrs. Edward Blackwood, for example, served as one of six members of the executive board of the Duluth FLP in 1925 and as a delegate to the state FLP convention in 1926.[103]

Despite the beginning of a coalition that cut across lines of ethnicity, religion, and gender, the Farmer-Labor Party in Duluth, like the Minnesota FLP as a whole, was largely Scandinavian throughout the 1920s. The early prominence of Scandinavian Americans like Henrik Shipstead, Magnus Johnson, and Floyd B. Olson attests to the importance of the Scandinavian base for the Farmer-Labor Party at the state level. The choice of Woodman Hall in the Scandinavian West End as a favorite site for Farmer-Labor meetings indicates the importance of Scandinavians locally. So, too, does a campaign appearance in Lincoln Park in the summer of 1928 by FLP Congressman Henrik Shipstead, an appearance at which Shipstead gave a speech that dealt heavily with Scandinavian history and included a recitation of the Swedish national anthem in Swedish.[104]

In winning the support of the Minnesota and Duluth AFL, the Duluth FLP added to its Scandinavian base the votes of a significant percentage of Duluth's Irish, Polish, and German voters. Many of these voters were Catholics. Throughout the 1920s, however, the Duluth FLP remained predominantly Protestant. Many working-class Catholics, in particular South Slavs and Italians, appear to have played little, if any, role in the local Farmer-Labor Party in the 1920s. With the exception of John Movern, who worked in the city clerk's office, served on the Duluth Americanization Committee, and acted as a leader in the Duluth Jugoslav-American Federation, no South Slavs or Italians appear as activists within the Duluth FLP during this period.[105]

The divide between Protestants and Catholics that had bedeviled the labor movement in Duluth since the 1890s continued to be an especially difficult issue. Like most of the "Americans" in the FLP, the Scandinavians were Protestants; often supporters of Prohibition; often members of the Masons or other lodges modeled on the Masons; tinged with the traditional anti-Catholicism of Protestants; and sometimes drawn to radical anti-Catholic organizations, like the American Protective Association of the 1890s and the Ku Klux Klan of the 1920s. We have already seen that anti-Catholics and perhaps Klan members were among the supporters of Carss, who seems to have been perceived as a representative of Anglo-Saxon, white, Protestant voters. In 1924, Leonard Hedman, the young Scandinavian American who had been one of the ringleaders in the lynching of the African American circus workers, wrote to Carss to apply for a job, mentioning a "heart to heart" talk he had had with Carss in the recent past.[106] While Hedman did not get the job and while there is no reason to think that Carss agreed with Hedman and certainly no reason to think he approved of Hedman's role in the lynching, Hedman's presumptions provide some evidence of how Carss and his supporters were perceived.

A letter from V. Bertoni, secretary of the Associated Italian-American Clubs of Northern Minnesota, illustrates this same impression of Carss from the other side of the Catholic/Protestant divide. Bertoni asks some direct and pointed questions about Carss's views on restrictions on Italian immigration and the proportional lack of political appointments given to Italians. Bertoni's letter was sent in early June 1924. Two months later, with the general election drawing near, Peter Belcastro, secretary of the Italian Americanization Club of Eveleth, wrote to Carss complaining of a lack of response to Bertoni's earlier letter, enclosing a copy of the letter and asking again for answers to the questions Bertoni had raised. Carss replied in a carefully worded letter, admitting that the lack of appointments suggested discrimination and rejecting the principle of discrimination on the basis of ethnicity as a foundation for appointments and immigration policy, but supporting an immigration policy that would favor prosperous immigrants over poor ones on the grounds that poor immigrants enable employers to undermine American wages.[107] Again, this exchange provides some evidence that the third-party movement behind Carss's election was viewed as northern European and Protestant, and perhaps tinged with racist and anti-Catholic prejudices.

The victory of Pal Brown, a KKK-endorsed candidate for St. Louis County Attorney, in the Farmer-Labor primary election in June 1926 lent credence to suspicions about the presence of religious bigotry in the Farmer-Labor movement.[108] Brown's opponent in the 1926 FLP primary was Sig Slonim, a Jew. Slonim, himself an immigrant, was a lawyer who had provided legal help to Socialists and IWWs since before World War I. Before training for the law he had done manual labor and had a strong record of support for labor rights, immigrant rights, and civil rights. In a campaign speech, Slonim addressed an issue that was emotionally charged for many working-class families in Duluth and St. Louis County:

> I have seen in strikes in this county lawful meetings illegally broken up with the consent of the authorities and at least without a protest from them. I have seen the homes of the working people and of the poor unlawfully entered and searched without legal warrant and there was not a sheriff or county attorney to prevent this violation of law. I have seen armed thugs shipped into the state in violation of law, sworn in as deputy sheriffs, and with the authority vested in them as such they served not the state, but private interests and against law abiding workingmen, whose only offense was in being on strike.[109]

Slonim's words harkened back to the strikes on the Iron Range in 1907 and 1916 and to the national steel strike of 1919, the Shopmen's strike of 1922, and a host of lesser strikes in Duluth from 1919 to 1922. Time and again, injunctions, imported strikebreakers, and imported "deputies" had been used by employers and the Citizens' Alliance to defeat strikes and break unions, all with the blessing and connivance of elected officials. A central aim of the Farmer-Labor Party was to wrest public power away from the control of the employers.

Slonim was defeated in the Farmer-Labor primary by a relatively small margin. Turnout for the primary election was low. Farmer-Labor activists, like R. H. Farley and O. E. Thompson, argued that many voters in Duluth and St. Louis County had been afraid to ask for Farmer-Labor primary ballots, fearing that poll officials friendly to the steel trust would report requests to employers, who would then retaliate against those voters. Farley and Thompson called for secret primary ballots so people could feel free to vote for the Farmer-Labor Party.[110] No doubt such fears did play a part in reducing the number of Farmer-Labor primary voters. On the Iron Range, where poll watchers friendly to the steel trust were likely to be present at polling places, progressive candidates sympathetic to immigrant iron-ore minors, like Victor Power, the mayor of Hibbing, had had better luck running as Republicans within the Republican Party. But it is also significant that the candidate who defeated Slonim was Pal Brown, the endorsed candidate of the anti-Catholic and anti-Jewish KKK.[111] The same divisions that had plagued labor politics in Duluth in the early 1890s remained. If the Farmer-Labor Party was to succeed in Duluth and St. Louis County, it would have to broaden its base of support beyond its strongly Protestant "American" and Scandinavian foundation. In particular, it would have to win the support of the large South Slav and Italian communities in St. Louis County if it was to succeed in its challenge to the pro-business philosophy of Duluth's governing elite.

west duluth on the move

WHILE THE FARMER-LABOR PARTY CHALLENGED BUSINESS LEAD-
ership throughout the 1920s, it was the business leadership that
prevailed, convincing itself and the voting public that American
families would prosper best under the benign hand of paternalistic
capitalism. In an essay written on the eve of the Depression, nationally prominent Duluth businessman Julius Barnes highlighted the
implications of this point of view for unemployment: "Unemployment which follows labor-saving installations, as well as unemployment which follows industry displacement, is a private charge on
the responsibility of business leadership."[1] The Depression of the

*Duluth businessman Julius Barnes, who endorsed the philosophy of paternalistic cap-
italism, was at one time national president of the Chamber of Commerce. Courtesy
Northeast Minnesota Historical Center.*

1930s cruelly undercut this commitment. The unfulfilled promise of corporate America produced a great loss of faith in business leaders and in the system of paternalistic capitalism they promoted.

At the same time, when the Depression arrived in 1929, America's immigrant working class had changed. Immigrants who had arrived before the First World War had learned how things worked in America and they had acquired experience in ethnically diverse coalitions. With their children, a new generation had appeared. Born in America, educated in American public schools, fluent in English, familiar with American history and American ways, and comfortable in the mixed ethnic environment of working-class Duluth, the sons and daughters of Duluth's immigrants stood ready to act on the historical stage. Drawing on the life experience, memories, and thoughts of their parents' generation, they used their own experience and their own understanding of Depression-era America to join with their parents to change America.

An understanding of the historical significance of the Depression for Duluth must begin with an appreciation of the impact it had on the economy of the city and the surrounding region. Even during the supposedly booming 1920s, chronic unemployment had plagued the city. This unemployment had served to discipline the labor force and buttress the campaign by the Citizens' Alliance to turn back local unions and reestablish the open shop. In May 1929, before the onslaught of the Depression, *Labor World* had complained again about the high unemployment and low wages found in Duluth, a complaint supported by Republican congressman William Pittenger, who asked for the government to provide relief to unemployed families in the city.[2]

In the months following the stock market crash of October 1929, unemployment in Duluth and on the Iron Range increased sharply. In April 1930, a nationwide census of the unemployed was initiated. A report based on this survey indicated that, among cities of more than 100,000, Duluth had the highest rate of unemployment in the nation, with more than 5,700 unemployed persons.[3] By March 1932, 11,716 people were unemployed in Duluth, more than 30 percent of the labor force.[4] That same year, in the area by the docks, a shack city made of scrap materials by homeless and destitute people was burned down by the police.[5]

Behind the great rise in unemployment was a precipitous decline in the iron-mining industry. While demand for basic consumer goods persisted, demand for steel for construction and for discretionary consumer goods fell sharply. With the collapse of the steel industry, the demand for iron ore plummeted, and much of Duluth's economy was tied to the steel and iron ore industries. From 1920 through 1930, iron ore constituted over 90 percent of the total tonnage shipped out of the port of Duluth.[6] In 1929, nearly forty-five million tons of iron ore was shipped from the ports of Duluth and Superior. In 1930, ore shipments fell to less than twenty-eight million tons. In 1931, shipments fell further, to around fifteen million tons. By 1932 shipments had virtually stopped.[7] This precipitous drop in shipments of iron ore had a devastating effect on employment in the iron mines on the range. It also was disastrous for the related industries based in Duluth: the ore docks, lake commerce, the railroads used to haul the ore, the railroad repair shops, and the foundries and metal fabricating shops that supplied parts and did repair work for the iron-mining industry and the railroads. The general decline of the steel industry, in turn, had a devastating effect on employment at the steel plant in Duluth and in the large scrap-iron industry located in Duluth. Unemployment in the metal products industries in Duluth had reached over 45 percent by the end of 1931.[8]

Loading grain in 1932. Grain shipments, at least, continued. Courtesy Minnesota Historical Society.

The steel plant in 1935 during the Depression and before the plant was organized. Courtesy Minnesota Historical Society.

During any depression, businesses typically face declining demand for their products. Faced with such conditions, businesses must either cut back on production or win customers away from rival firms. Since cuts in production threaten profits and the very survival of firms, hard times have traditionally been periods of intense competition as firms struggled with their rivals to retain customers and markets for their products. In the past, such competition had often led to wage cuts designed to lower production costs and allow a firm to undersell its competitors. One of the central ideas of the managed capitalism espoused by men like Elbert Gary had been the idea that companies should avoid such downward competition when faced with hard times, instead working out cooperative arrangements for sharing the reduced markets that would allow existing firms to weather the financial storm and avoid the anarchy of all-out competition. This arrangement also allowed businesses to respond to hard times in ways that were consistent with their paternalistic commitment to their workforce to avoid ruinous layoffs and wage cuts.

In the early days following the 1929 stock market crash, big businesses tried to avoid ruinous downward competition, promising to maintain wages. In the rubber industry, the six-hour day was adopted to spread the work among the employees. U.S. Steel took a somewhat different approach, rotating its employees in and out of work, thereby maintaining 94 percent of its workforce as late as January 1931.[9] But this commitment could not be sustained. For one thing, not all sectors of American industry accepted the idea that businesses should respond to the Depression by trying to maintain wages and employment. Also, small businesses operating in highly competitive markets had problems applying the paternalistic capitalism of giant companies like U.S. Steel. For many businesses, market-sharing arrangements were virtually impossible to enforce and, in any case, small businesses often lacked the capital reserves necessary to maintain wages and employment. The survival of such firms made wage cuts and layoffs necessary, and once started, they led to a snowballing series of cuts and layoffs. In Duluth, wage cuts were announced for longshoremen in May 1931. Wage cuts for bakers and painters followed later that month.[10]

In the critical steel industry, the first wage cuts were announced by the National Steel Corporation in May 1931. These cuts did not directly affect employees of the industry in Duluth, which was controlled by the U.S. Steel Corporation. U.S. Steel executive James Farrell denounced the National Steel wage cuts as a betrayal of the responsible management of the steel industry long championed by Elbert Gary and U.S. Steel: "I think it is a pretty cheap sort of business when ... [men] are working three days a week and then [they] cut that three days a week another ten percent.... Now that is not the idea of the old line companies."[11] But not even the mighty U.S. Steel could maintain the line on wages. The company was forced to announce a 10 percent reduction in wages effective October 1, 1931, on top of the reductions in hours already imposed by the system of employee rotation at work.[12] Further wage cuts were imposed at the steel plant in Duluth at the end of March 1934.[13]

Most of the unemployed people in Duluth were from working families with substantial roots in the city.[14] The prolonged unemployment and wage cuts associated with the Depression pushed many of these families over the line, forcing them to seek outside help to provide food, clothing, and shelter. The upsurge in demand for relief services strained and eventually overwhelmed the network of private charitable agencies serving the city of Duluth. The Community Fund, the umbrella organization developed by leaders of the business community in the 1920s, was $27,000 short of estimated need by the end of October 1930.[15] In 1924 the total yearly payments of the Community Fund amounted to $69,000. In 1932 the fund needed $35,000 for the two months of November and December alone. Leaders of the Community Fund asked for federal aid.[16]

At the beginning of the Depression, the only source of available public funds for relief was St. Louis County. Like the private agencies, the county was overwhelmed by the need for relief assistance. In 1927 expenditures for relief and county government amounted to a little over four million dollars in St. Louis County. By 1936 these expenditures had tripled to over twelve million.[17] Increases in payments for direct relief by the county Poor Commission made up a substantial part of this overall increase. In 1929, direct relief payments amounted to a little over $64,000. In 1935, payments for direct relief amounted to nearly $1.7 million, with another $1.7 million going for "work relief," a category not on the records until 1934.[18] Still, this huge increase in county expenditures fell far short of the amount needed to meet the needs of St. Louis County families. A 1937 report to the state legislature stressed the continued need for federal and state assistance, especially in the three large cities of St. Paul, Minneapolis, and Duluth.[19] As the Depression deepened, the proportion of public relief payments coming from outside the city and county increased dramatically.[20]

The 30 percent unemployment rate that plagued Duluth created needs that swamped existing private and public relief agencies. The effort by these agencies to meet those needs, however insufficient, intensified demands on both voluntary charitable payments and the tax payments made by the businesses and individuals who remained at work. As the Depression continued, the tax and charitable demands increased, threatening to pull under those businesses that had continued to operate. Soon a battle developed between those who wanted to increase tax rates to maintain or increase public spending and those who wanted to cut public spending to maintain or reduce tax rates.

Leading the fight to hold the line on taxes was the Taxpayers' League of St. Louis County. Organized in June 1921, the Taxpayers' League employed M. W. Dewees as its executive secretary and had a board of directors made up of many of the leading businessmen of Duluth, some of whom, like Royal Alworth, were also members of the Citizens' Alliance.[21] The Taxpayers' League called itself "a bureau for governmental research."[22] The league, however, was clearly more than a research institution. In a June 1934 letter to its members, the league described itself as "a non-political, citizens' agency, organized to promote effective citizenship, study public business, co-operate with officials, and specifically to work for economy and efficiency in governmental affairs."[23] Here the advocacy role of the league was clear. Later in this same letter, Executive Secretary DeWees said that the League was "the only citizens' agency maintaining a day to day contact with local governments." The *Labor World*, which opposed the league on tax issues, complained that the Duluth City Council was under the control of the Taxpayers' League and called the league a branch of the Citizens' Alliance.[24] Opposition to the Taxpayers' League included the *Labor World*, the unions, the Farmer-Labor Party, community clubs, and the Parent-Teacher Association of Duluth.

These two sides battled throughout the early 1930s. On the one side were the business leaders of Duluth, trying to keep businesses afloat and competitive by cutting wages and holding the line on taxes. On the other side was a coalition of forces struggling to maintain wages and finance relief programs by increasing taxes. If this popular coalition had numbers on its side, the business leaders had the financial levers of the banks on their side, as well as the inertia of tradition, which acknowledged the leading role of business leaders in the life of the city.

In March 1932, the Taxpayers' League began to press for cuts in city taxes, while at the same time the Duluth Chamber of Commerce tried to get the county board to reduce taxes.[25] Rebuffed in these efforts, a group of leading businessmen formed a special Committee of 77 to campaign for cuts in taxes and spending at all levels of government. The committee was modeled on similar committees formed in New York, Minneapolis, St. Paul, and elsewhere. Many of the men on the Duluth Committee of 77 were also members of the Citizens' Alliance and the Taxpayers' League. The group won an early victory when it persuaded the school board to cut spending on the schools.[26] Organized labor responded by recruiting a slate of candidates to run for school board against the board members who had supported the cuts. The labor candidates were pledged to maintain teachers' salaries and school programs. In the May elections of 1932, the labor candidates won.[27]

Fearing that spending and taxes would exhaust the resources of a shrinking tax base, one month later the Taxpayers' League and the Committee of 77 proposed a change in the city charter that would put a limit on the tax rates that could be levied by governmental bodies. That proposal was defeated.[28] The issue was revisited in the school board elections of May 1933. Again the Taxpayers' League, supported by the steel company, urged that school spending be brought under control by cutting programs and teachers' salaries. The slate of candidates backed by the Taxpayers' League was rivaled by a labor-backed slate, and once again the labor slate won. For the first time in the history of the city, the labor movement had won a majority on the school board.[29]

Still, it is one thing to vote to maintain wages and programs and quite another to find the resources to pay for them. As Depression conditions held and tax rates climbed, tax delinquency rates began to rise, further eroding the tax base for schools and governmental functions. Where the tax delinquency rate had stood at 3.5 percent before the beginning of the Depression in 1928, by 1933 the rate had risen to 22.2 percent.[30] The *Labor World*, now under the editorship of Anne McEwen, the daughter of longtime owner and editor William McEwen, who had died unexpectedly in February 1933, charged that property owners were deliberately withholding taxes to force cuts in government programs.[31] In November, the paper ran a story charging that U.S. Steel Corporation, which had called for cuts in school spending in April, was among those property holders delinquent in its tax payments. The story appears to have been true.[32]

Nevertheless, faced with mounting indebtedness, two school board members from the labor-backed majority joined other board members to impose further cuts on the schools.[33] *Labor World* denounced the two school board members as traitors and called on Duluth workers to defend the schools, but it was to no avail. Deeply in debt, by March 1934 the schools were unable to get further loans from the banks without agreeing to yet more cuts and holding the line on taxes.[34] That year the demoralized labor forces lost the school board elections in the spring and the Taxpayers' League stepped up the pressure for further cuts in school programs in the fall.[35]

Despite these victories for the Taxpayers' League, by 1935 tax rates in Duluth were the highest in the history of the city.[36] The two sides battled on, with the league, supported by the *News Tribune* and the *Herald*, trying again to gain public support for an amendment to the city constitution to prevent further tax hikes, a campaign that once again lost by a wide margin.[37] Business leaders argued that many people on relief were not truly in need, that taxes were simply too high, and that local businesses forced to pay such taxes could not compete. The popular coalition opposing the business leaders argued that human needs were real, that monies must be found to pay for relief for distressed families, that busi-

nesses in Duluth could afford to pay more, and that business leaders were putting profits before people. A Minnesota tax and finance
survey done in 1937 seems to support the view that the tax base in
St. Louis County could have supported more public spending. The
study classified the eighty-seven counties of Minnesota into seven
categories, each depending on the relative ability of the county to
finance relief programs and basic governmental functions. St. Louis
County received an "A" rating because it was "not only financially
capable of continued performance of established governmental
functions," but it was also "in a much better financial position, relatively speaking, to pay for practically all of the costs of new programs originated by both the Federal and State governments."[38]
The study showed that per capita taxes in St. Louis County were
lower than per capita taxes in Ramsey and Hennepin counties, and
in its "Summary of Recommendations" it urged that all three counties rely less on bank loans and more on increases in tax rates to
fund relief programs.[39]

Stress on St. Louis County taxes and finances would have
been even greater had it not been for the federal funds coming into
the region through the Works Progress Administration (WPA) and
other federal programs. Initiated in 1935, the WPA put the unemployed to work building roads, parks, and schools and making
other public improvements. The WPA also paid unemployed men
and women to write and produce plays, to create works of art, to
do historical research, and to provide special classes for working
and unemployed men and women. Begun locally in July 1935, by
the end of 1936, over seven million dollars in federal WPA funds
had been paid out in St. Louis County.[40] This infusion of federal
funds to employ the unemployed relieved some of the pressure on
county welfare programs. It also provided a source of income for
young people, predominantly young men, who otherwise would
have had none. Wages ranged from forty-two to one hundred dollars per month, with the lower rate paid to the common laborer and
the higher rate paid to skilled professional laborers.[41] For families
on the economic edge, this extra income, small as it was, made a
big difference.

The WPA was often criticized as a boondoggle for lazy men.[42]
The work was ridiculed as "make work" and WPA workers were
often caricatured as standing around leaning on their shovels. But
in fact a great deal of useful work was done. Within six years WPA
workers in the Duluth district had built forty-three new bridges,

WPA workers from Duluth take a break from fighting a fire in the Pequaywan Lake region in 1936. Courtesy Minnesota Historical Society.

repaired eighteen other bridges, constructed forty-five miles of sidewalks and eighteen miles of curbing, built ninety-two new public buildings, repaired an additional one hundred and sixty-eight buildings, made additions to seven buildings, repaired seventy-eight schools, constructed four new parks and made repairs to seventeen others, built seventeen playgrounds and repaired ten, built twenty-four new athletic fields and made repairs to seven, constructed ten new utility plants and repaired three, built forty-one miles of storm and sanitary sewers, built thirteen dams, and constructed fourteen thousand feet of retaining walls. In addition, women WPA workers made nearly seventy-nine thousand garments for the county welfare board to distribute to needy people, prepared and served over eleven thousand hot lunches for school kids, provided one hundred and thirty-six families of disabled homemakers with housekeeping assistance, and provided nursery schools for local children at Adams, Emerson, and Irving schools. In addition WPA workers prepared historical records for local institutions, repaired nearly forty thousand books for the schools, did historical research, and produced crafts, art work, and plays.[43] Among the buildings constructed by the WPA in Duluth were fieldhouses at Memorial Park, Wheeler Field, Portman Square on Raleigh Street, and in the Ordean school district. WPA workers also built LaFayette House on Park Point, the Duluth Airport, and Wade Stadium (originally known as the All Sports Municipal Stadium). Extensive improvements were also made to Skyline Parkway by WPA crews.[44]

The WPA was not without its critics, however. Although the Duluth AFL was generally supportive of the WPA, unions in the building trades protested the use of nonunion WPA workers to build Wade Stadium.[45] Another criticism came from the Labor Advancement Association, an AFL umbrella organization that managed an organizing drive in Duluth in the early 1930s. In a letter to St. Louis County Commissioner H. A. Anderson, the association went on record opposing the practice of employing married women who had husbands who were steadily employed on public works projects.[46] Similar objections had been raised regarding the employment of women in the schools and in city government. In a handwritten note to the Trades Assembly, "An Unemployed" complained about unfairness at the Federal Building, where Oscar Lindgen was employed as a fireman and his wife (unnamed) was

Children in the WPA nursery school at Irving School in Duluth, 1937. Courtesy Minnesota Historical Society.

also employed as a charwoman.[47] A similar complaint came from unemployed teachers, who urged the Trades Assembly to pass a resolution calling on the School Board to "request" that "married women teachers who [we]re not dependent upon their own earnings for a livelihood" to take a year's leave of absence to open up jobs for unemployed male teachers. While the Trades Assembly itself may not have approved this resolution, similar resolutions were approved by some unions and by some AFL organizations.[48]

Another criticism of the WPA and other smaller public works programs came from Isaac Moore, president of the First and American National Bank of Duluth, affiliated with Northwest Bancorporation. Moore reported that his friends thought the WPA "need[ed] a thorough revamping if it [wa]s to be continued." Moore went on to say that "the impression of my associates and myself is that there are a great many people obtaining financial assistance from government sources who are not entitled to it. The very general opinion is that a vast army of people are being converted into helpless paupers who are not willing to earn a living, but who formerly were compelled and able to do so."[49] Despite such criticisms, the WPA was extremely popular with the general public, which rejected Moore's view of it. Reflecting this popular support, politicians fought to preserve federal funding for WPA programs. A meeting of state legislators, mayors, and relief officials in March 1937 brought calls for more federal funding for the WPA.[50] In practice there seemed to be no real alternative. With a small recovery apparently under way in the summer of 1937, a local newspaper headline proclaimed that industry was finding jobs in the private sector for some local WPA workers.[51] However, this involved only 141 out of some 4,707 WPA jobs and at least some of these workers had go back on the WPA rolls when they were laid off a few months later.[52] The following year, 1938, still found some twelve thousand families in St. Louis County dependent on WPA wages for a living.[53]

Clayton Videen was among the many in Duluth whose lives were deeply affected by the Depression, the WPA, and the constellation of economic, political, and cultural changes of the Depression era.[54] Videen was thirteen in 1925 when his family moved to Duluth. His father worked at the steel plant and sometimes as a yard man for the railroad before he was laid off from the steel plant. Even during the 1920s, work at the steel plant was unsteady and Videen's family lived an economically precarious existence in the West End. In 1931, with his father laid off from the steel plant and unable to find work in Depression-era Duluth, Videen's parents left Duluth. Clayton, age nineteen, stayed behind.

With good paying jobs hard to find, Videen got by on what he could find. He worked for the YMCA for a while, at a shelter for transients at Fifth Avenue West, and later for the Postal Telegraph Company. He lived for a time at the "castle" at 301 East Third Street and later moved to a room at 228 North First Avenue West. Without cooking facilities and unable to afford a meal in an expensive restaurant, Videen favored the inexpensive "skid row" restaurants that catered to unemployed and marginally employed men. Among Videen's favorites were the Twin Ports Cafe, Collins Lunch, and Coney Island, then (as now) located on East Superior Street. A diary entry for August 6, 1931, describes a meal in a Finnish restaurant: "I ordered pork chops, which were listed on the bill of fare at twenty-five cents. The waitress brought me a couple of chops, each as large as my hand, two huge boiled potatoes with gravy, three thick slices of tomato, all the bread and butter I could eat (white or rye), coffee and apricot sauce. Boy! That's a meal."[55] Other days, when the money had run out, Videen simply did not eat.[56]

Yet, like most young people, Videen somehow found the money he needed to party. With Prohibition still the law of the land, Videen and his friends frequented a number of "blind pigs," where a person could either bring in his own alcoholic beverage or purchase them from local bootleggers. The 101 Club in Oliver, Wisconsin, just across the bridge from Gary-New Duluth, was a wide-open club with a dance floor and a band that played several nights a week. It was a rough and noisy place where fights were not uncommon. Another popular place was Dante's near Fairmount Park in West Duluth. Dante, a short, wiry Italian, had converted part of the first floor of his home into a beer joint and he made his own beer. On the weekends, when business was brisk, he enlisted the help of his two daughters, but "woe to the customer who made any advances, either physical or verbal," Videen says. "I once saw him threaten a transgressor with an iron pipe three-feet long."[57] Dances were also popular and Videen and his friends frequented such places as Camels' Hall, Foresters' Hall, the Glencoe, the Dreamland, the Shrine, and the Finn Hop at the Finnish Athletic Club.

Like many of his generation, Videen and his brother decided to leave Duluth for the West Coast. The trip began in September 1934, partly as a search for a better job and partly for sheer adven-

ture. But riding the rails proved to be a cold, hungry, and dangerous business and the only work the Videens could find was in a
work camp for unemployed young men run by the state of California. Looking for something better (and more adventurous), Videen
and his brother signed on to a Swedish oil tanker going from California to Japan in March 1935. This, too, proved to be hard work
and did not pay well. When the tanker returned to the West Coast
in May 1935, the Videens made their way back to Duluth.

In Duluth, Videen got involved in an adult education class in
short story writing. The Roosevelt administration had begun funding such classes in 1934 as a way to put unemployed teachers to
work. Videen also joined a Creative Arts Club, which included painters, sculptors, photographers, and writers. In his classes and in the
Arts Club Videen was exposed to a lively array of ideas about arts,
politics, and culture. Looking back on this time of his life, Videen
writes,

> I was in a new world, one I never knew existed. New
> ideas dripped like diamonds; every conversation was a
> real adventure. We were sailing along with the New Deal,
> as the Roosevelt Administration was called. Cultural
> values and inspirations were in their ascendancy. New
> ideas were welcome. We were living in days of hope, in a
> political climate that has not been equaled since.[58]

It is ironic that the Great Depression should have given rise
to such days of hope. Clayton Videen's sense of hope and excite-
ment were shared by many of his generation, who saw the Depression as the end of one age and the beginning of another. The world
of their parents had come crashing down, and as the new generation, they were to be the creators of the new world that would
take its place. In Duluth, the Farmer-Labor Party and the Congress
of Industrial Organizations (CIO) unions provided institutional
frameworks within which energized people acted to change the
world. Clayton Videen was a part of it. Involved in creative writing,
research work for the WPA Federal Writers Project, and local theater, he also joined the Duluth Youth Council, worked with the CIO
to hold a peace rally, and became active in the Farmer-Labor Party.
By November 1942, when Clayton married his wife, Gen, and left for
San Francisco, where he would eventually build a successful business, Duluth was a very different place than it had been before the
Depression.

When the Depression of the 1930s had settled down on Duluth, like geological strata reflecting the history of the Earth, the economic, political, and social strata of the city reflected the patterns established by its earlier development. At the top of the social structure were English-speaking people who were mostly Protestant and who were either descendants of the "American" pioneers who had founded the city or people who had come to Duluth as representatives of the eastern capitalists who had invested heavily in the city. At the bottom of the social structure were members of the ethnically and religiously diverse industrial working class, who provided the manual labor needed at the ore docks, the coal docks, the steel plant, the lumber mills, the railroads, the railroad shops, the lumber camps, and the myriad manufacturing shops needed to supply and maintain the iron ore and lumbering industries. Between these two groups was an array of skilled tradesmen, professionals, and businessmen who came from a variety of "American" and immigrant backgrounds.

The Depression shook this whole social structure. The economic collapse deprived thousands of households of the income they needed to meet basic daily needs. Younger families were hit especially hard. The crisis undermined faith in business leaders. Voters, especially those in working-class households, turned in increasing numbers to the revolutionary Communists or to the Farmer-Labor Party, which promised major reforms. Many working men and women also turned to the labor movement, hoping to finally succeed in organizing unions to provide them with some protection from the blind forces of the market and from the arbitrary power of employers.

Radicals took advantage of the economic crisis to recruit support. Having alienated potential allies within the Farmer-Labor Party in the mid-1920s and under orders from Moscow to present a more radical alternative, local Communists attacked the popular Farmer-Labor Governor Floyd B. Olson as a "crook, a fraud, and a liar," and denounced the Farmer-Labor Party as "reactionary."[59] Communist electoral campaigns did clearly address the desperate plight of many working-class families. A 1930 Communist campaign flyer entitled, "Don't Starve! Fight! Vote Communist!" lists fourteen demands. Among them are cash relief of fifteen dollars per week for each unemployed adult and three dollars per week for each dependent; free gas, water, and electricity for the unemployed; a moratorium on evictions of unemployed families; and the opening of the Armory, vacant apartments, and other public buildings to shel-

Duluth Communist Party campaign literature. Courtesy Northeast Minnesota Historical Center.

ter the unemployed.[60] While the Communists never succeeded in winning mass support in the western half of the city away from the Farmer-Labor Party, they did gain a reliable base of about one thousand voters.[61]

Demanding "Jobs or Relief," the Communists also mounted direct-action responses to the Depression. In 1930, local Communists began to organize the unemployed. With significant federal relief programs still three years off and city-supported public works programs woefully inadequate to meet the needs of unemployed families, more and more families turned to the Communist-led Unemployed Council in Duluth as the strongest champion of relief. By 1933 the local unemployed movement appears to have taken on the characteristics of a genuinely popular movement, involving the active participation of significant numbers of people outside the core of Communist activists. A February rally in 1933 involved marchers from New Duluth, Gary, West Duluth, and the West End who converged on the government center and elected delegates to represent them before city and county commissioners.[62] A similar 1932 Communist-organized "Hunger March" of farm families from the surrounding area drew 1,500 people to the government center in Duluth.[63] Communists also organized farmers and workers to stop evictions of destitute families.

WORKERS! DOWN TOOLS ON MARCH 6th

Demonstrate with your unemployed Brothers and Sisters on International Unemployment Day.

Duluth Court House Square Mar. 6th
3:30 P. M.

Thousands of workers are walking the street in Duluth looking for work. These unemployed workers are a part of the army of over 6,000,000 unemployed in this country. More thousands swell the army of unemployed daily, as the economic crisis deepens.

While vast numbers of these workers face starvation and misery without the slightest bit of relief from the bosses or their government, unemployment is striking at the vitals of all the employed workers.

The bosses are using unemployment as a club to break down the living standard of those that remain at work by further speedup, wage-cuts, miserable conditions and consequently unemployment for many more thousands.

Tens of thousands of workers thruout the country as well as in Duluth have already, and are demonstrating for work or wages and unemployed relief, only to be met by the bosses police clubbings, tear gas, arrests and other means of terror.

The workers in Duluth, under the leadership of the Trade Union Unity League and the Communist Party who have demonstrated at the City Hall with their demands and answered with police attack and the arrest and the conviction of the leaders in the demonstration, have shown their militancy and understand the role of the bosses and their government.

The attempt of the Mayor and the bosses of Duluth to mislead the workers in their fake relief program, in order to try to break up the united efforts of the workers organized to fight against unemployment, and the rotten conditions of the employed workers, must be met by the workers in Duluth with stronger organization under the leadership of the Trade Union Unity League and the Communist Party.

On March 6th, millions of workers thruout the world will demonstrate against unemployment, and against the capitalist system which breeds unemployment.

Workers of Duluth, employed and unemployed, demonstrate on March 6th at the Court House Square at 3:30 P. M.

EMPLOYED WORKERS!! DOWN TOOLS ON MARCH 6th

Fight for:
Work or wages.
7 hour day—5 day week, no wage cuts.
Abolition of all vagrancy laws.
Prohibition of the employment of children under 16 year of age.
Emergency relief for the unemployed from government funds; city, state and federal

Abolition of all private employment agencies.
6 hour day for all young workers under 18.
Against capitalist wars! For the defense of the Soviet Union!
Demonstrate your solidarity with the millions of employed and unemployed workers thruout the world.
Build the unemployed councils.
JOIN THE COMMUNIST PARTY.

Auspices: Communist Party U.S.A., Duluth Section, Dist. No. 9.

Duluth Communists call for a demonstration on behalf of the unemployed in 1930. Courtesy Northeast Minnesota Historical Center.

Communist rally at the Civic Center in Duluth, 1931. Courtesy Northeast Minnesota Historical Center.

Though such vigorous attempts to address unemployment, hunger, and evictions won the Communists some support, most working-class families in Duluth pinned their hopes on reforms promised by the Farmer-Labor Party and on a revived labor movement. In marked contrast to the labor peace imposed by the Citizens' Alliance in the 1920s, the early 1930s saw a marked increase in strikes and labor organizing in Duluth. Particularly important for the mass of unorganized workers was a strike by unorganized longshoremen in spring 1931.

The struggle on the docks was fierce. In the early 1900s, the International Longshoremen's Association (ILA) had been a powerful union at the head of the lakes. But the ILA's hold on the docks had been broken by the anti-union drive that began in 1907. Sporadic activity on the docks by the IWW during the First World War had failed to establish any lasting organization and the open-shop drive of the early 1920s had swept away the last remnants of ILA organization among the roughly one thousand "muscle men" working on the docks. Only small locals of tugmen, marine firemen, marine engineers, and dredgers survived. Throughout the 1920s the employers paid well, but backed up by the Citizens' Alliance and Pinkerton detectives, they also crushed any attempt at organizing. Men suspected of union sympathies were fired. Bosses expected favors; for example, E. L. Slaughter, a young man working on the docks in 1930, was expected to hang storm windows at his boss's home.[64] Wage cuts announced in 1931 provoked the longshoremen into action. Employers responded by getting injunctions against picketing from the courts and by hiring strikebreakers. Police chief Barber deployed his men to enforce the order of the court and to protect the scab crews from union harassment. The result was a melee involving the police and some five hundred rock-throwing longshoremen. Eventually, despite strong objections from the Citizens' Alliance and with help from Mayor Snively and federal officials, a settlement was reached.[65]

Such violent confrontations were not unusual for labor conflicts in the United States prior to the 1930s, when the law permitted employers to refuse to bargain with employees and to hire replacement workers. Supported by a popular mandate in the election of 1932, President Franklin D. Roosevelt launched a series of programs aimed at lifting the country out of the Depression and bringing a "new deal" to the American people. Among these programs was the National Recovery Act, which aimed to end the "downward competition" in wage rates that had been provoked by the Depression. The National Recovery Act also included a system of voluntary employment codes. Employers who promised to adhere to the standards on minimum wages and maximum hours displayed the Blue Eagle of the National Recovery Administration. The National Recovery Act also provided for the Public Works Administration, which put unemployed people to work on federally funded projects. And buried in the act was section 7a, which for the first time in U.S. labor law history gave federal approval to the right of trade unions to organize and bargain collectively. While the labor provisions of the NRA ultimately failed to live up to the hopes of labor activists, the right to organize proclaimed in section 7a nevertheless set in motion a torrent of activity among working men and women who were hard pressed by the conditions created by the depressed economy.

In Duluth, there were strikes at Diamond Calk and Horseshoe, Cutler-Magners Cement, and among milk-truck drivers, tugmen, cold-storage workers, and laundry "girls"—all demanding union recognition. There were also organizing drives among beauty operators, street railway employees, bartenders, auto mechanics, coal- and ore-dock workers, at Patrick Knitting Mill, and among area lumberjacks.[66] For the most part, these were unskilled workers laboring in industries that had long and successfully resisted attempts to form unions. Large numbers of the workers involved were immigrants or children of immigrants who had seen earlier organizing efforts crushed. By affirming the right of workers to organize, section 7a seemed to remove the recourse to court-ordered injunctions that employers had used for so long to beat back unions in these basic industries.

The upsurge in labor activity in Duluth was part of a national pattern. During the 1920s, with business leaders lauded as architects of American prosperity and with militant opposition to labor unions from organizations like the Citizens' Alliance, membership in AFL unions had fallen from nearly five million in 1919 to fewer than three million in 1933. In the upsurge in labor activity in 1933 and 1934, AFL membership increased by nearly 900,000.[67] Responding to wage cuts, Depression conditions, and the apparent green light provided by section 7a of the National Recovery Act, workers in unorganized industries once again struggled to gain union recognition and collective bargaining power.

The upsurge in labor activity presented both an opportunity and a challenge to the American Federation of Labor. It was an opportunity to regain lost members and enroll new ones, but at the same time, the large and rapid expansion of membership threatened its existing trade union structure. Under the leadership of Samuel Gompers and William Green, the AFL had focused on organizing skilled workers into trade unions according to their specific skill. Critics of the AFL had long argued that modern industrial technology had made this "trade unionism" obsolete and ignored the mass of workers, many of them immigrants or women, working in America's basic industries. Under pressure from increasing grass-roots militancy and calls for industrial unions within the AFL coming from labor leaders like John L. Lewis of the United Mine Workers, in July 1933 national AFL president William Green agreed to an organizing drive in steel, auto, rubber, and other basic industries.[68] But the AFL still struggled with how to fit unskilled workers in basic industries into its federation of craft unions. Should workers at Diamond Calk and Horseshoe in Duluth be assigned to different unions depending on the specific task they performed, with some going to the machinists and some to the teamsters? This had been the traditional approach of the AFL, which was sensitive to the jurisdictional claims of its affiliated unions. But by dividing the workforce in a particular plant into many separate unions, this method made it almost impossible for workers to form powerful unions capable of compelling employers to engage in collective bargaining. On the other hand, to take all workers into any one existing craft union would likely lead to serious jurisdictional disputes between unions and to swamping the existing craft union with workers who did not share the particular needs or outlook of the skilled laborers traditionally represented by the trade union.

The AFL attempted to sidestep this problem by forming "federal unions" that would take in all workers at one plant. These federal unions would be directly affiliated with the national AFL, rather than with one of its established trade unions. Local 18650, organized at Diamond Calk and Horseshoe in September 1933, was one of these federal locals. Federal unions of iron miners were also formed in Virginia and Mountain Iron in February 1934.[69] However, leaders of the existing craft unions, determined to protect their jurisdiction over particular skills like operating a machine or driving a truck, often insisted on carving up the newly formed federal unions, thereby undermining grass-roots unity and solidarity. These jurisdictional conflicts destroyed many of the federal unions formed in 1934 and 1935. The Diamond Calk union survived.[70]

Beyond the jurisdictional difficulties, many of the leaders of the AFL were clearly less than enthusiastic about taking in masses of unskilled workers in basic industries. In Duluth, Anne McEwen, like John L. Lewis, had been urging the AFL to organize the unorganized since taking over *Labor World* in June 1933. She publicly expressed her frustration at the conservative leadership of the national AFL, and at one point urged her readers to ignore the advice of national AFL president Green. On another occasion she remarked that Frances Perkins, Secretary of Labor in the Roosevelt administration, had displayed more courage than Green.[71] But most of the leadership of the local AFL was closer to Green than to Lewis or McEwen. The Duluth AFL was slow to react to Depression conditions and the rising tide of grass-roots militancy. Only after four years of the Depression, in March 1934, did local AFL leaders finally announce a "Labor Forward" campaign. The campaign appears to have been provoked by an attempt to create a company union at the steel plant in Duluth. Such company unions were one way that businesses could appear to comply with the NRA codes without really engaging in collective bargaining. However, unlike the proponents of industrial unions, like Lewis, who favored the creation of a single union at the steel plant, the Labor Forward campaign brought in organizers from twenty existing craft unions, apparently to organize the unorganized workers at the steel plant into existing craft unions, an approach that would have divided workers at the plant into many separate unions.[72] Neither U.S. Steel nor the Labor Forward campaign succeeded at the steel plant. The idea of carving up the workforce into many craft unions went nowhere and the proposal to create a company union was overwhelmingly voted down by the employees.[73]

Radicals were involved in several of the unions organized in Duluth between 1933 and 1935. Communist organizers were involved in a strike at the Cutler-Magners cement plant in October 1933.[74] Communists were also involved in the formation of an AFL-affiliated union at Western Paint and Varnish, a subsidiary of the Marshall Wells Company. Organizing at Western Paint was spearheaded by Ernest Pearson, formerly of the IWW and a member of the Scandinavian Socialist local who had joined the Communist Party.[75] Having organized sufficient support among the employees, in December 1935 Pearson and Ed Drill, a younger left-wing activist working at the plant, approached management with a demand for union recognition and contract negotiations. The company responded with a lockout and the union countered by calling a strike. Eventually the union won recognition and a contract. The Western Paint local was affiliated with the AFL as a federal union, but the union retained its radical leadership—a leadership that viewed the conservative heads of the Duluth AFL as having betrayed the organizing attempt at Western Paint. (Pearson and Drille both believed that local AFL leaders had promised Seth Marshall that none of his company's plants would be organized.)[76]

Similar distrust of the AFL was present in the Timber Workers union, which was organized in the fall of 1935 and the spring of 1936. The AFL had long ignored the plight of the lumberjacks, who faced some of the worst conditions of any laborers in the area. Duluth was the command and supply center for the men and equipment for lumber camps in the surrounding area of northern Minnesota, northern Wisconsin, and northern Michigan. In fall 1935 a strike that began in a camp near Gheen began to spread among the lumber camps in northern Minnesota. Joe Liss and other IWWs were among the early leaders of the strike, along with Communist Party activists.[77] In Duluth, a benefit fundraiser was held by the local Finnish American Athletic Club, and IWW lumberjacks wounded in an organizing drive in Idaho spoke at the Finnish Work People's College in Smithville.[78] The 1935 strike failed, but the nucleus of a union survived to fight again. The union, based in Duluth, was Local 2776 of the International Sawmill and Timber Workers Union.[79] Although affiliated with the AFL and eventually with the Duluth Federated Trades Assembly, Local 2776 was led by radicals who had little in common with, and no trust of, the conservative leaders of the AFL. Martin Kuusisto, a Communist from Duluth who was active in organizing the union, later recounted this period: "Certainly the AFL didn't give a darn. They couldn't care less about the unorganized, unskilled workers."[80] This split between the conservative AFL and the radical unions formed in Duluth between 1933 and 1935 would prove to be a serious difficulty later in the 1930s.

In 1935, determined to put a lid on the local labor movement, the Citizens' Alliance led a fight against Local 19509 at Duluth Linen Supply. In April 1934, the unionized women working at Duluth Linen Supply had been said to be making the best wages for women in Duluth.[81] In August of that year, the union, all of whose officers were women, won a one-day strike.[82] But with the Supreme Court of the United States ruling that the National Recovery Administration was unconstitutional in May 1935, the company broke off relations with the union. In August 1935, the union, consisting of thirty women and eight men, went on strike. The central demand was for union recognition.[83]

The Linen Supply strike took on enormous symbolic importance. In 1934 the nation had experienced a great wave of labor unrest. In that single year there were over 1,800 work stoppages involving over 1.5 million workers.[84] Nationally prominent strikes in Toledo, San Francisco, and Minneapolis had resulted in serious violence and loss of life. Many employers viewed these developments with alarm. Convinced that unionization and collective bargaining were fundamentally incompatible with their ability and right to manage their own firms, these employers were determined to turn back the wave of labor activism. On the other side, men and women who saw their economic well-being as dependent on the arbitrary will of the bosses were determined to seize this opportunity to assert their rights as human beings.

In Duluth, the *Labor World* saw the Linen Supply strike as a fight to the finish between organized labor and the Citizens' Alliance. Noting that Duluth Linen Supply had turned control of the strike over to A. Foster, secretary of the Citizens' Alliance, the Duluth Federated Trades Assembly put out a pamphlet starkly framing the strike as a battle between the Citizens' Alliance and organized labor, calling on all labor unions to aid the strikers. Headlines in the *Labor World* proclaimed, "We Accept the Challenge," and aid for the "laundry girls" came from the Coal Dock Workers, the Longshoremen, the Electrical Workers, and the Minnesota Federation of Labor.[85] The Nicollet Tavern, a union establishment, supplied food to the striking laundry girls.[86] On the other side, the Citizens' Alliance hired scab crews and armed guards to protect them. Foster, the Citizens' Alliance secretary, told the union that he would "die with a shotgun in my hand rather than recognize your union."[87]

In January 1936, despite litigation and some violence, the strike was finally settled with the union winning recognition and a contract.[88] But as important as the Linen Supply strike may have been, Duluth Linen, with its thirty-eight employees, was dwarfed by the still unorganized U.S. Steel, which owned the steel plant, the cement plant, the ore docks, and the DM&IR railway. The powerful steel trust had succeeded in evading the NRA and in fighting off an attempt at organization by the Amalgamated Association of Iron, Steel, and Tin Workers in June 1934, despite strong grassroots support for unionization.[89] While workers in West Duluth had made significant gains, with new unions formed at Diamond Calk, Western Paint, and on the coal docks, the steel industry, so important in Duluth, remained unorganized. Organization of the union at the steel plant would come only with the help of the Steelworkers Organizing Committee of the CIO.

The situation in Duluth was typical of the nation at large in the mid-1930s where, despite the wave of grass-roots activism, basic industries like steel, automobiles, rubber, and electrical manufacturing remained unorganized. John L. Lewis and others who had been urging the AFL to take more strenuous action feared that a historical opportunity for labor would be lost. In October 1935, the American Federation of Labor held its annual convention in Atlantic City. Lewis and the supporters of industrial unionism "lost vote after vote on the convention floor" to conservative union leaders who favored the traditional craft union approach and who "reaffirmed traditional [negative] views of mass production workers."[90] In November 1935, frustrated with the AFL leadership, Lewis, David Dubinsky, Sidney Hillman, and other labor leaders who shared a commitment to organizing industrial unions in basic industries formed the Committee for Industrial Organization (CIO) (later renamed the Congress of Industrial Organizations). William Green and other AFL leaders denounced the CIO as a dual union that threatened to split the American labor movement. The CIO leaders, still officially operating as heads of unions within the AFL, ignored these criticisms and pressed ahead with plans for major organizing drives. Lewis recruited a corps of able organizers and in 1936 they formed the Steel Workers Organizing Committee (SWOC) and turned to the task of organizing the steel industry.

In August 1936, SWOC began an organizing drive in the Great Lakes region with Van Bittner, the regional director, in charge.[91] Bittner's first step was to make contact with local men who had already shown an interest in forming a union at the steel plant. Earl Bester was a key early contact. Bester was the son of an English immigrant working in the copper mines of Michigan's Upper Peninsula in the years before World War I. His father, a member of the Western Federation of Miners, was blacklisted after the failed strike of 1913. After serving in World War I, Earl Bester came to Duluth, where he worked for U.S. Steel at the Mesabi Railway yards. Fired for refusing to scab during a strike, he was given a second chance and hired at the steel plant in Duluth in 1921 as a crane operator. Having been involved with the IWW, Bester had become a Socialist around 1920. At the steel plant he became active in what remained of the AFL's Amalgamated Association of Iron, Steel and Tin Workers' Union. The Amalgamated, which had been a powerful union late in the nineteenth century, had been badly beaten by the steel trust in the national strikes of 1892 and 1919. Fingered by a labor spy in 1928, Bester and eleven other union members were fired, though two months later he was hired back at a lower status. Laid off as a result of the Depression in 1931, Bester was back working again in the steel plant in 1936, when he was recruited by Bittner to become an SWOC organizer.[92]

Other local activists recruited by SWOC to help organize the steel industry in the Duluth region were William Hartman, Martin Maki, and Joe Van Nordstrand. Maki and Van Nordstrand were both Communists. Maki and his wife, Toini, had grown up in the Finnish Communist movement on the Iron Range. In the early years of the Depression, he had helped organize the Communist-led hunger march from Virginia to the Duluth Court House. After that, he had turned to doing organizing work among the iron ore miners on the range.[93] Joe Van Nordstrand, operating under the alias of Joe Moreland, had been the organizer for District Nine of the Communist Party.[94] Like Maki, Van Nordstrand was an able and committed organizer who had developed extensive contacts among Communist and non-Communist labor activists in the region. Hartman was a gifted local organizer who worked at Interlake Iron; like Bester, he stood outside the Communist Party.

Cooperation between SWOC and the Communist Party was the result of an understanding reached at the national level between John L. Lewis, the driving force behind the CIO, and the national leaders of the American Communist Party.[95] Locally such cooperation built on work already done by Communist Party activists. Communists had been quietly trying to organize a union at the steel plant throughout the latter half of the 1920s. Arnie Arnio was a Communist involved in this work. Born in Finland in 1904, he had witnessed the miners' strike on the Iron Range in 1916. He was also involved in the railroad shopmen's strike in Duluth in 1922. Though he did not himself work at the steel plant, he was active in a Communist Trade Union Education League (TUEL) group in Morgan Park and West Duluth. During the 1920s members of this TUEL group met secretly with men who worked at the steel plant, with groups of South Slav and Italian workers from the steel plant turning out for these meetings.[96] Out of these efforts came a group of contacts who would later become a significant part of the nucleus for the union that would be formed at the steel plant in 1936.[97]

The work of local organizers like Bester and Arnio paved the way for the SWOC organizing drive in the steel plant that began in August 1936. The long and successful anti-union stance of U.S. Steel hung over the organizing effort. Earl Bester, now with a family to support, got a guarantee from SWOC that they would provide him a job if he was fired.[98] Contacts were made quietly by word of mouth to minimize danger to the men. Employees at the steel plant, long disgruntled by the antilabor stance of U.S. Steel, the abuses of power by foremen and higher management, and the invasive system of company spies, were eager to sign up with SWOC organizers. The company, getting word that the organizing drive was succeeding, tried to head off the union with a pay raise. By now, however, the long-accumulated sentiment in favor of a union was too strong. By September 16, with a membership of over four hundred, SWOC granted a charter to Local 1028, originally organized as a local of the Amalgamated Association of Iron, Steel and Tin Workers. The original officers for the local included William Hartman, president; George Bell, vice president; Joe Van Nordstrand, financial secretary; Harold Setter, treasurer; and Robert Huston, recording secretary.[99] Hartman and Van Nordstrand were on the staff of the regional SWOC, and the other men worked at the steel plant. In February 1937, Local 1028 elected a new slate of officers, made up entirely of men who worked in the steel plant, with Al Overton as president.[100] In March 1937, as part of a national settlement between the CIO and U.S. Steel, local employees came under their first union contract.[101]

The achievement of a contract and union recognition was almost universally welcomed in West Duluth and in Gary-New Duluth. Nearly everyone in these communities either worked at the steel plant or had relatives or neighbors who worked there. Many had lived through the Iron Range strikes of 1907 and 1916 and the national steel strike of 1919. They knew about the long hours at the plant, the insecurity of employment, the system of labor spies, the abuses of bosses who expected bribes for continued work or favorable treatment, and the invasive paternalism of the steel company. Union recognition and a union contract brought a seniority system and a grievance system that finally gave a degree of security and autonomy to steel company employees. The union was almost universally welcomed.[102]

Following the breakthrough at the steel plant, new unions appeared rapidly in several of the manufacturing shops of the West End, West Duluth, and Gary-New Duluth. In addition to the locals at the steel plant and the cement plant, new SWOC locals appeared at the Coolerator plants in West Duluth and New Duluth, at the Mesaba Ore Docks, at Clyde Iron, Marine Iron, National Iron, and at the scrap-iron yards.[103] Since all of these shops had something to do with the metal trades, all were organized originally as locals of the Amalgamated Association of Iron, Steel and Tin Workers, an old AFL union. However, unlike the Amalgamated of the nineteenth century, which was made up of highly specialized and skilled crafts, the new locals were industrial unions that included both skilled craftsmen and unskilled laborers. There were some tensions between these two groups. At National Iron, for example, skilled molders wanted to revive their old craft unions, which had

National Iron, Clyde Iron, and Marine Iron were among the metalworking shops organized by the Steel Workers Organizing Committee drive in Duluth. Photograph by Hugh
McKenzie; courtesy Northeast Minnesota Historical Center.

gone moribund during the open-shop 1920s, while the unskilled
men (who outnumbered the molders two to one) wanted to form
a new, inclusive, industrial local. A SWOC organizer met with the
men at the VFW bar to talk things over. Admiring the fighting spirit
of CIO head John L. Lewis and recognizing the need for a stronger union, the skilled men agreed to throw their lot in with the
new local.[104] The new SWOC locals brought union recognition and
union contracts to the manufacturing shops of western Duluth for
the first time in the history of the city. They also brought together
an ethnically and generationally divided membership galvanized by
SWOC's inclusively militant outlook.

Following the successful organization of the steel plant, the
next major labor battle in Duluth came at the two Coolerator plants.
Coolerator employed around 1,800 workers. Labor World identified
a strike at Coolerator in December 1936 as the first CIO strike in
the city and identified Coolerator Local 1096 as an Amalgamated
local organized by SWOC.[105] In fact, organization of the local began
well before the arrival of the SWOC in Duluth, with local radicals
playing a key role. The organizing effort at Coolerator was led by

Glenn Pearson, who was born on Raleigh Street in 1914 and lived there until about 1940. The son of parents active in the labor movement, Pearson was raised on Socialism and radical politics. At sixteen he served as chair of the Duluth Junior Farmer-Labor Party. Out of high school, he went to work at Coolerator, an ice-box manufacturing plant owned by Marshall-Wells.

Coolerator operated around the clock, with four six-hour shifts and seven-day work weeks. Pay was thirty-seven and a half cents per hour. In a single year, fifty-six fingers were lost in the plant. "We worked like the dickens and you might get fired in the morning and hired back in the afternoon.... That was their method of discipline, and everybody knew it," recalled Pearson.[106] In late 1935 or early 1936, Herman Griffith persuaded Glenn Pearson to try to organize a union at Coolerator. Griffith, an interior decorator, was an open Communist. He had helped Ernie Pearson organize the Western Paint local in 1934 and would have known Glenn Pearson through Ernie Pearson, Glenn's father. A twelve-man organizing committee was formed, which met in the garage of a carpet dealer who refurnished furniture. When the twelve men were found out, they were fired. But by December 1936, the union had enough members to call a strike. With the Wagner Act now in place, the company was forced to enter into negotiations with the union, eventually agreeing to union recognition, a 30 percent wage increase, new safety measures, and the restoration of jobs to the fired members of the organizing committee.[107]

Following rapidly on the December Coolerator strike was a major strike by lumberjacks in northern Minnesota, northern Michigan, and northern Wisconsin. Lumberjacks had organized Local 2776 of the AFL Carpenters and Joiners International during the sporadic strikes among timber workers in 1935. The vast majority of timber workers, however, remained unorganized and it was not until late 1936 that the union was really born as a powerful organization. With the strike, begun in January 1937, the lumberjacks finally won the union recognition that had eluded them for so long.

According to one study, at the end of the nineteenth century the timber industry employed sixty percent of all wage earners in the state of Minnesota.[108] Great stands of white pine covered much of the state, yielding as much as 150,000 board feet of lumber from a single acre of land. By 1910 most of the white pine was gone and the industry entered a steep decline. By 1932 production had fallen to only 7 percent of its peak year, the great sawmills of the past had given way to small portable mills, and the industry was dominated by independent contractors who hired their own men, ran their own camps, and sold wood to the large lumber companies. In the late 1930s there were around 250 such camps in the state of Minnesota, employing at most several hundred men per camp.

The industry was highly competitive and prices were set by the lumber companies. The small contractors competed among themselves to supply the wood at the stipulated price and make enough profit to stay in business. Contractors were forced to reduce their production costs as much as possible. The development of this system of independent contractors eroded gains won in the aftermath of the IWW-led "revolt of the timber beasts" in 1917. By the mid-1930s, conditions in the lumber camps were as bad as ever: "muzzle-loader bunks" were so close together that they could only be entered by crawling in from the foot; there were straw-stuffed gunny sacks for mattresses; sixty men were packed into dark, close, unventilated bunkhouses; and there were no bathing or washing facilities, but plenty of lice and bedbugs.[109]

These were the conditions that provoked the strikes of 1935. The experience of 1935, however, had made it clear that strikes against independent contractors could not improve conditions since "the individual contractors were unable to grant concessions even if they so wanted."[110] What was needed was an industry-wide collective bargaining agreement. With this end in view, organizers called a meeting of representatives from lumber camps across the region to discuss a fight for an industry-wide settlement.

The meeting was held the last week of December in an old employment office on Michigan Street in Duluth. Delegates came from sixteen camps in the surrounding area and represented some 1,500 lumberjacks. While the meeting was officially a meeting of Timber Workers Local 2776, most of the delegates represented unorganized men. The delegates drew up a list of demands, including a minimum of fifty cents per hour, an eight-hour day, washing and bathing facilities in each camp, compliance with state regulations regarding industries, and union recognition. When the contractors refused to accede to these demands, a strike was called. By January 5, logging operations were shut down in 70 percent of the camps in the surrounding area. With temperatures dipping to 40 degrees below zero, striking lumberjacks flooded into the Bowery area in Duluth around Michigan Street and Fifth Avenue West.

Many of the men had no money. In some cases logging contractors had confiscated the backpacks in which the men carried their worldly belongings, holding them as security against debts for transportation and food contracted by the men while working in the camps. Emergency food kitchens were established. Many small businessmen contributed to the support of the striking lumberjacks. The Finnish Nicolett Tavern owners, Mr. and Mrs. Urpo Kyto, who had provided food for the striking laundry girls, donated their entire one-hundred-room hotel to the striking lumberjacks for the duration of the strike.[111]

Known for drinking and carousing when in town with money in their pockets, lumberjacks were seen differently by some who knew them firsthand. Many of the "Knights of the Winding Way" were men who had come to America to rise in the world, but who had ended up going nowhere. Wandering from camp to camp, with nothing to show for their hard labor, dispirited, ashamed to let

Meeting of Timber Workers Local 29 in Duluth, 1946. Seated at the table with gavel in hand is Ilmar Koivunen. Photograph by Gallagher Studio; courtesy Minnesota Historical Society.

their families know what had become of them, timid, gentle, and self-mocking in their humor, many lumberjacks were men of culture and education who, unable to express themselves in English, had endured the miserable conditions in the camps and the abusive treatment of some of the bosses.[112] While many of the lumberjacks were Finns and Scandinavians, Irish and "American" men were also found in the camps. American Indians also worked as lumberjacks. At one point both the president and vice president of the Timberworkers' Local, Fred Lequier and Jim Rogers, were American Indians.[113] Organizer Ilmar Koivunen, a Finnish Communist who would later serve as president of the Timber Workers Union, confirmed the gentleness of the lumberjacks, at least while they were sober, and noted that business agents for the union who sometimes traveled to remote areas with three or four thousand dollars on them were never robbed.[114]

Some of the lumberjacks involved in the 1937 strike had also taken part in the IWW strike in 1917. Two of the strike leaders in 1937, Joe Liss and Oscar Rissberg, were among these old Wobblies.[115] In 1917 the lumberjacks' strike had been broken by scab crews and gunmen hired by the lumber companies and aided by law enforcement officials. Things were different in 1937, with Elmer Benson of the Farmer-Labor Party sitting in the governor's chair in St. Paul. Instead of sending deputies to break the strike, Benson sent a truckload of grapefruit to the striking lumberjacks and used the power of his office to persuade the Timber Producers' Association to sign a contract with the union.[116]

Not everyone in Duluth was so supportive. During the strike, the Duluth newspapers "played the role of experts at confusion," wrongly announcing several different times that the strike was over.[117] To keep the lumberjacks informed about the true state of the strike, Joe Liss enlisted the help of Irene Paull to publish a newsletter that would enable Local 2776 to communicate with the striking lumberjacks and the public at large. Paull, a Duluth Communist, was married to attorney Henry Paull, who would go on to do a substantial amount of legal work for the Timber Workers Union and who was badly beaten up in July 1937 by vigilantes led by a lumber company foreman.[118] After the strike was successfully settled and Timber Workers Local 2776 became established as one of the largest unions in the area, Irene Paull, now joined by Sam Davis, another Communist from Duluth, began producing *The Timber Worker*, a weekly newspaper published by Local 2776 for

Henry Paull, recognized by his peers as a skilled attorney, provided legal services to the Timber Workers and to other left-wing causes. Courtesy Mike Paull.

Irene Paull was both a radical activist and a gifted writer of journalism and fiction. Courtesy Mike Paull.

its members. Written with spirit and humor, the newspaper celebrated the newfound strength of the lumberjacks and preached a militant solidarity with all working people.[119]

With its recent victories at the steel plant, Coolerator, and in the lumber camps, in spring 1937 the labor movement in Duluth was stronger than it had ever been before. Beneath the surface, however, there was a developing rift that would deeply divide the local labor movement for over a decade. As early as August 1936, William Green, the national president of the AFL, had suspended the ten CIO unions from the AFL, charging them with practicing dual unionism. National CIO leaders took no official action and continued to act as a committee of leaders of AFL unions.[120] In spring 1937, Green decided to force the issue, ordering local AFL bodies to expel all CIO unions. Accordingly, by order of William Green, in June 1937 the Duluth Federated Trades Assembly expelled the nine

MIDWEST LABOR

(Successor to The Timber Worker)

Published every Friday by Midwest District Council No. 12 of the International Woodworkers of America, (Affiliated with Committee for Industrial Organization).

Room 14, Winthrop Bldg., Duluth, Minn., Phone: Melrose 1002
(325 West First Street)

MIDWEST DISTRICT COUNCIL EXECUTIVE BOARD:
President, Oscar Risberg, Duluth; Vice President, Herman Olson, Park Falls, Wis.; Secretary-Treasurer, Matt Savola, Ironwood, Michigan.
BOARD MEMBERS: Minnesota—James Rogers, Ilmar Koivunen, Herbert Johnson; Wisconsin—Victor Lundmark, Wallace LaFay, Fred Nordin; Michigan—George Rahkonen, Wilho Wilkilla, Lester Stolberg.

NEWSPAPER MANAGEMENT COMMITTEE:
Matt Savola, Ernest Tomberg, Charles Jarvi, P. R. McGraw.

Editor P. R. McGraw

OFFICIAL ORGAN OF:
Minnesota Lumber and Sawmill Workers Local No. 29 (C.I.O.)
Wisconsin Lumber and Sawmill Workers Local No. 72 (C.I.O.)
Michigan Lumber and Sawmill Workers Local No. 15 (C.I.O.)
Duluth Steel Plant Lodge Local No. 1028 of the Amalgamated Association of Iron, Steel and Tin Workers (C.I.O.)
Duluth Western Paint and Varnish Union (C.I.O.)
Letonia, Minn. Miners Lodge Local No. 1442 of Amalgamated Association of Iron, Steel and Tin Workers (C.I.O.)
Clyde Iron Works, Local No. 1424 of the Amalgamated Association of Iron, Steel and Tin Workers (C.I.O.)

SUBSCRIPTION — — — — — — — — $1.50 PER YEAR

NOVEMBER 25, 1937

The Workers and Farmers

Editorial information for Midwest Labor *for November 25, 1937, listing early CIO unions in Duluth. Courtesy Labor World.*

CIO locals that up to that point had been formed in Duluth. The unions expelled were the Amalgamated Clothing Workers Local at the Patrick Knitting Mill, the Clyde Iron Local, the Textile Workers at the Klearflax Rug Factory, Local 1210 at the Cement Plant, Local 1028 at the Steel Plant, the Newspaper Guild, the American Tar and Chemical Workers Union representing workers at Interlake Iron and Zenith Furnace, the National Iron Local, and a local of the United Automobile Workers that had been organized among mechanics working in auto repair shops in Duluth. (The Coolerator Local had been expelled earlier, supposedly on jurisdictional grounds.) There was no protest after the expulsion order was read.[121] The expelled CIO unions immediately announced their intention to form their own central labor body.

The CIO Duluth Industrial Union Council held its founding meeting on June 21, 1937.[122] The expelled CIO unions were almost immediately joined by the large Coolerator Local and by the Western Paint Local, whose radical leadership undoubtedly sympathized with the CIO. Indeed, Edwin Drill from the Western Paint Local was elected as the first president of the CIO Council at the founding meeting. Other unions soon followed Western Paint in leaving the AFL for the CIO. Among them were the National Maritime Local, which had been formed among sailors on the Great Lakes; the Marine Iron, Ore Dock, and Paper Calmenson Scrap Iron locals, each formed as Amalgamated locals with ties to SWOC; two unions of WPA workers; and the Timber Workers Union. Now organized as Local 29 of the CIO International Woodworkers of America,

The Duluth Industrial Union Council, a delegated body of all C.I.O. Unions in the City of Duluth is laying plans for the Convention of all state C.I.O. unions to be held in Minneapolis December 10th, 11th and 12th. Officers of the Council are as follows: Seated: Ralph J. Bondy, Secretary-Treasurer; P. R. McGraw, Secretary; Ervin Drill, President; Richard Schoenberger, Vice President; Genevieve Simon, Reading Clerk. Standing: Nels Strand, Trustee; Ed. Drill, Trustee; E. Westin, Sergeant at Arms; Roy B. Tritchler, Trustee. They are the first officials of the C.I.O. Council established after expulsion of C.I.O. unions by the A.F.L.

First elected officers of the CIO Council in Duluth. From Midwest Labor, *October 15, 1937. Courtesy Labor World.*

10-ACT Floor Show

AND
"FRENCHY" La BROSSE'S
Famous Swing Orchestra

Royal Entertainment
At Commoner's Price

Only 40c
Per Person

LOIS BROOKS
Mistress of Ceremonies heads the show.

GREET the DELEGATES TO THE CIO STATE CONVENTION

SAT. NITE
MAY 13th

SPALDING HOTEL
AUSPICES DULUTH CIO INDUSTRIAL COUNCIL.

"Frenchy" La Brosse's Orchestra played for many CIO functions. J. W. La Brosse was a CIO activist in the pattern shop at Clyde Iron Works. This notice is from Midwest Labor, *May 12, 1939. Courtesy* Labor World.

the Timber Workers brought with them their newspaper, renamed *Midwest Labor*, which became the voice of the CIO in Duluth.[123]

With the Timber Workers, the Steel Plant local, the Cement

Plant local, the Coolerator local, and the Marine Iron local, the Duluth CIO included the largest unions in the area. With *Midwest Labor*, the Duluth CIO had its own newspaper. The CIO unions also had strong popular support throughout the West End, West Duluth, and Gary-New Duluth. The Steel Workers Organizing Committee had begun its work in Duluth in August 1936. It found a reservoir of support for industrial unionism deeply rooted in the history of Duluth and the surrounding area. Building on this reservoir of support and the past work of local activists, SWOC organizers had set to work. In less than a year, a powerful coalition of industrial unions had been established. At the first convention of the Minnesota CIO, held at the Dyckman Hotel in Minneapolis in December 1937, CIO leaders from Duluth played leading roles. Representing Steel Plant Local 1028, SWOC organizer Joe Van Nordstrand from Duluth was elected vice chairman of the Minnesota CIO. In a prepared greeting to the assembled delegates, Van Nordstrand spoke with pride about Steel Plant Local 1028 and with confidence about the future ahead: "Our Lodge, the first union organized under the great C.I.O. campaign, extends greetings and a clear expression of confidence that with the coordination of the great C.I.O. membership in Minnesota we will be able to go forward all together to unity in the labor movement, better working conditions for all Minnesota labor and ... [to] the complete organization of Minnesota Labor."[124]

the popular front

WHEN JOE VAN NORDSTRAND TOOK OFFICE AS THE NEWLY elected vice chair of the Minnesota CIO, he was a paid organizer for the Steel Workers Organizing Committee (SWOC), a representative of Local 1028 of the Amalgamated Association of Iron, Steel, and Tin Workers, and a leader of the CIO Industrial Union Council in Duluth. He was also a member of the Communist Party, who, under the name of Joe Moreland, had been serving as organizer for District Nine of the party before going on staff as a SWOC organizer for the CIO.

Van Nordstrand was not the only Communist playing an active role in the CIO in Duluth. Ilmar Koivunen and Martin Kuusisto of Timber Workers Local 29 were both Communists. Ernie Pearson, one of the key organizers of the Western Paint and Varnish Local, was a Communist. Ernie's son Glenn, organizer and leader of the large Coolerator Local was, if not himself a Communist, close to the Communist Party, as were Edwin and Ervin Drill, the leaders, respectively, of the Western Paint and the Steel Plant Locals. Joe Paszak, a leader of the Cement Plant Local, was a Communist. Ed Drill and Joe Paszak would both serve terms as president of the CIO Council in Duluth. Pat McGraw, from the Coolerator Local, who would serve as a secretary for the council, was, if not a party member, at least very close to the Communists. Two of the local CIO unions, the National Maritime Union representing Great Lakes sailors in Duluth and the Fur Workers, had significant Communist Party leadership at the national level. *Midwest Labor*, the weekly CIO newspaper published in Duluth, was edited by Sam Davis, the 1934 candidate for governor of Minnesota on the Communist Party ticket. Communist Party member Irene Paull was a regular writer for *Midwest Labor*, and a number of Finnish Communists, Ilmar Koivunen among them, served on the newspaper's editorial board.[1]

age Hike

"No Sales Tax"

) Gets
ise for
Crews

nn.—A 52 per
piece rates was
esota Local 29
al Woodwork-
IO; at the four
erated by the
timber opera-
Grand Marais.
ates went into
ay, Sept. 23.

Friday
as granted last
men in the
oted the night
y would leave

'ollowing the

JOE VAN NORDSTRAND

LABOR BOARD TO

Defen
Air
Fun

MINNEAPOI
hart, internat
tive of the U
dicted last W
federal grand
ing alleged i
regard to the
onstrations.
posted the ne
and he was r
Charge again
"conspiring" t
28 of the relie
Wishart's ac
demonstration
speaking to r
demonstrating
serving on t
Committee. V
opposed viole
and he urged
to be provoke

Joe Van Nordstrand (Joe Moreland) in Midwest Labor, *September 29, 1939. Courtesy* Labor World.

While Communist Party members constituted only a fraction of the membership of CIO unions in Duluth and were a minority among those active in the local CIO Industrial Union Council, they held key leadership positions within a number of the Duluth unions and within the CIO Council. These leaders enjoyed strong support from a wider circle of activists and rank-and-file union members. With the notable exception of Sam Davis, the Communist Party memberships of these CIO leaders were not known to union members or the public at large, who considered these CIO leaders to be progressives who cooperated with a wider circle of supporters within the CIO and the Farmer-Labor Party to advance a shared set of aims.

Communist involvement in the labor movement in Duluth resulted in part from a decision made by the Soviet-dominated Communist International, the Comintern, at the Seventh Comintern Congress in August 1935. Having taken an ultra-radical stance in the late 1920s and early 1930s, and having grown alarmed by the rise of fascism in German and Italy, the Comintern decided in 1935 to form alliances with more moderate forces in political and labor movements around the globe. In Duluth this meant that the Communists turned from denouncing Floyd B. Olson and the Farmer-Labor Party to cooperating with the Farmer-Laborites. It also meant leaving behind the Communist strategy of the late 1920s, which was to form radical unions independent of the AFL, in favor of cooperating with the AFL. In Duluth, local Communists studied the work of Georgi Dimitroff, the Bulgarian Communist who championed the change of direction within the Comintern. Acting in accordance with this change of direction, local Communists became active within the Farmer-Labor Party and the local labor movement. They played important roles in organizing several of the federal unions that joined the AFL in 1935, like the Western Paint, Coolerator, and Timber Workers locals, and in SWOC when it was formed in 1936 as a CIO committee working within the AFL.[2] When the AFL expelled the newly formed CIO unions, most of the Communists then active in the labor movement found themselves in the CIO.

Reflecting the new Comintern policy of seeking unity with all progressive forces, however, the Communists continued to reach out to the AFL, seeking cooperation between the AFL and the CIO unions and pursuing an eventual restoration of unity in the labor movement. This general orientation of the Communists after 1935 to seek cooperation with all "progressive forces" is known as the policy of the "Popular Front." During the Popular Front period, the Communists postponed revolutionary goals to the distant future, concentrating instead on organizing a broad alliance of all "progressive" forces working for peace, justice, racial equality, and the amelioration of poverty.

To build such progressive movements, during the Popular Front period the Communist Party created a number of organizations designed to enlist non-Communists in social movements to further these progressive ends and foster unity between Communists and progressive non-Communists. Among the earliest of these "front" organizations was the American League against War and Fascism.[3] In October 1935 the league sponsored a Lake Superior Conference against War and Fascism at the Moose Temple Auditorium in Duluth. Participating in the conference was an impressive array of local organizations, including churches, labor unions, and Farmer-Labor clubs. Among the prominent people involved were Rabbi Harvey Wessel, Reverend Henry Adlard, Reverend Lewis

Dunnington, and nationally known Duluth novelist Margaret Culkin Banning.[4] Herman Griffith was the person responsible for putting this conference together. The son of a prosperous businessman and himself a successful interior decorator, Griffith had the kind of education and social connections that made him well-suited to the work of building cooperative movements. He was publicly known to be a Communist, having announced his membership in the Communist Party at a meeting of the Trades Assembly, where he had asked to speak on behalf of an antiwar association.[5]

The American Youth Congress (AYC) was perhaps the most successful of the united front organizations within which the Communists participated. The AYC was an umbrella organization with which other youth organizations were affiliated. In addition to the Young Communist League (YCL), the AYC included the Young People's Socialist League (YPSL), the Boy Scouts, the Girl Scouts, the Young Zionists, the YMCA, the YWCA, and a wide variety of church youth groups.[6] Like the American League against War and Fascism, the AYC passed resolutions condemning fascism and supporting peace. But the organization also addressed the pressing economic problems facing young people in the Depression era, supporting, for example, passage of the American Youth Act, which would have provided vocational training and public works jobs at twenty-five dollars a week for young people who were unemployed.[7] The organization had the support of Eleanor Roosevelt and other prominent people. By 1939, its affiliated youth groups included nearly five million members. Although the vast majority of these members were not Communists, Communists played leading roles in the activities of the AYC.

The experience of Leata Wigg was typical of many youth who joined the AYC. Wigg graduated from high school in 1935. After a year at Duluth Junior College, she enrolled at the University of Minnesota. Her parents were not politically active, but Wigg got caught up in progressive political activity as a university student. She demonstrated against the Japanese invasion of Manchuria and joined the boycott of silk stockings popular on college campuses at that time. She joined the campus Farmer-Labor youth group and worked for the election of Elmer Benson in 1936. Along with thousands of other students, she heard Clarence Hathaway, secretary of the Communist Party of Minnesota, speak at the Minneapolis Auditorium. She joined picket lines where workers were on strike and went door to door registering voters. Eventually she joined the YCL and became active in the work of the AYC. In 1938 she attended a YCL summer camp in New York. When she returned to Duluth in 1939, she began serving as secretary of the Duluth Youth Council, which was affiliated with the AYC. It was through the Duluth Youth Council that Leata Wigg met her future husband, Glenn Pearson, who worked at Coolerator, was a leader of Local 1096, and was active in the CIO Council.[8]

Not surprisingly, theirs was not the only romance born in the Youth Council in Duluth. George and Rhoda Dizard also met there. George Dizard was in high school from 1932 to 1936. His parents were immigrants, his father from Switzerland and his mother from Denmark. His mother, who had worked in a boardinghouse in New Duluth, imparted a strong sense of racial equality and love of peace to him. His father was unemployed during the Depression and the family briefly moved to Milwaukee in search of work. Dizard worked spotting pins in a bowling alley. There he picked up radical ideas from an old Norwegian man and from his reading of the critique of capitalism by Episcopal Bishop William Montgomery Brown. After returning to Duluth, Dizard endured the humiliation of being offered charity tickets for noontime meals, which he refused. Like Wigg, Dizard joined with other radical students at Central High School to arrange a forum on the Japanese invasion of Manchuria and the Italian invasion of Ethiopia. Herman Griffith was one of the three speakers at the forum. After graduating from high school, Dizard enrolled at the Teachers College in Duluth. Forced to leave for lack of money, he found work upgrading railroad tracks and digging ditches on a National Youth Administration project, a kind of WPA for young people.[9]

Rhoda Levine grew up in the Jewish community in Duluth. She was a cousin of Irene (Levine) Paull and Stanley (Yank) Levine, who were both active in left-wing circles in Duluth in the 1930s. Like her cousins, Rhoda Levine came from a relatively nonpolitical family. Her parents were active members of the Orthodox Temple at Third Avenue East and Third Street and her father was a successful businessman. But like Irene Paull, Rhoda Levine applied the social justice values learned from her Jewish upbringing to the problems of the Depression-era world. By the late 1930s she was active in the Youth Council in Duluth, arranging for an appearance in Duluth of a student from India who would speak on the social problems of the world from an Indian point of view.[10] Rhoda Levine met George Dizard at a Youth Council meeting in Duluth and they were married in December 1940.

A number of young people from Duluth attended a meeting

of the American Youth Congress in Lake Geneva, Wisconsin, in the summer of 1940. Leata Wigg, Glenn Pearson, George Dizard, and Anne Gerlovich packed into Glenn Pearson's new Buick and drove straight through.[11] This group played an important part in the life of the Popular Front in Duluth, supporting the newly formed unions and winning support from the CIO Council for the work of the Youth Council.[12] All of them played active roles in the Farmer-Labor Party in Duluth. Glenn Pearson was a leader at the Coolerator local. George Dizard would become one of the few Popular Front leaders active within the AFL, representing the Federal Local at Diamond Calk in the Trades Assembly and serving on a number of AFL committees.[13] Leata Pearson and Rhoda Dizard took time to care for their families in the early 1940s, but they supported the union activities of their husbands and remained politically active in the Farmer-Labor Party and a variety of other causes. Anne Gerlovich, the daughter of a Socialist father, worked for a number of years at the Klearflax Rug factory in West Duluth, where she was active in her union, Textile Workers Local 4, and in the Duluth and Minnesota CIO Councils. In 1942 she served as one of nine members of the Executive Board of the Minnesota CIO. Later Gerlovich married

Interior of Klearflax Linen rug factory, 1919. Courtesy Minnesota Historical Society.

Klearflax work crew, circa 1930. Courtesy Herbert Widell.

Roger Hargrave, a Lincoln Brigade veteran of the Spanish Civil War and secretary to Congressman John Blatnik.[14]

Along with the defeat of fascism and the preservation of peace, racial equality was one of the goals of the Popular Front. Particularly important were some legal defense battles waged in support of African Americans, whose legal and civil rights had been grossly abused. In Duluth, Communist Party members Alma Folely and Irene Paull led the fight to save the Scottsboro Boys, nine black youths convicted of raping two white women despite a lack of credible evidence and a deeply flawed trial. Harvey Klehr and John Haynes, two historians who are highly critical of the Communist Party, concede that "[f]or many black Americans the party was the only predominantly white organization willing to confront Southern racism head-on."[15]

Although the African American community in Duluth was not large and most factories in Duluth refused to hire blacks, African American men had been working at the steel plant since at least 1916. Some of these men were active in the CIO in Duluth, including Lee Wiley. He served as grievance officer for Local 1028 and played an active role in the Duluth CIO Industrial Union Council. Nary Joseph was another African American who was an active member of Local 1028.[16]

Blacks who worked at the steel plant were excluded from Morgan Park and lived in Gary-New Duluth, often in some of the worst available housing.[17] South Slavs working at the steel plant were also excluded from Morgan Park and lived in Gary-New Duluth. They tended to deny that there was any hostility or discrimination directed against African Americans in the steel plant or in Gary-New Duluth.[18] Nonetheless, black workers were relegated to the less desirable jobs. Many of them were assigned to work in the coke ovens, a job that was hot, dirty, and unhealthy. At least one South Slav claimed that blacks worked there because they liked the heat.[19] Another South Slav, noting that many of the black families brought to Duluth to work at the steel plant in 1917 had left Duluth in the early 1920s, attributed this exodus to dislike of the cold weather, without any mention of the 1920 lynching and the subsequent hardening of local attitudes toward African Americans.[20] Similar insensitivity to racism was apparent in the persistence of "black face" acts in vaudeville shows put on by the Gary Athletic Club in the 1920s.[21]

Insensitivity to racism was not limited to Gary-New Duluth. Indeed, discrimination against African Americans was prevalent throughout the whole of Duluth in the 1920s and 1930s. After the lynchings of 1920, black students at the Teachers' College could not be placed as student teachers in the public schools in Duluth and black workers were gradually driven out of jobs as waiters in

Blackface vaudeville from a show at the Gary Athletic Club, 1931. From Gary Athletic Club anniversary booklet, 1980. Courtesy Northeast Minnesota Historical Center.

hotels, restaurants, and clubs, as well as on ships on the Great Lakes. With the exception of the steel plant, most factories refused to hire black workers. African Americans were segregated in many movie theaters and forced to sit in the balconies. Many hotels and restaurants in Duluth would not serve African Americans and discrimination in housing was widespread.[22]

Most white Duluthians simply took these conditions for granted. If they were noticed at all, they were simply accepted as the way things were. Popular Front activists, however, challenged these long-standing discriminatory practices. SWOC activists demanded equal treatment for black workers at the steel plant, insisting on uniform wage rates and a seniority system for bidding on open positions. Popular Front leaders also carried this concern for racial justice and civil rights into the CIO Council. The left-led National Maritime Union (NMU), representing sailors in Duluth, had insisted on integrated crews in its deep-sea organizing, a position that left it open to race-baiting by U.S. Steel when the NMU tried to organize the Great Lakes.[23] In May 1942, with the country united in support of American armed forces in World War II, the Duluth CIO Council passed a resolution protesting the segregation of Negro draftees. The council also called for Negro representation on the local wartime Civilian Defense Council and it brought the fight against racism home, investigating reports of discrimination and taking action on a case involving an African American CIO member at the Hi-Spot restaurant in Duluth.[24] Popular Front activists persuaded the CIO Council to donate money to the NAACP.[25] A number of Popular Front activists joined the NAACP, with Ernie Pearson serving on the NAACP Board of Directors as a representative of the CIO Council.[26] Rhoda Dizard served on the Advisory Committee of the Duluth Interracial Council.[27] Edward Nichols, a longtime black activist in Duluth whose wife served as chair of the Interracial Council, later commented on the role of Communists among these Popular Front activists in Duluth: "The Communists tried to infiltrate into the National Association [NAACP] branch [in Duluth].... But I felt this way. I didn't give a darn who they were as long as they were willing to come along and help us in our cause. So we took them in. We took them in. And we kept control, but they helped us in our work."[28]

An appearance by Paul Robeson in Duluth illustrated both Popular Front support for racial equality and African American support for the Popular Front. Robeson, an athlete, singer, and actor, was one of a number of prominent African Americans who appreciated the support for racial justice that came from the Popular Front and he willingly aligned himself with it. During a strike at the Garon Knitting mill, then located in Duluth's West End, Robeson came to Duluth for a concert. The next day he showed up on the picket line maintained by the American Clothing Workers (ACW) local and sang two of his favorite labor songs for the women on the line. When Mr. Garon, the owner of the mill, invited Robeson up for a visit, Robeson replied that he would be happy to do so, but only after Garon signed a contract for better wages and working conditions. It should be noted here that despite Robeson's international renown, the staff at the Hotel Duluth, perhaps Duluth's finest hotel, refused to give him a room unless he used the back elevator. Earl Bester of the Steel Workers Organizing Committee, and Abe Polinski, a local businessman who shared the antidiscriminatory outlook of the Popular Front, were accompanying Robeson at the time. Bester credited Polinski with insisting on proper treatment of Robeson.[29]

Gender equality was not a conscious goal of Popular Front activists in the way that racial equality was. The feminist movement of the late nineteenth and early twentieth centuries had made significant advances. Along with the right to vote, women had gained the rights to own and control property, to be admitted to universities and professional schools, and to be divorced. Traditional gender roles persisted, however. The idea of gender equality had to some extent been eclipsed by the psychoanalytic claim that women were naturally destined for motherhood and a domestic existence. While psychoanalysis was less popular in left-wing circles than in the educated public as a whole, Popular Front activists, both men and women, tended to be like the general public in unquestioningly accepting traditional gender roles.

Within the CIO, most union members were men. Wives of union members joined women's auxiliaries, often meeting at the same time the men attended union meetings. The auxiliaries tended to perform support activities for the unions, ranging from providing coffee and donuts to men on picket lines to organizing social events and fund-raising. The Congress of Women's Auxiliaries (CWA) mirrored the CIO Council as an umbrella organization made up of representatives of the auxiliaries of the various CIO unions. Maney Pearson, wife of Ernie Pearson, was the longtime president of the CWA in Duluth.[30]

While the auxiliaries clearly played supportive roles, it would be a mistake to underestimate the importance of these organizations and the women who were active in them. The support functions played by the auxiliaries were crucial to the success of the unions. They helped to maintain the morale, solidarity, and resources necessary to keep the unions alive and capable of taking effective action. Women in leadership roles in the auxiliaries also developed important skills, ranging from the ability to run meetings and conduct fund-raising campaigns to public speaking and interaction with the mass media. Many women from the auxiliaries used these leadership skills in other organizations. Maney Pearson, for example, served a term on the executive board of the state Farmer-Labor Association (FLA) and Anne Gerlovich served on the executive board of the Minnesota CIO.[31] As these examples show, while the auxiliary system assigned women separate and unequal roles, women's activities were not restricted to those roles.

Nonetheless, with some notable exceptions, women were largely excluded from visible leadership roles in the CIO, the FLA, and other organizations within which the Popular Front was active. In this respect, the Popular Front organizations were no different from virtually all other organizations spanning the political spectrum. Gender separation and gender roles were simply features of the times, and they would not be widely questioned until the revival of feminism in the late 1960s and early 1970s, a time when Maney Pearson would talk about the injustices suffered by women and would become a spokeswoman for the Equal Rights Amendment.[32]

Some women did play important public roles outside the women's auxiliaries. Irene Paull, who wrote for and sometimes edited *Midwest Labor*, is a prominent example. Although women held jobs outside the home in unionized plants, in theory they were members of the unions with all the powers that membership brought. In practice, however, this was often not the case. In some factories there were even separate salary scales for men and women, a system that Popular Front leaders in the unions opposed and in some cases overcame.[33] Most leadership positions in the unions were held by men, even in unions like the American Clothing Workers (ACW), where most of the workers were women. There were some exceptions. In addition to Anne Gerlovich, who was active in Textile Workers Local 4, a member of the Duluth CIO Council, and served on the state CIO Executive Board, Pearl Larson served as representative of the ACW to the CIO Council.[34] Women also represented the Fur Workers on the council.[35]

Like the CIO, the Farmer-Labor movement provided an arena within which a number of women played leadership roles. With the exception of Lakeside, neighborhood clubs of the Farmer-Labor Association in Duluth were male-only affairs.[36] The women had their own separate clubs. But delegates from both the men's clubs and the women's clubs had formally equal status at the city-wide and county-wide conventions, where they sat alongside delegates from labor and farm organizations. While men held most of the leadership roles at city, county, and state conventions, some women were elected to fill these positions and a number of women played leadership roles at a high level within the Farmer-Labor Association.

A closer look at the annual meeting of the Duluth Farmer-Labor Women's Club in February 1938 identifies some of the women active in the Farmer-Labor movement in Duluth and provides a somewhat richer sense of what Duluth's Popular Front was like. Mrs. Ruth Siegler was elected president, replacing Mrs. Viena Johnson, who had served two previous terms. Mrs. Siegler's husband had been a leader in the railroad shopmen's strike in 1922. Although there is no evidence that either of the Sieglers was a Communist Party member, they were among the much larger circle of non-Communists who agreed with the goals of the Popular Front and who worked with others, including Communists, to reach those goals. The Sieglers had moved to Duluth in 1918. They built a house in Lakeside and were active in a church there. With young children in the 1920s, Ruth Siegler was not politically active, but later on she was. "In the 30s I was a delegate practically to every convention, state conventions and all," she recalled.[37]

The first vice president of the Farmer-Labor Women's Club was Pearl Griffith, wife of the openly Communist Herman Griffith. Pearl Griffith's name appears over and over as serving on Farmer-Labor committees of various kinds. The second vice president was Mrs. Robert Sermon. Her husband had been a Socialist since before the First World War. He had been active in the AFL Boilermakers Union before going into an engineering business of his own and had long been active on the left wing of the AFL and the right wing of the local Socialists. The secretary of the club was Miss Evelyn Sandberg. The treasurer was Sybl McGraw, wife of Pat McGraw, one of the key Popular Front leaders in the CIO. Delegates to the

Farmer-Labor county convention included Viena Johnson, Ruth Siegler, Maney Pearson, Mrs. Carl Falk, and Mrs. Sven Nelson. Alternate delegates were Mrs. Ed Drill, Mrs. O. H. Tarun, Mrs. E. R. Backstrom, and Mrs. Ingworth Erickson. Along with many others not mentioned here, nearly all of these women would play a significant part in the Farmer-Labor Party in Duluth over the course of one or two decades.[38] Only Pearl Griffith's husband was known to be a Communist. Viena Johnson, Ruth Siegler, Mrs. O. H. Tarun, and Mrs. Ingworth Erickson had all been active in the Farmer-Labor Party long before Communists entered the party in 1935. Like Ruth Siegler, Mrs. Tarun and Mrs. Erickson had husbands who were active on the left wing of the AFL, Otto Tarun from the Carpenters and Ingworth Erickson from the Machinists. Both men had been active in Farmer-Labor politics since the mid 1920s and Mrs. Erickson herself had served as president of the Progressive Women's League at that time.[39] Women like Siegler, Tarun, Erickson, and Johnson had been pursuing policies like those embraced by the Popular Front well before the Communists adopted a policy of forming a Popular Front around those issues. In a sense, then, it is more true that the Communists joined with them than that they joined with the Communists.

The same could be said of Viena Johnson, whom historian John Haynes identifies as a hard-core member of the Communist-dominated Popular Front.[40] Viena Rakel Pasanen grew up the daughter of Finnish immigrants in northern Minnesota. Her parents were radicals; as a child she was familiar with *Industrialisti*, the Finnish IWW newspaper, and she went with her parents to hear Socialist Party leader Eugene Debs speak. As a child she played the violin at meetings in the Finn Hall. Her parents were active in the Finnish co-op movement and in the struggle for industrial unions. From her youth, Viena Johnson acquired the belief that the AFL was unresponsive to the needs of immigrant industrial workers. When the Finnish-American labor movement split into Socialist, Communist, and IWW factions in 1919, her parents appear to have belonged to the IWW group, though Johnson describes herself as having become a Socialist in her youth and says that she came into the Farmer-Labor Party as a Socialist. Having studied violin at the Bush Conservatory in Chicago, she married George Johnson, a construction engineer, and moved to Duluth in the early 1930s.

Johnson quickly became a popular speaker at Farmer-Labor events, appearing with Floyd B. Olson on a platform in Fair-

For STATE SENATOR
57TH DISTRICT

Mrs. Viena P.
JOHNSON

Endorsed by FARMER - LABOR Ass'n.

Prepared and circulated by Mrs. Viena P. Johnson in her own behalf.

Running in the East End, Viena Johnson was never expected to win this campaign, but she played a leadership role in the Farmer-Labor Party in Duluth and Minnesota. Courtesy Minnesota Historical Society.

mount Park before a crowd of twenty-five thousand people.[41] She appeared on many platforms in Duluth. She was a frequent speaker at an annual Farmer-Labor summer festival held in Lincoln Park. She was one of the speakers at a rally for the striking Linen Supply girls in 1936, and a speaker on behalf of Republican Spain at both the IWW-connected Finnish-American Athletic Club Hall and at the Communist-connected Workers' Hall. She was a speaker against war and fascism at a meeting of the women's auxiliary of the Coke and Gas Workers Union of Interlake Iron, and at a meeting of the Slovene National Benevolent Society in Ely. She was invited to speak on the labor movement, Farmer-Labor politics, and the role of progressive women at a youth summer camp held at the Mesaba Co-op Park on the Iron Range near Cherry. She spoke at a meeting of the Chippewa Farmer-Labor Unit in Cloquet, also working with Herman Griffith, Mrs. Clarence Hemmingsen, and Governor Benson to address some Indian issues and to include Indian speakers at a Farmer-Labor rally in Duluth. She spoke at a peace rally sponsored by the Youth Council of Duluth and was herself a member of the Duluth Peace Council chaired by Judge Bert Fesler and Rev. L. L. Dunnington. She was a frequent speaker on politics on radio station WEBC.[42]

Soon after her arrival in Duluth, Viena Johnson was protesting against racial discrimination after seven hotels in Duluth, including all of the prominent ones, refused a room to a black scholar from New York. In 1934, she ran unsuccessfully on the FLP ticket for the Minnesota state senate seat from the wealthy East End. In 1935 she was one of the prominent speakers participating in the Lake Superior Conference against War and Fascism organized by Herman Griffith. In 1936, Johnson served as the FLP campaign manager for the city of Duluth. She was a two-term president of the Duluth Farmer-Labor Women's Club, a member of the Central Committee of the FLP in Duluth, and a member of the Executive Committee of the Eighth Congressional District of the FLP. Recommended by the St. Louis County FLP, she was named to the board of the Minnesota State Teachers College, eventually serving as board president. She also served on the Women's Advisory Committee for the WPA, overseeing projects involving women. In 1941 she became the Farmer-Labor Association's state secretary-treasurer and left Duluth for the Twin Cities.[43]

While far from complete, this list of activities gives a sense of the range of issues that Popular Front activists addressed. It should also be noted that Viena Johnson did all of this with two preteen daughters at home. While this level of activity was surely not typical of rank-and-file supporters of the Popular Front, it was not atypical of activists in leadership positions. Viena Johnson was a personal friend of Ernie and Maney Pearson, of Herman and Pearl Griffith, of Art and Ruth Siegler, and of many other Popular Front activists. Together they saw themselves as engaged in a struggle between the forces of light and the forces of darkness. They shared a sense of the historical importance of their time as a crossroads between an unjust past and a possibly better future. They poured their time, energy, and resources into this struggle. A sense of this self-perception is conveyed in a letter written by congressman-elect John T. Bernard to his campaign manager in Duluth, Viena Johnson:

> I find myself at a loss as to how to answer your splendid letter of congratulations. Knowing the sentiments and principles which are burning so ardently within you, I feel that I can talk to you as to one of my own kind. The only way that I can possibly repay you for your splendid support and co-operation is by giving you this pledge—that I shall do everything in my power, that I shall fight until the very end, so that right shall rule over might. The faith and confidence which those thousands of people have placed in me will never be betrayed. Two years from now when you will be reading my record in Congress, I assure you that you will be rather proud of it.[44]

This sense of being involved in a struggle between right and might in part reflected the crisis of the Depression in the United States, of the apparent worldwide collapse of free-market capitalism, and of the rise of fascism in Europe. But the passion that filled this self-understanding was also fueled by the personal history of individuals, their families, and their ethnic communities. For Viena Johnson and many other Popular Front activists, the work in which they were engaged was a continuation of the struggle for justice their immigrant parents had been engaged in. Like Viena Johnson, Ilmar Koivunen, Martin Kuusisto, and Martin Maki had all grown up in the radical Finnish community with a keen sense and acceptance of their parents' radical values. Glenn Pearson, the son of longtime Duluth radical Ernie Pearson, was also raised on Socialism.[45] Anne Gerlovich was the daughter of Carl Gerlovich, a crane operator at the steel plant and a Socialist.[46]

Other key people in the CIO and the Farmer-Labor Party who were active in the Popular Front coalition in Duluth were older people who themselves had connections to the radicalism of the past. Joe Liss and Oscar Rissberg, activists in the Timber Workers Local 29, had been Wobblies. Arnie Arnio had been radicalized by the IWW strike on the Iron Range in 1916 and had entered the Communist movement in the early 1920s. Einar Bjork, a Swedish immigrant who had served several terms as president of Local 1028, was the son of a Swedish Socialist.[47] O. P. Langdahl, an FLP candidate for the state legislature in 1936, had been active in the Duluth Scandinavian Socialist Local during the World War I era, as had Emil Strandin, campaign manager for the Arrowhead Farmer-Labor Club in the 1936 campaign, and Mr. and Mrs. Carl Falk.[48] Carl Carlson was secretary of the Arrowhead Farmer-Labor Club in 1936 and one of the most important Farmer-Labor figures in Duluth. He was also a leader of statewide importance in the Good Templars Lodge. During World War I he had been openly critical of the war and had written a defiant reply to a threatening letter sent to him by the local public safety commission.

O. E. Thompson, a leader of the old Scandinavian Socialist Local, was another important figure in the Farmer-Labor movement in the 1930s, serving on the committee of the Lake Superior Conference against War and Fascism. Sig Slonim, another Farmer-Labor activist in the 1930s, was a longtime Socialist who had been the lead lawyer in Duluth defending the IWWs during the miners' strike of 1916. Robert Sermon, also a Socialist and an FLP activist in the 1930s, had been a member of the left-wing AFL Boilermakers Union during the World War I era.[49] Michael O'Rourke, active in the FLP during the 1930s, was an Irish railroad engineer who had thrown his lot in with the Scandinavian Socialist Local before the First World War. Several of these men—Carl Carlson, O. E. Thompson, Robert Sermon, and Michael O'Rourke—served together on the executive board of the Central Political Committee of Labor and Farmers of Duluth and Southern St. Louis County in 1936.[50]

A sense of historical mission was part of the self-consciousness of both leaders and rank-and-file activists within the CIO and the FLP. Irene Paull spoke about this under the heading "We Are Pioneers" in her popular "Calamity Jane" column in *Midwest Labor* in August 1937, shortly after her husband, union attorney Henry Paull, had been beaten up by vigilantes:

> Dozens of Jacks have told me what this Union means to them. That before the Union, life was hardly worth liv-

ing, and now a new and shining path spreads out before them. Well, brothers, I thank you because your Union has opened up a shining path not only for you, but also for me. For once in my life I have the chance to change a system that I've always hated, to help my brothers build a future for themselves and the men who will come after them, to help to make out of this beautiful country a better America for my own child to live in. Our forefathers were the pioneers who carved a nation out of this wilderness. But are we not also pioneers, we who are building unions of the working class, we who are developing a Farmer-Labor movement ... are we not pioneering in a wilderness of greed and injustice and human misery, and will we not carve, inch by inch, through a jungle of vigilante beasts and barbarous police, a new America? An America that will belong to the people who built it ... with happiness, security, and plenty for all?[51]

A similar sense of the historical significance of the unions and the Farmer-Labor movement is present in work done during the 1930s as part of the Workers Education Project under the auspices of the WPA in Duluth. Sponsored by local unions, labor history courses were frequently offered, along with courses in the English language, parliamentary procedure, accounting, and other topics. Unemployed men with skills in research and writing were also put to work chronicling the history of the labor movement in northeastern Minnesota.[52]

This sense of history reached down to rank-and-file activists. In December 1936, local activists organized a reunion of the Scandinavian Socialist local. In an article in *Midwest Labor*, lumberjack John D. Nelson recalled the progressive labor politics of the club; members' outrage at the lynching of the antiwar Finn, Olli Kiukkonen, in Lester Park in 1918; and the Wobblie past of the recently deceased Farmer-Labor governor, Floyd B. Olson.[53] Another example of this sense of history was a meeting of steel plant Local 1028 in October 1938. Matt Daley was a speaker at the meeting, where he was made an honorary member of the local. Eighty years old and a union man for forty-four years, Daley talked about his experiences as a steelworker during the strike in Homestead, Pennsylvania, in 1892, a strike in which his wife was killed by a militiaman's bullet. Under the sponsorship of the Scandinavian Local, then affiliated with the Communists, Daley had been a frequent speaker at Woodman Hall in the early 1920s.[54] A sense of history is also evident in the numerous testimonials from rank-and-file union members about how the unions had finally put an end to many of the unfair labor practices they and their families had experienced in the past.[55]

While correcting the unfair conditions facing working men and women and their families in northern Minnesota provided the foundation of support for the Popular Front in Duluth, Popular Front leaders consistently urged their supporters to join a variety of "progressive" causes. Farmer-Labor and CIO groups lent their support to organizations fighting against fascism and in favor of peace and racial justice. *Midwest Labor* urged its readers to support China in its struggle against Japanese imperialism.[56] It supported a protest at Leif Erickson Park against the German invasion of Czechoslovakia.[57] It condemned anti-Semitism at home and abroad.[58] It celebrated the victory of Joe Louis, an African American, over Max Schmeling, a German prizefighter who had expressed his Nazi sympathies.[59] It supported the Republican cause in Spain, frequently providing news of local men fighting in the Republican ranks.[60] It ran features on problems faced by working women, offered rebuttals to the charges that women were taking jobs that ought to have gone to male heads of families, and supported Popular Front activists working against the dismissals of women from WPA jobs.[61] It publicized the indignities and poor conditions faced by unemployed men housed at the Bethel, a charitable institution for indigent men.[62] It publicized the problem of substandard housing in Duluth and the need to create affordable housing for the poor.[63] It talked about the problems faced by young people, the need for recreational facilities for youth, and the importance of providing financial assistance to young families.[64] After cuts to WPA jobs for the unemployed were proposed in 1938, *Midwest Labor* provided sympathetic portraits of families dependent on WPA jobs, supported Popular Front activists in fighting the proposed cuts, and supported the Workers' Alliance, a union of WPA workers that fought on behalf of their members and all unemployed workers.[65]

The Depression, the wave of labor unrest, and the success of Farmer-Labor gubernatorial candidate Floyd B. Olson in 1932 and 1934 had drawn significant numbers of newcomers into the FLP in Duluth. Many of these newcomers were sympathetic to the outlook of the Popular Front, and they gave their support to Popular Front activists within the FLP. By spring 1935, seeing that the local FLP had slipped out of its control, the local AFL severed its official connection to the FLP in Duluth, reaffirming its traditional nonpartisan position.[66] This left the local FLP largely in the hands of activists sympathetic to the orientation of the Popular Front. With the establishment of the CIO unions and the CIO Industrial Union Council, leaders of the Popular Front in Duluth gained a second important base of support. The 1936 election of Popular Front supporter Elmer Benson to succeed the recently deceased Floyd B. Olson as governor gave Popular Front leaders a powerful ally in St. Paul. By late 1937 and early 1938, the Popular Front in Duluth appeared to be in a position to strongly influence, if not control, the fate of the city.

Indeed, to some extent, the real governing power in Duluth had slipped into the hands of Popular Front leaders. One example of this is the Coolerator Union. Because of the depressed economic conditions, layoffs were common at the Coolerator plant. Officials at the welfare department, however, would not give any benefits to laid-off workers. The issue was taken up by Coolerator Local 1096. When the next layoffs came, the union shut down the plant and union members went down to the welfare department office en masse, refusing to leave until the laid-off workers were enrolled on relief lists. Here we have an action that borders on an extra-legal exercise of power. As union leader Glenn Pearson put it in looking back on this incident, "We sort of kind of run the town a little bit you know."[67]

Joe Paszak, a leader of the Cement Plant Local 1210 and a long-time president of the CIO Industrial Union Council, told another story that makes a similar point. Some destitute people had walked four miles to get to Duluth to ask officials at the Welfare Department for assistance. Paszak and Yank Levine, a Popular Front activist who was a brother of Irene Paull, went with them. The official they saw told them it was too close to the five o'clock closing time and they would have to come back the next day. Paszak sent Levine to the Timber Workers' Hall and the National Maritime Union (Sailors') Hall to get some men. When he returned with nineteen men, they blocked all exits from the building, refusing to leave until the destitute people were enrolled for assistance. The sheriff, who was up for reelection, did nothing.[68]

The 1938 strike by the Newspaper Guild provides another example of the Popular Front in action. The Newspaper Guild rep-

Ernie Pearson and Joe Paszak at the first CIO convention in Duluth on Labor Day, 1937. Pearson led the organization of Western Paint and Varnish and was something of an elder statesman among radicals in Duluth. Paszak was a longtime president of the CIO Industrial Union Council. Courtesy Minnesota Historical Society.

resented reporters and other white-collar employees of the *News Tribune* and the *Herald*. Organized in 1933, the guild had left the AFL and affiliated with the CIO, aligning itself with the Popular

Front in Duluth. The strike began in early April when Joseph Jordan, representing Joseph and Victor Ridder, the New York–based owners of the two newspapers, rejected union demands. After strikers had shut the newspapers down for several weeks, management decided to reopen the plant, using the management team to put out a newspaper. But pickets for the guild and their supporters from other CIO unions blocked printers and other blue-collar workers from the print shop from entering the plant.[69] With negotiations at an impasse, management called on Public Safety Commissioner Len Culbertson and the police department to protect employees attempting to enter the plant. The guild responded by calling for more help from the CIO unions. Timber workers, sailors, and men and women from other CIO unions joined the guild picket lines. Armed police manned sandbag barricades outside City Hall on the hill across the street from the newspaper building. On Monday, May 23, with four to five hundred pickets parading in front of the newspaper building and many more supporters watching from across the street, police in riot gear attacked with tear gas and night sticks.[70]

Both sides dug in. Guild supporters promised to form a stronger picket line the next morning and Commissioner Culbertson vowed to protect the rights of the publisher and those employees who wanted to work. With a very real threat of bloodshed, both sides appealed to Governor Benson to intervene. Benson, acting as he had done earlier in the Timber Workers strike to support organized labor, ordered National Guard units in the state to intervene to protect the guild pickets from the police. Without other recourse, the publisher was forced to negotiate a settlement. It was a major victory for the guild and the Popular Front.[71]

In late April 1938, with tension mounting around the Newspaper Guild strike, *Midwest Labor* issued a call for a May Day demonstration for Saturday, April 30, at the Civic Center in Duluth, just across the street from the marching guild pickets. Among the signers endorsing the demonstration call were Viena Johnson, Herman Griffith, Ed Drill, Glenn Pearson, Ilmar Koivunen, Robert Sermon, William Higbee, and other Popular Front leaders.[72] While significant, the May Day demonstration pales in significance in comparison with the Labor Day celebration by the CIO unions in September of that year, when a record crowd of ten thousand was reported to have attended the Labor Day festivities in Fairmount Park.[73] Even allowing for exaggeration in this report, the crowd was clearly

Police use tear gas against massed pickets during the Newspaper Guild strike, May 23, 1938. Photograph by Hugh McKenzie; courtesy Northeast Minnesota Historical Center.

immense, much larger than that attending the Labor Day celebration sponsored by the AFL unions in Leif Erikson Park.[74]

Another enormous crowd participated in the "Parade of Progress" mounted by Popular Front leaders and their union supporters on behalf of Farmer-Labor candidates in the November election of 1938. With Governor Benson leading the way and the Duluth CIO unions in the rear, the parade made its way from the Civic Center to the armory. Marching between the governor and the CIO unions were bands and floats, veterans' organizations, women's organizations, Cloquet and Grand Portage Indians, Iron Range unions, Young Democrats, Proctor railroad workers, some AFL unions, delegations from surrounding towns, the Gary-New Duluth Club, and members of the Workers Alliance.[75]

Clearly the Popular Front had deep and broad support in Duluth. To a large extent, this support came from men and women who had been on the unrecognized margins of American life in the 1920s. In the 1920s, "Americans" had worried about the "aliens" in their midst. The open doors of America had been shut to future immigration in 1924, ethnic groups had been evaluated on grounds of their supposed capacity for Americanization, and coordinated efforts had been taken to Americanize the "foreigners" already here. If the 1920s saw a celebration of America, it was an America of Anglo-Saxon origins and Protestant Christianity. The "American Plan" was the paternalistic capitalism of the great corporations.

In the 1930s, a new conception of America and what it meant to be an American came to the fore. According to this new conception, Poles, Serbs, Negroes, and Indians were Americans, too. Catholics and Jews were as American as Protestants, and any form of ethnic, religious, or racial discrimination was "un-American." According to this new conception, Americans had a right to expect decent jobs, homes of their own, and access to schools and cultural opportunities. And according to this new conception, American workers had rights. The old system, which gave arbitrary powers to employers and supervisors, was seen as an un-American relic of

Farmer-Labor Party Governor Elmer Benson speaks at the Minnesota State Convention of the Farmer-Labor Party in Duluth during the campaign of 1938. Courtesy Minnesota Historical Society.

a hierarchical past, inconsistent with the American principle of the rights of the common person. The multiethnic working class of the West End, West Duluth, and Gary-New Duluth embraced this new conception of what it meant to be an American, a conception that was fundamental to the vision of America offered by Popular Front activists in the CIO and FLP.

A pamphlet written by Irene Paull conveys the power of this conception of what it meant to be an American for the Popular Front and its supporters. The pamphlet is entitled "Joe Paszak ... American." It was published in January 1943 on the occasion of Paszak's leaving Duluth to join America's armed forces during World War II.[76] Joe Paszak was the son of Polish immigrants. He had worked in the steel plant and the cement plant, participated in the CIO organizing drive in Duluth, and had served as president of the Cement Plant Local 1210 and the CIO Council in Duluth. Just before joining the armed forces, Paszak had given a talk on WEBC radio in Duluth that was picked up by national outlets. In that talk, Paszak had stressed the evils of anti-Semitism abroad and at home, and the importance of defeating fascism.[77]

"I met him on the picket line"—"Joe Paszak ... American" begins with these words. "Joe was raised among the smokestacks of Gary, West Duluth." As a youth, Paszak played basketball on an all-Slav team in Gary where "he could out jump anybody on the bank boards." He was the "squarest shooter on the team," the pamphlet says, both literally and figuratively:

> That's Joe Paszak. Is it a delegation to protest Jim Crow against a Negro worker? Joe Paszak, first on the floor! Is it a grievance of a woman on relief? See Joe Paszak. Do a bunch of fellows want to organize? Go ask Joe. What of it? That's just square shooting ... helping your fellow man get his rights. Just plain American to Joe.

These words made sense to a lot of people in western Duluth, people who knew firsthand the discrimination experienced by immigrant families, people who knew Joe Paszak and what he stood for.

CHAPTER NINE

the embattled popular front

THE POPULAR FRONT ADVOCATED INDUSTRIAL UNIONS, UNEM-
ployment insurance, old-age pensions, minimum-wage laws,
reduction of the working day, and health and safety rules. It also
championed peace, civil liberties, racial equality, and an inclusive vision of America. Support for some or all of these proposals came from Socialists, IWWs, and AFL progressives, but it also
came from members of the consumer cooperatives, the International Order of Good Templars, the Croatian Fraternal Union, and
the Slovene National Benefit Society (SNPJ). These organizations
and their ideas had deep roots in Duluth's multiethnic industrial
working class. Many people from immigrant, working-class, western Duluth entered into mainstream politics and the labor movement in the early 1930s. Under the aegis of the New Deal and the
labor-friendly policies of Farmer-Labor governors Floyd B. Olson
and Elmer Benson, these people joined the new unions springing
up all over the western half of the city and became active in the
Farmer-Labor Party. By late 1934 they had already transformed the
labor movement and the FLP in Duluth. These new faces were not
entirely welcome.

The FLP in Duluth had its origins in the coalition of left-wing
activists within the AFL and independent Socialists outside the AFL
who formed the Union Labor Party in Duluth in February 1918. It
was not until 1919, after the successful congressional campaign of
William Carss and after the Minnesota Federation of Labor decided
to enter into third-party politics, that leaders of the Trades Assembly in Duluth joined the third-party movement. And it was not until
1924 that the Duluth AFL gained firm control over the local FLP.

The Central Labor Political Committee (CLPC) of Duluth and
Proctor was the control center for the Farmer-Labor movement
in Duluth from 1924 into the 1930s. Delegates elected from AFL
unions, the Railroad Brotherhoods, and the ladies' auxiliaries of

both organizations served on the CLPC, where they screened and endorsed candidates to run on the Farmer-Labor ticket. The influx of new members in the early 1930s changed the Duluth FLP, making it more diverse and less Protestant and Scandinavian. It also brought with it support for different leaders (some of them Scandinavian), who contested with the conservative heads of the AFL for control of the FLP. Among these new leaders were Carl Carlson, head of the Scandinavian Good Templars for the state of Minnesota; John Kobi, a Socialist active in the SNPJ and the Yugoslav Socialist Federation; and Frank Puglisi, who, with the help of his Uncle Tony Puglisi, had successfully contested with pro-Mussolini forces for leadership of the Italian-American Club in Duluth.[1]

As early as September 1930 a resolution was introduced in the AFL Trades Assembly calling for the assembly to withdraw from the CLPC on the grounds that "[t]he Central Labor Political Committee has come to be controlled largely by persons not identified with the Federated Trades Assembly and organized labor as represented by the American Federation of Labor."[2] The AFL faced a fundamental difficulty in its relationship to the Farmer-Labor movement as a whole. On the one hand, it viewed the Farmer-Labor Party as essentially the party of the AFL and the Railroad Brotherhoods. On the other hand, Farmer-Labor candidates could not win on AFL votes alone. They needed support from Duluth's middle class and from Duluth's large unorganized and ethnically diverse industrial working class. Neighborhood clubs, like the West End Farmer-Labor Club and the Central Duluth Political Club, represented organizations through which the FLP could enlist the support of individuals who were not part of the organized AFL unions. As early as 1925, delegates representing these two clubs appear to have gained positions on the Duluth CLPC, casting votes in proportion to their membership alongside the CLPC-affiliated unions and Railroad Brotherhoods.[3] While in 1925 this left the AFL unions and Railroad Brotherhoods in firm control of the CLPC, as the FLA neighborhood clubs grew dramatically in the early 1930s and as new unions not controlled by the conservative leadership of the Trades Assembly sprung up, AFL control of the CLPC was threatened.

The Trades Assembly did not act on the proposal to disaffiliate from the CLPC in 1930, but tensions continued between the conservative AFL leadership and other forces increasingly active in the CLPC. In April 1931, William McEwen, the prominent AFL and Farmer-Labor leader in Duluth, came out in a radio address in support of the reelection of Chauncey Peterson to the state legislature. Peterson had served as a Farmer-Labor legislator from 1923 to 1931. But he had also been named in Frank Palmer's *Spies in Steel* as a secret informant to the steel trust. By unanimous vote, the CLPC instructed its secretary to write a letter to the Trades Assembly requesting that the assembly require McEwen to appear at its next meeting to "explain the statements made against the labor movement of Duluth" in his radio address.[4]

This letter to the assembly, written on CLPC letterhead, was signed by Ingworth Erickson and Milton Carlson, the CLPC's vice president and secretary. Erickson was a machinist who worked in the unorganized railroad shops who had long been active in the Farmer-Labor movement in Duluth.[5] Carlson was active in the Cabinet Makers and Sawmill Workers Union Local 1284, a union that organized in 1916 but never won a contract until 1937, and one that included a number of Scandinavian Socialists.[6] Members of such unions in unorganized industries, particularly among the Railroad Shopmen who had gone through the losing fight with U.S. Steel's repair shops in 1922, were not happy supporting someone identified as a spy for the steel trust. Accordingly, the Machinists, the Carmen, and Shopmen's System Federation Local 148 all sent letters to the Trades Assembly protesting AFL support for Peterson, with the Carmen going so far as to disaffiliate from the Trades Assembly.[7] These radicalized railroad shop unions, many of them affiliated with the AFL, nonetheless tended to side with Popular Front forces against conservative AFL leaders throughout the 1930s. From them came activists like Ingworth Erickson, Arthur Siegler, and John Kobi, each an active supporter of the Popular Front in the 1930s.[8]

One of the "persons not identified with the Federated Trades Assembly and organized labor as represented by the American Federation of Labor" whose appearance on the CLPC was particularly troubling to AFL leaders was O. E. Thompson. An article in *Labor World* in March 1929 blamed Thompson for the defeat of CLPC-endorsed candidate Arthur Siegler in the primary of that year. Thompson, president of the Central Farmer-Labor Club, had run for mayor on a Communist-backed ticket rivaling the CLPC-endorsed candidates.[9] Three years later, in 1932, the non-AFL forces within the CLPC had become strong enough to name this same O. E. Thompson as the campaign manager for the FLP's own city-wide electoral campaign.[10]

In 1933 and 1934 the AFL hold on the CLPC weakened further, with the calls for the annual CLPC meeting including not only FLA neighborhood clubs, but other "progressive organizations" as well.[11] The call for the 1935 annual meeting included a proposal to amend the constitution of the CLPC to formally permit this arrangement.[12] With non-AFL forces now in control of the CLPC, this constitutional proposal was carried. The newly constituted and renamed Executive Committee of the Central Committee of Labor and Farmers of Duluth and Southern St. Louis County was firmly in the hands of the Popular Front. It included some progressive AFLers like Milton Carlson of the Cabinet Makers, O. H. Tarun of the Carpenters, and R. C. Sermon of the Boilermakers, as well as a majority made up of non-AFL progressives, including Carl J. Carlson, O. E. Thompson, Michael O'Rourke, Mrs. Carl Johnson, and Tony Puglisi.[13] Persuaded by AFL conservatives Henry Pereault and Elling Munkeby, the Duluth Federated Trades Assembly responded by withdrawing entirely from the existing screening and endorsing body and organizing a new screening body made up exclusively of delegates from AFL unions, railroad brotherhoods, and ladies' auxiliaries. The new Central Labor Political Committee was to be independent of the Farmer-Labor Party and run on a "nonpartisan" basis, though it would "work jointly on campaigns" with the organization of the Farmer-Labor clubs.[14] In effect, the AFL had abandoned control of the FLP to the Popular Front and established a rival body that could either end up working jointly on campaigns or could run a slate of candidates of its own, opposed to the endorsed FLP slate.

It was at this point that the Communists adopted the policy of the Popular Front, plunging into the local labor movement, helping to organize unions at Western Paint and the Coolerator plant, forming front organizations like the American League against War and Fascism, and joining the neighborhood clubs and "progressive" organizations affiliated with the Central Committee of Labor and Farmers of Duluth and Southern St. Louis County. Though the ban on Communists enacted at the state convention of the FLP in 1925 remained on the books, the Popular Front liberals now in control of the Central Committee and Farmer-Labor neighborhood clubs made no effort to enforce the ban. Though numerically small, the Communists were able, through the concerted action of their members, to play an important role in the Popular Front they formed with the non-Communist progressives.

The entry of the Communists into the local FLP stiffened AFL opposition to the progressives, who had already gained control of the Farmer-Labor movement in Duluth. The AFL had long opposed any cooperation with Communists. As early as March 1935, before the decision to break with the progressives and form a separate, AFL-controlled screening and endorsing committee, the Farmer-Labor Women's Club drew criticism for scheduling Marion LeSueur to speak at Washington Junior High School. LeSueur, who had been active in third-party politics since the days of the Non-Partisan League, was denounced as a "red." Anne McEwen, who had taken over as editor of *Labor World* following the death of her father, William McEwen, dismissed this charge as reactionary.[15]

Anne McEwen herself was sympathetic to the progressives within the Farmer-Labor movement. She had supported the formation of the Committee for Industrial Organization within the AFL and openly criticized national leaders of the AFL for lack of vigorous leadership. In the spring and summer of 1935, as conservative AFL leaders were trying to pull back from cooperation with the FLP progressives, McEwen supported such cooperation. For example, as editor of the *Labor World* she supported Julius Emme in his fight with conservative leaders of the Minnesota Federation of Labor. Emme, a supporter of industrial unions, had held a position as secretary of the Minnesota State Industrial Commission. He had been fired from this position, ostensibly because of criticisms he had made of the adverse rulings of a judge regarding a strike in Albert Lea. Supporters of Emme maintained that he was the victim of the machinations of the state officers of the Minnesota Federation, who wanted to get rid of him because of his support for industrial unionism. Anne McEwen strongly supported Emme in the *Labor World*, running articles and editorials critical of the state officers of the Minnesota Federation. When, by a vote of nineteen to thirteen, the Trades Assembly passed a resolution demanding that McEwen apologize for these attacks, she refused, instead printing articles in *Labor World* supportive of Emme.[16] Infuriated, the Trades Assembly passed a resolution calling on the board of the newspaper to require editor McEwen to "make a complete retraction." Again, McEwen refused to comply.[17]

The two most important leaders of the opposition to the Popular Front progressives within the Trades Assembly were Robert Olson and Henry Pereault. Olson came out of the Motion Picture Operators union. He was active in the affairs of the AFL in Duluth throughout the 1920s and was president of the Federated Trades Assembly in 1935. In 1938 he became president of the Minnesota Federation of Labor, a post he would hold until 1953.[18] Pereault had been active in the affairs of the Trades Assembly since 1900 when he joined the Duluth Cigarmakers Union. He was a three-time president of the Trades Assembly in Duluth and in 1914 he was elected as a vice president of the Minnesota Federation of Labor, a position he held almost continuously until his death in 1947. Although he had played some part in the Farmer-Labor movement in Duluth in the mid- to late twenties, Pereault's heart was with the nonpolitical trade unionism of his fellow cigarmaker, Samuel Gompers, the longtime national head of the AFL. It was Pereault who led the fight in the Trades Assembly in favor of withdrawing from the old endorsements committee, which had come under the control of Farmer-Labor progressives, championing a return to the AFL's traditional "nonpartisan" position.[19]

As the summer of 1935 progressed, Olson and Pereault led a

Of Cuban heritage, cigar maker Henry Pereault was active in the local labor movement from 1900 until his death in 1946, serving in numerous capacities including several terms as president of the Trades Assembly. Courtesy Labor World.

fight within the Duluth AFL against the emerging Popular Front coalition. In early June, Olson proposed that the Trades Assembly take over publication of the *Labor World* and later that month he proposed that the assembly name a new board with greater control over the newspaper.[20] *Labor World* editor Anne McEwen remained defiant, appearing on a platform with Popular Front progressives at the annual Farmer-Labor summer festival in Lincoln Park.[21] By this time, alarmed at left-wingers entering into the AFL through some of the newly formed unions, the national AFL reminded all affiliated bodies that they would be held to the AFL rule banning Communists.[22] In November, the Minnesota Federation of Labor announced that it was bringing this war on "reds" to Minnesota.[23] During this same spring and summer, the Popular Front leaders of the FLP further provoked the AFL by distributing a letter suggesting that local AFL leaders had sold out to big business. Progressives also attempted to block a routine endorsement of Robert Olson and tried to prevent the seating of Phil DeMore, a member of the Executive Board of the new AFL Central Labor Political Committee, at an FLP convention on the grounds that he was part of a nonpartisan organization.[24]

The week following this last affront, the Lake Superior Conference against War and Fascism was held at the Moose Temple Auditorium. The conference included several local religious leaders and a number of local luminaries, such as the author Margaret Culkin Banning, but its sponsors included such left-wing organizations as the International Workers Order, the Finnish Workers Club, and the Head of the Lakes Section of the Communist Party. Further, the chairman of the committee in charge of the event was none other than Herman Griffith, the self-proclaimed Communist. Listed as endorsing this conference was Anne McEwen, the embattled editor of *Labor World*. Within the month, the Trades Assembly had removed McEwen and named Arthur Ramberg as the new editor of *Labor World*. In Ramberg's hands, *Labor World* would become an important weapon in the battle against the Popular Front.

An article in the *St. Paul Pioneer Press* stated that McEwen had been "dismissed with the 'Red' purge of the American Federation of Labor in Minnesota."[25] While there was clearly a kernel of truth in this, it is important to be clear about just what that kernel was. There is no evidence to suggest that Anne McEwen was a member of the Communist Party. She belongs in the category of progressives who were willing to work with the Communists on

d centered his attention large-
the commerce clause in finding
t valid.
clause was an issue in the Su-
court's NRA decision, but
urt made its decision on oth-
unds and was silent regarding
ause.
ce the clause appears in the
tution, the first time as a re-
on on the Federal government,
cond time as a restriction on
ates. In language it is sim-
itself.
r shall any person . . . be
ed of life, liberty, or prop-
without due process of law,
'.says the Fifth amendment.
r shall any state deprive any
of life, liberty, or property,
it due process of law . . .
he Fourteenth amendment.

Application Extended.

the Fifth amendment has
to mean much more than a
ainst the mere condemnation
rivate house and lot without
nsation, and the Fourteenth
uch more than safeguard the
of emancipated Negroes, the
e for which it was drawn.
judicial interpretation a "per-
lso is a corporation.
the clause, by gradual judi-
nterpretation, has been read
ncept of "liberty of contract"
in varying degrees has been
o prevent government inter-
e with wages, hours, prices.
er one decision relating to
ause was founded the entire
can system of public utility
tion.
er it the Supreme court in
ave a black eye to so-called
mic planning" and experi-
l legislation.
two years later the same
upheld a New York law per-
g the fixing of a minimum
for milk.

Has Tried to Draw Line.

ecision after decision passing
nimum wage laws, maximum
week laws, licensing laws,
tory laws, price-fixing laws,
urt has attempted to mark the
between the "due process"
which would make the rights
perty absolute and the indef-
police power" of state gov-
nts to legislate for the "safe-
alth, morals and general wel-

y New Deal laws have at-

ments of war and their tree dwellings. The warriors in the fore-
ground are re-enacting in dance the
events of a previous battle. Below
is shown the story of primitive production the world over as illustrated by a domestic scene from the
life of the Hopi Indians. The wom-
en are shown engaged in pottery
and basket making.

Duluth Woman Editor Ousted In 'Red' Purge

ANNE McEWEN.

Duluth, Nov. 30.—Miss Anne Mc-
Ewen, editor of the Labor World
of Duluth, has been dismissed with
the "Red" purge of the American
Federation of Labor in Minnesota.
The Labor World was founded
40 years ago by her father, the late
William E. McEwen, Minnesota
state conservation commissioner,
at one time State Labor commissioner, secretary-treasurer of Minnesota's state Federation of Labor
for sixteen years and father of the
state's workingmen's compensation

DR. JOHN R. M(WILL SPE(

Former General Sec
to Have 'World Ou
Topic Tuesd

Dr. John R. Mott, for
secretary of the Nation
the Young Men's Christ
tions, and for more
than 35 years a
leader in young
men's organiza-
tions, will come to
St. Paul Tuesday.
He will be the
principal speaker
at the seventy-
ninth annual
meeting of the St.
Paul Y. M. C. A.
at noon Tuesday
in the auditorium
of the Central Y.
M. C. A., Ninth
and Cedar streets.
His topic will be
'The Present
World Outlook".
Dr. Mott's decoration
the Distinguished Serv
the United States to t
the Order of the Cro
lem and total eleven
service to mankind. H
thor of thirteen books
ber of other publicat
with religious, ethical
tional problems.
Presiding at the ses
Roy B. Million, chairm
nual meeting committ
Beckman, president of
Y. M. C. A., will give th
port and Dr. T. H.
treasurer, will make

St. Paul Pioneer Press *article on the "purge" of Anne McEwen. Courtesy* St. Paul Pioneer Press.

issues of common concern. The immediate cause of her downfall was that she endorsed a conference against war and fascism that was also endorsed by Communists.[26] But there were deeper reasons. Over the entire period of her tenure as editor of the *Labor World*, Anne McEwen had consistently sided with Popular Front progressives inside and outside the AFL against the conservative leadership of the Duluth Federated Trades Assembly and the Minnesota Federation of Labor. It is for this reason that Robert Olson had initiated steps to gain greater control over *Labor World* in early June, well before the national or state campaigns against "reds" were announced.

This point is of some importance because it indicates that the battle between supporters and opponents of the Popular Front was not merely over Communist influence. By the end of 1935, the Farmer-Labor movement in Duluth was already deeply divided into two factions. While the allegiance of Communists with one side surely exacerbated the conflict, it was not the cause of the conflict, and while the battle against Communism was one reason for the downfall of the Popular Front, it was not the only one.

One of the other causes for the growing split within the FLP involved matters of patronage. This was one of the issues raised in a major attack on the area FLP in *Labor World* in March 1936, after Ramberg took over as editor. A number of the Popular Front progressives had been rewarded for their work on behalf of the Farmer-Labor Party with appointments to various state offices. Prominent among them were Carl Carlson, named state grain inspector, O. E. Thompson, named state food inspector, and Robert Sermon, named state boiler inspector.[27] All three were leaders of the progressive faction contesting the AFL conservatives for control of the FLP. *Labor World* used the patronage issue to attack the Popular Front progressives, deriding them as "patronage boys" and depicting them as a small clique bent on using the FLP to serve their personal ends, rather than the causes of laborers and farmers: "Organized labor, which has been responsible for the growth and success of the Farmer-Labor movement in St. Louis county, is being forced aside by office holders and petty politicians who are rapidly gaining control of the Farmer-Labor association."[28] While patronage-related corruption was indeed a problem within the Minnesota Farmer-Labor Party, care must be taken in assessing the AFL charge that patronage boys were taking over the FLP for their own interest.[29] Whatever their shortcomings may have been, Carlson, Thompson, and Sermon were far from mere political opportunists. Each had been active in progressive politics for decades and had a long record of involvement in the Farmer-Labor movement, as had Sig Slonim, a Duluth attorney also mentioned in the AFL attack on the "patronage boys."

In addition to patronage, the AFL returned to the issue of Communist influence within the FLP. The March 1936 *Labor World* raised the issue, pointing to Communist influence at the recent state convention of the FLP in Virginia.[30] Noting that Communists had been seated as delegates to the convention and that Joe Moreland, the organizer for District Nine of the Communist Party, was both a delegate and a member of the resolutions committee, the District Council of the International Longshoremen's locals in Duluth, led by E. L. Slaughter, threatened that its locals would withdraw support for the FLP unless the party rid itself of the Communists.[31]

The *Labor World* attack on the FLP also focused on irregularities at the Virginia convention:

> Organized labor delegates expressed disgust with the manner in which the convention was conducted. There was almost a total lack of parliamentary procedure. Delegates were seated regardless of credentials or whether or not their organizations were in good or bad standing. Speakers from the floor were not required to state their names or the organization they purported to represent. Many non-delegates participated in the convention business. Voting on resolutions and on the election of officers was done haphazardly.[32]

Popular Front leaders of the FLP responded apologetically to the growing disaffection of the AFL. John T. Bernard, who had been reelected as chair of the St. Louis County FLP, publicly apologized to P. F. DeMore, whose seating had been contested by Popular Front activists at the special convention in Duluth the previous fall. The St. Louis County FLP also promised to enforce the ban on Communists within the FLP, still officially in place since 1925, replacing Joe Moreland as a delegate to the state convention with Leo Koski.[33] When AFL leaders objected that Koski had himself been expelled from the Duluth Truck Drivers' union because of his affiliation with the Communist Party, Koski insisted that he was no longer a member.[34]

Not placated by these overtures, the Duluth Trades Assembly registered an official protest against the seating of nine local delegates at the state convention of the Farmer-Labor Party. The nine contested delegates were O. E. Thompson, Mrs. Frank Wanner, George R. Johnson, Francis A. Shoemaker, A. A. Siegler, Henning Borg, Joseph Moreland, Leo Koski, Robert Sermon, and O. H. Tarun. The assembly charged Moreland and Koski with being Communists; they objected to the others on the grounds that officeholders and government employees should have been barred from serving as delegates. All nine were part of the Popular Front coalition. Some, like Siegler, Borg, Sermon, and Tarun, had long played prominent roles within the AFL itself. It is an indication of the hardening position of AFL leaders that objection would be made against such men.

In November 1935, at the urging of Henry Pereault, the reconstructed AFL Central Labor Political Committee had passed a resolution forbidding city, county, or state employees from holding any position on its board. The objection to most of the nine delegates appears to have rested on an attempt to extend this principle outside the CLPC to the FLP as well. But the idea that government employees should have been banned from positions on Farmer-Labor committees appears to have been invented as a way to dislodge Popular Front activists from influential positions within the FLP. No such ban had been enforced against William McEwen following his appointment to the state Conservation Commission by Governor Olson in 1931.[35]

In April, *Labor World* retracted some criticisms of Carl Carlson and the Popular Front–controlled Central Farmer-Labor Club and then proposed a harmony dinner with AFL leaders to resolve their differences.[36] Despite these attempts to overcome the split, the division within the Duluth FLP remained, with the proposed harmony banquet postponed indefinitely.[37] The Popular Front wing of the party seemed to have forgotten its promise to break with the Communists. It scheduled Elmer Benson to speak at Lincoln Park under the sponsorship of the (Communist) Finnish Workers' Club. It also scheduled Benson and the FLP congressional candidate, John Bernard, to speak at Communist-connected Mesaba Park on the Iron Range. This event was also sponsored by the Finnish Workers Federation and included the United Front Band from Ironwood, Michigan, as the entertainment.[38] Disgusted with the Popular Front leaders' cooperation with the Communists, when the local Popular Front–controlled FLP sponsored a festival at Lincoln Park chaired by Carl Carlson, the Trades Assembly disavowed all association with the festival, despite the fact that the dying Floyd B. Olson was the scheduled speaker.[39] As the fall elections rolled around, the AFL and FLP set up separate campaign headquarters. And although the AFL supported Frankin D. Roosevelt and all the statewide FLP candidates, it did not endorse John Bernard and, in fact, it sharply attacked him, as well as Carl Carlson and O. E. Thompson, soon after the election was over.[40] In January 1937, though the AFL did send delegates, AFL leaders again complained that the FLP county convention was under the control of the patronage boys, with AFL organizer William Wright demanding that control of the FLP be returned to the trade unions.[41]

At this point the leaders of the Trades Assembly were politically isolated and ineffectual. Many of the longtime leaders of the AFL in Duluth were aligned with the Popular Front within the FLP. For example, the convention call for city progressives to plan for the elections of 1937 was signed by longtime AFL men O. H. Tarun of the Carpenters and Robert Sermon of the Boilermakers. And while the AFL's CLPC decided to adopt a policy of neutrality, making no endorsements, many of the AFL unions went ahead and endorsed the entire FLP slate.[42]

The formation of the CIO and the Duluth Industrial Union Council strengthened the Popular Front by giving it an institutional base that complemented the base already established within the FLP and by winning new grass-roots support for the FLP among the newly formed CIO unions. But it also increased the hostility of the AFL to the Popular Front. While some within the AFL, like Julius Emme and Anne McEwen, had welcomed the CIO, Duluth AFL leaders like Robert Olson and Henry Pereault saw the CIO industrial union movement as a dual unionism that betrayed the American labor movement. Following directives from the national AFL, in Duluth the CIO unions were expelled from the Trades Assembly in June 1937. The local vote was close, however, reflecting the relative isolation of the conservative leadership of the Trades Assembly.[43] Now, with the CIO unions and the CIO Council outside the AFL, the bad feeling between the AFL and CIO intensified.

The conflict was particularly intense along the waterfront, where immigrant radicals had long enjoyed significant support. The upsurge in the labor movement in 1933–35 had created a number of new unions on the Duluth waterfront affiliated with the International Longshoremen's Association (ILA) and with the ILA District Council in Duluth. With the formation of the CIO as a separate organization, the question of whether to remain with the AFL or go over to the CIO became an issue in some of these newly formed unions. With charges of raiding coming from both directions, ulti-

Robert Olson (cigar in hand) and E. L. "Buster" Slaughter, two of the leaders of the anti–Popular Front AFL unions in Duluth. Courtesy Northeast Minnesota Historical Center.

mately the AFL got the Coal Dock Workers and the CIO got the Ore Dock Workers.[44]

On the AFL side, the conflict on the waterfront was led by E. L. (Buster) Slaughter, a young, active, and effective organizer on behalf of the ILA and the AFL. Slaughter shared the conservative AFL view that the CIO had betrayed the fundamental principle of labor solidarity by organizing itself as a dual union in competition with the AFL. He was also militantly anti-Communist. Slaughter worked aggressively to gain contested ground from the CIO. In the spring of 1938 there was intense conflict between the AFL and CIO over control of the scrap-iron yards and around the Newspaper Guild strike. Slaughter played a major role in both of these conflicts.

The scrap-iron yards in Duluth were a big business. Scrap iron was collected for melting down and reuse. In 1937, over 381 thousand tons of scrap iron were processed in the yards, with a value of over $5.5 million.[45] Organized as a local of the SWOC, Scrap Iron Local 1425 left the AFL for the CIO along with a number of other unions in the summer of 1937. Over the course of the following year, the AFL and the CIO battled for control of scrap-iron workers. The first round of that battle took the form of a jurisdictional dispute at the Paper-Calmenson yard over skilled crane operators and firemen claimed by Local 516 of the Operating Engineers, an AFL union. In January 1938, the National Labor Relations Board ruled in favor of the CIO, holding that ten of the fourteen skilled men had signed CIO cards and should be included in Local 1425.[46]

Initially Local 1425 met with great success, winning a pay raise from 37 to 57 cents per hour. However, by spring 1938, demanding a pay cut and an end to seniority rights, the employers initiated a lockout.[47] When the lockout had dragged on for two months, some of the men working at the Paper-Calmenson yard wanted to return to work. Advised by AFL organizer Slaughter, 140 of the 200 locked-out men formed a union of their own, applied for an AFL charter, and voted to return to work.[48] On Thursday, May 6, police in riot gear escorted twenty-five of these men through the Local 1425 picket line, which had been reinforced by Timber Workers and men from other CIO unions. Four of the CIO pickets were arrested, including Ernest Audette, Stanley Mistkowski, Vilho Uusitalo, and Adron Coldiron, a SWOC organizer.[49] Speaking for the CIO, SWOC director Henry Burkhammer charged, "There is no question but treacherous elements within the A.F. of L. have joined hands with the employers in an effort to defeat this strike."[50] Defending Slaughter and the AFL, the *Labor World* replied that the strike had already been defeated and that Slaughter did not manipulate the men. The police, the paper argued, did not protect a back-to-work movement; they "simply did their duty to protect the rights of good, honest working men of Duluth."[51]

Slaughter was also involved in the Newspaper Guild strike, which was going on at the same time. The Newspaper Guild claimed to represent reporters and other office workers at the newspapers. Pressmen, typographers, and printers had long been represented by AFL unions. With the guild strike underway, Slaughter supported the effort by some of the office workers protesting the right of the guild to represent them. Though Robert Olson, president of the Trades Assembly, backed Slaughter in this initiative, many within the Trades Assembly did not. When the Allied Printing Trades, representing the pressmen, printers, and typographers, presented a resolution on the floor of the assembly requesting the office workers to withdraw their protest against guild representation, the resolution failed to get the necessary two-thirds vote, but it did win a 48 to 35 majority in the assembly itself.[52] Further, Slaughter's own union, ILA Freight Handlers Local 1279, by a close vote passed a resolution condemning Slaughter's role in the affair, a resolution it later rescinded under orders from the ILA International.[53]

The significant opposition coming from the Trades Assembly and from within his own union indicates the difficulty that Slaughter faced keeping the waterfront unions aligned with the AFL. From the time of the Knights of Labor through the IWW strikes of the World War I era, waterfront workers had shown more than a little sympathy for radical ideas. Some of this sympathy persisted into the 1930s. The National Maritime Union (NMU), which represented Duluth sailors on the Great Lakes, was identified by the Dies Committee of the U.S. Congress as a Communist-controlled union.[54] And there were clearly some members of Slaughter's own Freight Handlers Local 1279 who were sympathetic to the left. Local 1279 had been one of the organizations endorsing the Lake Superior Conference against War and Fascism and, in an act of solidarity with a CIO union that went against the current of opinion stemming from the national AFL and the local leaders of the Trades Assembly, the members of Local 1279 refused to unload ships that ignored an NLRB ruling certifying the CIO's NMU for collective bargaining.[55]

In an interview done many years later, Slaughter talked about the Communist threat to the waterfront unions during the early days of the CIO. Even before he went to work on the docks in 1920, Slaughter had witnessed IWW activity around the docks as a youth. He rejected the IWW then as being made up of men unwilling to work and willing to use intimidation against men who did want to work, considering them unpatriotic and the bane of real unions. He viewed the Communists in the same light. "I hated them guys," he recalled years later.[56] Nonetheless, Slaughter was a militant trade unionist, without any trace of the corruption that sullied ILA leaders elsewhere. He was an effective organizer and his ILA members provided help to other unions, often providing the "muscle" to prevent scabs from crossing picket lines.[57]

In discussing the role of the Communists, Slaughter mentioned how a group of Communists would control a meeting by forming a "red diamond" on the floor of the hall, with one Communist stationed near each side, one toward the front, and one toward the rear. Spread out in this way they would appear as unconnected individuals, and by supporting what one another said, they could often steer what happened in a meeting. Reports by FBI informants present at Communist meetings confirm Slaughter's account. At one meeting of local Communists, for example, a detailed plan was worked out for how the Communists could gain control of a convention of the Eighth District of the FLP in August 1944. In this case it worked. With one minor exception the Communists succeeded in getting every one of their planned slate elected, even though they were numerically a small group on the convention floor.[58]

Slaughter was convinced that the Communists intended to use such methods to gain control over the waterfront unions because of their potential strategic value to the cause of the Soviet Union. His solution was to drive every single Communist out of the ILA union locals. He was also willing to use ILA muscle against the Communists on their home turf. In a 1980 interview, Slaughter spoke openly about ILA men attacking the office of the local Communist organization. He mentioned four such attacks: one against an office "next to the incline" at Seventh Avenue West and Superior Street in the late 1920s or early 1930s, another later against an office in the basement of the New York Hotel, another against a Communist meeting at Camels Hall, and a fourth against an office of *Midwest Labor* on the third or fourth floor of the Palladio building, where editor Sam Davis was beaten up.[59] There was no police action mentioned in any of these attacks. Indeed, Slaughter comments that after one such attack he was approached by an FBI man who simply asked that the next time the ILA did that, would they please bring the Communist files to him instead of throwing them all over the place. It is unclear to what extent this violence was reciprocated from the other side. A *Labor World* article from October 1937 mentions CIO use of terroristic methods in raids on AFL unions in the Twin Cities. But while the same article mentions CIO raids on AFL unions in Duluth, especially along the waterfront, it

Duluth native Sam Davis was editor of Midwest Labor and Communist Party candidate for governor of Minnesota. From Työmies, June 28, 1937. Courtesy Työmies Society.

makes no mention of the use of violence.[60] Still, the interview with Slaughter, though it mentions no specific incidents, strongly suggests that there was an ongoing threat of violence on both sides.[61]

A rough and tumble anti-Communism of a somewhat different sort played a significant role in the gubernatorial campaign of 1938. Incumbent Governor Elmer Benson was closely aligned with the Popular Front. He had used the power of his office to force employers to settle in both the Timber Workers strike and the Newspaper Guild strike and had frequently appeared on platforms with John Bernard, the Popular Front congressman elected to represent the Eighth Congressional District of Minnesota. In Congress, Bernard had been an outspoken radical, inserting articles from the *Daily Worker*, the newspaper of the Communist Party, into the *Congressional Record*, joining CIO workers at a sit-in strike at an auto plant in Flint, Michigan, and, alone in the U.S. House of Representatives, supporting arms sales to Republican forces during the Spanish civil war, a position that brought the Catholic Church to actively campaign against Bernard in the congressional campaign of 1938.[62]

Benson's forthright and sometimes undiplomatic support of Popular Front politics, and his willingness to use the power of the governor's office to support the labor movement, angered conservatives and alienated some of those who had supported him as Floyd B. Olson's successor in 1936. Along with charges of corruption in the patronage system employed by the FLP, anti-Communism played a major role in the campaign to defeat Benson in 1938. In "Are They Communists or Catspaws?" a pamphlet written for the 1938 campaign, former congressman Ray Chase accused Governor Benson and his closest aides of knowingly or gullibly giving undue influence to Communists and Communist ideas in Minnesota. For the most part the pamphlet is a miserable exercise in the fallacy of guilt by association, but there was no doubt that Benson, like other Popular Front progressives, was willing to work with Communists. The pamphlet also carried anti-Semitic overtones in its depiction of prominent Jewish aides to Benson as sinister figures.[63]

The gubernatorial campaign of 1938 was a major confrontation between Benson, supported by the powerful Popular Front wing of the FLP, and the enemies of the Popular Front rallying around the young, charismatic Republican, Harold Stassen. The Republicans mounted an aggressive campaign focused on charges of corruption and Communist influence in the Benson administration. To win the election, the FLP needed the support of the right wing of the FLP under the influence of the AFL unions. But in Duluth, the AFL leadership was incensed with John Bernard because of his strong support for the CIO and his association with the Communists. Although less angry at Benson, local leaders of the Trades Assembly also saw Benson as belonging to the Popular Front camp and at least some of them supported Stassen.[64] In September, the Minnesota Federation of Labor (AFL) finally did endorse Benson, making it difficult for local AFLers to continue supporting Stassen.[65] Nevertheless, the AFL in Duluth gave Benson little support. In the months of September and October, *Labor World* devoted its front page and its headlines to attacking Bernard and defending his Republican challenger, William Pittenger. Statements of support for Benson from local unions were relegated to the back pages and six weeks went by before the Minnesota Federation's endorsement of Benson was mentioned anywhere in the paper.[66]

The Popular Front forces appealed to those elements within the local AFL they thought they could win over. In October Benson spoke to a crowd of three thousand at the Shrine Auditorium as part of a "No Wage Cut" campaign supported by the railroad unions, which had long played a prominent part in the FLP in Duluth. Noting FDR's plea for unity in the labor movement, *Midwest Labor* reported on a meeting with CIO union leaders at which Otto Tarun, secretary of the Carpenters union, expressed hope for unity between the AFL and CIO.[67] Tarun was one of the AFL leaders who had consistently lined up with the Popular Front. The Carpenters in fact broke with the Trades Assembly, endorsing Bernard for Congress instead of Pittenger.[68] Teamsters Local 346, led by Fred Smith, another AFL leader who usually lined up with the Popular Front, also endorsed Bernard and went so far as to withdraw from the CLPC, charging AFL leaders with splitting the FLP.[69] Other AFL locals endorsing Bernard included the Cabinet Makers and Sawmill Workers unions, several of the federal unions formed in the early 1930s, the Railroad Carmen and the Machinists—both unions radicalized by the shopmen's strike of 1922—and even some of the ILA locals.[70]

In 1938 as in 1936, the AFL and the FLP had separate campaign headquarters in Duluth. E. L. Slaughter was the official head of the AFL Benson campaign in Duluth, but he appears to have devoted most of his energy to attacking Bernard. In an interview done years later, he mentions both Bernard and Benson in the context of expressing his hatred for Communists.[71] The official FLP cam-

Issued by Volunteer Committee for Progressive
Farmer-Labor Candidates, Leonard Olson, Sec.

Send
JOHN T.
BERNARD
BACK TO
Congress
(Over) 1

*Campaign card for reelection of John T. Bernard. As a U.S. Congressman from the
Eighth District of Minnesota, Bernard had been openly left wing and strongly supportive of the CIO organizing drive. Courtesy Pearson family.*

paign in Duluth ended with a torchlight parade followed by a rally
at the armory on Friday, November 4. Governor Benson and Congressman Bernard led the parade and a radio broadcast by President Roosevelt rounded out the program at the armory. The parade
included some AFL and railroad unions, but did not include representatives from the Trades Assembly. In the end, Benson carried
St. Louis County by a narrow margin, but lost the Eighth District
and the state. Bernard was also defeated. It was a major setback
for the Popular Front. Writing in the *Labor World*, editor Ramberg expressed sorrow that Benson had lost, blamed his defeat on
the clique that had stolen the FLP from organized labor, and took
credit on behalf of the AFL for Pittenger's victory over Bernard.[72]
In 1940, Ramberg again supported the Republican, Pittenger, as the
best candidate to defeat the CIO man, Bernard.[73]

    The campaign to defeat Benson had shown that the FLP was
vulnerable to charges that it had been infiltrated by Communists.
Ramberg sought to drive that point home in the weeks after the
election of 1938, deriding party leaders who had welcomed "known
Communists, Communist sympathizers and half-baked radicals
and parlor pinks" into the party and letting leaders know that the
AFL expected some action to dislodge these elements.[74] In December, the FLP state Central Committee did act, banning Communists
from state and local FLP organizations and calling for the revoca-

tion of charters from organizations that ignored the ban. Despite this, the *Labor World* noted that under the leadership of Herman Griffith and Eveleth attorney Morris Greenberg, Popular Front forces maintained control of the St. Louis County FLP.[75] Similarly, at the Eighth District convention in January, Herman Griffith was elected to the key post of district secretary, and Morris Greenberg and Rudolph Rautio, both strong supporters of the Popular Front, were elected to represent the district on the state Central Committee of the FLP.[76] In disgust, the Duluth Central Labor Political Committee of the AFL officially withdrew from the FLP.[77]

The Communist issue would bedevil the party for the next decade. It also became a problem for the CIO. John L. Lewis had welcomed Communist organizers into the CIO, and in the Duluth area, Joe Van Nordstrand and Martin Maki had played key roles in the organizing work done by SWOC. But as early as late 1937, Henry Burkhammer and William Hartman, non-Communists within the local SWOC, had managed to force Van Nordstrand and Maki out of their positions.[78] While the two would remain active within the CIO and secret Communists and assorted independent radicals remained active in many SWOC locals, SWOC would become the base for anti-Communist agitation within the Duluth and Minnesota CIO.

In fall 1939, *Labor World* charges that the CIO was Communist influenced gained support from the U.S. House Committee on Un-American Activities, newly formed under the chairmanship of Congressman Martin Dies of Texas. Representatives of the Dies Committee investigating Communist activity made their way to Duluth, where they were welcomed by the ILA District Council, headed by E. L. Slaughter.[79] A report issued by the Dies Committee in early 1939 identified eleven unions as seriously tainted with Communist influence. Among them were the National Maritime Union and the Fur Workers, both with locals affiliated with the Duluth CIO Council.[80] *Labor World* went further than this, depicting the whole CIO as a tool of Soviet Communism aimed at destroying the American labor movement.[81]

The charge that American Communists were subservient to the Soviet Union was not hard to sustain. From late 1936 into August 1939, the Communists strongly supported the efforts of democratic countries to resist fascism in Germany and supported FDR's foreign policy of aligning the United States with England and France against Germany. But following the signing of a nonaggression pact between Germany and the Soviet Union in August 1939, Communists in the United States took their cue from Moscow and drastically altered their position, depicting the antifascist rhetoric of FDR and other Western leaders as warmongering, and they campaigned to keep the United States out of the war.

Most Popular Front activists in Duluth followed the Moscow line. *Midwest Labor* ran numerous articles and editorials against American involvement in the war.[82] Peace rallies were organized in Duluth in April and June of 1940 with Viena Johnson and even District SWOC Director Henry Burkhammer among the featured speakers.[83] The Duluth CIO Council provided support for local Youth Council delegates involved in peace work and it approved the preparation of a CIO peace resolution to be presented at the Fairmount Park Peace Rally in June.[84] The CIO Council also supported distribution of "The Yanks Are Not Coming" antiwar buttons and, with some dissent, passed a resolution calling for publication of a pamphlet against the Lend Lease legislation supported by the Roosevelt administration, which they said was leading toward American involvement in the war.[85]

More controversial was Popular Front support for the USSR in its invasion of Finland in late 1939. Andy Johnson, a former business manager for *Midwest Labor*, played a particularly prominent role in supporting the Soviet Union in its "Winter War" against Finland. Such support for Soviet aggression alienated many Finnish Americans from the Popular Front.[86] *Midwest Labor* itself was more circumspect in dealing with the issue, publishing letters supporting the Soviet invasion, but also publishing a letter against it.[87] At an FLP convention in Virginia in February, more than half the delegates walked out in protest over Communist efforts to force through a resolution supporting the USSR in its invasion of Finland. Among those who walked out were such stalwarts of the Popular Front as Sig Slonim, R. C. Sermon, and O. E. Thompson.[88] In Duluth, the General Relief Association for Finland was established to aid the Finns against the Soviets. Despite shrill Communist opposition, the relief effort drew widespread support. Viena Johnson, a pillar of the Popular Front in Duluth, served on the executive committee of the Relief Association, an indication of how isolated the Communists were on this issue and also a clear sign of Johnson's non-Communist credentials.[89] While Popular Front supporters retained control of the St. Louis County and Eighth District FLP, in Duluth they temporarily lost control of the Central FLA Club and at the state level "right wing" opponents of the Popular Front prevailed at the state convention of the FLP.[90]

The entanglement of the Communists in support of unpopular foreign policy positions dictated by Moscow also provided the basis for a challenge to Communist influence within the Minnesota CIO. Joe Van Nordstrand, who had been serving as state CIO secretary, was a more or less open member of the Communist Party. At the Minnesota CIO convention in 1940, recognizing that his support was waning, Van Nordstrand stepped down to assume a position with the Fur Workers. Communists and their Popular Front allies supported Leonard Lageman of the United Electrical Workers, a Twin Cities–based union, to succeed Van Nordstrand. Lageman was a Communist Party member, but his membership was not publicly known.[91] Because of their criticism of FDR in the wake of the nonaggression pact between Germany and the Soviet Union, Popular Front forces within the CIO were vulnerable to a challenge from CIO activists loyal to the president and his foreign policies. These foreign policy issues figured prominently at the convention, with Popular Front supporters managing to get the convention to oppose conscription and support a Peace Conference planned for Chicago. Opposition to the Popular Front came largely from the SWOC locals. Among those asking to be recorded as voting against support for the peace conference were representatives from a number of SWOC locals, including Jack Liston, Ben Anderson, and Ronald Carlson from Duluth Local 1028 and Bill Hartman from the SWOC staff in Duluth.[92] Paul Lee, a SWOC organizer based in Duluth, seconded the nomination of Walter Brock, from a SWOC local outside Duluth, to run against Lageman. In the end, Lageman won by a vote of 129 and one half to 59 and one half.[93] Pat McGraw, a leader of the Popular Front within the CIO in Duluth, was elected as state vice president from the Duluth area and Popular Front activists Joe Paszak and Anne Gerlovich were elected as representatives from the Duluth area to the state Executive Board.[94] Despite the challenge, in the CIO as in the FLP, the Popular Front had maintained its leadership position. Nevertheless, an organized opposition was beginning to take shape.

the fall of the popular front

WHILE THE POPULAR FRONT HAD WEATHERED THE STORM IN both the FLP and the CIO between 1938 and 1946, it now faced organized opposition on both fronts. Difficulties for Popular Front supporters were eased somewhat by the German invasion of the Soviet Union in late June 1941. Before the invasion, Popular Front activists in Duluth were openly hostile to the foreign policy of FDR, which tilted in favor of England and France against Germany. After Germany invaded the USSR, American Communists, clearly revealing their subservience to Moscow, quickly reverted to their earlier position of ardent support for FDR and the anti-Nazi coalition with England and France. A July peace conference that Popular Front activists called for before the German invasion of Russia never happened.[1] From that point until the end of the war, the foreign policy issues that had threatened to isolate left-wing forces politically in the FLP and CIO ceased to be a problem, though they would reemerge in the postwar period in different guise.

Nevertheless, the Popular Front now faced organized opposition in Duluth. Local 1625, a SWOC local made up of men and women working at the Marine Iron Shipyard, went so far as to disaffiliate from the CIO Council in 1943 after anti-Communists were defeated by supporters of the Popular Front in a contested election for CIO Council officers.[2] Support for the Popular Front within the Duluth CIO remained strong enough to give it a potentially powerful base for action, but Popular Front support for the war effort led local leaders to avoid strikes or confrontations that would disrupt production. And with the Duluth AFL having withdrawn its support from the FLP, the party was unable to make significant gains in electoral politics in the war years, even though Popular Front supporters retained control of the organization. In the 1942 elections, the AFL endorsed Republican Joseph Ball for the U.S. Senate and Republican William Pittenger for Congress, while the *Labor*

World editor, Arthur Ramberg, with the support of E. L. Slaughter and other AFL leaders, ran for Railroad Commissioner in the Republican primary.[3] With support from the AFL, the Republican Party won in the fall elections, returning to its traditional position of dominance in Duluth and leaving the Popular Front forces firmly in control of an ineffectual FLP.

Like the rest of America, Duluth threw its heart and back into the war effort. As in World War I, the shipyards in Duluth and Superior had been converted to wartime production. In February 1942, with ten thousand people still unemployed in Duluth, Barnes Duluth Shipyard in Riverside began work on sections for eight tankers.[4] By June the finished tankers *Tarentum* and *Mannington* were launched. The vessels were christened by Mrs. Catherine Walzynski, mother of Andrew Aloise Walzynski, and Catherine McQuade Berg, sister of Robert Cameron Berg, both men from Duluth who had been killed in action at Pearl Harbor.[5] Through war bonds and "Buy a Bomber Shows," Duluthians contributed cash, lives, and labor to the war effort.[6]

Despite unity in support of the nation's war effort, however, political maneuvering continued beneath the surface during the war

In addition to 230 ships built in the Twin Ports during the war, a number of Great Lakes freighters, like these of the popular NMU-organized "Poker Fleet," were called up for service. Several Poker Fleet boats were lost during the war. Photograph by Hugh McKenzie; courtesy Northeast Minnesota Historical Center.

years. The Farmer-Labor Party never recovered from its defeat in 1938. Behind popular Governor Stassen, the Republican Party successfully redefined its image, embracing the progressive reforms of the New Deal era, and promising to administer them without the

Coolerator Steelworkers Local 1096 sponsored this float to support the war effort. Courtesy Pearson family.

War bond rally at the Coolerator plant. Courtesy Pearson family.

Popular Front activists Ernie Pearson and Anne Gerlovich, now part of the united Democratic-Farmer-Labor Party, admire campaign posters for Franklin D. Roosevelt for president and Byron G. Allen for governor. Courtesy Pearson family.

inefficiency, corruption, and Communist influence charged against former Governor Benson and the Farmer-Laborites. In the elections of 1940 and 1942, the FLP remained in second place, with the Democrats running a weak third.

Concerned that Minnesota might be lost to the Republicans in the presidential contest of 1944, the Roosevelt administration wanted to see Farmer-Laborites and Democrats unite in Minnesota. Roosevelt turned to his supporters in the national CIO to help bring this about. Unity was also supported by Elmer Kelm, state chairman of the Democratic Party in Minnesota. The Communists, who had bitterly attacked Roosevelt during the period of the Soviet-German nonaggression pact between August 1939 and July 1941, now focused their efforts on reelecting him and supported unification in Minnesota. They pressured their allies in the Popular Front to accept the unity proposals urged by the Roosevelt administration, the Democratic Party of Minnesota, and the CIO.[7]

In the spring of 1944, overriding the resistance of many Popular Front activists, unity was achieved.[8] Democrats, meeting in their state convention in St. Paul, invited delegates attending a simultaneous FLP convention in a different hotel nearby to come and join them. John Moriarity, a Democratic delegate from Duluth, watched as the Farmer-Labor delegates marched into the convention hall. What struck him was the marked difference in dress and appearance between the Democratic delegates, most of whom were professionals, and the Farmer-Labor delegates, many of whom came from blue-collar occupations.[9] While no major gains were won in the 1944 elections, in 1945 the new Democratic-Farmer-Labor Party (DFL) managed to elect the young Hubert Humphrey as mayor of Minneapolis. Energetic and ambitious, Humphrey would play a significant role in shaping the new party in Minnesota and Duluth.

The first major test for the newly united DFL in Duluth was the congressional campaign of 1946. The campaign pitted incumbent Republican William Pittenger against DFL nominee John Blatnik. Blatnik was from Chisholm on the Iron Range. He came from a Slovenian family and did not speak English until he entered school at age five. After high school, he went to Winona State, where able students from poor families could get affordable training to become teachers. He worked his way through Winona State, grad-

John Blatnik, 1940. Photograph by Propotnick Studio; courtesy Northeast Minnesota Historical Center.

uating with honors in 1935, and in 1937 landed a job teaching high school chemistry in Chisholm. He immediately became active in Farmer-Labor politics and was elected to fill the last two years of the Minnesota Senate term left vacant by the death of his good friend, Richard Kelly. During the war, Blatnik served in the Office of Strategic Services, a precursor to the CIA, parachuting behind enemy lines into Yugoslavia, where he used his knowledge of Slavic languages to establish a strategically valuable connection with anti-fascist forces fighting under Yugoslav Communist leader Marshal Tito. Decorated for his wartime services, Blatnik was picked by the now-united DFL to run for Congress in 1946.[10]

The DFL endorsed Blatnik early in the campaign. He was opposed in the primary by William McKinnon, a member of the Brotherhood of Railway Trainmen who had run strongly against Pittenger in 1944, but who was opposed by the Popular Front wing of the DFL. The AFL made no endorsement in the primary.[11] Blatnik won the primary, which was held on July 8, with *Labor World* predicting a bitter fall contest between Republican William Pittenger and Blatnik, but making no endorsement. Eventually, the AFL did endorse Blatnik, but the endorsement did not come until late in the campaign and a significant number of AFL members openly supported Pittenger.[12]

Pittenger had been in office since he had defeated FLP congressman William Carss in 1930 with the exception of one term, when he was defeated by FLP candidate John Bernard in 1936. In 1938, Pittenger had regained his congressional seat by taking advantage of the split between the right and left wings of the FLP, attacking Bernard as a radical under Communist influence and winning the support of opponents of the Popular Front within the FLP and AFL. In 1946, Pittenger tried to use this same anti-Communist theme in his contest with Blatnik. While in Yugoslavia during the war, Blatnik developed a personal friendship with Marshal Tito. After the war Blatnik had occasionally praised Tito for his role in the struggle against fascism. Blatnik was also supported by the Popular Front wing of the FLP. Further, it was rumored that, in exchange for Popular Front support, Blatnik had promised to appoint Herman Griffith as his personal secretary once elected.

The public praise for Tito, the support of the Popular Front, and the rumored connection with Griffith were exploited by Pittenger, who tried to brand Blatnik as a Communist sympathizer. A campaign ad in the *Labor World* tried to turn AFL dislike for Bernard against Blatnik, calling him "experiment number two" in radicalism and foreign ideology.[13] In an address before a Duluth veterans group, Pittenger said that "Titoism" was an issue in the Eighth District and that Blatnik was "supported by the Communists" and "would follow the Communist line" if elected.[14] Both the *Duluth Tribune* and the *Duluth Herald* endorsed Pittenger and echoed his attack on Blatnik as soft on Communism. The *Herald* ran articles under the headlines, "Blatnik Raps War Veteran" and "Vet Replies to Blatnik." The *Tribune* ran a campaign ad framed as "a letter from an ex-marine to his brother now in service," charging Blatnik with supporting Tito's Communism and with having close ties to Elmer Benson and Herman Griffith. An editorial also reminded readers of the rumor that Blatnik would appoint Herman Griffith as his private secretary.[15] According to one source, the publisher of the Duluth newspapers even threatened to withhold ad space from Oreck's department store and Minnesota Woolens because the Oreckovsky and Polinski families, the Jewish owners of these businesses, had endorsed Blatnik because he was supported by outspoken critics of anti-Semitism.[16]

This time Pittenger's attacks backfired. At an appearance at a crowded Shrine Auditorium in which Senator Claude Pepper of Florida spoke on Blatnik's behalf, Blatnik charged Pittenger with political cowardice and disavowed any Communist views. The Blatnik campaign also ran a series of "Vets for Blatnik" talks over the radio, the first given by paratrooper George Ebinger countering Pittenger's charge that Blatnik was hostile to veterans. Even the *Labor World*, though it never endorsed Blatnik, ran a series of articles defending Blatnik from Pittenger's red-baiting attacks.[17] On Election Day Blatnik won an impressive victory. Noting that the Eighth District of Minnesota was one of the few districts in the whole country where a liberal replaced a Republican, the *Labor World* credited the victory to an overwhelming "labor" vote.[18] While there was indeed an overwhelming labor vote, the real basis for Blatnik's victory lay more with the CIO and the DFL than with *Labor World* or the AFL. Henry Morin, the old Democrat who had tried to persuade Carss to run as a Democrat in 1920 and who was now at home in the united DFL coalition against the Republicans, credited the CIO for Blatnik's success on the Iron Range and credited Gerald Heaney, the emissary of the Humphrey Democrats, for Blatnik's success in Duluth. Morin went on to warn against lingering Republican sentiment in the Duluth AFL.[19] Blatnik himself credited the

Popular Front activists at a social gathering in the 1940s. Herman Griffith stands at far left in the back; Anne Gerlovich is seated in the armchair in front of him. Courtesy Pearson family.

CIO with his victory in 1946 and rebuked those in the Duluth AFL who wanted to return to the Republicans in 1948.[20]

The election of John Blatnik to Congress in 1946 was the last great victory of the Popular Front in Duluth. Though Blatnik's support was much broader than the Popular Front, the Popular Front was an important part of the winning coalition and Popular Front leaders did indeed have close ties to Blatnik. While the rumor that Herman Griffith would become the new congressman's personal secretary proved false, that appointment did go to Roger Hargrave, a professor of political science at Duluth State Teachers College, a Lincoln Brigade veteran of the Spanish civil war, and the husband of Popular Front activist Anne Gerlovich.[21] Having retained control of the FLP and the CIO after the challenge of the early 1940s, having successfully led the FLP into the merger with the Democrats without giving up leading positions within the DFL, and having successfully elected a man with close ties to Popular Front leaders to Congress, the Popular Front in Duluth could view the situation in late 1946 with some satisfaction. Trouble, however, was looming on the horizon.

During World War II, both the AFL and the CIO had made "no strike" pledges. With resources diverted to producing war materials, there were significant shortages of many consumer goods. During the war a system of price controls and rationing had kept inflationary pressure at bay, but with the removal of price controls after the war, prices shot up, causing the purchasing power of the average paycheck to decline and provoking a wave of strikes. In addition to trying to make up for wages lost to rising prices, American workers and their unions pressed for better contractual agreements regarding pensions, vacation time, and medical care. With 35 percent of the American workforce organized, many of these strikes were disciplined, union-led, and designed to improve contractual terms.[22] The wave of strikes was supported by a strong grass-roots militancy, generating what at least one historian has described as an almost festive and carnival-like atmosphere in which working people celebrated the power that the strong unions created in the 1930s and early 1940s had given them.[23]

In response to this aggressive postwar labor movement, conservatives began to demand action to limit the power of the unions. In the eighteen months following the Japanese surrender, over seventy bills were introduced in Congress to try to limit union powers.[24] One proposal, floated in 1946, would have given the government power to conscript striking workers into the armed forces.[25] The conservatives' position was strengthened by their victories in the congressional elections of fall 1946, and in June 1947 they succeeded in enacting the Taft-Hartley Act. According to one of its sponsors, Republican Representative Fred Hartley of New Jersey, the act returned America to the conditions that had prevailed before the passage of the Wagner Act in 1935. While Hartley exaggerated, Taft-Hartley did significantly weaken the unions and in doing so, undermined a powerful base of support for the Popular Front in Duluth's CIO.

Another threat to the Popular Front came from the resurgence of anti-Communism after World War II. With the United States and the Soviet Union allied during the war, the anti-Communist movement of 1938–1941 had abated. At Tehran and Yalta, the wartime allies had reached agreements on the shape of the postwar world, one that envisioned spheres of interest dominated by each power and peaceful cooperation in the years ahead. Serious differences developed between the USSR and the Western allies over the implementation of these agreements, however. American perceptions of the USSR quickly changed from wartime ally to cold war enemy. Concomitantly, the campaign against Communists as internal allies of the USSR began to heat up. In Minnesota, this meant a renewal of the campaign against the Popular Front, now part of the

DFL. The *Labor World* returned to the anti-Communist theme in 1946, expressing worries about "Commies" within the federal government, attacking the CIO as soft on Communism, and covering national AFL vice president Matthew Woll's threat to picket Hollywood films made by "treasonable" stars and writers.[26]

The Federal Bureau of Investigation also stepped up its surveillance of local Communists. As early as February 1940, with the cooperation of the Duluth Police Department, the FBI had local reds under watch. By early 1941 individuals had been identified who "should be considered for custodial detention in case of a national emergency." In 1944 an informant turned over to the FBI a list of all local subscribers to the Communist newspaper, *The Daily Worker*. Another informant reported on merger negotiations between Democrats and Farmer-Laborites, identifying Herman Griffith, Irene Paull, Ernest Pearson, Sam Davis, and an unidentified African American from Duluth as among Communists present at the meeting.

After the end of the war, the level of attention paid to Communist activities increased dramatically. FBI informants were present within the local Communist Party, the DFL, and the unions. A November 1, 1946, report written by FBI agent Erling Habro on the Communists in Duluth relied on the input of nine informants. Phone taps were placed at Communist Party and CIO headquarters in St. Paul. Informants in Steelworkers Local 1028 identified Communist activists in the union for the FBI. Records of the checking accounts of Irene Paull and Herman Griffith were turned over to the FBI. Meetings of the Progressive Club in Duluth and the Duluth Civil Rights Congress were monitored. With the nation entering into the McCarthy-era concern over Communist threats to American security, plans for custodial detention that had been vague in 1940 began to take on chilling detail. To update information on subjects considered for detention, Duluth police were asked to confirm places of residence and employment for each local red. By November 1947, individuals had been identified who were to be seized in the event of a national emergency and agents were advised to learn to recognize these individuals by sight. Fingerprints of local Communists were collected with help from cooperative local agencies. In July 1950, the FBI issued contingency orders for the arrest of named individuals in the event of an emergency, designating specific agents as responsible for the arrest of specific individuals and advising those agents to establish detailed plans of action for what was to be done with the spouse and children of the arrested persons. Agents replied with memos to superiors confirming that arrangements for these arrests were in place.[27] FBI agents also interrogated local Communists and their families.[28]

Communists also came under increasing pressure within the CIO. When Philip Murray replaced John L. Lewis as national head of the CIO, he made his acceptance of the position conditional on the CIO's acceptance of an anti-Communist resolution.[29] While Murray cooperated with Communists throughout the war years, in 1946, with anti-Communist fever mounting throughout the country, Murray saw a need for the CIO to do something to undercut the charges of Communist influence hurled against it. At a meeting of the CIO executive board in November, just after the elections that saw Republican critics of the CIO gain strength, Murray told the assembled board members that some CIO unions were substantially influenced on questions of foreign affairs by Communists and that this influence made the CIO an easy target for its enemies.[30] With the passage in June 1947 of the Taft-Hartley Act, which included provisions barring Communists from holding offices within unions, Murray saw the need to take action against the Communists within the CIO and he began to maneuver cautiously against them.[31]

In Minnesota, the campaign against Communists within the CIO was linked to the campaign against Communists within the DFL. The merger between the Democrats and the Farmer-Labor Party had been consummated at a time when the Popular Front was in control of the FLP. By 1947 a serious rift had developed between the Popular Front and the non–Popular Front wings of the DFL. Popular Front and anti–Popular Front forces battled for control of both the DFL and the CIO. With Popular Front forces having won control of the DFL convention and statewide leadership positions in 1946, Hubert Humphrey, the emerging leader of the anti–Popular Front movement in Minnesota, turned to Philip Murray and the CIO for help combating the Popular Front. Planning to run for the U.S. Senate in 1948 and needing the support of the CIO in Minnesota, Humphrey met with Murray in 1947. Murray, also wanting to weaken Communist influence within the CIO, agreed to help and sent Darrell Smith to Minnesota. Ostensibly working for Humphrey, Smith was at least partially supported by money secretly supplied by the CIO.[32] At the same time, Murray and other national CIO leaders hostile to the Communists supported anti-Communist activists within the CIO in a bid to take leadership of the Minnesota CIO away from the Popular Front. The key to the defeat of the Popular Front within the Minnesota CIO was the defection of Rodney Jacobson, secretary-treasurer of the Minnesota CIO, from the Popular Front to the anti–Popular Front side. With Jacobson's support and with help from the national CIO, opponents of the Popular Front were able to engineer a change in the makeup of the executive board of the Minnesota CIO that gave greater control to anti-Popular Front supporters. The three representatives on the state executive board from the Duluth area, Ilmar Koivunen of the Timber Workers, Edwin Drill of the Duluth CIO Council, and Hilding Schoen of the CIO public employees' union, were all stalwart supporters of the Popular Front.[33]

The final nail in the coffin of the Popular Front came with the 1948 election. President Truman firmly supported a foreign policy aimed at confronting the Soviet Union. The Popular Front favored a continuation of wartime cooperation with the Soviets. In December 1947 Henry Wallace announced that he would run against Truman as an independent third-party candidate. Wallace favored a more cooperative approach to Russia. Elmer Benson, leader of the Popular Front faction in Minnesota, which was in control of the state offices of the DFL, announced that the Minnesota DFL would send its national delegates to the convention of Wallace's independent party (later named the Progressive Party), rather than to the convention of the national Democratic Party supporting Truman.[34]

With the Wallace campaign threatening to pull votes away from Truman and throw the election to the Republicans, Philip Murray and the national CIO leaders ordered all CIO state organizations and central bodies to refrain from supporting the Wallace campaign. This put the Popular Front leaders in the Minnesota CIO in a difficult position. If they persisted in supporting Wallace, they would be violating national CIO policy. *Minnesota Labor*, the successor to *Midwest Labor* as the newspaper of the CIO in Minnesota, defied Murray's order, running stories in support of Wallace. The executive board of the state CIO immediately fired Ray Munson, the newspaper's editor. Joe Paszak, the representative of the Duluth CIO Council on the executive board, voted against the firing.[35] The anti–Popular Front leadership of the Minnesota CIO now got resolutions affirming the national CIO's ban on support for Wallace from both the executive board and the political action committee of the state CIO. Defiant Popular Front activists within the CIO responded by forming a "Minnesota Committee to Back Wallace," with Ilmar Koivunen of Duluth as president and Joe Paszak of Duluth as a member of the executive board. The anti–Popular Front forces, now in control of the state CIO, expelled Koivunen, Paszak, and three other Popular Front activists from the state executive board of the Minnesota CIO.[36]

Although they had been driven from the state CIO board, Popular Front leaders still retained control of the Duluth CIO Industrial Union Council. Indeed, they found sufficient support within that council to pass resolutions opposing the national CIO policy and the actions of the Minnesota CIO in expelling Wallace supporters. When the national CIO ordered the Duluth Council to rescind these resolutions, the Duluth CIO ignored the order. With the local CIO council now in open opposition to both the national and the state CIO, several local unions began to resist the Popular Front leadership in the Duluth CIO. Steel Plant Local 1028 passed a resolution opposing the Wallace campaign. Coolerator Local 1096, now under the control of local leaders reflecting the anti-Communist stance of the national leadership of the Steel Workers, demanded that Joe Paszak either stop supporting Wallace or resign as president of the CIO Council.[37]

The anti–Popular Front locals banded together to form the Duluth CIO Political Action Committee (PAC), with affiliated locals switching their per capita dues from the CIO Council under Popular Front control to the PAC, which was independent of the Popular Front and in line with national and state CIO policy. This Duluth CIO PAC was headed by Glenn Peterson from Local 1028. With the backing of Philip Murray, Peterson would later be named president of the Minnesota CIO and given the charge "to clean out the Commies."[38] One by one the CIO unions in Duluth switched their allegiance from the Popular Front-controlled CIO Council to the anti–Popular Front PAC. Local 4 from the Klearflax plant led the way, followed by the Steelworkers Locals 1028, 1096, and 1424 (the Clyde Iron Local). Other unions followed suit, including the Brewers, the Newspaper Guild, and the UAW Auto Mechanics Union. Altogether, three-quarters of the Duluth CIO Council's membership was gone, leaving the Popular Front leaders in control of a council reduced to a shadow of its former self. On Labor Day, only 150 people showed up to the official CIO Council event in Fairmount Park, while over 1,000 attended the rival event sponsored by the Steelworkers in Lincoln Park.[39]

The anti–Popular Front Duluth CIO PAC made the election of

Hubert Humphrey to the U.S. Senate its top priority. As a supporter of the hard-line anti-Soviet foreign policy of the Truman administration, Humphrey was anathema to Popular Front leaders in Duluth. For his part, Humphrey had been working to dislodge the Popular Front from its control of the DFL as early as 1946, when he was supposedly allied with the Popular Front in support of Blatnik. In October of that year, in the midst of the campaign to elect John Blatnik to Congress, Humphrey ally Orville Freeman wrote to Earl Bester, acting district director for the Steelworkers and director of the CIO PAC during the campaign, asking him to recommend someone to be appointed as an officer in the Young DFL of Minnesota. The letter expressed the hope that the Young DFL "might serve to rectify some of the problems we are facing at present" and he requested the recommendation of persons who would "have had some experience in dealing with the kind of people we must displace from leadership in the Party."[40]

The Young Democrats had existed in the prewar years, but the organization had gone under during the war, with many young people serving in the armed forces. The prewar organization had been open to people between the ages of eighteen and forty. With a core of able young supporters, Humphrey aimed to resurrect this organization under the control of his supporters as a base for mounting a challenge to the Popular Front leadership of the DFL. A founding convention for the Young DFL was held in Minneapolis in November 1947. The convention was clearly orchestrated by Humphrey and his supporters, among them Orville Freeman, Arthur Naftalin, Eugene McCarthy, Donald Fraser, and, from Duluth, Gerald Heaney. Humphrey supporters entered the convention as part of an "Independent Progressive Caucus" whose aim it was "to assume leadership of a party once great and once the spearhead of sincere liberals in Minnesota" and "to wrest control from leadership *now discredited*." Members of this Independent Progressive Caucus came with a predesignated slate of candidates for officers and with a printed page of instructions emphasizing the need to follow the lead of experienced floor leaders. The page was stamped with the admonition "do not bring this along to the convention."[41]

Francis Smith, a St. Paul attorney who had been active in the Young Democrats before the war and who had provided legal advice to the Democratic Party of Minnesota during negotiations over the merger with the FLP, wrote a report to the DFL Central Committee concerning the November convention of the Young Democrats.

Smith was himself an anti-Communist. He had once objected to the merger with the FLP on the grounds that "the Reds are actually dominating the Farmer-Labor Party."[42] But here Smith aligned himself with the Popular Front in its struggle with Humphrey supporters. He wrote a scathing denunciation of the Young DFL convention, pointing out that Humphrey supporters had packed the convention with students from the nearby campus, that "delegates" were never asked to show credentials, and that the practice of voting by districts, traditionally followed by the prewar Young Democrats and specifically required by the DFL's leadership charge to the Young DFLers, was not followed. Smith concluded his report by saying, "this writer feels that from both a legal and a moral standpoint that the State Executive Committee of the Democratic-Farmer-Labor Party of Minnesota should unhesitatingly refuse to recognize the alleged organization of Younger Democratic-Farmer-Labor Clubs of Minnesota, set up at the November 9, 1947, gathering."[43]

The political hardball between Humphrey and the Popular Front created serious difficulties for men like Congressman John Blatnik and Steelworkers District Director Earl Bester. Each had long worked alongside Popular Front leaders in the labor movement and the Farmer-Labor Party, and Popular Front support had played a significant role in getting Blatnik elected to Congress. In a later interview, Bester commented on the close relations that he and the Steelworkers had to the Popular Front, saying that they could go along with ninety percent of what the local Communists wanted.[44] For both Bester and Blatnik, a break with the leaders of the Popular Front would be politically and personally difficult.

But in December 1947, an angry Hubert Humphrey forced the issue. He wrote a letter to Bester complaining about attacks made on him by Herman Griffith, the leader of the Popular Front forces in Duluth and in the Eighth Congressional District. Humphrey begins his letter by complaining about the unfairness of Griffith's attack. Having mentioned Bester's defense of Griffith in the past, Humphrey reminded Bester of Griffith's obvious loyalty to the needs of the Soviet Union. Humphrey then goes on to press Bester and Blatnik to come out clearly in support of himself. Humphrey continues:

> Now if Blatnik's supporters are going to knife me, then
> I'm going to have to let my supporters do as they see fit
> in retaliation.... Make no mistake about it—I am person-

ally for John Blatnik.... [But] I can guarantee you that there is plenty of grumbling right in your home town over the tactics of some of the DFL Executive Committee.... I'm not going to write any more this time, Earl. I just want you to think this through. I'm going to start counting my friends. I want to know where they are, and where they stand.... I tell you, Earl, I'm so fed up with this business of being knifed by the left wing, or should I say, the Commie brethren, that I'm not going to tolerate it any longer."[45]

At the time he received this letter, Bester may have thought he could avoid breaking with either side. Even in a report to Washington one month later, Bester evaded the coming crisis, saying there was no interest in Wallace's third-party effort in Minnesota and that all local unions were going along with the national CIO PAC. Two months later, with the battle between the Wallace forces and the Humphrey forces heating up, Bester still tried to avoid taking sides. He wrote a letter to Blatnik rebuking him for criticisms of the Marshall Plan, which, though pleasing to the Popular Front, would alienate the Steelworkers in Locals 1028 and 1096 in Duluth, who supported the plan. Bester urged Blatnik to follow a policy of strict neutrality, saying nothing that could be construed as an endorsement of one side or the other. He concluded by telling Blatnik he thought Humphrey was the best hope to defeat Ball.[46] By May 1948, Blatnik was finding it difficult to stay neutral. He begged Bester and other DFL leaders in Duluth independent of the Popular Front to "keep me out of this."[47]

A leaflet distributed by Popular Front activists at a Yugoslav Federation picnic in Eveleth increased the pressure on Blatnik. The leaflet, issued by the Eighth District DFL, which remained under the control of the Popular Front, supported Jim Schields, Humphrey's Popular Front opponent in the DFL primary for U.S. Senate. It also called Humphrey a Trojan horse for the Republicans, a sell-out, an opponent of Blatnik, a phony liberal, and a faker. An enraged Humphrey wrote to Gerald Heaney, his lieutenant in Duluth, instructing Heaney to tell Bester that this sort of thing had to stop: "I want Blatnik to come out for me 100 percent and I want it damn quick."[48] Though his anger is understandable, Humphrey need not have been anxious about the election. In the DFL primary Humphrey defeated Shields by a ratio of 8 to 1.[49]

Earl Bester (here holding the sign while photographed next to Hubert H. Humphrey at the DFL convention in 1948) tried to avoid the break with the Popular Front, but in the end supported Humphrey. Courtesy Minnesota Historical Society.

Despite the drubbing, the battered Popular Front forces pressed ahead, focusing on the third-party campaign of Henry Wallace for president. As announced earlier by Elmer Benson, Popular Front supporters aimed to send delegates from the state convention of the Minnesota DFL to the national convention of Wallace's Progressive Party, rather than to the national convention of the Democratic Party. This strategy depended on maintaining Popular Front control of the Minnesota DFL. For this to happen, control of the Eighth District DFL convention was crucial because the district was one of the strongholds of the Popular Front. Although the Popular Front controlled the DFL in the Eighth District at the beginning of 1948, the growth of organized opposition within the CIO and the DFL had weakened its position substantially. Also of great importance was the role of John Moriarity, chairman of the St. Louis County DFL. Moriarity was not himself a member of the Popular Front and had come into the DFL as a Democrat. However, he had been willing to cooperate with Popular Front forces in Duluth and St. Louis County since the merger in 1944 and had been elected chairman of the county DFL as someone acceptable to the then-

A combat veteran of World War II and labor lawyer, Gerald Heaney led the Humphrey forces in Duluth and the Eighth District of Minnesota, out-organizing his Popular Front opponents. Courtesy Judge Gerald Heaney.

strong Popular Front. As county chair, Moriarity was courted by the Humphrey faction of the party, represented in Duluth by Gerald Heaney, who, like Moriarity, came into the DFL from the Democratic side of the merger. The Humphrey forces were successful. By the time of the convention, Moriarity had clearly resolved not to follow the Popular Front into Wallace's Progressive Party.

With both sides doing their best to turn out supporters, attendance at precinct caucuses prior to the county convention was high. At the caucuses, delegates were elected to attend the county convention. For thirteen of Duluth's seventy-five precincts, conflicting credentials were submitted for delegates from each side. Chairman Moriarity appointed a credentials committee with an anti-Wallace majority. In a heated atmosphere, with Wallace supporters packing the room where the committee met, the credentials committee sifted through the conflicting slates submitted from the precincts in question, refusing to seat a relatively small number of Wallace supporters with credentials that were apparently forged. Chairman Moriarity also refused to seat fifty-one other delegates who were ruled to be supporters of a third party and therefore not eligible to be seated at the convention. By the time the convention convened, it was apparent to all that the Popular Front was in the minority position. In fact, it would have been in the minority position even if all contested delegates had been seated on the convention floor. Seeing that it had lost control of the convention, the Popular Front group walked out shortly after the convention opened, joining the excluded Wallace supporters to form a convention of its own in a room rented ahead of time in a Duluth hotel. Altogether, the Popular Front Wallace convention included approximately one hundred and eighty-seven people, whereas the anti–Popular Front controlled convention included three hundred and three people. The Popular Front–controlled Eighth District Executive Committee tried to salvage the situation by recognizing the Wallace convention as the legitimate convention of the St. Louis County DFL, but this ploy proved to be of no avail when the state convention of the DFL recognized the anti-Wallace convention.[50]

Having walked out of the DFL, Duluth's Popular Front plunged ahead with the campaign to elect Henry Wallace as president on the Progressive Party ticket, but the election was a disaster for the Popular Front. Wallace received only 2.3 percent of the vote in the state of Minnesota, which had once been a Popular Front stronghold. Humphrey, on the other hand, won an impressive victory in the U.S. Senate race, overwhelming Republican Joseph Ball and winning the first major office for liberal forces since the FLP victories of 1936. With Popular Front supporters having left the party, the DFL was now firmly in the hands of the anti–Popular Front liberals. And though Popular Front supporters remained in control of the Duluth CIO Council, the council had been reduced to a hollow shell.

Further losses would follow. By December 1948 only 10 percent of Duluth's CIO members remained in the CIO Council under Popular Front control. Under the direction of national officers of the CIO the Duluth Council was reconstituted. Elections were held in February 1949. Clifford Rohlf, an anti–Popular Front activist from the Coolerator Local with ties to Earl Bester and John Blatnik, was elected chair of the new council, winning over Erwin Drill, the Popular Front candidate, by a margin of 3 to 2. The once-powerful Popular Front had lost its base of support in the CIO, as well as in the DFL.

Individual Popular Front activists remained. With strong support from his Cement Plant Local, Joe Paszak continued to play an active role in the new CIO Council, as did Erwin Drill, Hilding Schoen, Pat McGraw, Ernie Pearson, Maney Pearson, and Glenn Pearson. Popular Front activists prodded the council to act on a variety of social issues, calling for an investigation of unemployment, defending the civil liberties of the foreign-born, contributing to an NAACP Legal Defense Fund, maintaining county relief funding, supporting the formation of a fair employment practices commission, and protesting racial discrimination. The Popular Front even retained enough influence to persuade the council to protest the stand taken by Senator Humphrey on a particular bill.[51]

Still, pressure against the Popular Front continued within the CIO. Having once gotten the upper hand, anti-Communists within the CIO were determined to drive all Communists and their allies out. Earl Bester, who had broken with the Popular Front under pressure from the Humphrey forces, wrote to the CIO in Washington, thanking them for help electing an all right-wing slate in Minnesota in 1948 and talking about the job ahead "to get these birds cleaned out."[52] And with Phil Murray's blessing, Glenn Peterson of Steelworkers Local 1028 was named president of the Minnesota CIO to do just that.[53]

The Western Paint Local, one of the oldest of the Popular Front–led locals in Duluth, retained its left-wing leadership. By 1949 the local was affiliated with the United Gas and Chemical Workers (UGCW) Union as Local 79. Under a provision of the Taft-Hartley Act, unions with Communist officers were excluded from the protections of the National Labor Relations Board. In September 1949, the reconstituted Duluth CIO Council received a communication from the UGCW International asking that the council not seat delegates from Local 79 until notified to do so by the international. The international used this ploy to exert pressure on Local 79 to rid itself of its left-wing leadership. The matter was sent to the Duluth CIO Executive Board for discussion. The board recommended compliance with the UGCW request and, by a narrow vote of eleven to ten, the Duluth CIO Council accepted this recommendation.[54]

Gradually, many of the left-wingers dropped out. When the Coolerator plant closed, Glenn Pearson went into business cleaning Venetian blinds.[55] Ernie Pearson died in 1951 during the height of the anti-Communist excesses of the McCarthy era. Herman Griffith gave a eulogy for his old friend, frightening many of those present with the dangerous candor of his use of the word "comrade."[56]

Ernie's wife, Maney, was in her late 50s when Ernie died, and she got a job at the Nopeming tuberculosis asylum. According to her daughter-in-law, Leata Pearson, she was fired, blacklisted by the Humphrey forces because of her radical politics.[57] Henry Paull died of a heart attack in 1947. With the death of her husband and the defeat of the Popular Front in Duluth, Irene Paull moved to Minneapolis, where she continued to work for civil rights during the McCarthy era.[58] Ilmar Koivunen left the Timber Workers in 1948. He bought a garage in Tamarack, Minnesota, and ran a Ford dealership there. When he refused to testify against Harry Bridges, the West Coast Longshoremen leader accused of being a Communist, Ford Motor Company canceled his dealership. Koivunen was left with a repair shop and gas pumps. FBI agents started visiting neighbors and customers, scaring away his business. In 1952 Koivunen sold out and moved to the West Coast, where he got a job as a longshoreman.[59] Herman Griffith continued in business as an interior decorator. Martin Kuusisto, Joe Paszak, and George Dizard held on to positions within their unions, sustained by rank-and-file support against all efforts to remove them.[60]

An anticlimactic finale of sorts was provided by the trial of Henry Olsen and Ervin Drill. In March 1951 the two produced the first issue of *Rank and File Duluth Steelworker*, an underground newspaper distributed at the steel plant. A second issue appeared in April. In May of the same year, with a National Labor Relations Board Ruling in hand giving employers the right to fire employees discharged by their unions as Communists, Local 1028 brought formal charges against Olsen and Drill. The charges were filed by Glenn Peterson, W. N. Beaudin, Al Overton, and John McCauley. The statement of charges read as follows:

> Ervin Drill and Henry M. Olsen are charged with contributing to an anonymous publication entitled "RANK AND FILE, DULUTH STEELWORKER," not authorized by the United Steelworkers of America, Local Union No. 1028, which publication circulated amongst the membership false reports, and misrepresentations and which slandered and did willfully wrong a member of the International Union.

In May and June a trial was conducted at Steelworkers Hall on Central Avenue, with Stanley Roginski presiding. Drill did not even show up, sending a note verified by a physician that he was ill, leaving poor Olsen to face his accusers alone. A transcription of the entire proceeding, running to sixty-four pages, was made by Evelyn K. Coe. It makes clear that the real issue on trial was Communism. Throughout the proceeding the accusers and the accused addressed one another by their first names. At once comic and sad, the transcription provides a revealing portrait of the time. There is nothing in the records to indicate the outcome of the trial.[61]

after the fall

THE ELECTION OF 1948 MARKED A TURNING POINT IN THE HIS-
tory of Duluth. From the violent confrontation with police in 1889
to the victories of the Farmer-Labor Party and the CIO in the 1930s,
the struggle waged for respect and economic security by Duluth's
ethnically mixed industrial working class was a constant theme
in the history of the city. While always representing minority perspectives, radicals from the Knights of Labor, the Socialist Party,
the IWW, and the Communist Party played a leavening role in this
sixty-year struggle. In 1948 anti-Communists captured control of
the DFL in Duluth and by 1950 Communists were largely driven
out of the organized labor movement in the city. While the expulsion of the Communists turned on the connection of the American Communist Party with Soviet Russia, it also marked the end
of an organized radical perspective within the labor movement
in Duluth.[1] But beyond this, the Communist expulsion marked a
deeper change in the nature of the labor movement in Duluth. By
1948, Duluth's multiethnic industrial working class had won its
long struggle for respect and economic security. The victories won
by the FLP and CIO in the 1930s had changed everything. With John
Blatnik as their representative in Congress and powerful unions as
their representatives in collective bargaining, Duluth's working
class had achieved its long-sought goals. With the battle won, it
was now possible for working-class families to enjoy the fruits of
their long historical labors.

Gradually, however, economic and social forces eroded the
gains won by working-class families. Foremost among these forces
was the gradual dismantling of the industrial base that supported
working-class Duluth. Interlake Iron, Western Paint, Coolerator,
Clyde Iron, Klearflax, Diamond Tool, the scrap-iron yards, the knitting mills, and the lumber camps are all gone now. Between Morgan
Park and Gary, where the U.S. Steel complex once employed thou-

sands, nothing remains but asphalt strips trailing off into weeds and wildflowers.

With the decline of industrial Duluth, families that for two or three generations had found work in the shops scattered over the western half of the city had to create new ways of life. Many people left Duluth altogether, with the population of the city gradually falling from a high of over one hundred thousand to the present eighty thousand or so.[2] The decline of industrial Duluth also brought with it the loss of many unions. The once powerful CIO unions are now all gone. With the decline of the unions, working-class families lost much of the economic security that had been won by their parents and grandparents.[3] They also lost much of their influence over the political life of Duluth, with the remaining unions, largely based in the building trades and public-service sectors, forced to acquiesce to economic and political leadership coming from the city's business community.[4]

From this perspective it might seem that the long historical struggle waged by the immigrant labor movement in Duluth had ultimately had little effect on the city. A case could be made for this view, that the changes of the 1930s were only transient phenomena, brief upheavals that soon subsided to leave the city pretty much as it had always been and leaving a demoralized working class that had lost its vision and sense of purpose. There is more than a kernel of truth to this pessimistic assessment of the legacy of the labor movement in Duluth, but it is not the whole story.

In the first place, it is important to remember that the decline of industrial Duluth did not happen overnight. It was a long, drawn-out process. Men coming home from World War II took up good union jobs. They married and raised families in West Duluth. Like their parents and grandparents, they strongly identified with their unions and with the DFL. In 1959 Steelworkers Local 1028 waged a strike that lasted 118 days.[5] And while many did not speak the Swedish or Slovenian of their grandparents, most had some sense of their ethnic heritage and the importance of ethnicity in the past. They worked, raised their families, and served their communities. The lucky ones made it to retirement before the shop closed down. They were proud of their wartime service, proud of the comfortable life their labor had provided for their families, and proud of themselves as men of standing in the life of the community. Men and women of this generation were in many ways the beneficiaries of the long struggle waged by their parents and grandparents. If they were less tempted by radicalism than their parents or grand-parents had been, it is because they understood the magnitude of what had been accomplished.

But there were limits to this consciousness. The loss of a radical perspective deprived the labor movement of some of its moral force and critical understanding. The radical perspective put the struggle for labor's rights within a broader moral context. During the era of the Popular Front, the Duluth CIO Council was in the forefront of the struggle for racial justice. After the expulsion of the radicals, there are reports that African Americans attempting to join picket lines were turned away by fellow unionists from Local 1028.[6] Perhaps the sense of victory, the sense that labor's long battle had been won, left organized labor less sensitive to the other injustices around it. In any case, there was a self-satisfied turn away from the proselytizing moral solidarity of the past, a turn that left the labor movement vulnerable to the erosion caused by the decline of industrial Duluth.

The loss of a radical perspective also deprived the labor movement in Duluth of a certain understanding of its situation. The immigrant radicalism of the whole period spanning from the 1880s to the 1940s included an intellectually sophisticated under-standing of labor's place in the global capitalist order. The labor radicals placed the unions within a broader context of class struggle, a context within which, as the Knights of Labor said, "An injury to one is an injury to all." Newspapers like *Työmies*, *Industrialisti*, *Truth*, and *Midwest Labor* provided useful analysis and a guiding vision to activists within the labor movement. After 1950 this level of understanding virtually disappeared. By the 1980s in Duluth the sophisticated class-consciousness of the 1930s had given way to an almost purely geographic consciousness, one that pitted West against East, but had little understanding of what that opposition was about.[7]

Nonetheless, some legacy remains of the long struggle waged by Duluth's multiethnic industrial working class. Duluth remains a union town. With 30 to 35 percent of its labor force organized, Duluth remains among the most organized cities in the country. In 1997 labor activists in Duluth launched a living wage campaign.[8] The campaign aimed at getting the city council to require businesses receiving financial support from the city to pay employees a living wage. Union members themselves stood to gain nothing from the campaign since they already received union wages. In looking beyond self-interest, the living-wage campaign harkened back to the moral solidarity of the past. It found strong support throughout the city of Duluth, giving a radical edge to local politics that had been missing for decades. It replaced the geographic divide between East and West Duluth with a line drawn on principled grounds between labor on the one side and the Chamber of Commerce on the other, a line that resonated with the struggles of the past.

Still, the living-wage campaign did not exactly replicate the divisions of the past. The Duluth of 1997 was different from the Duluth of 1937. The industrial city of the past had redefined itself as a medical, educational, and retail center. The living-wage campaign found strong support in West Duluth. But it also found strong support in East Duluth, now home to many of the professionals working in the city's hospitals and universities. Without the legacy of the past, however, the living-wage campaign would not have found the degree of support that it did. In a sense, the campaign breathed new life into the moral embers of the past. In the elections of fall 1997, labor-supported candidates won all eight of the hotly contested seats for city council and school board.

Despite some losses in the years since 1997, the reenergized labor movement remains a force to be reckoned with in local politics. In the election of 2002, following the death of Senator Paul Wellstone, a political figure rooted in the progressive wing of Minnesota's DFL, 425 progressive activists door-knocked in Duluth neighborhoods. Two years later, in the presidential campaign of 2004, Duluth activists mounted an even more massive effort. Some 650 volunteers knocked on doors to get out the vote, sweeping the historically low-turnout inner-city precincts three times. This unprecedented effort paid off. At the end of the day, 90 percent of the registered voters in the city had voted, including some six to eight thousand new voters. The turnout rate in Duluth was higher than in any other city in the nation, with the Democratic candidate, John Kerry, winning every precinct in the city. One of the central organizers of this campaign and one of the activists responsible for the reenergized labor movement in Duluth was Erik Peterson. In analyzing the process that led up to this 2004 election effort, Peterson pointed to the importance of the living-wage campaign of 1997, a campaign that realigned local politics around radical issues of social justice.[9]

The revitalized labor movement in Duluth is deeply indebted

to the many men and women who have given their time and energy. Some of these activists lacked personal roots in Duluth and it took their conscious planning and enormous effort to achieve what has been accomplished. But seeds must be sown in fertile ground. It is this fertile ground that is the real legacy of the immigrant labor movement in Duluth. Probably everywhere on this earth there are men and women who would respond to calls for social justice framed in terms of labor's rights. But there are more of them in Duluth than elsewhere. For many people in Duluth, labor's rights are family values, a precious part of what has been inherited from the past.

notes

introduction

1. Herbert Gutman is a historian who did groundbreaking work in the study of the American working class and the forms by which resistance to the emerging industrial order found expression in the cultural traditions and actions of groups of American workers. See his collection of important essays, *Work, Culture, and Society in Industrializing America: Essays in American Working-Class and Social History* (New York: Alfred A. Knopf, 1976).

2. David Montgomery, *The Fall of the House of Labor* (Cambridge: Cambridge University Press, 1987) provides a rich account of this process in the steel industry.

3. Gary Gerstle, *American Crucible: Race and Nation in the Twentieth Century* (Princeton: Princeton University Press, 2001), describes the tension between civic nationalist and racial nationalist visions of America, both of which often worked against certain ethnic groups.

4. See, for example, Lars Olsson, "Evelina Johansdotter, Textile Workers, and the Munsingwear Family: Class, Gender, and Ethnicity in the Political Economy of Minnesota at the End of World War I," in Philip J. Anderson and Dag Blanck, eds., *Swedes in the Twin Cities: Immigrant Life and Minnesota's Urban Frontier* (St. Paul: Minnesota Historical Society Press, 2001), 77-90.

5. The term comes from Gary Gerstle, *Working Class Americanism: The Politics of Labor in a Textile City* (Cambridge: Cambridge University Press, 1989).

6. On the connection between Duluth and Butte, see Richard Hudelson, "Jack Carney and the Truth in Duluth," *Saothar* 19 (1994): 135-36.

7. On Butte, see David M. Emmons, *The Butte Irish: Class and Ethnicity in an American Mining Town, 1875-1925* (Urbana: University of Illinois Press, 1989).

8. Lizabeth Cohen, *Making a New Deal: Industrial Workers in Chicago, 1919-1939* (Cambridge: Cambridge University Press, 1990), provides a powerful account of this process in Chicago.

9. On the radical Swedes in Chicago, see Per Nordahl, *Weaving the Ethnic Fabric: Social Networks among Swedish-American Radicals in Chicago 1890-1940* (Umeå: Umeå University, 1994). On radical Swedes in Duluth, see Richard Hudelson, "The Scandinavian Local of the Duluth Socialist Party: 1910-1924," *The Swedish-American Historical Quarterly* 44 (1993): 181-90.

10. Nordahl focuses on the development of networks within the radical Swedish community and for this reason it is difficult to say that his work specifically supports this inward turn. The importance in Chicago of Swedish "enclaves"

as a form of self-protection against competition and hostility to immigrants is mentioned by Ulf Beijbom in his introduction to *Swedes in America*, ed. Ulf Beijbom (Växjö: Swedish Emigrant Institute, 1993), 11, though this does not imply a denial of outward-looking action as well. In the same volume, Lars Wendelius, in "Swedish-American Organizations as Cultural Institutions: The Case of Rockford, Illinois," draws a related contrast between Chicago and Rockford. "What distinguishes the two communities from each other," he says, "is just that the radical popular culture was allowed to play a more important part in Rockford than in Chicago" (48).

11. David Brody, *Steelworkers in America: The Nonunion Era* (Cambridge: Harvard University Press, 1960), provides a classic study of the industry after the fall of the nineteenth-century unions. Steelworkers in Duluth faced many of the same problems as steelworkers elsewhere, but they lacked the past that shaped the experiences of steelworkers in towns further east.

12. Robert H. Zieger, *The CIO, 1935–1955* (Chapel Hill: University of North Carolina Press, 1995), 254.

chapter 1. labor roots

1. For several other references to this claim, see Matti Kaups, "Europeans in Duluth: 1870," in Ryck Lydecker, Lawrence J. Sommer, and Arthur J. Larson, eds., *Duluth: Sketches of the Past* (Duluth: American Bicentennial Commission, 1976), 71–81.

2. On the panic of 1857, see Anne Stultz Bailey, "The Towns That Became Duluth," in Lydecker et al., *Duluth*, 106; see also Kaups, "Europeans in Duluth," 71.

3. Cited in Kaups, "Europeans in Duluth," 71.

4. Stuart V. Bradley, "Duluth in the 1870s," in Lydecker et al., *Duluth*, 240–41.

5. Ibid., 241.

6. Kaups, "Europeans in Duluth," 73.

7. *The Duluth Minnesotian*, May 1, 1869.

8. Bradley, "Duluth in the 1870s," 241. On General Sargent's position as head of Jay Cooke's bank, see Cecil H. Meyers, "Banking in Duluth," in Lydecker et al, *Duluth*, 221–22.

9. Kaups, "Europeans in Duluth," 71.

10. *The Duluth Minnesotian*, April 23, 1870.

11. Kaups, "Europeans in Duluth," 72.

12. Dwight Woodbridge and John Pardee, *History of Duluth and St. Louis County* (Chicago: C.F. Cooper and Co., 1910), 1:347.

13. See Meyers, "Banking in Duluth," 222; Bailey, "The Towns That Became Duluth," 101; and Bradley, "Duluth in the 1870s," 244–45.

14. Richard O. Sielaff, tables 1 and 2 in *Lake Traffic at the Port of Duluth-Superior*, research study no. 1. Duluth: Port Authority of Duluth, 1955. Available at the Northeast Minnesota Historical Center (NEMHC). Figures for years prior to 1883 exclude the port of Superior.

15. *R. L. Polk and Company's Duluth and Superior City Directory, 1887–1888* (Duluth: R. L. Polk and Co., 1887), 27.

16. Lawrence J. Sommer, "Forgotten Industries of Duluth," in Lydecker et al., *Duluth*, 201.

17. *Duluth and Superior City Directory*, 25.

18. J. C. Ryan, "The Duluth Lumber Industry," in Lydecker et al., *Duluth*, 167.

19. Quoted by Walter Van Brunt in *Duluth and St. Louis County, Minnesota* (Chicago and New York: American Historical Society, 1921), 1:266.

20. *London Financial Times*, November 22, 1889; *New York Observer*, January 24, 1889; *New York Evening Post*, April 1889; *Harper's Weekly*, August 17, 1889; and *Cosmopolitan*, February 1889. These references come from Dora Mary Macdonald, *This Is Duluth* (Duluth: Duluth Board of Education, 1950), 100.

21. Lakeside and Lester Park file at the NEMHC.

22. Woodbridge and Pardee, *History of Duluth*, 155.

23. Bailey, "The Towns That Became Duluth," 89.

24. Ibid., 93.

25. Ibid., 102, quoting Woodbridge and Pardee, *History of Duluth*, 194.

26. For a description of the early Rice's Point and West End, see the *Duluth News Tribune*, July 29, 1956. The *Sanborn Insurance Atlas* for 1885 shows the saloons, boardinghouses, and "shanties" that haphazardly covered the base of Rice's Point at that time (NEMHC).

27. Kaups, "Europeans in Duluth," 73–74. The figures apply only to the north shore settlement then known as Duluth. Foreigners were also present in other settlements that would eventually make up the city of Duluth. For example, there were an additional 516 Swedes in Oneota and Fond du Lac. See Matti Kaups, "Swedish Immigrants in Duluth, 1856–1870," in *Perspectives on Swedish Immigration*, ed. Nils Hasselmo (Chicago: Swedish Pioneer Historical Society, 1978), 169.

28. Meyers, "Banking in Duluth," 221. The agreement to build the railroad involved a commitment by the citizens of St. Louis County to approve $150,000 in government bonds. On this, see Frank A. King, "Railroads at the Head of the Lakes," in Lydecker et al., *Duluth*, 181.

29. Kaups, "Europeans in Duluth," 72–73.

30. *Duluth News Tribune*, July 29, 1956, 14B.

31. Kaups, "Swedish Immigrants," 158.

32. Ibid., 159.

33. Van Brunt, *Duluth and St. Louis County* 1:186.

34. Timo Riippa, "Finns and Swede-Finns," in June Drenning Holmquist, ed., *They Chose Minnesota: A Survey of the State's Ethnic Groups* (St. Paul: Minnesota Historical Society Press, 1981), 314.

35. Bradley, "Duluth in the 1870s," 241.

36. Kaups, "Europeans in Duluth," 75.

37. Ibid., 77.

38. This estimate comes from the exhibit on Swedish emigration to the Americas found at Emigrant House in Växjö, Sweden. This exhibit was prepared under the direction of Ulf Beijbom, one of the foremost scholars of this emigration.

39. Riippa, "The Finns and Swede-Finns," 306.

40. Sommer, "Forgotten Industries," 201–2.

41. Philip Foner, *History of the Labor Movement in the United States* (New York: International, 1955), 2:12.

42. Shelton Stromquist, *A Generation of Boomers: The Pattern of Railroad Labor Conflict in Nineteenth-Century America* (Urbana: University of Illinois, 1987), 5.

43. Foner, *History of the Labor Movement*, 12.

44. Stromquist, *Generation of Boomers*, 4–10.

45. Quoted in Foner, *History of the Labor Movement*, 13–14.

46. Leon Fink, *Workingmen's Democracy: The Knights of Labor and American Politics* (Urbana: University of Illinois, 1985), 4.

47. Ibid., 9.

48. *Duluth Weekly Tribune*, July 8, 1881, 4.

49. Jonathan Garlock, *Guide to the Local Assemblies of the Knights of Labor* (Westport, Conn.: Greenwood, 1982), 233–34, 543.

50. *Duluth Directory 1884–85*, 63. On the role of this hall in the life of the labor movement in Duluth, see George C. Engberg, "The Knights of Labor in Minnesota," *Minnesota History* 22 (1941), 376.

51. Engberg, "Knights of Labor," 374; *Industrial Age*, March 24, 1888, 2. *Industrial Age* is available on microfilm at the Minnesota Historical Society (MHS).

52. No known copy of the *Voice of Labor* exists; an advertisement for the newspaper appears on the last page of the *Duluth and Superior Directory, 1889–90*.

53. Foner, *History of the Labor Movement*, 20.

54. *Duluth Weekly Tribune*, August 19, 1881, 4; and August 17, 1883, 4.

55. *Duluth Weekly Tribune*, May 19, 1882, 4.

56. *Duluth Weekly Tribune*, May 18, 1883, 4.

57. *Duluth Weekly Tribune*, October 26, 1883, 4.

58. *Duluth Weekly Tribune*, August 22, 1884, 2.

59. *Duluth Weekly Tribune*, January 25, 1988; and July 18, 1884, 4.

60. The U.S. average of 282 working days per year comes from Foner, *History of the Labor Movement*, 20. With the limitations imposed by Duluth's climate, it may be that the average number of working days per year in Duluth was fewer than this.

61. *Duluth Weekly Tribune*, January 25, 1884, 3.

62. Foner, *History of the Labor Movement*, 20.

63. For the view that laborers were doing well, see the *Duluth Weekly Tribune*, September 21, 1883, 2.

64. *Duluth Weekly Tribune*, March 14, 1884, 2.

65. *Duluth Weekly Tribune*, March 21, 1884, 3.

66. *Duluth Weekly Tribune*, December 19, 1884, 4.

67. *Duluth Weekly Tribune*, November 28, 1884, 1.

68. *Duluth Weekly Tribune*, February 5, 1886, 3.

69. *Duluth Weekly Tribune*, July 8, 1881, 4. The identification of "Whiffet" as W. S. Woodbridge can be found in the *Duluth Weekly Tribune*, May 11, 1883, 4.

70. *Duluth Weekly Tribune*, October 21, 1881, 4; and May 10, 1882, 4.

71. *Duluth Weekly Tribune*, December 8, 1882, 4.

72. Garlock, *Guide to the Local Assemblies*, 234.

73. Ibid., 637.

74. The first mention of the hall appears in the *Duluth Directory, 1884–1885*, 63.

75. *Duluth Weekly Tribune*, March 12, 1886, 3.

76. Ibid., 2.

77. Ibid.

78. *Duluth Weekly Tribune*, April 23, 1886, 1.

79. Accounts of these two strikes and the quoted passages are from the *Duluth Weekly Tribune*, May 28, 1886, 1–2, 4.

80. Engberg, "Knights of Labor," 379.

81. Garlock, *Guide to the Local Assemblies*, 234.

82. Engberg, "Knights of Labor," 371. Schweiger appears to have been from Duluth and to have written to the Knights' national paper about the whiskey. Judging from the city directory, "Brother Schweiger" was likely Joseph Schweiger, an assistant health inspector.

83. *Duluth Daily Tribune*, May 27, 1888, 2; and May 29, 1888, 4.

84. *Duluth Weekly Tribune*, April 23, 1886, 3.

85. *Industrial Age*, March 24, 1888, 2.

86. *Duluth Evening Herald*, May 30, 1888, 3.

87. *Duluth Evening Herald*, June 5, 1888, 3; and June 8, 1888, 1. There is a photo and brief description of MacDonald in Rhoda R. Gilman, *The Story of Minnesota's Past* (St. Paul: Minnesota Historical Society Press, 1989), 131.

88. See the coverage of MacDonald's talk given in the *Lake Superior News*, June 9, 1888, 2.

89. On the dance in Superior, see the *Duluth Evening Herald*, August 2, 1888, 4.

90. Except where otherwise noted, this account of the strike is taken from the *Lake Superior News*, August 4, 1888, 5. A bound copy of this volume is available at the Northeast Minnesota Historical Center (NEMHC).

91. *Lake Superior News*, August 4, 1888, 5.

92. An account of this meeting can be found in the *Lake Superior News*, August 11, 1888, 3.

93. *Duluth Daily Tribune*, July 3, 1889.

94. *Duluth Daily Tribune*, July 3, 1889. The *Duluth Daily News* (July 3, 1889, 4) estimated the number of strikers at over one thousand.

95. *Duluth Daily Tribune*, July 3, 1889.

96. *Duluth Daily News*, July 4, 1889, 4.

97. *Duluth Daily Tribune*, July 4, 1889.

98. Ibid.

99. *Duluth Daily News*, July 2, 1889, 2; and July 3, 1889, 2. On July 4, page 1 of the *Daily News* reported the stabbing of a laborer on West Michigan Street. The man was working for Wolf and Truax, one of the contractors engaged in street improvements.

100. *Duluth Daily News*, July 5, 1889, 4.

101. Ibid., 3.

102. Ibid.

103. Ibid., 1.

104. *Duluth Evening Herald*, July 5, 1889, 1; see also *Duluth Daily News*, July 5, 1889, 3.

105. *Duluth Daily Tribune*, July 6, 1889.

106. Ibid.

107. Ibid., 3.

108. Ibid.

109. Ibid.

110. Ibid., 1.

111. *Duluth Daily Tribune*, July 7, 1889. The identification of Johnson and Mack as Finns can be found in the report of the coroner's inquest in the *Duluth Daily Tribune*, July 11, 1889. The *Duluth Evening Herald* reported that Mack had a wife and four children in Finland (July 8, 1889, 1).

112. The names, with slightly different spellings in some cases (such as *Hakin* for *Haken*, and *Halford* for *Alfred*), can be found in the *Duluth Daily Tribune* on July 7, 1889, and in the *Duluth Evening Herald* on July 8, 1889, 1. The initial report in the *Duluth Daily Tribune* states that "the ringleader of the strikers, a Polander whose name could not be learned" was struck by a rifle ball. Given the report on the coroner's inquest, this man was probably Ed Johnson, a Finn.

113. *Duluth Evening Herald*, July 8, 1889, 1; and July 10, 1889, 1.

114. On Pastor Dahl, see the *Duluth Daily News*, July 7, 1889, 4. On Fitzsimmons, see the *Duluth Evening Herald*, July 8, 1889, 1.

115. *Duluth Daily Tribune*, July 7, 1889, 1. For other accounts of these events, see "Riot and Bloodshed," *Duluth Daily News*, July 7, 1889, 4; and "Strikers Still Strike," *Duluth Evening Herald*, July 6, 1889, 1.

116. *Duluth Evening Herald*, July 6, 1889, 1.

117. Ibid. The *Duluth Daily Tribune* (July 7, 1889) agreed the strikers had probably fired first, but admitted that there were contrary reports.

118. *Duluth Evening Herald*, July 8, 1889, 1.

119. *Duluth Evening Herald*, July 6, 1889, 1.

120. *Duluth Evening Herald*, July 8, 1889, 1.

121. *Duluth Daily News*, July 7, 1889, 4.

122. *Duluth Daily Tribune*, July 8, 1889.

123. *Duluth Daily News*, July 9, 1889, 4.

124. *Duluth Daily Tribune*, July 8, 1889.

125. Ibid.

126. *Duluth Daily Tribune*, July 9, 1889.

127. *Duluth Daily Tribune*, July 9, 1889, 4; *Duluth Daily News*, July 9, 1889, 4.

128. *Duluth Daily Tribune*, July 9, 1889. Apparently no one considered the mayor's ban on public gatherings to apply to the meeting called by the chamber of commerce.

129. *Duluth Evening Herald*, July 8, 1889, 1.

130. *Duluth Daily Tribune*, July 10, 1889.

131. *Duluth Daily News*, July 7, 1889, 4.

132. *Duluth Daily News*, July 9, 1889, 2. The account provided by the *Duluth Daily*

News regarding Swanstrom's position is not altogether clear. Still, given the context and subsequent events, it is clear that Swanstrom opposed the mayor.

133. The *Duluth Daily News* was sharply critical of the mayor at this time; see, for example, the attack on the mayor in the July 2, 1889, issue.

134. *Duluth Daily Tribune*, July 7, 9, and 10, 1889.

135. *Duluth Daily Tribune*, July 9, 1889. The *Duluth Daily Tribune* for July 10, 1889, continues the attack on Swanstrom, Burke, and the editor of the *Duluth Daily News*.

136. *Duluth Daily Tribune*, July 11, 1889.

137. *Duluth Daily News*, July 9, 1889, 2.

138. *Duluth Daily Tribune*, July 9, 1889, 2.

139. *Duluth Daily News*, July 13, 1889, 4.

140. For examples of McLean's letters, see the *Duluth Daily News* for July 7 and July 9, 1889.

141. *Duluth Daily News*, September 19, 20, 1889.

142. Court Records, District Court, Eleventh Judicial District, State of Minnesota, County of St. Louis, n.d.

143. William E. McEwen, "History of the Duluth Police Department," unpublished manuscript, 15 (NEMHC). McEwen was an eyewitness to the battle between the strikers and the police. He later became a leader of the labor movement in Duluth and the state of Minnesota.

144. Ibid., 16.

chapter 2. from labor town to steel trust

1. On the sources of support for Davis, see the *Duluth Evening Herald*, February 1, 1890, 1; and the *Duluth Daily Tribune*, February 2, 1890, 1. Leading support for Davis came from the *Industrial Age*, the newspaper of the Knights of Labor; businessman and city councilor E. G. Swanstrom, political leader of the strongly Swedish West End; M. F. Wesenberg, editor of the Swedish newspaper, *Skandinav*, published in Duluth; J. H. Baker, leader of Carpenters Union 361, a local assembly of the Knights of Labor; and W. H. Burke and S. A. Thompson, formerly of the *Duluth Daily News*.

2. *Duluth Daily Tribune*, January 26, 1890, 1.

3. *Duluth Daily Tribune*, January 28, 1890, 4.

4. *Duluth Daily Tribune*, January 29, 1890, 3.

5. The resolution blamed the *Duluth Daily Tribune* for printing the story about the inadequacy of the $1.50/day wage rate. On Hall's resolution, see the Chamber of Commerce Papers at the Northeast Minnesota Historical Center (NEMHC).

6. These quotations are attributed to Davis supporters by an article printed in *Scandia* and quoted by the *Duluth Daily News* (morning edition) of February 4, 1890. Both *Scandia* and the *Duluth Daily News* opposed Davis. Apparently Burke and Thompson, associated with the *Duluth Daily News* during the strike and then in the Davis camp, were no longer with the *News*. The *News* called *Scandia* "the representative of the better class of Norwegians, Swedes and Danes of Duluth," in contrast to the Scandinavian laborers sup-

porting Davis. It should also be kept in mind that *Scandia*, supporting the Norwegian candidate Hall, was a Norwegian paper, and that *Skandinav*, the Swedish newspaper edited by Wesenberg, supported Davis, the candidate of the Swedish "boss," Swanstrom.

7.   *Duluth Daily Tribune*, February 2, 1890.

8.   *Duluth Daily Tribune*, February 2, 1890. This letter also claimed that Swanstrom was the owner of *Scandinav*.

9.   *Duluth Daily Tribune*, February 3, 1890.

10. *Duluth Daily Tribune*, February 2, 1890. In addition to being the editor of the Swedish, pro-labor newspaper *Skandinav*, M. F. Wesenberg was one of the early leaders of the Populist Party in Duluth. For the identification of *Skandinav* as a union labor paper, see *Scandia*, October 29, 1896. For Wesenberg's role in the Populists, see *Union Workman*, May 28, 1892, 3.

11. *Program Book and Address Calendar*, Northwest Grand Lodge of the International Order of Good Templars (IOGT), December 1941–May 1942, 3.

12. *1857–1957, In Commemoration of the One Hundredth Anniversary of the Northwest Grand Lodge, IOGT*, 1957 (MHS).

13. Across the bay from Duluth, in Superior, Wisconsin, a Good Templars Lodge is listed as one of the locals of the Superior Trades and Labor Assembly in the early 1890s. See the "Superior Trades and Labor Assembly Dues Book, 1893–1896," 19 (Area Research Center, Superior Public Library, Superior, Wisconsin).

14. Woodbridge and Pardee, *History of Duluth*, 2:444.

15. *Duluth Daily Tribune*, February 3, 1890.

16. *Duluth Daily Tribune*, January 30, 1890, 3.

17. *Duluth Sunday Tribune*, February 2, 1890.

18. Quoted in John M. Blum et al., *The National Experience: A History of the United States* (New York: Harcourt, Brace and World, 1963), 484.

19. Quoted in *The Union Workman* (Duluth), May 21, 1892, 1. The *Union Workman* was a short-lived organ of the AFL Trades Assembly in Duluth; see also the *Union Workman* for January 30, 1892, 2.

20. *Scandia*, May 8, 1891.

21. On the APA in general, see Humphrey J. Desmond, *The A.P.A. Movement* (New York: Arno Press, 1969); on the APA in Duluth, see 68–69.

22. For the nonrenewal of McGolrick, see Woodbridge and Pardee, *History of Duluth* 2:466. On the blocked sale of land, see Whitney Evans, Neil Storch, and Bill Beck, *Our Diocesan Century* (Duluth: Duluth Diocese, 1989), 65. For evidence of other APA action against the Irish in Duluth, see Holmquist, *They Chose Minnesota*, 139; and the *Duluth Daily News*, March 18, 1892.

23. Desmond, *The A.P.A. Movement*, 9, 45, 46.

24. Blum, *The National Experience*, 487.

25. *Labor World*, April 25 and May 23, 1896.

26. The best account of Akin can be found in Mary C. Pruitt, "Lady Organizer: Sabrie G. Akin and the *Labor World*," *Minnesota History* 52, no. 6 (Summer 1991): 206–19. A brief biographical sketch was also printed in *Labor World* (March 10, 1900, 1) following her death.

27. *Labor World*, April 25, 1896, 3, 5.

28. *Labor World*, July 18, 1896, 11, 13.

29. For a history of the Twentieth Century Club, see Rose Alice Johnson, *1898–1988: The History of the GFWC Twentieth Century Club of Duluth Minnesota* (Duluth) (NEMHC).

30. *Labor World*, March 10, 1900. For more on Akin's connection with the Twentieth Century Club, see Pruitt, "Lady Organizer."

31. *Labor World*, January 12, 1901, 1; and January 19, 1901, 4.

32. *Labor World*, August 29, 1896, 16. Important local leaders included C. M. Thomas of the Streetcar Workers, James Murray of the Waiters' Union, Henry Dworschack of the Cigar Makers, William McEwen of the Plumbers, and James Nichols, the AFL organizer who had replaced Applehagen, who died in 1895.

33. *Labor World*, September 12, 1896, 3.

34. On Bryan's appearance in Duluth, see *Labor World*, October 17, 1896, 1. On the Lyceum strike, see "History of the Duluth Labor Movement," *Labor World*, October 25, 1979, 5.

35. *Labor World*, October 24, 1896, 1.

36. Both quotations are from Ronald Huch, "Typhoid Truelson, Water and Politics in Duluth, 1896–1900," *Minnesota History* 47, no. 5 (Spring 1981): 191.

37. Ibid., 192–93.

38. *Evening News*, July 6, 1889, 1.

39. See the *Evening News* (special edition), July 8, 1889, 2; and the *Daily News*, July 13, 1889, 1.

40. An account of the discovery of iron ore and the establishment of the Jackson Mine can be found in Harlan Hatcher, *A Century of Iron and Men* (Indianapolis: Bobbs-Merrill, 1950), 21–37. David Walker, *Iron Frontier: The Discovery and Early Development of Minnesota's Three Ranges* (St. Paul: Minnesota Historical Society, 1979), provides an overview of the history of the iron-mining industry in Minnesota.

41. George B. Sargent, *Lecture on the West* (Davenport: Luse, Lane and Co., 1858), 16, 17.

42. Allan Nevins, *John D. Rockefeller* (New York: Charles Scribners, 1940), 393–97.

43. Gerald G. Eggert, *Steelmasters and Labor Reform, 1886–1923* (Pittsburgh: University of Pittsburgh Press, 1981), 79; Robert Hessen, *Steel Titan: The Life of Charles M. Schwab* (New York: Oxford University Press, 1975), 24, 62–63.

44. Ida Tarbell, *The Life of Elbert H. Gary: The Story of Steel* (New York: D. Appleton and Company, 1925), 118–25; Nevins, *John D. Rockefeller*, 418–22.

45. Tarbell, *Life of Elbert H. Gary*, 124–25.

46. Hatcher, *A Century of Iron and Men*, 181.

47. Ibid.

48. Ibid., 191–92.

49. Eggert, *Steelmasters*, 143.

50. Hatcher, *A Century of Iron and Men*, 163–64.

51. *Iron*, December 2, 1892, 500, quoted in Kenneth Warren, *The American Steel Industry 1850–1970: A Geographical Interpretation* (Oxford, England: Clarendon Press, 1973), 73.

52. Quoted in Tarbell, *Life of Elbert H. Gary*, 156. On Carnegie's own views see Eggert, *Steelmasters*, 12–13.

53. On Schwab, see Hessen, *Steel Titan*, 74–75. On Corey and Dinkey, see Eggert, *Steelmasters*, 138.

54. Lewis Corey, *The House of Morgan* (New York: G. Howard Watt, 1930), 278.

55. Arnold R. Alanen, "Early Labor Strife on Minnesota's Mining Frontier, 1882–1906," *Minnesota History* 52, no. 7 (Fall 1991): 247–63, 248.

56. *Labor World*, January 2, 1897, 7.

57. *Labor World*, January 16, 1897, 13.

58. Alanen, "Strife," 248.

59. See Alanen, "Strife," for an account of these early strikes. See also Rudolph Pinola, "Labor and Politics on the Iron Range of Northern Minnesota" (Ph.D. diss., University of Wisconsin, n.d.), 12–39.

60. *Labor World*, April 11, 1896, 8.

61. *Labor World*, May 23, 1896, 11; and June 20, 1896, 5 and 15. At this time, the secrecy of the vote was not protected and mining company employees could see how miners voted.

62. *Labor World*, May 9, 1896, 13. L. M. Bowers managed Rockefeller's Bessemer Steamship Company, the largest ore fleet in the world; see Nevins, *John D. Rockefeller*, 408–9. Nevins also says that Bowers "showed an inveterate hostility to any interference with the open shop, and Bowers took rigid views of labor management. He belonged to a dying age in the relationship of capital and labor" (668).

63. *Labor World*, May 9, 1896, 13. For the quotation from Truelson, see Huch, "Typhoid Truelson," 193.

64. Eggert, *Steelmasters*, 36.

65. *Labor World*, May 4, 1901, 1.

66. Tarbell, *Life of Elbert H. Gary*, 161–62.

67. *Labor World*, August 31, 1901, 4; and November 2, 1901, 3.

68. *Labor World*, May 17, 1902, 1.

69. *Labor World*, August 2, 1902, 1.

70. Ibid.

71. Ibid.

72. Brody, *Steelworkers in America*, 118, 123.

73. See the biographical sketches for William J. Olcott, Herbert Brown, Hermon L. Dresser, and John H. McLean in Woodbridge and Pardee, *History of Duluth*, vol. 2.

74. *Labor World*, May 12, 1900, 2. The Boycott bill was introduced at the legislature at the urging of Duluth businessmen; see *Labor World*, February 2, 1907, 6.

75. The quote comes from Millard Gieske, *Minnesota Farmer-Laborism: The Third Party Alternative* (Minneapolis: University of Minnesota Press, 1979), 54.

76. On the general lack of labor discipline throughout the United States, see David Montgomery, *Fall of the House of Labor*, 269–75. On the situation in Duluth in the early 1900s, see the reflective article in *Labor World*, February 2, 1907, 6.

77. Montgomery, *Fall of the House of Labor*, 269–75.

78. Ibid., 289.

79. *Labor World*, January 4, 1908, 4.

80. On this open shop drive in Duluth, see *Labor World*, December 14, 1907, 1; January 4, 1908, 4; January 25, 1908, 1; February 29, 1908, 1; March 21, 1908, 4; and April 8, 1911, 4.

81. *Duluth: The New Steel City* (Duluth: The Public Affairs Committee of the Commercial Club, 1910). Available at the Duluth Public Library.

chapter 3. class struggle and ethnic conflict

1. For a discussion of the tax deal, see Arnold Alanen, "Morgan Park: U.S. Steel, and a Planned Company Town," in Lydecker et al., *Duluth*, 111–12.

2. "We Were All Once Immigrants," supplement to the *Duluth News Tribune*, February 4, 1979, 73 (on recruitment in Europe) and 87 (on the percent of foreign-born employees).

3. *Duluth News Tribune*, July 18, 1907, 3.

4. For accounts of the strike on the range, see Pinola, "Labor and Politics," 21–28; and Carl Ross, *The Finn Factor* (New York Mills, Minn.: Parta Printers, 1982), 109–14. The claim that twenty thousand miners were involved comes from *Labor World*, July 27, 1907, 1.

5. Ross, *Finn Factor*, 113.

6. *Labor World*, August 3, 1907, 1.

7. *Labor World*, August 3, 1907, 1; and August 17, 1907, 1.

8. Ross, *Finn Factor*, 113.

9. *Labor World*, August 3, 1907, 1.

10. For accounts of this meeting, see the *Duluth News Tribune*, August 19, 1907; and *Labor World*, August 24, 1907, 6.

11. Ross, *Finn Factor*, 10.

12. Hans R. Wasastjerna, ed., *History of the Finns in Minnesota* (Duluth: Minnesota Finnish-American Historical Society, 1957), 210.

13. Ibid., 212.

14. Ibid., 213.

15. Riippa, "Finns and Swede Finns," 298.

16. *St. Croix Avenue* (Superior, Wisconsin: Työmies Society, 1992) by Lauri Lemberg, a Finnish immigrant who became a major figure in the cultural life of Duluth's Finns, is a fictional story based on life in the Finnish immigrant community in Duluth. One of the significant characters in the book is Saara Mönkkönen. Widowed as a young woman, she manages to buy a restaurant on St. Croix Avenue and runs it as a successful business. Probably written in the 1950s, *St. Croix Avenue* gives a rich description of both the physical and cultural aspects of the Finnish community in Duluth.

17. Wasastjerna, *History of the Finns*, 214.

18. For a sense of the common roots of these movements, see Ross, *Finn Factor*, 36–54. For a sense of the idealism common to them, see Carl Ross, "The Utopian Vision of Finnish Immigrants: 1900–30," in *Scandinavian Studies* 60 (1988): 481–96.

19. Ross, *Finn Factor*, 66–68. On the early commitment of the Duluth Local to Marxist positions, see 63.

20. *Duluth News Tribune*, July 22, 1907, 1.

21. On "Hall Socialism," see Ross, *Finn Factor*, 70–71. One of these two newspapers, *Socialisti*, would soon become the IWW newspaper, *Industrialisti*. Votes for Socialist and Communist candidates will be discussed in later chapters.

22. Louis Dworschak, a member of the Duluth Cigar Makers Union, ran as the SLP candidate for comptroller of Duluth in 1901. Edward Kritz of the Boilermakers Union ran as the SLP candidate for alderman in 1902. Henry Dworschak of the Typographers Union also gave support to the SLP position within the AFL. See *Labor World*, February 9, 1901; February 8, 1902; and June 21, 1902.

23. *Labor World*, August 1, 1896; August 29, 1896; December 5, 1896; June 16, 1897.

24. *Labor World*, December 13, 1902, 1; December 20, 1902, 3; December 5, 1903, 8; December 19, 1903, 8.

25. On early Jewish business leadership in Duluth, see W. Gunther Plaut, *The Jews in Minnesota: The First Seventy-Five Years* (New York: American Jewish Historical Society, 1959), 132–36.

26. Hyman Berman, "The Jews," in Holmquist, *They Chose Minnesota*, 495.

27. Berman locates the principal Russian Jewish settlement in Duluth in the West End, between Twelfth and Twenty-Fourth Avenues (ibid., 495). All things considered, it appears that the East Third Jewish settlement was larger.

28. Irene Paull, "Duluth Kasrilevka," in *Irene: Selected Writings of Irene Paull* (Minneapolis: Midwest Villages and Voices, 1996), 30. In *The Jews in Minnesota*, W. Gunther Plaut, while acknowledging the differences between the "Western" and "Eastern" Jewish communities, argues that in Duluth these differences were less severe than elsewhere and he points to cooperation between these groups in the formation of a "mixed" B'nai B'rith lodge in Duluth as early as 1897 (137). Plaut concludes that "[o]f the three major Minnesota communities which saw the development from a unitary to a dual Jewish community structure, Duluth was the first to foreshadow the ultimate third step: the reunification into one single Jewish community" (139).

29. Ruby Kamatos, "Profiles of Industrial Duluth" (master's thesis; University of Minnesota Duluth, 1961), 81. Lithuanian Jews also established businesses in many of the Iron Range towns north of Duluth. See "We Were All Once Immigrants," *Duluth News Tribune*, February 4, 1979, 87.

30. Records for this organization have been lost. For a very brief history of Branch 353 and mention of a second Duluth Branch 503, see *Jewish Fellowship News: A Collection of Memories Celebrating Jewish Life in the Northland*, ed. Phil Myzel and Harry Bergal (Duluth: Jewish Fellowship News, n.d.), 19. A letter from the Duluth local signed by Secretary Matthew H. Schneider of 515 East Fifth Street requesting aid for garment workers in New York City appears in the files of the Duluth Federated Trades Assembly (DFTA). See DFTA Papers, January 23, 1913 (MHS).

31. *Duluth News Tribune*, June 23, 1917, 3.

32. Michael Brook, "Radical Literature in Swedish America: A Narrative Survey," *Swedish Pioneer Historical Quarterly* 20 (1969), 117. On the level of activity, see *Truth*, September 19, 1919. *Truth* was published in Duluth from

1917 to 1923 and is available on microfilm at the Minnesota Historical Society (MHS). For more on the Scandinavian local, see Hudelson, "The Scandinavian Local."

33. In *Truth*, a newspaper published by the Scandinavian Local, editor Jack Carney claimed a membership of four hundred (October 3, 1919, 2). The estimate of six hundred members comes from the reminiscence of John D. Nelson in "Son of Mother Svea Recalls Duluth's Progressive Past," *Midwest Labor*, August 1937, 3. The estimate of an active membership of forty comes from an interview with Dr. William Wickstrom, whose father, John Wickstrom, was one of the leaders of the local. A typed record of this interview, done by Richard Hudelson (September 24 and November 13, 1991), is available at the Northeast Minnesota Historical Center (NEMHC).

34. These observations are based on a reading of *Truth*, the newspaper sponsored by the local from 1917 to 1923.

35. *Truth*, September 28, 1922, 3.

36. Wickstrom, interview with Hudelson (NEMHC).

37. *Duluth Weekly Record*, June 22, 1912.

38. *Duluth Weekly Record*, September 14, 1912.

39. William E. Towne, "The Class War in Duluth," *International Socialist Review* 13 (October 1912): 328, 330.

40. On the hours involved, see the story on the strike in the *Herald*, September 9, 1912.

41. For a detailed account of the strike, see Susan Perala-Dewey, "The Streetcar Strike of 1912: Duluth under Dictatorship" (unpublished manuscript, NEMHC).

42. "Prepared for Strike," *Duluth Herald*, September 13, 1912.

43. Towne, "Class War," 329–30.

44. These references to the *Duluth News Tribune* coverage of the strike are taken from Perala-Dewey, "Streetcar Strike," 6. The depth of anti-Semitism that existed in some quarters in Duluth is indicated by the fact that in the midst of this crisis, the Street Railway Company refused to honor a contract for scab labor signed by an agency in Minneapolis on its behalf when it was discovered that the man hired was Jewish. On this account, see *Labor World*, October 12, 1912, 1.

45. *Duluth Herald*, September 11, 1912.

46. *Duluth Herald*, September 13, 1912.

47. *Duluth News Tribune*, October 7, 1912.

48. *Duluth News Tribune*, September 12, 1912; *Superior Telegram*, September 12, 1912.

49. This account of the ore dock strike is heavily indebted to David Wegge, "Industrial Workers of the World: Duluth-Superior 1911–1913" (unpublished manuscript, NEMHC). The two deaths occurred immediately when the accident happened. A third man may have died later. An article in *Labor World* (August 9, 1913, 1) puts the number of deaths at three.

50. *Superior Telegram*, August 1, 1913, 1.

51. *Duluth News Tribune*, August 2, 1913, 1.

52. *Superior Telegram*, August 2, 1913, 3.

53. *Labor World*, August 10, 1912, 1.

54. Wegge, "Industrial Workers," 4–5.

55. On Cannon's involvement, see the *Duluth News Tribune*, August 8, 1913, 4.

56. *Labor World*, August 16, 1913, 3.

57. For an account of these proposals and responses, see Wegge, "Industrial Workers," 6–7.

58. *Duluth News Tribune*, August 5, 1913, 4.

59. *Duluth News Tribune*, August 6, 1913, 4; *Labor World*, August 9, 1913, 1.

60. *Duluth News Tribune*, August 7, 1913, 1.

61. *Duluth News Tribune*, August 8, 1913, 1.

62. *Superior Telegram*, August 8, 1913, 6; and *News Tribune*, August 8, 1913, 4.

63. *Duluth News Tribune*, August 9, 1913, 1.

64. For an account of this incident, see Wegge, "Industrial Workers," 15–17.

65. *Duluth News Tribune*, August 11, 1913, 4.

66. *Duluth News Tribune*, August 12, 1913, 1.

67. *Superior Telegram*, August 12, 1913, 5.

68. Wegge, "Industrial Workers," 19.

69. *Labor World*, August 16, 1923, 1.

70. Charles Leinenweber, "The American Socialist Party and the New Immigrants," in George Pozzetta, ed., *Immigrant Radicals: The View from the Left* (New York: Garland, 1991), 319.

71. *Solidarity*, July 15, 1911, 1.

72. *Duluth News Tribune*, July 9, 1911, 7; *Solidarity*, July 15, 1911, 1; and August 26, 1911, 1.

73. On racial and ethnic prejudices within the American Socialist Party, see Leinenweber, "American Socialist Party."

74. Melvyn Dubofsky, *We Shall Be All: A History of the Industrial Workers of the World* (Chicago: Quadrangle Books, 1969), provides a widely acclaimed history of the IWW.

75. Ross, *Finn Factor*, 68–69.

76. Ibid., 141.

77. Ibid., 141–42.

78. On Johnson's connection with the Socialists, see the "Christmas Greetings" list of names in *Truth*, December 24, 1920.

79. *Labor World*, April 26, 1913, 6.

80. The text of the letter with the names of the signers was published in the *Duluth Herald* on October 14, 1914. On the county referendum supporting the expulsion, see George Leidenberger, "Reformers and Revolutionists: The Socialist Party in Minnesota, 1910–1919" (unpublished B.A. thesis, Macalester College, St. Paul, 1987), 148. For a letter from Richard Jones to Carl D. Thompson of the national office of the Socialist Party explaining the trouble caused by radicals in control of the local Socialist Party, see Jones to Thompson, September 19, 1914, Socialist Party Papers, A167, reel 5. Available at the William R. Perkins Library, Duke University, Durham, N.C.

81. Daniel Bell, "The Background and Development of Marxian Socialism in the United States," in Donald Drew Egbert and Stow Persons, eds., *Socialism and American Life* (Princeton: Princeton University Press, 1952), 1:288–89.

82. *New Times*, January 2, 1915. Quoted in Leidenberger, *Reformers and Revolutionists*, 149.

83. *New Times*, December 9, 1916; and January 27, 1916. See Leidenberger, *Reformers and Revolutionists*, 143.

84. *Labor World*, June 26, 1915, 1.

85. *Labor World*, July 24, 1915, 6.

86. *Labor World*, November 27, 1915, 6.

87. *New Times*, March 11, 1916. See Leidenberger, *Reformers and Revolutionists*, 151–52.

88. *Labor World*, December 25, 1915, 1; and January 15, 1916, 1, 6. The campaign lasted at least through February 1916. See also *Labor World*, January 29, 1916, 8; and February 12, 1916, 6.

89. Quoted by Mary Marcy, "The Iron Heel on the Mesaba Range," *International Socialist Review*, August 1916, 75.

90. *Duluth Herald*, June 22, 1916.

91. See Carl Nykanen, "The Western Federation of Miners," unpublished manuscript done as part of the Duluth Workers' Education project of the Minnesota Work Projects Administration, 25 (NEMHC).

92. Quoted by Michael Karni, in "Elizabeth Gurley Flynn and the Mesabi Strike of 1916," in George Pozzetta, ed., *Immigrant Radicals: The View from the Left* (New York: Garland, 1991), 248; *News Tribune*, June 23, 1916.

93. Marcy, "Iron Heel," 75–76.

94. On Myron, see *Duluth Herald*, July 4, 1916; and the *Duluth City Directory* (1915), 657.

95. *Labor World*, July 8, 1916, 1.

96. Nykanen, "Western Federation," 21, 23.

97. On the disposition of the three cases, see *Duluth Herald*, December 15. On the supposed deal, see Helen C. Camp, *Iron in Her Soul: Elizabeth Gurley Flynn and the American Left* (Pullman: Washington State University Press, 1995), 74.

98. See, for example, *Labor World*, July 22, 1916, 1; and August 12, 1916, 1.

99. A copy of this report was printed in the *Duluth Herald*, August 16, 1916, 11.

100. The quotations from the West report are taken from Nykanen, "Western Federation," 22–23.

101. This quote is from the Clayton Videen notes taken from the version of the West report published in the *Duluth News Tribune* on September 3, 1916. The Videen notes are available at the Minnesota Historical Society.

102. Quoted by Nykanen, "Western Federation," 19.

103. *Duluth Herald*, July 6, 1916.

104. Marcy, "Iron Heel," 80. For information on IWW activity at the Duluth ore docks, see *Labor World*, July 1, 1916, 6.

105. *Duluth Herald*, June 30, 1916; *Duluth News Tribune*, July 19, 1916.

106. *Duluth Herald*, June 30, 1916.

107. *Labor World*, July 1, 1916, 6.

108. *Duluth News Tribune*, August 1, 1916. Quoted in Pinola, *Labor and Politics*, 35–36. In the text Pinola attributes this claim to the *Duluth News Tribune*; in the note it is attributed to the *Duluth Herald*.

chapter 4. war and revolution

1. *Posten*, March 23, 1917, 4.

2. "Military Service Records," Minnesota War Records, St. Louis County Branch, Duluth.

3. *Posten*, April 13, 1917, 4. See Sture Lindmark, *Swedish-America, 1914–1932* (Uppsala: Läromedelsförlagen, 1971), 78.

4. Lindmark, *Swedish-America*, 120–21.

5. Ibid., 110–11.

6. *Duluth Herald*, April 23, 1917. Soon after this event a special holiday was proclaimed in Duluth by Mayor Magney. Everyone took half the day off to attend a big patriotic demonstration. For information on this topic, see *Posten*, April 27, 1917.

7. Lindmark, *Swedish-America*, 123.

8. Ibid., 64.

9. Ibid., 104.

10. Ibid., 66–67.

11. Ibid., 93–94.

12. Carl H. Chrislock, *Watchdog of Loyalty: The Minnesota Commission of Public Safety During World War I* (St. Paul: Minnesota Historical Society Press, 1991), 55–56.

13. Minnesota Commission of Public Safety (MCPS) Papers, St. Louis County file, May 1918 (MHS).

14. On the speakers, see ibid. On the Gustav Johnson speech, see the St. Louis County File, April 5, 1918 (MHS).

15. MCPS Papers, "Alien Registration Lists" (MHS).

16. In a letter dated November 19, 1918, an Olmsted County official recommended forbidding even this single hour. See MCPS Papers, St. Louis County file (MHS).

17. This regulation is mentioned in a June 5, 1917, letter to Issac Frazier. See MCPS Papers, Correspondence with Counties, St. Louis County file (MHS).

18. *Labor World*, February 17, 1917, 2.

19. Correspondence with Counties, May 1, May 5, and May 7, 1917, MCPS Papers, St. Louis County file (MHS).

20. *Labor World*, May 5, 1917, 4.

21. William Prince to Henry Libby, April 13, 1918, MCPS Papers, St. Louis County file (MHS).

22. William Prince to H. J. Scharr, March 16, 1918, MCPS Papers, St. Louis County file (MHS).

23. Chrislock, *Watchdog of Loyalty*, x and 196–99.

24. On the Finns, see Ross, *Finn Factor*, 145. On the Swedes, see Lindmark, *Swedish-America*, 79.

25. Ross, *Finn Factor*, 146.

26. On the Scandinavian local, see Hudelson, "The Scandinavian Local," and "Jack Carney and the Truth in Duluth."

27. MCPS Papers, Correspondence with St. Louis County file, October 31, 1917 (MHS).

28. Ross, *Finn Factor*, 149.

29. Lindmark, *Swedish-America*, 123–24. There was a major case involving draft resistance by members of the Rockford local of the Scandinavian Socialist Federation. *Truth*, the newspaper published by the Duluth group, shows that there was close contact between this Rockford group and the Duluth group.

30. *Duluth News Tribune*, March 9, 1919.

31. Lindmark, *Swedish-America*, 123.

32. *Duluth Herald*, June 13, 1917.

33. Jane Perry Clark, *Deportation of Aliens from the United States to Europe* (1931; New York: Arno Press and the New York Times, 1969), 217.

34. *Duluth Herald*, June 21, 1917, 1.

35. "Agent's Reports to Winters," file cards, MCPS Papers, June 11, 1917 (MHS).

36. MCPS Papers, July 13, 1917, St. Louis County file (MHS).

37. Ibid., August 15, 1917.

38. Ibid., n.d. The reply by Prince is dated September 5, 1917.

39. "Agent's Reports to Winters," file cards and D. J. G. file, MCPS Papers (MHS).

40. *Labor Leader*, June 28, 1917. A copy of the vagrancy ordinance can be found in *Proceedings of the City Council of the City of Duluth for 1917*, 237 (NEMHC).

41. *Labor Leader*, June 28, 1917, 1. For Flynn's own account, see Elizabeth Gurley Flynn, *Rebel Girl* (New York: International, 1982), 228–29.

42. *Duluth News Tribune*, June 24, 1917, 1–2A; and *Herald*, June 28, 1917, 5.

43. *Posten*, August 17, 1917, 6.

44. The quotations and the account of Little's death are from Flynn, *Rebel Girl*, 232.

45. *Duluth Herald*, August 4, 1917, 14.

46. *Labor World*, July 7, 1917, 6.

47. *Duluth Herald*, July 31, 1917, 3.

48. "Agent's Reports to Winters," D. J. G. file, no. 45, August 18, 1917. MCPS Papers (MHS).

49. *Duluth News Tribune*, Aug. 19, 1917, 1; *Posten*, Aug. 24, 1917, 8.

50. Prince to Pardee, August 21, 1917, MCPS Papers, St. Louis County file (MHS).

51. *Duluth News Tribune*, August 19, 1917, 1 , 11A.

52. William Preston, Jr., *Aliens and Dissenter: Federal Suppression of Radicals, 1903–1933* (1963; Urbana: University of Illinois, 1994), 118, 123.

53. Ross (*Finn Factor*, 150) mentions Laukki. Laukki and the others are listed in *Ahjo* [The Forge] 4, no. 2 (Kesäkuu [June] 1919), 52–57. *Ahjo* was a Finnish language serial published by the Work People's College in Duluth.

54. Chrislock, *Watchdog of Loyalty*, 298.

55. *Duluth News Tribune*, May 28, 1918, 1 and 14A.

56. Swedes did indeed support the NPL in the voting booth. In the 1918 gubernatorial election, Swedes favored Lindbergh over the incumbent Swedish American governor J. A. A. Burnquist. See Chrislock, *Watchdog of Loyalty*, 69.

57. McGee's quotations are from ibid., 299.

58. Ibid., 300.

59. Lindmark, *Swedish-America*, 120–21.

60. On the many Socialists in this neighborhood, see MCPS Papers, "Agent's Reports to Winters," B file, D. J. G. reports, June 25, 1917. The agent was mistaken in claiming that the Scandinavians did not support the IWW.

61. *Labor World*, May 26, 1917, 6.

62. *Labor World*, June 30 1917, 1.

63. June 28, 1917, 1, 4. *The Labor Leader* is available on microfilm from the Minnesota Historical Society.

64. *Labor Leader*, June 22, 1917, 1.

65. "Agent Reports to Winters," June 24–28, 1917 (MHS).

66. *Labor World*, August 25, 1917, 4.

67. See, for example, *Labor World*, August 4, 1917, 4; August 11, 1917, 4; and August 18, 1917, 4.

68. *Labor World*, August 18, 1917, 4.

69. *Labor World*, August 18, 1917, 6.

70. J. G. O'Neill to Frank Crassweller, March 30, 1918, MCPS Papers, St. Louis County file, folder 6 (MHS).

71. *Truth*, November 16, 1917, 1. The *News Tribune*, November 13, 1917, 1A, estimated the crowd at five hundred.

72. *Truth*, November 16, 1917, 4.

73. *Truth*, January 4, 1918, 4.

74. *Truth*, February 22, 1918, 3.

75. *Duluth News Tribune*, September 11, 1918, 6.

76. *Duluth News Tribune*, October 1, 1918, 1; *Herald*, October 1, 1918, 6.

77. *Truth*, December 7, 1917, 2.

78. *Truth*, December 27, 1918, 3.

79. *Truth*, November 15, 1918, 1, and November 22, 1918, 1.

80. *Truth*, October 3, 1919, 2. The Duluth group joined the Communist Labor Party (CLP), one of two organizations that later merged to form the Communist Party of the United States. The CLP insignia began to appear on the masthead of *Truth* in December 1919.

81. *Duluth News Tribune*, January 4, 1920, 1; and January 6, 1920, 1. Jack Carney was an Irishman recruited by the Scandinavian Socialists in Duluth to edit *Truth*. Carl Haglund, along with Carney, played a leadership role in the budding Communist movement in Minnesota.

82. *Truth*, January 23, 1920, 1.

83. *Truth*, January 16, 1920, 4.

84. *Truth*, January 23, 1920, 4; and April 23, 1920, 6.

85. *Truth*, October 15, 1920, 2, 3. Bloor was invited back a month later; see *Truth*, November 26, 1920, 2. On the refusal to allow Minor to speak, see *Herald*, November 19, 1920, 1.

86. These names are all taken from the pages of *Truth*. Bentall took over editorial duties in October 1920. Carney moved to Butte, Montana, to edit a Communist daily newspaper published there.

87. *Truth*, November 25, 1921, 2; and January 20, 1922, 1. Flynn was scheduled to appear again in February 1922. See *Duluth Herald*, February 1, 1922, 14.

88. The Duluth local was quite active on the Sacco and Vanzetti case. See *Truth*, July 8, 1921, 1; July 22, 1921, 1; November 25, 1921, 2; May 5, 1922, 2; June 30, 1922, 3; and August 18, 1922, 1.

89. *Truth*, April 14, 1922; and September 28, 1922, 3.

90. *Truth*, September 9, 1921, 3.

91. Ross, *Finn Factor*, 163–64.

92. Ross, *Finn Factor*, 164, 182.

93. Dubofsky, *We Shall Be All*, 463.

94. *Truth*, August 27, 1920.

95. Auvo Kostianen, *The Forging of Finnish-American Communism, 1917–1924: A Study in Ethnic Radicalism* (Turku, Finland: Turun Yliopisto, 1978), 47n18. On Laukki's embrace of Communism, see Ross, *Finn Factor*, 142.

96. *Duluth Herald*, May 2, 1921, 17.

97. *Truth*, August 5, 1921, 3. On Hardy, see Dubofsky, *We Shall Be All*, 463.

98. *Truth*, June 16, 1922, 4.

99. *Truth*, June 30, 1922, 2.

100. *Truth*, June 23, 1922, 2; and June 30, 1922, 4. On Foster, see Edward P. Johanningsmeier, *Forging American Communism: The Life of William Z. Foster* (Princeton: Princeton University Press, 1994), 175.

101. On the Superior Workers' Hall, see *Truth*, May 19, 1922, 2.

102. *The Worker*, April 15, 1922, 5. On the action of the national Scandinavian Socialist Federation to affiliate with the Workers' Party, see *Truth*, November 17, 1922, 1.

103. *Truth*, April 28, 1922, 2; September 15, 1922, 2; and October 13, 1922, 3.

104. *Truth*, August 4, 1922, 1. On Niskin's connection with the Young Women's Hebrew Association, see *Truth*, September 1, 1922, 3.

105. *Truth*, December 8, 1922, 2.

chapter 5. americanization

1. On the exclusion of South Slavs from Morgan Park in the pre–World War I era, see Marjorie Hoover's interviews with Father Dragicevich, Steve Balach, and Mr. and Mrs. Alex Smolnikar. Copies of all interviews cited here by Hoover can be found in the "Duluth: Miscellaneous South Slavs" file of the Ethnic History Project Papers (MHS).

2. Dragicevich, interview with Hoover (MHS).

3. *Duluth Ripsaw*, February 23, 1918, 3.

4. Dan Bastie and Mr. and Mrs. Alex Smolnikar, interview with Hoover. Hoover's interview with Ann Bubalo gives a more favorable account of Stowe and Morgan Park schools (MHS).

5. Jacqueline Rocchio Moran, "The Italian Americans of Duluth" (master's thesis, University of Minnesota, 1979), 120.

6. Ibid., 124. On Raleigh Street, see Claire W. Schumacher, *The Raleigh Street Saga: Shattering the Legend* (Duluth: Zenith City Publishing, 1990).

7. *Herald*, July 6, 1889, 1.

8. Rudolph Vecoli, "The Italians," in Holmquist, *They Chose Minnesota*, 454.

9. Ibid., 458.

10. Moran, *Italian Americans*, 63–64.

11. Both pieces can be found in Paull, *Irene: Selected Writings*, 30.

12. "That's Right Friends …," *Duluth Budgeteer*, June 4, 1975.

13. Moran, *Italian Americans*, 120–21.

14. Zlatovski, "The Autobiography of an Anti-Hero," unpublished manuscript available at the Immigration History Research Center (IHRC), University of Minnesota; and interview by Richard Hudelson with Trudy Chern, who grew up in the Jewish community in Duluth, March 23, 1997 (NEMHC).

15. On the origins of the St. Louis County Public Safety Commission, see the May 1, 1917, letter from Pardee to Eva in the MCPS Papers, St. Louis County, Correspondence with Counties File (MHS). On the origins of the local Americanization Committee, see the "Report of the Secretary" by A. B. Clarfield, Executive Secretary of the Duluth Americanization Committee, December 16, 1918, in Americanization of Aliens Reports, War Records (NEMHC).

16. See the letterhead of the Americanization Committee of the city of Duluth in the Americanization of Aliens Reports, War Records (NEMHC).

17. Annual Report of A. B. Clarfield, Executive Secretary, Americanization Committee of the City of Duluth, 1918–1919, 9, in the Americanization of Aliens Reports, War Records (NEMHC).

18. "Suggestions to Employers," Americanization of Aliens Reports, War Records (NEMHC).

19. For Roosevelt's views, see the "motto" he penned, which was adopted by the Northwest Warriors in Duluth (*Duluth Herald*, November 13, 1920). For an account of Roosevelt's views stressing the tension between "racial nationalist" and "civic nationalist" currents, see Gerstle, *American Crucible*.

20. A copy of the report, written by executive secretary Albert Clarfield, can be found in the Americanization of Aliens Reports, War Records (NEMHC).

21. On these early classes, see the fundraising letter written by Judge William Cant, chairman of the Duluth Americanization Committee, during World War I. Though there is no date on the letter, it is evident that it was written while the war was still in progress. Americanization of Aliens Reports, War Records (NEMHC).

22. Americanization Committee Financial Statement for the period from September 1, 1918, to March 5, 1919 (Americanization of Aliens Reports, War Records, NEMHC). This confirms the April 23, 1942, letter from Ethel Bird to Helen Beavers in which she recounts the opening of the Little Gray House and says, "My guess is that it was started on war funds." International Institute Collection (NEHMC).

23. Letter from Bird to Beavers (NEHMC).

24. Annual Report of the Americanization Committee of the City of Duluth by Albert Clarfield, executive secretary, August 1, 1919, 7–9. Americanization of Aliens Reports, War Records (NEMHC).

25. Mrs. Nickoloff's comments are in the James Steele Papers (MHS).

26. International Institute Collection (NEMHC).

27. Like the Gary Center, the Raleigh Street Neighborhood House began life as a

project of the Duluth Americanization Committee. In fact, the Raleigh Street Center did not officially come under the wing of the International Institute until 1930. On the origins of the Raleigh Street Neighborhood House, see the letter from Ethel Bird to Helen Beavers, April 23, 1942, and the interview with Joe Bucsko in Schumacher, *Raleigh Street Saga*, 32. On the downtown work, see letter from Bird to Beavers (NEMHC).

28. Unless otherwise noted, references to the activities of the institute are taken from the International Institute Collection at the NEMHC. The records of the institute are organized in chronological order.

29. Interview with Mary Puglisi Talarico in Schumacher, *Raleigh Street Saga*, 25; see also the photos of the sports teams on 32–33.

30. Interview with Julia (Dolly) Puglisi Carlson in Schumacher, *Raleigh Street Saga*, 78.

31. Mrs. Orescanin, interview with Margaret Hoover, Ethnic History Project Papers (MHS). There are also several references to the "Mason's clinics" in the International Institute Papers at NEMHC

32. Schumacher, *Raleigh Street Saga*, 25.

33. Moran, *Italian Americans*, chapter 5.

34. *Duluth Herald*, October 15, 1923, 12.

35. Papers of the Italian American Club of Duluth, Immigration History Research Center (IHRC)

36. Ibid.

37. Albert B. Clarfield, "The Americanization of the Foreign Born in Duluth: A Typical American Community" (unpublished master's thesis, University of Minnesota, 1920), 53.

38. *Labor World*, September 26, 1925, 6.

39. Clippings file, International Institute of Duluth (NEMHC).

40. For an account of the movie theater scene in Duluth, see Christine E. Ranta, "Dearie ... Do You Remember?" in *Take A Look*, ed. Gerda E. Woelffer (Duluth: Duluth Manuscript Club, 1983).

41. Schumacher, *Raleigh Street Saga*, 143.

42. Wickstrom, interview with Hudelson (NEMHC).

43. Carl Ross, interview with Hy Berman (MHS).

44. On Chumich, see Schumacher, *Raleigh Street Saga*, 153. See also the newspaper clipping and photo of Chumich in the Duluth Steelworkers Local 1028 papers (MHS).

45. Ross, interview with Berman (MHS).

46. "Gary Athletic Club: Fiftieth Anniversary Reunion Program," 1979 (NEMHC).

47. Vecoli, "The Italians," 456.

48. Ibid., 452.

49. In 1908, a district attorney in St. Paul held up applications for citizenship papers from some seventeen Finns on the grounds that Finns were not white men but Mongols, and hence ineligible for U.S. citizenship because of the Oriental Exclusion Act. Duluth District Judge W. A. Cant reversed this ruling on the grounds that "if the Finns were originally Mongols, modifying influences have continued until they are now among the whitest people in Europe." See Ross, *Finn Factor*, 115.

50. Woman's Christian Temperance Union file (NEMHC).

51. Bessie Lathe Scovell, *Yesteryears: History of the Minnesota Woman's Christian Temperance Union, 1877-1939* (St. Paul: Bruce Publishing Company, 1939).

52. Kathleen Edith Kerr, "Female Empowerment: A History of the Minnesota Woman's Christian Temperance Union, 1900 to 1910," unpublished manuscript (St. Paul: Macalester College, 1992), 109-110 (MHS). Kerr quotes a report from the *White Ribboner*, March 1907, 4.

53. Quoted in Sidney Ahlstrom, *A Religious History of the American People* (New Haven: Yale, 1972), 902.

54. Quoted in Edward Behr, *Prohibition: Thirteen Years that Changed America* (New York: Arcade, 1997), 227.

55. See the program for this convention in the Woman's Christian Temperance Union file (NEMHC).

56. Wyn Craig Wade, *The Fiery Cross* (New York: Simon and Schuster, 1987), 172.

57. Quoted in Ahlstrom, *Religious History*, 748.

58. Ibid.

59. Ibid, 900.

60. Wade, *Fiery Cross*, 168.

61. *Duluth Herald*, May 27, 1918, 1.

62. Wade, *Fiery Cross*, 176-77.

63. Mary Ann Clawson, *Constructing Brotherhood: Class, Gender, and Fraternalism* (Princeton: Princeton University Press, 1989), 218.

64. Ibid.

65. Ibid., 130.

66. *Minnesota Fiery Cross* (published in St. Paul), February 22, 1924, 1 and 4 (MHS).

67. *Minnesota Fiery Cross*, March 14, 1924, 4.

68. *Minnesota Fiery Cross*, April 11, 1924, 3; and April 4, 1924, 4.

69. David M. Chalmers, *Hooded Americanism* (New York: Doubleday, 1965), 149-51.

70. Wade, *Fiery Cross*, 199.

71. Ibid., 179-80.

72. *Duluth Herald*, June 7, 1965, 9.

73. *Labor World*, April 18, 1925, 1.

74. Ku Klux Klan, Membership Lists for 1925 and 1926, Papers of Bishop Thomas Welch, Archives of the Duluth Diocese, Duluth.

75. *Labor World*, April 11, 1925, 1.

76. *Labor World*, May 9, 1925, 1.

77. *Labor World*, August 8, 1925, 5.

78. *Labor World*, October 3, 1925, 1-2.

79. *Labor World*, March 6, 1926, 1-2. See also the *Duluth Herald*, June 7, 1965, 9.

80. *Labor World*, June 26, 1926, 1.

81. The story of the whole incident and the quotation from the KKK bulletin are from *Labor World*, July 17, 1926, 1.

82. *Labor World*, August 7, 1926, 1.

83. *Labor World*, August 7, 1926, 1; and July 24, 1926, 1. There was something to McEwen's claim that in the South the Scandinavian Lutherans would not have been accepted as equals in the Klan. In Indiana, for example, foreign Protestants were enrolled in the American Krusaders, an organization formed by the Klan, but distinct from the Klan itself. On this topic, see Kathleen M. Blee, *Women of the Klan: Racism and Gender in the 1920s* (Berkeley and Los Angeles: University of California Press, 1992), 169.

84. *Labor World*, December 25, 1926, 1; and April 30, 1927, 2. See also the *Duluth Herald*, June 7, 1965, 9.

85. On this affair, see *Labor World*, May 7, 1927, 1–2; May 14, 1927, 1; May 21, 1927, 1; May 28, 1927, 1; and June 11, 1927, 1.

86. Ahlstrom, *Religious History*, 901. On KKK support for the law, see Wade, *Fiery Cross*, 199.

87. Ahlstrom, *Religious History*, 884.

88. Ibid., 885.

89. On the adoption of this motto by the local Warriors, see the *Duluth Herald*, November 13, 1920.

90. This account of the fire is taken from "The Great Fire—A Taste of War," written by William E. Caulkin, a witness to the fire and also president of the St. Louis County Historical Society (War Records, NEMHC).

91. Ibid., 4 and 1.

92. This narrative relies heavily on the account of the lynching provided by Michael Fedo in his book *Trial by Mob* (Duluth: Norshor, 1993).

93. On the testimony of the examining physician, see Fedo, *Trial by Mob*, 146–49 and 179; the *Duluth Ripsaw*, June 26, 1920, 1; and the letter from Walter White, Assistant Secretary of the New York NAACP, July 23, 1920, in the papers of Governor J. A. A. Burnquist (Minnesota State Archives, box 83, file no. 648c). On the implausibility of the whole story and conjectures about possible motives behind it, see Fedo, *Trial by Mob*.

94. Fedo, *Trial by Mob*, 16.

95. Ibid. On the working-class character of the mob, see 44; on Murnian, see 72; on Hedman, see 46.

96. Ibid., 57–58. In private correspondence with the author after this book was written, Fedo said that the idea that the mob was motivated by anger at black workers displacing white workers in the steel industry was mentioned by many of the people he interviewed.

97. Edward Nichols, interview with David Taylor, July 17, 1974, 16–17, Minnesota Black History Project (MHS).

98. *Twin City Star*, June 3, 1916.

99. See the collection of interviews done by Marjorie Hoover for the Minnesota Ethnic History Project (MHS).

100. See, for example, Eggert, *Steelmasters*, 135–36.

101. Brody, *Steelworkers in America*, 266–67.

102. On black residents in the Gary-New Duluth area and the employment of black workers in the coke ovens, see the Hoover interviews with Amelia Thomas and Ann Bubalo. Edward Nichols worked as a hod carrier; see his interview with Taylor, 7 (MHS).

103. In his interview with Taylor, Nichols mentions discrimination at the plant (7), Taylor and the reunion (17), and says that white workers lived in Morgan Park. This was not true of the South Slav and Italian workers at the steel plant at the time but, in the race theories of the time, South Slavs and Italians were often considered nonwhite.

104. Fedo, *Trial by Mob*, 177.

105. These occupational identifications come from ibid., 44–48. The *Duluth City Directory* for 1920 confirms these identifications in most cases and raises no conflicting occupational identifications.

106. Morgan's name is on a list of those indicted for participation in the lynch mob. Identification of his occupation is based on the *Duluth City Directory* for 1920.

107. Fedo, *Trial by Mob*, 18.

108. *Labor World*, July 17, 1920, 1.

109. Fedo, *Trial by Mob*, 45, 48.

110. Ibid., 152.

111. Ibid., 132.

112. *Labor World*, July 3, 1920, 10; and July 10, 1920, 8. It should be noted that this explanation of the lynching is advanced in the context of defending the pro-labor Commissioner Murnian against the efforts of unnamed members of the Commercial Club to blame Murnian.

113. For an account of the legal struggle following the lynching and the formation of the NAACP chapter in Duluth, see Steven Hoffbeck, "Victories Yet to Win: Charles W. Scrutchin, Bemidji's Black Activist Attorney," *Minnesota History* 55 (Summer 1996): 59–75.

chapter 6. the farmer-labor party

1. Blum et. al., *The National Experience*, 573–74.

2. William E. Culkin, "The First Thirty Days of the War in St. Louis County," unpublished manuscript, 18 and 27 (NEMHC).

3. *Labor World*, April 21, 1917, 6.

4. *Labor World*, April 28, 1917, 6.

5. *Labor World*, May 5, 1917, 4, 6.

6. *Labor World*, May 19, 1917, 6; and May 26, 1917, 6.

7. *Labor World*, June 30, 1917, 1.

8. *Labor World*, July 21, 1917, 1.

9. *Labor World*, August 11, 1917, 4; and August 18, 1917, 4.

10. *Labor World*, August 18, 1917, 6. The Machinist Local returned to the fold in January 1918 (*Labor World*, January 5, 1918, 6). The Boilermakers were sufficiently alienated from McEwen and the *Labor World* that they supported the founding of the alternative Socialist newspaper, *Truth*, in the spring of 1917. On this development, see *Two Harbors Socialist*, June 22, 1917, 5.

11. *Labor World*, November 17, 1917, 6. On the presence of the Finnish IWWs in Local 64, see *Labor World*, September 13, 1919, 3. On the wildcat nature of this strike, see *Truth*, November 2, 1917, 1. *Truth* also mentions a strike at this time by sheet-metal workers in Duluth.

12. *Labor World*, May 18, 1918, 1; and June 29, 1918, 6.

13. *Truth*, August 9, 1918, 2; *Labor World*, August 3, 1918, 3.

14. *Labor World*, August 17, 1918, 6.

15. *Labor World*, March 8–22, 1919, and May 3, 1919. On the molders' strike, see *Truth*, March 14 and March 21, 1919. The molders appear to have included a significant number of Scandinavian Socialists. *Truth* (May 23, 1919) attacked *Labor World* for running Clyde Iron ads during the strike. In June, *Labor World* reported that the struggle against Clyde Iron continued and that the company had been put on an "unfair" list to be circulated outside Duluth because of its resort to strikebreaking tactics (June 25, 1919, 6).

16. *Labor World*, August 9, August 16, and September 13, 1919; *Truth*, August 8, August 22, September 12, and September 19, 1919.

17. *Labor World*, August 9, 1919, 1 and 4; August 30, 1919, 1.

18. Edward P. Johanningsmeier, *Forging American Communism: The Life of William Z. Foster* (Princeton: Princeton University Press, 1994), 112.

19. On Foster, see ibid.

20. Brody, *Steelworkers in America*, 100–101.

21. Ibid., 98.

22. Ibid., 125.

23. Ibid., 116–18. The classic exposé of labor spies employed by the steel industry is Frank Palmer, *Spies in Steel: An Exposé of Industrial War* (1928; Denver: Labor Press, 1927).

24. Johanningsmeier, *Forging American Communism*, 128.

25. Brody, *Steelworkers in America*, 265.

26. Johanningsmeier, *Forging American Communism*, 133.

27. See, for example, *Duluth Herald*, September 11, 1919, 15; and September 22, 1919, 1.

28. *Labor World*, September 27, 1919, 1.

29. Ibid.

30. The account of the Citizens' Alliance in Duluth offered here is heavily indebted to William Millikin, *A Union against Unions: The Minneapolis Citizens Alliance and Its Fight against Organized Labor, 1903–1947* (St. Paul: Minnesota Historical Society Press, 2001). Millikin generously shared research in progress.

31. *Duluth Herald*, October 3, 1919, 6.

32. *Labor World*, October 11, 1919, 4.

33. Millikin, *Union against Unions*, 175. On the connection with the Russell Detective Agency, see *Labor World*, April 9, 1921.

34. On these various confrontations, see "Special Bulletin," Duluth Citizens' Alliance, April 1, 1921. This bulletin somehow made its way into the papers of Robert Olson, a leader of the AFL in Duluth (Robert Olson Papers, MHS). See *Labor World*, April 30, 1921, 4; and July 30, 1921, 6.

35. *Labor World*, July 9, 1921, 1; July 17, 1926; September 25, 1926; May 22, 1927; October 29, 1927; October 4, 1930, 1.

36. For brief accounts of this strike and the circumstances surrounding it, see Johanningsmeier, *Forging American Communism*, 180–85; and Montgomery, *Fall of the House of Labor*, 399–410.

37.   *Labor World*, July 15, 1922, 1. Coverage of the local strike in *Labor World* began on July 8, 1922. See also *Truth*, July 7–September 15, 1922, for coverage of the strike locally.

38.   *Labor World*, August 12, 1922, 1.

39.   *Labor World*, August 12, 1922, 6. Later *Labor World* claimed that Arthur Ziegler was chair of the Federated Shop Crafts in Duluth during the shopmen's strike of 1922 (April 5, 1924, 1). In any case, both Jensen and Ziegler appear to have played leadership roles during the strike.

40.   On the blacklists of striking shopmen from the 1922 strike, see *Labor World*, March 31, 1923, 5, where it is claimed that the D&IR and the Northern Pacific railways, but not the Great Northern, still maintained them.

41.   *Labor World*, July 21, 1923, 4.

42.   Montgomery, *Fall of the House of Labor*, 406.

43.   "Special Bulletin," April 1, 1921; and January 15, 1923, letter from President L. C. Harris to the members of the Citizens' Alliance (Robert Olson Papers, MHS). See also *Labor World*, August 21, 1926.

44.   See *Labor World*, July 13, 1929, 1.

45.   Duluth Citizens' Alliance, January 1929 (NEMHC).

46.   For a biography of Chester Congdon, see Roy O. Hoover, *A Lake Superior Lawyer* (Duluth: Superior Partners, 1997). For a biographical sketch of Guilford Hartley drawn from his notes and from writings by his grandson, David Hartley, see "The Life and Times of Guilford Graham Hartley," unpublished manuscript (NEMHC).

47.   On the overseas operations, see Hoover, *Lake Superior Lawyer*, 104–17. In her novel *Mesabi* (New York: Harper and Row, 1969), Duluth author Margaret Culkin Banning gives a picture of the confident, energetic, and substantial world of Duluth's industrial and commercial leaders in the period 1920–1950.

48.   Sydney E. Ahlstrom, *Religious History*, 905.

49.   Quoted by David Brody, "The Rise and Decline of Welfare Capitalism," in *Change and Continuity in Twentieth-Century America: The 1920s*, ed. John Braeman, Robert H. Bremner, and David Brody (Columbus: Ohio State University Press, 1968), 147, 149.

50.   Julius H. Barnes, *The Genius of American Business* (Garden City, N.J.: Doubleday, Page, and Company, 1924).

51.   On Barnes, see *Genius of American Business*, 12–13; and Julius Barnes, "The Growing Responsibilities of Business," an address delivered before the U.S. Chamber of Commerce and printed in *The Duluthian* (Duluth: Duluth Chamber of Commerce, November 1929), 14–20 (NEMHC).

52.   *Duluth News Tribune*, May 28, 1918, 1, 14A.

53.   For Carney's attack on the Non-Partisan League, see *Truth*, February 22, 1918, 4; May 10, 1918, 4; May 17, 1918, 3; June 28, 1918, 4; July 5, 1918, 4; and October 25, 1918, 4.

54.   *Labor World*, March 23, 1918, 6.

55.   *Labor World*, March 30, 1918, 1.

56.   *Labor World*, May 18, 1918, 3.

57.   *Labor World*, June 15, 1918, 6.

58.   *Labor World*, August 3, 1918, 1.

59. Carl H. Chrislock, *The Progressive Era in Minnesota 1899–1918* (St. Paul: Minnesota Historical Society, 1971), 172.

60. Ibid., 177.

61. John Thompson to W. L. Carss, October 8, 1918. William Leighton Carss Papers (MHS).

62. Chrislock, *Progressive Era*, 178; and *Labor World*, August 31, 1918, 19; October 26, 1918, 4; and November 2, 1918, 4.

63. William Leighton Carss Papers (MHS).

64. Helen Rawlings to "Dear Lady," June 16, 1920, William Leighton Carss Papers (MHS).

65. See the letter from A. W. Kloepfel (January 15, 1923) and the supporting letter from O. J. Larson (June 7, 1923), William Leighton Carss Papers (MHS).

66. C. K. Davis to Carss, March 8, 1928; and E. Jackson to Carss, January 12, 1929, William Leighton Carss Papers (MHS).

67. J. H. Bacon to Carss, August 28, 1925, William Leighton Carss Papers, (MHS).

68. On Socialist opposition to the Union Labor Party and Lichten, see *Truth*, February 21, 1919. On Johnson and Lichten, see *Labor World*, February 1, 1919, 6; and December 6, 1919, 3.

69. *Labor World*, April 5, 1918. See also the James A. Farrell file at the NEMHC.

70. *Labor World*, March 8, 1919, 6.

71. On Murnian and Farrell, see *Labor World*, March 22, 1919, 1, and also the files on these men at the NEMHC.

72. *Labor World*, April 5, 1919, 1.

73. *Labor World*, April 12, 1919, 3.

74. *Labor World*, May 24, 1919, 6; and June 7, 1919, 6.

75. *Labor World*, July 26, 1919, 2.

76. *Labor World*, September 20, 1919, 5; and October 25, 1919, 6.

77. *Labor World*, February 7, 1920, 6.

78. "Convention Minutes and List of Delegates," St. Paul, 1920, Farmer-Labor Association of St. Paul Papers (MHS).

79. *Labor World*, June 19, 1920, 1. On the crowds at Woodman Hall, see *Labor World*, June 19, 1920, 12.

80. *Labor World*, November 6, 1920, 1.

81. In his 1918 campaign, Carss was well aware of the importance of Democrats' votes. His files for that campaign contain lists of Democratic activists. Henry Morin, a Democratic activist, tried to convince Carss to run as a Democrat in 1922. See Henry Morin to Carss, April 17, 1922, in the William Leighton Carss Papers (MHS).

82. For a more detailed discussion of the process by which the Farmer-Labor Party and Farmer-Labor Association came into existence, see Chrislock, *Progressive Era*, 191–93.

83. For an account of this episode, see Irving Howe and Lewis Coser, *The American Communist Party: A Critical History* (New York: Praeger, 1962), 118–27.

84. Farmer-Labor Association of St. Paul Papers (MHS).

85. Chrislock, *Progressive Era*, 192–93.

86.   *Labor World*, March 8, 1924, 4; and April 19, 1924, 1.

87.   *Labor World*, June 7, 1924, 4, 6.

88.   *Labor World*, September 13, 1924, 6.

89.   Howe and Coser, *American Communist Party*, 136–37; on the Minnesota Communists, see the footnote on 131–32. Clarence Hathaway, head of the Communist Party in Minnesota, was on good terms with William Mahoney prior to the June convention and his name appears on official Farmer-Labor letterhead announcing the conference.

90.   *Labor World*, August 2, 1924, 6.

91.   Chrislock, *Progressive Era*, 193.

92.   Farmer-Labor Association of St. Paul Papers (MHS). Charles Olson of Duluth, an AFL activist, was the Farmer-Labor candidate for secretary of state in this same 1926 campaign.

93.   Ibid.

94.   Susan Perala-Dewey, "The Farmer-Labor Party in Duluth, MN," unpublished research paper, 13 (NEMHC).

95.   *Labor World*, March 19, 1927, 1; and April 9, 1927, 1.

96.   Farmer-Labor Association of St. Paul Papers and William Leighton Carss Papers (MHS).

97.   *Labor World*, September 3, 1927, 1; and September 10, 1927, 10.

98.   The newspaper originally appeared under the name *Labor Leader*; the name of the paper was changed in October 1917.

99.   Information on the Boilermakers, the Machinists, and the Shopmen comes from *Truth*, *Labor World*, and the Farmer-Labor Association of St. Paul Papers. On Siegler, see Steve Trimble and Tom O'Connell's 1977 interview with Ruth Siegler, available at the MHS. On Siegler's role as chair of the Federated Crafts in the Shopmen's strike, see *Labor World*, April 5, 1924, 1.

100.   Farmer-Labor Association of St. Paul Papers (MHS).

101.   Perala-Dewey, "Farmer-Labor Party," 7.

102.   Farmer-Labor Association of St. Paul Papers (MHS).

103.   Ibid.

104.   *Labor World*, June 23, 1928.

105.   S. Sloven was elected as a local delegate to the state Farmer-Labor convention in 1926. Farmer-Labor Association of St. Paul Papers.

106.   Leonard Hedman to Carss, August 25, 1924, William Leighton Carss Papers (MHS).

107.   William Leighton Carss Papers (MHS).

108.   *Labor World*, June 26, 1926, 1. William McEwen, himself a Presbyterian, was a persistent and harsh critic of the KKK and anti-Catholicism.

109.   *Labor World*, June 5, 1926, 1.

110.   On Thompson, see *Labor World*, July 26, 1926, 6. On Farley, see R. H. Farley to J. A. Barron, February 23, 1927, DFTA Papers (MHS).

111.   *Labor World*, June 26, 1926, 1.

chapter 7. west duluth on the move

1. Julius Barnes, "The Growing Responsibilities of Business," in *The Duluthian* (Duluth: Duluth Chamber of Commerce, November 1929), 20.

2. *Labor World*, May 11, 1929, 1; and June 1, 1929, 1.

3. *Labor World*, September 13, 1930, 1. For information regarding this survey and others conducted in the early 1930s, see *An Analysis of Three Unemployment Surveys in Minneapolis, St. Paul, and Duluth*, ed. Alvin Hansen, Nelle M. Petrowski, and Richard Graves (Minneapolis: University of Minnesota Press, 1932). Another study headed by Hansen claims 5,723 unemployed in Duluth as of April 1930. See *The Decline of Employment in the 1930–31 Depression in St. Paul, Minneapolis, and Duluth*, ed. Alvin Hansen, Dreng Bjornaraa, and Tillman M. Sogge (University of Minnesota Employment Stabilization Research Institute 1, no. 5 [June 1932], 32).

4. Hansen, *The Decline of Employment*, 33.

5. Sam Davis Papers, Biographical Information, Correspondence, Miscellaneous Papers, 1919– (MHS).

6. Sielaff, "Lake Traffic at the Port of Duluth-Superior," table B.

7. "Statistical Report of Marine Commerce of Duluth Minnesota and Superior Wisconsin," 1913–31 (NEMHC).

8. For data on unemployment in the metal products industry and other industries in Duluth, see Hansen, *Decline of Employment*, table 7, 14.

9. David Brody, "The Rise and Decline of Welfare Capitalism," in *Change and Continuity in Twentieth-Century America: The 1920s*, ed. John Braeman, Robert H. Bremner, and David Brody (Columbus: Ohio State University Press, 1968), 165–67.

10. *Labor World*, May 9 and May 16, 1931.

11. Quoted by Brody, "Rise and Decline," 172.

12. Ibid; *Labor World*, September 26, 1931.

13. *Labor World*, March 31, 1934.

14. Hansen, *Analysis of Three Unemployment Surveys*.

15. Duluth Community Chest Fund, October 29, 1930, Duluth Clippings files, Duluth Public Library.

16. Duluth Community Chest Fund, April 18, 1925, and November 3, 1932, Duluth Clippings files, Duluth Public Library.

17. "Relief Data," Minnesota State Planning Board, box 3, 1927–36 (MHS).

18. These figures are from a statement by the Taxpayers' League of St. Louis County to its members for June 1, 1937. Taxpayers' League of St. Louis County, Annual Report Collection, 1924–37 (MHS).

19. Report of the Interim Committee on Social Legislation and Relief to the Legislature of the State of Minnesota, 1937, 19–20 (MHS).

20. "Receipts—Public Welfare," Minnesota State Planning Board, box 3, 1927–36 (MHS).

21. The date of organization is mentioned in the June 1, 1937, statement to its members by the Taxpayers' League of St. Louis County, Annual Report Collection, 1924–37 (MHS).

22. Letterhead of the Taxpayers' League of St. Louis County (MHS).

23. Taxpayers' League of St. Louis County, Annual Report Collection, 1924–37 (MHS).

24. *Labor World*, December 1, 1934, 4.

25. *Labor World*, March 5, 1932, 1; and March 12, 1932, 1.

26. *Labor World*, April 16, 1932, 1. For the names of the members of the Duluth Committee of 77, see *Labor World*, April 30, 1932, 2.

27. *Labor World*, May 21, 1932, 1.

28. *Labor World*, June 25, 1932, 1.

29. *Labor World*, April 22, 1933; May 6, 13, and 20, 1933; and August 12, 1933.

30. This figure on the tax delinquency rate comes from the June 1, 1937, letter to members from M. W. DeWees, executive secretary of the Taxpayers' League, Taxpayers' League of St. Louis County Papers (MHS). The figure is corroborated by a slightly higher figure found in a report sent by Walter Borgen, St. Louis County Auditor, to Harry Fiterman, director of a tax and finance survey conducted by the state of Minnesota. See St. Louis County file, Minnesota Planning Board, Box 1 (MHS).

31. *Labor World*, May 27, 1933, 1.

32. *Labor World*, November 11, 1933. The taxes were paid within a week of this story; see *Labor World*, November 18, 1933.

33. *Labor World*, September 23, 1933, 1.

34. *Labor World*, March 31, 1934, 1.

35. *Labor World*, April 7, 1934, 1; and September 29, 1934, 1.

36. *Labor World*, October 19, 1935, 1.

37. *Labor World*, April 11, 1936, 1; May 23, 1936, 1; June 6, 1936, 1; June 20, 1936, 1.

38. "Analysis of the Comparative Financial Status of the Eighty-Four Rural and Three Urban Counties of Minnesota and Their Ability to Contribute to the Established Local Governmental Functions," 9. On the "A" rating for St. Louis County, see p. 11. Minnesota State Planning Board (MHS).

39. Per capita taxes for the three counties can be found in the folder labeled "County Financial Data," box 1. The summary of recommendations is in the folder labeled "Three Cities: Minneapolis, St. Paul and Duluth," box 3, Minnesota State Planning Board (MHS).

40. On the start of the WPA in the Duluth area, see *Duluth Herald*, February 24, 1943. On expenditures in St. Louis County through 1936, see Minnesota Works Progress Administration Division of Finance and Statistics, "Cumulative Federal Expenditures by County and District for WPA to December 31, 1936," Minnesota Planning Board (MHS).

41. "WPA Birthday," *Duluth News Tribune*, June 29, 1941.

42. On this criticism and a reply, see *Labor World*, September 26, 1936, 2.

43. "WPA Birthday."

44. A useful survey of the WPA in Duluth is Dorothy Herman, "The WPA in Duluth, Minnesota: A Pictorial and Written Over-View," 1977 (unpublished manuscript, NEMHC). There are also newspaper clippings files on the WPA at the Duluth Public Library and the NEMHC.

45. *Labor World*, September 21, 1939, 1.

46. See October 3, 1935, Leo Brett to H. A. Anderson. St. Louis County Commissioners file 1 (NEMHC).

47. November 27, 1932, DFTA Papers (MHS).

48. January 13, 1932, DFTA Papers (MHS).

49. Isaac Moore to Harry Fiterman, November 17, 1936, St. Louis County File, Minnesota State Planning Board (MHS).

50. *Duluth Herald*, March 17, 1937.

51. *Duluth News Tribune*, July 16, 1937.

52. *Duluth Herald*, October 12, 1937.

53. "WPA Birthday."

54. The account of Videen's experiences that follows is based on his own unpublished manuscript, "The Hard Life and Good Times of Clayton A. Videen." A copy of this manuscript is available at the NEMHC. An interview with Mr. Videen, conducted by Richard Hudelson, is also available on audio tape at the Historical Center and a collection of Mr. Videen's papers is available at the MHS.

55. Videen, "Hard Life and Good Times," 63.

56. Ibid., 119.

57. Ibid., 60.

58. Ibid., 73.

59. John Haynes, *Dubious Alliance: The Making of Minnesota's DFL Party* (Minneapolis: University of Minnesota, 1984), 12.

60. "Program of the Communist Party in the Duluth Municipal Election" (1930). Copies of this four-page flyer are available at the NEMHC and the MHS. For further information on the unemployment and anti-eviction work of the Communists in Duluth, see the Sam Davis Papers (MHS).

61. *Labor World*, July 19, 1930, 1.

62. *Labor World*, February 4, 1933, 1.

63. *Labor World*, July 2, 1932.

64. Edward L. Slaughter, oral history interview (MHS).

65. For an account of the history of the ILA, the conditions on the docks in Duluth, and the longshoremen's strike of 1931, see ibid. On the settlement of the strike, see *Labor World*, May 16, 1931, 1.

66. *Labor World*, September 23, 1933, 1; October 21, 1933, 21; November 4, 1933, 1; June 16, 1934, 1; June 30, 1934, 1; September 1, 1934, 1; October 28, 1933, 2; February 16, 1935, 1; May 30, 1935, 1.

67. Robert Zieger, *American Workers, American Unions, 1920–1985* (Baltimore: The Johns Hopkins University Press, 1989), 22, 31.

68. *Labor World*, July 1, 1933, 1; ibid., 41.

69. *Labor World*, September 23, 1933, 1; and February 3, 1934, 4. The union at Diamond Calk was the first federal union formed in Duluth in the 1930s. That there was some confusion about this is indicated by the announcement of the formation of the union in the *Labor World* (September 23, 1933, 1), where the union is said to be both a federal union and a local of the General Drivers Union. It was in fact a federal union.

70. Zieger, *American Workers*, 32, 38.

71. *Labor World*, August 19, 1933, 1; August 26, 1933, 1; March 24, 1934, 2; July 28, 1934, 1.

72. *Labor World*, March 17, 1934, 1. The local AFL leaders involved in the Labor

Forward campaign are identified in *Labor World*, April 14, 1934, 1. See also April 28, 1934, 1.

73. *Labor World*, March 17, 1934, 1. In 1936, following the passage of the Wagner Act, a company union, the "Employee Representation Plan," was established at the steel plant in Duluth. On this development, see the Einar Bjork, 1977 interview with Martin Duffy (MHS). Bjork was one of the founding members of Local 1028.

74. *Labor World*, October 21, 1933, 1.

75. On Ernest Pearson's IWW past and his membership in the Communist Party, see the interviews by Hyvärinen and Frenkel with Glenn Pearson and Leata Pearson in the Oral History Collection of the MHS. Though he was not himself Scandinavian, Ernie Pearson's name appears in *Truth* as someone who was actively involved with the Scandinavian Socialist Club in Duluth between 1917 and 1923. It appears likely that Pearson joined the Communist Party when the members of the Duluth Scandinavian Socialist Club joined as one of the founding locals of the Communist Labor Party in late fall 1919.

76. Ed Drille, interview by Carl Ross, October 14, 1987 (MHS).

77. *Labor World*, September 7, 1935, 1; September 14, 1935, 1; September 28, 1935, 1. On the role of Joe Liss and the Communist Party, see the 1968 interviews by Irene Paull with Martin Kuusisto and Ilmar Koivunen, both Communist Party activists who were involved in organizing the lumberjacks (MHS).

78. *Labor World*, October 12, 1935, 1; *Labor World*, November 14, 1936, 1.

79. *Labor World*, May 30, 1936, 4, mentions John Couture, president of Local 2776, speaking on the abuse of lumberjacks by some employers who would not pay them for work done.

80. Kuusisto interview with Paull.

81. *Labor World*, April 21, 1934, 1.

82. *Labor World*, September 1, 1934, 4.

83. *Labor World*, August 31, 1935, 1. The union appears to have been reorganized, as *Labor World* identifies it as Local 166 of the Laundry and Dry Cleaners Union, with Carl Dahlberg as president and Angeline Pavlich as vice president (*Labor World*, August 31, 1935, 4, and September 7, 1935, 1).

84. Zieger, *American Workers*, 33.

85. See DFTA Papers, September 9, 1935; *Labor World*, September 7 and 14, 1935; and DFTA Papers for September 14, 18, 23, 24, and 27, 1935. There is no date on the pamphlet.

86. *Labor World*, September 7, 1935, 1.

87. *Labor World*, September 14, 1935, 6; and September 7, 1935, 1.

88. *Labor World*, January 18, 1936, 2. For accounts of the violence and court cases, see *Labor World*, October 5, 1935, 1; and October 26, 1935, 1.

89. *Labor World*, July 7, 1934, 1; and July 28, 1934, 4. On company unions, see *Labor World*, July 22, 1933, 1; and May 17, 1934, 1. A company union had been formed among clerical workers for the DM&N railway. See Brotherhood of Railway Clerks to DFTA, September 28, 1935, DFTA Papers (MHS).

90. Zieger, *American Workers*, 43.

91. *Labor World*, August 1, 1936, 1.

92. There are two interviews with Earl Bester in the MHS collection. One was done by Jack Spiese in 1967 and is available in the Earl Bester Papers; the

other, done by James Dooley and Martin Duffy in 1974, is available in the Oral History Collection. See also the 1980 interview with Earl Bester and Joe Paszak done by Jean Johnson (MHS).

93. Toini Maki, interview with Irene Paull, September 1968 (MHS).

94. On the role of Martin Maki and Joe Van Nordstrand as SWOC organizers, see Bester, interview with Dooley and Duffy (MHS). Van Nordstrand's connection to the Communist Party was a poorly kept secret. He had worked openly in Minnesota as a Communist under the name of Joe Moreland. Information about his specific role as organizer for District Nine of the Communist Party comes from Carl Ross, who was himself active in the party during the 1930s.

95. Zieger, *American Workers*, 54–55. An interesting first-person account of this understanding is offered by Len De Caux, a Communist Party member who became the national publicity director for the CIO. See De Caux, *Labor Radical: From the Wobblies to the CIO* (Boston: Beacon Press, 1970), 219–21.

96. See Arnold Arnio, interview with Carl Ross in 1987 (MHS). See also George Zlatovski, "The Autobiography of an Anti-Hero," unpublished manuscript, 84–86 (IHRC).

97. Prior to 1928, the Communists cooperated with the non-Communists within the Amalgamated. From 1928 to 1935, when the Communists were attempting to form an independent radical alternative, they worked through the Mine, Mill and Smelter Workers Union (MMSW). On an attempt to organize an MMSW local at the steel plant in 1932, see Bester interview with Dooley and Duffy (MHS). On the formation of MMSW locals on the Iron Range, see *Labor World*, January 19, 1935, and March 9, 1935.

98. Bester, interview with Dooley and Duffy.

99. An account of the origins of Local 1028 is provided in *Midwest Labor*, September 17, 1937, 2. That article identifies a "Mr. Dolter" as being the first to sign a union card. Marco Bullyan also claimed this honor for Sam Angelo and himself (see Schumacher, *The Raleigh Street Saga*, 17). Given the necessary secrecy of the organizing drive, a number of different people might well have thought themselves the first to sign. In any case, there were already remnants of the old Amalgamated Local and the Communist-led Mine, Mill and Smelters Local still present in the plant before the SWOC drive even began. Cards from both the Amalgamated and the MMSW were turned over to SWOC (Earl Bester Papers, MHS).

100. The officers were Al Overton (president), Nels Strand (vice president), Ervin Drill (recording secretary), Thomas H. DeNio (financial secretary), John Neely (tresurer), and A. N. Albrecht, K. Whelan, and R. MacMillan (trustees). See *Midwest Labor*, September 10, 1937, 1.

101. *Midwest Labor*, September 17, 1937, 2.

102. Interviews done by Marjorie Hoover for the Minnesota Ethnic History Project include many testimonials in support of the union. See, for example, her interviews with Dan Bastie, Anthony and Anna Matkovich, Nick Borovak, Mr. and Mrs. Alex Smolinker, John Howden, and J. B. Wiener. The only comment against the union among those interviewed by Hoover came from Father Francis Schweiger, who was a priest in New Duluth from 1932 to 1937. Father Schweiger said that he never could see why the men wanted a union because things were going well for them, but he himself mentioned the role of his predecessor, Father Pirnat, in influencing who would and who would not be hired at the steel plant, an influence also mentioned by others interviewed by Hoover.

103. *Midwest Labor*, October 29, 1937, 2, provides a list of locals participating in an Amalgamated Convention in Duluth. The issue for July 22, 1938, provides a list of Duluth CIO unions, most of which originated in 1937. The history of their formation can be traced in *Midwest Labor*.

104. Herbert Widell, interview with Richard Hudelson (NEMHC).

105. *Labor World*, December 5, 1936, 1.

106. Glenn Pearson, interview with Virginia Hyvärinen and Susanna Frenkel, 1988, 6 (MHS). Additional material on the Pearson family, the Coolerator Local, the CIO, and Duluth radical politics can be found in a 1988 interview with Leata Pearson, Glenn Pearson's wife, by Hyvärinen and Frenkel, and in a 1978 interview with Maney Pearson by Barbara Sommers. All of these interviews are available at the MHS.

107. Glenn Pearson, interview by Hyvärinen and Frenkel.

108. Fred Natus, "The Timber Industry of Northern Minnesota," unpublished manuscript prepared for the Workers Education Program in Duluth, n.d. (NEMHC).

109. Ilmar Koivunen, along with Edith Koivunen, interview by Irene Paull, 1968 (MHS).

110. Natus, chapter 3 (there is no consistent pagination to the manuscript).

111. Ibid.

112. Ibid.

113. Kuusisto, interview by Paull (MHS). Lequier was also French Canadian.

114. Ibid.

115. Ibid. Martin Kuusisto, another leader of the Timber Workers' Union, also discusses the role of Joe Liss.

116. Koivunen, interview by Paull. On Benson's role in the strike, see also Kuusisto's interview with Paull (MHS).

117. The quoted phrase is from Natus, chapter 3.

118. On Irene Paull's role, see her 1968 interview with Kuusisto and Steven Trimble's 1977 interview with her (24–25). On the attack on Henry Paull, see the letters and telegrams from local CIO unions and Farmer-Labor clubs in the Governor Elmer Benson Papers (Executive Letters, 1937 file, MHS). See also *Midwest Labor*, October 21, 1938, 1, and November 11, 1938, 3, on legal action brought by Henry Paull against his attackers and against several lumber companies alleged to have been behind the attack.

119. *The Timber Worker*, later to become *Midwest Labor*, is available on microfilm at the MHS.

120. Zieger, *American Workers*, 44–45.

121. *Labor World*, June 19, 1937, 1. On the expulsion of the Coolerator Local, see *Labor World*, February 20, 1937.

122. Duluth Industrial Union Council Papers (MHS).

123. See the list of CIO unions in *Midwest Labor*, July 15, 1938, 2.

124. Proceedings of the First Annual Convention of the Minnesota State Industrial Union Council (Minneapolis, December 1937), 9 (MHS).

chapter 8. the popular front

1. On Ilmar Koivunen and Martin Kuusisto, see their interviews with Irene Paull. On Ernie Pearson, see Leata Pearson's 1988 interview with Hyvärinen and Frenkel. On Glenn Pearson and Pat McGraw, see Glenn Pearson's 1988 interview with Hyvärinen and Frenkel. On Edwin and Erwin Drill, see Edwin Drill's 1987 interview with Carl Ross. On Joe Paszak, see his 1988 interview with Hyvärinen and Frenkel. On Sam Davis, see the Sam Davis Papers. On Irene Paull, see her 1977 interview with Steve Trimble, as well as her interviews of Ilmar Koivunen and Martin Kuusisto, cited above. All interviews cited above are available at MHS. On the National Maritime Union and the Fur and Leather Workers Union, see Klehr, *Heyday*, 237–38.

2. On the effect of a pamphlet by Dimitroff on local Communists, see Trimble's interview with Irene Paull (MHS).

3. The American League against War and Fascism was actually formed in 1933. For a discussion of the history of this organization, see Howe and Coser, *American Communist Party*, 348–54.

4. *Labor World*, October 26, 1935, 6.

5. *Labor World*, August 4, 1934, 1. This announcement resulted in Griffith's expulsion from the meeting.

6. On the AYC, see Klehr, *Heyday*, 319–23.

7. Howe and Coser, *American Communist Party*, 359–60.

8. Leata Pearson, interview with Hyvärinen and Frenkel (MHS).

9. George Dizard, interview with Ross, 1987 (MHS).

10. There is some information on Rhoda Dizard in the George Dizard and Family Papers at the MHS. On the student from India, see *Midwest Labor*, December 15, 1939, 2.

11. Leata Pearson, interview with Hyvärinen and Frenkel (MHS).

12. Minutes of the Duluth CIO Council, February 6, 1940; February 20, 1940; March 19, 1940, Duluth CIO Industrial Union Council Papers (MHS).

13. George Dizard and Family Papers (MHS).

14. On Anne Gerlovich, see Maney Pearson's interview with Barbara Sommer (NEMHC). See also the *Minnesota CIO Yearbook 1942* (MHS).

15. Klehr and Haynes, *Heyday*, 77.

16. Paszak, interview with Hyvärinen and Frenkel (MHS).

17. Nichols, interview with Taylor (MHS).

18. On the attitudes of South Slavs toward their black neighbors, see Paszak, interview with Hyvärinen and Frenkel, and Hoover's interviews with South Slavs in Duluth conducted for the Minnesota Ethnic Studies Project (MHS).

19. Bubalo, interview with Hoover. Amelia Thomas, another South Slav interviewed by Hoover, also mentions the concentration of black men in the coke plant (MHS).

20. Thomas, interview with Hoover (MHS).

21. Gary Athletic Club Fiftieth Anniversary Reunion pamphlet (NEMHC).

22. Nichols, interview with Taylor (MHS).

23. Charles P. Larrowe, *Maritime Labor Relations on the Great Lakes* (East Lansing: Michigan State University, 1959), 63.

24. Minutes for August 4, 1942; April 12, 1943; July 27, 1943; and December 28, 1943, Duluth CIO Industrial Union Council Papers (MHS).

25. Minutes for May 17, 1943, Duluth CIO Industrial Union Council Papers (MHS). See also later donations to support work for racial justice: April 19, 1949; June 7, 1949; December 6, 1949. By 1949, Popular Front leaders had already lost control of the CIO Council. Nonetheless, the minutes show that it was at their instigation that the council acted on these matters.

26. NAACP File (NEMHC).

27. Copy of letter from Chesta E. Mitchel, executive director, to Reverend Roy E. Burt, January 10, 1946, Duluth Interracial Council File (NEMHC).

28. Nichols, interview with Taylor (MHS).

29. Paszak, interview with Hyvärinen and Frenkel; Bester and Paszak, interview with Johnson (both MHS).

30. On the CWA in Duluth, see Maney Pearson, interview with Sommer (NEMHC).

31. On Maney Pearson, see ibid. On Gerlovich, see the Minnesota CIO *Yearbook 1942* (MHS).

32. Maney Pearson, interview with Sommer (MHS).

33. Drill and Dizard interviews with Ross (MHS).

34. Minutes for November 7, 1940, show Larson among ACW representatives resigning from the council, Duluth CIO Industrial Union Council Papers (MHS).

35. CIO Industrial Union Council Papers, minutes, November 3, 1942 (MHS).

36. On Lakeside, where there was a mixed-gender Farmer-Labor club, see Ruth Siegler's 1977 interview with Steve Trimble and Tom O'Connell (MHS).

37. Ibid.

38. Mrs. Frank Wanner, Mrs. Carl Falk, and Mrs. Philip DeMore are among other women whose names appear frequently in local newspaper accounts of the Farmer-Labor movement in Duluth in the 1930s.

39. See the unity convention call to Farmer-Labor groups signed by Mrs. Erickson, March 30, 1925, DFTA Papers (MHS).

40. Haynes, *Dubious Alliance*. Haynes does not claim that Johnson was a member of the Communist Party, but he sees her as someone who unfailingly went along with positions taken by Communists.

41. Viena Hendrickson Papers (MHS); later in her life, Viena Johnson married Paul Hendrickson. There are two biographical sources in these papers: a brief handwritten biographical sketch in pencil and a folder of family and biographical data, including a 1973 interview of Viena Hendrickson by Tim Madigen.

42. There are numerous announcements, letters, and newspaper clippings regarding speaking engagements in the Viena Hendrickson Papers (MHS). Other mention of public speeches can be found in *Labor World*, January 4, 1936, 1; November 14, 1936, 1; July 7, 1937, 1; and July 27, 1939, 1.

43. Viena Hendrickson Papers (MHS).

44. John T. Bernard to Viena P. Johnson, November 14, 1936, Viena Hendrickson Papers (MHS).

45. On Koivunen, Kuusisto, Maki, and Pearson, see their interviews at the MHS.

46. A card for Carl Gerlovich can be found among subscription cards to *Proletaric* in the Jugoslav Socialist Federation Papers, 1900–1952, folders 150–51 (IHRC).

47. See Bjork interview with Duffy; and Arnio interview with Ross.

48. Langdahl's name appears repeatedly in *Truth*, the newspaper published by the Scandinavian Socialist Local. In a biographical sketch of Langdahl prepared for the 1936 campaign, there is a claim that Langdahl at some point served on the Board of Directors of *Truth* (Viena Hendrickson Papers, MHS). Emil Standin's name is one of those that appear on an invitation for a reunion meeting of the Scandinavian Socialist Local; it can also be found in the Viena Hendrickson Papers. The names of Carl and Hulda Falk appear in *Truth* in 1917, 1920, and 1921 and appear repeatedly in stories about the FLP in the 1930s in *Labor World* and *Midwest Labor*.

49. For examples of letterhead mentioning these names from the mid-1930s, see the Viena Hendrickson Papers (MHS).

50. Letterhead for the 1936 Central Labor Political Committee with the names of the executive committee can be found in the Viena Hendrickson Papers (MHS). "Shot by Some Unknown Man," an article in the *Superior Telegram* (May 11, 1909, 10), may throw some light on why Michael O'Rourke was aligned with the Scandinavian radicals instead of his fellow engineers. The article reports that seaman James O'Rourke had been shot to death during an altercation between striking seamen and special officers serving the Lake Carriers' Association. No charges were filed.

51. Irene Paull, *Midwest Labor*, August 13, 1937, 8.

52. Examples of such work are Natus, "The Timber Industry of Northern Minnesota"; Eino Krapu, "The Mining Industry of Minnesota"; and research by Clayton Videen on the strike of 1916 on the Iron Range. All are unpublished manuscripts available at MHS.

53. A postcard announcement of the reunion, dated December 6, 1936, can be found in the Viena Hendrickson Papers (MHS). John D. Nelson's article, "Son of Mother Svea Recalls Duluth's Progressive Past," appeared in *Midwest Labor*, August 27, 1937, 3.

54. *Midwest Labor*, October 21, 1938, 1. Daley was also active in Duluth in the early 1920s, when his name appears frequently in *Truth*.

55. For examples of this, see the remarks by the Scandinavian ore dock worker in *Midwest Labor*, September 3, 1937, 5; the remarks of the steel plant worker in *Midwest Labor*, September 17, 1937, 2; the interviews with Tony Mattovich, Nick Borvak, Mr. and Mrs. Alex Smolniker, Dan Bastie, John Howden, and J. B. Wiener done by Marjorie Hoover for the Minnesota Ethnic History Project (MHS); and the interviews with Joe Bucsko and Marco Bullyan in Schumacher, *The Raleigh Street Saga*.

56. *Midwest Labor*, September 10, 1937.

57. *Midwest Labor*, September 30, 1938, 2.

58. *Midwest Labor*, October 28, 1938, 3; March 3, 1939, 3; May 26, 1939, 4.

59. *Midwest Labor*, July 1, 1938, 4.

60. *Midwest Labor*, August 20, 1937, 6; October 15, 1937, 4; June 10, 1938, 4; August 19, 1938, 4; December 9, 1938, 1; December 16, 1938, 1.

61. *Midwest Labor*, August 26, 1938, 4; September 30, 1938, 3.

62. *Midwest Labor*, February 10, 1939, 2.

63. *Midwest Labor*, March 17, 1939, 2; April 21, 1939, 2.

64. *Midwest Labor*, September 30, 1938, 4; June 30, 1939, 4.

65. *Midwest Labor*, January 27, 1938, 1; June 23, 1939, 1 and 4; July 7, 1939, 1; July 21, 1939, 1; September 15, 1939, 1 and 2; September 29, 1939, 1. On the Workers' Alliance, see, for example, December 24, 1937, 1; and September 9, 1938, 1.

66. *Labor World*, March 2, 1935, 1; and May 4, 1935, 1.

67. Glenn Pearson, interview with Hyvärinen and Frenkel, 31 (MHS).

68. Paszak, interview with Hudelson, 1993 (NEMHC).

69. *Labor World*, April 28, 1938, 1; *Midwest Labor*, April 29, 1938, 1.

70. Accounts of this incident can be found in *The Guild Daily*, May 24, 1938, and in the *St. Paul Dispatch*, May 24, 1938. *The Guild Daily* was a newspaper put out by the striking Newspaper Guild during the course of the strike. A few numbers are available at the MHS. Another interesting account of the strike is provided by Glenn Pearson in his interview with Hyvärinen and Frenkel.

71. Papers relevant to the guild strike in Duluth, including many telegrams to the governor and statements by the governor, can be found in the Governor Elmer Benson Papers (MHS).

72. *Midwest Labor*, April 22, 1938, 1.

73. *Midwest Labor*, May 6, 1938, 3; September 9, 1938, 1.

74. *Labor World*, September 1 and 8, 1938.

75. *Midwest Labor*, November 4, 1938, 1.

76. Irene Paull, "Joe Paszak ... American," Minneapolis: Labor Coordinating Committee, 1943 (NEMHC).

77. On Paszak, see his interview with Hyvärinen and Frenkel. See also interview with Hudelson and the newspaper clippings file on Paszak, which include reports of the radio talk mentioned here (both at NEMHC).

chapter 9. the embattled popular front

1. On Carl Carlson, see *1857–1957 In Commemoration of the One Hundredth Anniversary of the Northwest Grand Lodge, I.O.G.T.*, published by the History Committee of the Northwest Grand Lodge in 1957 (39–40). On John Kobi and the entry of the Socialist Party of Minnesota into the FLP, see *Labor World*, April 9, 1932. On Kobi's connections to the SNPJ and the Yugoslav Federation, see the Duluth International Institute Papers (NEMHC) and the membership cards found in the papers of the Jugoslav Socialist Federation (IHRC). On Frank and Tony Puglisi, see interview with Frank Puglisi by Tom O'Connell (MHS). According to George Zlatovski, Tony Puglisi, an accomplished light-weight boxer, once served as a bodyguard for Communist Party activist Herman Griffith when Griffith was speaking to a meeting of Yugoslav and Italian steelworkers in Duluth. See George Zlatovski, *Autobiography of an Anti-Hero*, unpublished manuscript (IHRC).

2. September 11, 1930, DFTA Papers (MHS).

3. March 20, 1925, Farmer-Labor Association Papers (MHS). See also the financial statement for January–March 1931 in the DFTA Papers (MHS), which shows the Arrowhead FLA Club being taxed according to the per capita formula applied to CLPC-affiliated organizations.

4. April 9, 1931, DFTA Papers (MHS).

5. On Erickson's connection to the railroad shops, see the letter from the Railroad Carmen of April 24, 1931, and the copy of the letter to the Duluth City Council from the Railroad Shopmen of May 22, 1931, both in the DFTA Papers (MHS).

6. On the Cabinet Makers and Millmen's Union, see *Labor World*, March 13, 1941. John A. Johnson, for example, appears in a list of supporters of the Scandinavian Socialist Local that was published in *Truth* (December 24, 1920); he was also active in the Duluth Union Labor Party in 1919 and represented Local 1284 in the 1920 convention of the Working People's Nonpartisan League. Farmer-Labor Association of St. Paul Papers (MHS).

7. April 17, 1931 (Machinists); April 22, 1931 (Shopmen); April 24, 1931 (Carmen), DFTA Papers (MHS).

8. Erickson and Kobi were both signers of a letter from System Federation 148 to the Duluth City Council protesting the use of police against the Longshoremen, dated May 22, 1931 (DFTA Papers, MHS). On Siegler's role as a leader of the Federated Shopmen, see *Labor World*, April 5, 1924.

9. *Labor World*, March 23, 1929.

10. Central Labor Political Committee (CLPC) of Duluth and Proctor. "To All Progressive Organizations, Local Unions and F.L. Clubs," 1932, DFTA Papers (MHS). The CLPC letterhead document is signed by Thompson as campaign manager and by Milton Carlson as secretary of the CLPC.

11. January 3, 1933, and December 12, 1933, DFTA Papers (MHS).

12. December 31, 1934, DFTA Papers (MHS).

13. May 16, 1935, DFTA Papers (MHS).

14. See the "Report of Delegates to Central Labor Political Committee" by AFL leaders Robert Olson and Fred I. Brooks, which laments the AFL's loss of "non-partisan" status and the takeover of the old CLPC by a "small group within the city of Duluth that have no particular interest in either organized labor or the farmer" (1935), DFTA Papers (MHS). See also the minutes of the Trade Assembly at which the decision to form a separate screening and endorsing body was taken (1935), also in the DFTA Papers (MHS). The role of Henry Pereault and Elling Munkeby in leading the fight to reject participation in the newly constituted Central Committee, now controlled by Popular Front liberals, is cited in *Labor World*, March 2, 1935, 1. The new AFL organization was formed by October. See the letter from Earl Woolette to affiliated bodies dated October 7, 1935, DFTA Papers. On the make-up of the new AFL CLPC, see *Labor World*, November 9, 1935.

15. *Labor World*, March 9, 1935, 6.

16. *Labor World*, March 9, 1935, 4; March 23, 1935, 1; March 30, 1935, 1; April 6, 1935, 1 and 4; April 20, 1935, 1 and 4.

17. *Labor World*, April 20, 1935, 1.

18. On Olson, see the Robert Olson Papers, and Ralph Olson, "Robert Olson: Labor Leader," unpublished manuscript (both MHS).

19. March 2, 1935, 1. Elling Munkeby, who along with Pereault favored a separate and "nonpartisan" AFL endorsement committee, was active in the public employees union. On Pereault, see the Henry Pereault Papers (MHS). See also the biographical article on Pereault that appeared at his death in *Labor World* (March 13, 1947, 1). Pereault served as chairman of the AFL organizing drive in the mid-1930s, a drive that helped win the Duluth Linen strike, and he later worked at organizing retail clerks.

20. *Labor World*, June 1, 1935, 1; June 22, 1935, 1 and 3.

21. *Labor World*, July 27, 1935, 4.

22. *Labor World*, June 29, 1935, 3.

23. *Labor World*, November 2, 1935, 1.

24. *Labor World*, May 4, 1935, 3; and October 26, 1935, 1.

25. *St. Paul Pioneer Press*, December 1, 1935.

26. In fact she had participated in two such events, one earlier in 1934 as well as the one mentioned here. On this topic, see Herman Griffith to the Trades Assembly, October 22, 1934, DFTA Papers (MHS). See also Anne McEwen's remarks quoted in the *Minnesota Leader* account of her dismissal (December 7, 1935) (MHS).

27. On Carlson and Thompson, see *Labor World*, March 14, 1936, 1. On Robert Sermon, see the obituary in *Duluth Herald*, February 13, 1961. Viena Johnson, another prominent Popular Front leader, would only later be named to the Board of Control of the State College system.

28. This was one of the themes in a major attack on the local Farmer-Labor movement published in *Labor World*, March 14, 1936; the quote appears on p. 2.

29. Haynes, "Communists and Anti-Communists," points to the influx of patronage job holders into the FLA local clubs as one of the causes for the split between the FLA and the AFL in Duluth (57).

30. *Labor World*, March 14, 1936.

31. Ibid., 1.

32. Ibid, 4.

33. Ibid., 1, and *Labor World*, March 21, 1936, 1.

34. *Labor World*, March 21, 1936, 1.

35. On McEwen's appointment, see the account of his life that appeared at the time of his death in *The Minneapolis Journal*, February 2, 1933, 1–2.

36. *Labor World*, April 11, 1936, 1; and April 18, 1936, 1.

37. *Labor World*, May 23, 1936, 1.

38. *Labor World*, June 6, 1936, 3; and July 4, 1936, 1.

39. *Labor World*, July 4, 1936, 1; and July 11, 1936, 1.

40. *Labor World*, October 3, 1; October 10, 1; October 24, 1936, 1; December 19, 1936, 1.

41. *Labor World*, December 19, 1936, 8A; and January 2, 1937, 1.

42. *Labor World*, February 6, 1937, 1; February 13, 1937, 1; March 6, 1937, 8.

43. On the close vote regarding expulsion of the CIO unions from the Duluth Trades Assembly, see the interview with Edwin Drill by Ross, and the interview with Glenn Pearson by Hyvärinen and Frenkel. The vote would have been even closer had the Coolerator Local not been expelled earlier.

44. The National Labor Relations Board ruled in favor of the CIO on the ore docks in March 1938 and in favor of the AFL at the contested Inland Coal Dock in May 1938. See *Midwest Labor*, March 18, 1938, 2; and May 27, 1938, 1, and *Labor World*, May 26, 1938, 1.

45. *Midwest Labor*, March 14, 1938, 1.

46. *Midwest Labor*, January 21, 1938, 2.

47. *Midwest Labor*, March 14, 1938, 1.

48. *Labor World*, May 12, 1938, 1.

49. *Midwest Labor*, May 13, 1938, 1.

50. Ibid.

51. *Labor World*, July 7, 1938, 7.

52. *Labor World*, April 28, 1938, 1.

53. *Labor World*, April 28, 1938, 1; and May 12, 1938, 1.

54. On the Dies Committee on Communists in the NMU, see Klehr, *Heyday*, 249.

55. *Midwest Labor*, October 8, 1937, 1.

56. Edward L. Slaughter, interview with Sommer (MHS)

57. Ibid.

58. Informant's report for August 8, 1944, FBI Files, FOIA Request re. Herman Griffith (NEMHC).

59. Slaughter, interview with Sommer. An article on Slaughter in the *Duluth Budgeteer* (January 5, 1977) says this: "When the AFL was battling the CIO, Buster was very cute. He was out to embarrass the CIO so he had various handbills printed and distributed at CIO plants making fun of the union. Again, from time to time, a few bones were broken but the end result was a merger of the two powerful unions in the 1950s."

60. *Labor World*, October 9, 1937, 2.

61. At one point in Glenn Pearson's interview with Hyvärinen and Frenkel, he comments on a meeting with representatives of the Steelworkers International who were bent on taking over the Coolerator Local: "They had their goons and we had ours." This suggests a climate in which the threat of violence was not uncommon. Such a climate has a history in American labor relations much older than the Communist Party.

62. On Bernard, see John Haynes, "Communists and Anti-Communists," 57. In the 1978 documentary film, "A Common Man's Courage," producers John DeGraaf and Jim Mulligan present a sympathetic portrait of Bernard (MHS). On Catholic opposition to Bernard, see the interview with Tony Puglisi by Tom O'Connell (MHS).

63. Ray Chase, "Are They Communists or Catspaws?" (Anoka: published by author, 1938). The Ray P. Chase Research Bureau was supported by prominent Minneapolis businessmen, among them George Gillette, president of Minneapolis Moline; J. C. Hormel; James Ford Bell of Northwestern Bank; Colonel Robert McCormick, owner of the *Chicago Tribune*; and George Belden of the Citizens' Alliance. The bureau had as its avowed aim to "block the efforts of the present governor and his Communistic Jewish advisers to perpetuate themselves in power." On this and the anti-Communist and anti-Semitic aspects of the campaign of Hjalmar Peterson, Benson's opponent in the FLP primary, see Hy Berman, "Political Antisemitism in Minnesota during the Great Depression," *Jewish Social Studies* 38 (Summer/Fall 1976): 259. On anti-Semitic aspects of the campaign and anti-Semitic sentiment in Duluth during the campaign, see *Midwest Labor*, October 28, 1938, 3, and Irene Paull's interview with Trimble, Frank Puglisi's interview with O'Connell, and Joe Paszak's interviews with Jean Johnson and with Hyvärinen and Frenkel (MHS).

64. *Labor World*, August 18, 1938, 1.

65. *Midwest Labor*, September 16, 1938, 1.

66. It appears in *Labor World* on October 13, 1938, 2.

67. *Midwest Labor*, October 21, 1938, 1.

68. *Labor World*, October 27, 1938, 1.

69. *Labor World*, October 20, 1938, 1; *Midwest Labor*, October 28, 1938, 1.

70. A full list of the AFL locals endorsing Bernard can be found in *Midwest Labor*, November 4, 1938, 4. According to this same article, not a single AFL local endorsed Pittenger.

71. *Labor World*, November 3, 1938, 1; Slaughter, interview with Sommer.

72. *Labor World*, November 10, 1938, 1.

73. *Labor World*, October 3, 1940, 1.

74. *Labor World*, November 17, 1938, 1; December 8, 1938, 1.

75. *Labor World*, December 15, 1938, 1; December 22, 1938, 1.

76. *Labor World*, January 12, 1939, 1.

77. *Labor World*, January 12, 1939, 1.

78. Haynes, "Communists and Anti-Communists," 56.

79. *Labor World*, October 12, 1939, 1; November 2, 1939, 1. See *Labor World*, March 23, 1, for an example of earlier attacks on the CIO, this one based on nothing more than guilt by association.

80. *Labor World*, January 11, 1940, 5.

81. See, for example, *Labor World*, December 14, 1939, 3.

82. For examples, see *Midwest Labor*, September 8, 1939, 4, and October 20, 1939, 1.

83. *Labor World*, April 14, 1940, 1; and June 6, 1940, 1.

84. March 19, 1940, and June 4, 1940, Duluth Industrial Union Council Papers (MHS).

85. January 21, 1941, and February 4, 1941, Duluth Industrial Union Council Papers. Among those supporting the Roosevelt administration on Lend Lease was Fred Megill of the Newspaper Guild. The break with the Roosevelt administration also caused the local of the American Clothing Workers, which was under the national leadership of Sidney Hillman, a strong supporter of FDR, to temporarily withdraw from the council (November 7, 1940, Duluth Industrial Union Council Papers). On the antiwar buttons, see *Midwest Labor*, January 19, 1940, 4.

86. On the role of Andy Johnson and the alienation of Finnish Americans, see Haynes, "Communists and Anti-Communists," 59. On the alienation of Finnish American support for the Communists, see also Arne Halonen, *Minnesota's Help to Finland* (Minneapolis: Finnish Relief Fund, Inc., Minnesota Division, n.d.), 23 (IHRC).

87. *Midwest Labor*, December 8, 1939, 3.

88. *Labor World*, February 22, 1940, 1.

89. Halonen, *Minnesota's Help*, 19. On Communist criticism of the relief effort, see 23.

90. On the Central Club, see *Labor World*, March 28, 1940, 1. On the state convention, see *Labor World*, March 14, 1940, 1.

91. Haynes, "Communists and Anti-Communists," 60–61, provides a succinct overview of the CIO in Duluth and Minnesota in 1940.

92. *Proceedings of the Third Convention of the Minnesota State Industrial Union Council* (1940), 9 (MHS).

93. Ibid., 30, 34.

94. Ibid., 33.

chapter 10. the fall of the popular front

1. Haynes, "Communists and Anti-Communists," 61.

2. Ibid., 62–63. The local reaffiliated in May 1945.

3. *Labor World*, August 20, 1942, 1; October 29, 1942, 1; August 27, 1942, 3.

4. *Labor World*, February 26, 1942, 6; March 5, 1942, 1.

5. *Labor World*, June 4, 1942, 1.

6. The "Buy War Bonds" campaign was a constant throughout the war. On the "Buy a Bomber Shows," see *Labor World*, July 2, 1942.

7. For an account of these various forces, see John E. Haynes, "Reformers, Radicals, and Conservatives," in *Minnesota in a Century of Change*, ed. Clifford E. Clark Jr. (St. Paul: Minnesota Historical Society Press, 1989), 384.

8. Gieske, *Minnesota Farmer-Laborism*, 318–32, provides an account of the merger.

9. Moriarity, interview by Hudelson (NEMHC).

10. This sketch of John Blatnik is taken from *Citizens Look at Congress* (Washington, D.C.: Grossman Publishers, Ralph Nader Congress Project, 1972), 6. See also the interview with John Blatnik's brother, Frank Blatnik, done by Carl Ross, 1989 (MHS).

11. *Labor World*, June 20, 1946, 1.

12. On the endorsements of Blatnik and other DFL candidates, see *Labor World*, October 10, 1946, 1. On AFL support for Pittenger, see *Labor World*, October 31, 1946, 6.

13. *Labor World*, October 17, 1946, 6.

14. William Pittenger, "Titoism Is an Issue in the Eighth Congressional District," address by Congressman William A. Pittenger, Duluth, Minnesota, August 30, 1946. Excerpts from the address are available in the Earl Bester Papers, box 3 (MHS).

15. *Duluth Herald*, October 28, 1946, 8; and October 29, 1946, 7. *Duluth News Tribune*, October 30, 1946, 5; and October 31, 1946, 24.

16. Joe Paszak, interview by Hyvärinen and Frenkel (MHS).

17. On the Shrine Auditorium event, see *Labor World*, October 24, 1946, 1. On the Vets for Blatnik, see *Labor World*, October 24, 1946, 1; and October 31, 1946, 1. See the same two issues of *Labor World* for other articles favorable to Blatnik.

18. *Labor World*, November 7, 1946, 1.

19. Henry Morin to Earl Bester, December 17, 1948, Earl Bester Papers (MHS).

20. John Blatnik to Earl Bester, June 11, 1948, Earl Bester Papers (MHS).

21. On Hargrave, see Dizard interview with Ross (MHS). Dizard claims there was an agreement between Blatnik and Popular Front leaders regarding Hargrave's appointment.

22. Robert H. Zieger, *American Workers, American Unions, 1920–1985* (Baltimore: The Johns Hopkins University Press, 1986), 98–104.

23. George Lipsitz, *Rainbow at Midnight* (Urbana: University of Illinois Press, 1994), 20–21.

24. Ziegler, *American Workers*, 109.

25. Ibid.

26. *Labor World*, March 21, 1946, 4; April 11, 1946, 3; May 9, 1946, 3; July 18, 1946, 6; October 10, 1946, 1.

27. This information is taken from FBI records pertinent to Herman Griffith made available under the Freedom of Information Act and is available at the NEMHC.

28. Joe Paszak and Leata Pearson, interviews with Hyvärinen and Frenkel (MHS).

29. On Burkhammer, see Haynes, "Communists and Anti-Communists," 56. On Murray, see Ronald W. Schatz, "Philip Murray and the Subordination of the Industrial Unions to the United States Government," in Melvin Dubofsky and Warren Van Tine, eds., *Labor Leaders in America* (Urbana: University of Illinois, 1987), 251.

30. Schatz, "Philip Murray," 252.

31. For more on Murray's position at this time, see Haynes, "Communists and Anti-Communists," 64.

32. Ibid.

33. Ibid., 65. Haynes misidentifies Hilding Schoen; see the Duluth Industrial Union Council Papers, June 7, 1949, where there is mention of a leaflet attacking Schoen being distributed in Duluth. The leaflet, produced locally and distributed by the "Citizens [*sic*] Committee for Good American Government," identifies Schoen as an organizer for the United Public Workers (UPW) of America and claims that the UPW is a Communist-led union. A copy of the leaflet attacking Schoen can be found in the Earl Bester Papers, box 3 (MHS). For a reply from Schoen claiming that the charges made in the leaflet had been considered and dismissed by both President Truman and Philip Murray, see Earl Bester Papers, March 8, 1949 (MHS).

34. Haynes, "Communists and Anti-Communists ," 66.

35. Ibid.

36. Ibid., 67.

37. Ibid.

38. Glenn Peterson interview by Martin Duffy, 1977 (MHS).

39. Haynes, "Communists and Anti-Communists," 67–68.

40. Orville Freeman to Earl Bester, October 2, 1946, Earl Bester Papers (MHS).

41. Copies of the program of the "Independent Progressive Caucus" and the printed page of directions for the convention can be found in the Francis Smith Papers (MHS).

42. Gieske, *Minnesota Farmer-Laborism*, 261.

43. Francis Smith, "Minnesota Younger Democratic-Farmer-Labor Club Controversy," n.d., Francis Smith Papers (MHS).

44. Earl Bester, interview with Jack Spiese, 1967, Earl Bester Papers (MHS).

45. Hubert Humphrey to Earl Bester, December 9, 1947, Earl Bester Papers (MHS).

46. Bester to CIO PAC in Washington, January 27, 1948; Bester to Blatnik, March 25, 1948; both in Earl Bester Papers (MHS).

47. Blatnik to Bester, May 13, 1948, Earl Bester Papers (MHS).

48. Humphrey to Heaney, June 22, 1948. The letter and a copy of the offending leaflet are in the Earl Bester Papers (MHS). In fact, Blatnik did not commit to Humphrey until after the primary. See Haynes, *Dubious Alliance*, 209.

49. Haynes, "Communists and Anti-Communists," 69.

50. A copy of chair John Moriarity's report on the credentials disputes and the St. Louis County convention can be found in the Francis Smith Papers (MHS). A fuller account of these events can be found in Haynes, *Dubious Alliance*, 188–93.

51. February 15, 1949; March 15, 1949; April 19, 1949; May 17, 1949; June 7, 1949; June 21, 1949, Duluth CIO Industrial Union Council Papers (MHS).

52. February 10, 1949, Earl Bester Papers (MHS).

53. Glenn Peterson, interview with Martin Duffy (MHS).

54. September 20, 1949; October. 4, 1949, Duluth CIO Industrial Union Council Papers (MHS).

55. Glenn Pearson, interview with Hyvärinen and Frenkel (MHS).

56. Leata Pearson, interview with Hyvärinen and Frenkel (MHS).

57. Ibid.

58. Paull, interview with Trimble (MHS).

59. Koivunen, interview with Paull (MHS).

60. Kuusisto, interview with Paull; Paszak, interview with Hyvärinen and Frenkel; Dizard, interview with Ross. In "Liberals, Communists, and the Popular Front in Minnesota" (Ph.D. diss., University of Minnesota, March 1978), John Haynes provides an account of Dizard's successful effort to resist repeated attempts to force him out of a position of influence within the Diamond Calk AFL local.

61. The transcription of the trial along with the statement of charges, a copy of the NLRB ruling, and copies of the May and April issues of the *Rank and File Duluth Steelworker* are in the archives of the United Steelworkers of America, District 33, Pennsylvania State University.

epilogue

1. Scholarship on the history of the American Communist Party is currently embroiled in a debate between "traditionalists," who stress the role of the party as an agent of Moscow, and "revisionists," who stress the role of the party as part of a broad populist current in American history. A review of this debate sympathetic to the traditionalist perspective can be found in John Earl Haynes, "The Cold War Debate Continues: A Traditionalist Looks at Historical Writing on Domestic Communism and Anti-Communism," *Journal of Cold War Studies* 2 (Winter 2000): 76–115. For a review of the literature sympathetic to the revisionist side, see Michael Kazin, "The Agony and Romance of the American Left," *The American Historical Review* 100 (1995): 1488–1512. The history of Duluth offered here would seem to support the revisionist perspective, though as John Haynes points out in his article, studies focused on local conditions may tend to marginalize the peculiar nature of the American Communist Party.

2.   An exodus from Duluth began as early as World War II, when people left the city for military service or to work elsewhere in the booming defense industries. Leata Pearson, a Popular Front activist, mentions the importance of this in looking back on the history of the city. This war-related exodus began the break-up of the stable communities that had found collective strength and meaning in the unions and in the neighborhood clubs of the Farmer-Labor Association. See Leata Pearson, interview with Hyvärinen and Frenkel (MHS).

3.   Here we see the limits of what many labor historians have described as the "second New Deal," involving a shift from a radical program directly committed to the welfare of working families to a program of indirect support through macroeconomic policies aimed at promoting growth. While a rising tide may lift all boats, it does nothing for individuals and families cast adrift on the seas of capitalism. On the idea of a second New Deal and labor's accommodation to it, see Steve Fraser and Gary Gerstle, eds., *The Rise and Fall of the New Deal Order: 1930–1980* (Princeton: Princeton University Press, 1989); and Nelson Lichtenstein, *Labor's War at Home: The CIO in World War II* (Cambridge: Cambridge University Press, 1982).

4.   A study of the power structure in Duluth done in the 1970s shows that the boards of directors of leading businesses, banks, and civic clubs continue to include many representatives of families that were in those same positions in the early decades of the twentieth century. See Charles Dizard, "The Power Structure of Duluth," unpublished manuscript. (NEMHC).

5.   Einar Bjork, interview with Trimble (MHS).

6.   Remarks by Vernon Green at a "Racism in the Northland" workshop sponsored by the Center for Peace and Justice, College of St. Scholastica, Duluth, January 12, 1991. Here the history of Duluth supports the analysis of Gary Gerstle regarding the replacement of the fine-grained racism of 1920s America with the black/white racism of the post–World War II order. See Gerstle, *American Crucible*.

7.   Some notable expressions of this East versus West consciousness can be found in the controversy over extending the freeway through east Duluth in the late 1970s. On this topic, see Virginia Hyvärinen Papers, box 2, folders 9, 10, and 11, on Interstate 35. There is also a clippings file, with some brief accompanying remarks assembled by Ken Wagner, also at NEMHC. See also Mary Morse, "Rainbow at the End of the Highway: The Interstate Stops Here," *Lake Superior Magazine* (August–September 1992). Finally, on the fight against the extension of the freeway, see the oral history interview of John Peyton (NEMHC). For another indication of the East/West divide, see the map showing election results for the 1995 mayoral contest in the *Duluth News-Tribune*, November 8, 1995, 1.

8.   Among the key people in this living wage campaign were Al Netland, president of the AFL-CIO Central Labor Body; Erik Peterson, an organizer with AFSCME; Larry Sillanpa, editor of *Labor World*; and Buddy Robinson of the Senior Federation. The large contribution of the Senior Federation to this campaign exemplifies both the non-self-interested nature of the campaign and the living connection to Duluth's historic labor movement found in the lives of many of its members.

9.   Erik Peterson, "Coming Together: Promises and Pitfalls of Minnesota's Corporate Accountability Campaigns," in David Reynolds, ed., *Partnering for Change: How Unions and Community Groups Build Coalitions for Economic Justice* (Armonk: M. E. Sharpe, 2004). For data on the election results in Duluth, see the *Duluth News-Tribune*, November 4, 2004.

index

RICHARD HUDELSON teaches philosophy at the University of Wisconsin-Superior. He is the author of books, essays, and reviews about the history of social thought.

CARL ROSS (1913–2004) grew up in the left-wing Finnish community of Superior, Wisconsin. He served in state and national leadership roles within the Communist Party until he left the party in 1958 because of its failure to reform. After a career in business, he turned to scholarly work on Finnish-American history and is the author of several books.